GARDENING
THROUGH THE YEAR

GARDENING
THROUGH THE YEAR

IAN SPENCE

For Mum and Dad, in loving memory

LONDON, NEW YORK, MELBOURNE, MUNICH, DELHI

REVISED EDITION 2009
Editors Jo Godfrey Wood, Sarah Ruddick
US Editor Christine Heilman
Art Editor Peggy Sadler
Senior Editor Helen Fewster
Acting Project Art Editor Vicky Read
Managing Editor Esther Ripley
Managing Art Editor Alison Donovan
Associate Publisher Liz Wheeler
Production Editor Joanna Byrne
Production Controller Mandy Inness
Publisher Jonathan Metcalf
Art Director Bryn Walls

FIRST EDITION 2001
Project Editor Louise Abbott
Art Editor Alison Donovan
Managing Editor Anna Kruger
Managing Art Editor Lee Griffiths
DTP Designer Louise Waller
Media Resources Charlotte Oster, Romaine Werblow
Picture Research Sharon Southren

First published in Great Britain in 2001 by
Dorling Kindersley Limited, London

This revised edition published in 2009 by
DK Publishing
375 Hudson Street
New York, New York 10014

09 10 11 12 10 9 8 7 6 5 4 3 2 1

A catalog record for this book is available from the Library of Congress.

ISBN 978-0-7566-5645-4

DK books are available at special discounts when purchased in bulk for sales
promotions, premiums, fund-raising, or educational use. For details, contact:
DK Publishing Special Markets, 375 Hudson Street, New York, New York 10014
or SpecialSales@dk.com.

Printed and bound in Singapore by Star Standard

discover more at
www.dk.com

CONTENTS

Introduction

Gardeners are born optimists, always looking forward to the year ahead, convinced that they will achieve much more than in the previous year. But to get better results, gardeners need to plan ahead and have a good sense of timing and an awareness of the demands of each passing season. In essence, that's what this book is all about.

Gardening essentials include getting sowing and planting times right so the young plants we have nurtured in a warm environment are not put outside and then promptly killed by frost. And if a shrub is pruned at the wrong time, we may discover too late that we have cut off all this year's flowers. Mistakes like this can happen to any of us, no matter how expert we think we are, especially in the mad spring rush when our enthusiasm is fired by the cheering sight of the first snowdrops and daffodils, or the first seedlings germinating in a seed tray. One of my aims is to help you avoid some of the pitfalls.

Climatic conditions can vary widely—there can be a difference of a month or more from a plant flowering in the south of the country compared to in the north, so there can be no hard and fast rules on the timing of operations in the garden. Another consideration to take into account is the weather conditions at the time a particular job has to be done. If there is a foot of snow on the ground in late April, then you cannot sow seeds outside! This actually happened in my native Scotland in the mid-1980s. So the timing of operations in the garden will vary from month to month and from year to year.

In recent years there has been a notable change in our weather patterns, often with one season seeming to merge into the next. This may be the result of global warming, caused by excessive emissions of greenhouse gases such as carbon dioxide. Owing to milder conditions, plants tend to come into flower much earlier than in previous years. And plants that are considered tender are surviving our increasingly mild winters, while pests and diseases once killed off by snow and frost are now on the increase. We also seem to be experiencing extremes of weather, with parts of the country receiving considerable rainfall in short periods of time. This has led to widespread flooding in some parts of the country, and prolonged droughts in others. Patterns of work in the garden are changing, and we must adapt when planning which plants to grow and where to plant them.

It is often recommended that you keep a notebook handy and write down jobs as you do them, so that you can refer to your notes at a later date. But if your memory is anything like mine, this will be an incomplete record because you'll often forget to note down the jobs you have already done. I hope this book will make it easier to plan your time, not by dictating exactly what should be done when, but by giving general guidelines and realistic advice.

Despite what I have said about climate changes, try not to worry too much about the timing of jobs in the garden. Nature always seems to have a way of balancing things out, and even if you think you're very late sowing those hardy annuals or planting out the summer bedding plants, they can still surprise you by growing and flowering beautifully, just at the right time. Enjoy your garden and don't let it become a chore. Indeed, gardening may become a passion that lasts a lifetime, as it has for me. Happy gardening!

Ian Spence

The January garden

If you're under the impression that there's nothing to do and that the garden looks boring at this time of the year, think again! However harsh the weather may be, there are still plenty of plants that you can enjoy, and lots of jobs to get started on. And don't forget to help out any visiting wildlife in your yard— it's a tough month for them, too.

THINGS TO DO

Ensure that vulnerable plants are protected from the wintry conditions January brings. Where temperatures remain above freezing, stay on top of any winter-germinating weeds, and clear damp leaves away from the crowns of plants. You can continue with winter digging if soil conditions allow, but cover the ground to keep it reasonably dry.

Brush snow off heavily laden trees, shrubs, and hedges before the weight breaks branches, and check the supports of trees and shrubs. Prune wisteria and other vigorous climbers. Take hardwood cuttings of trees and shrubs that you wish to propagate, and plant deciduous hedging.

Sow some summer bedding under cover this month, as well as sowing sweet peas. Now is a good time to look through catalogs for seeds and summer-flowering bulbs. Check forced bulbs for growth, and take root cuttings from perennials.

Start sowing early vegetable crops under cover, and sprout early potatoes. Continue planting and winter-pruning of fruit in January, and protect fruit trees from bird damage in the Deep South and California. Force rhubarb this month in mild areas.

LAST CHANCE

Prune grape vines before the sap starts rising. Protect container plants from freezing spells, and insulate all outside faucets against the cold.

GET AHEAD

Warm up some soil with cloches for early seed-sowing outdoors. Clean all your pots and seed trays for spring sowing, and send the lawnmower off for servicing so that it's ready when you need it later on.

Honesty Seedheads of *Lunaria annua*, amid fern foliage rimmed with frost, catch the sun on a winter day.

Winter beauty

The month of January may find the garden asleep to the world, but there is more going on than you think. Evergreens can provide satisfying and reassuring silhouettes in a spartan landscape, while a covering of snow can bring true magic and may even do your garden some good.

Cold winds, frost, and heavy rains can often make it seem as if nothing much can be done in the garden now. But even though it is usually the coldest time of the year, January can be regarded as the most optimistic month. Those few plants that do dare to flower really are to be marveled at, and without the distraction of a riot of colorful blooms, it's a time to admire the beautiful silhouettes of bare branches, the intriguing colors and textures of bark, and the reassuring solid forms of the evergreens. And a garden covered in snow is always good to look at, too.

A delightful sight Pearly snowdrops and golden winter aconites make perfect partners in the garden during the month of January.

Watch the weather forecasts

A blanket of snow can actually be good for the garden, killing off unwanted pests and protecting plants from severe frost. Do, however, keep an eye on the weather forecasts and look out for warnings of heavy snowfall or sharp frosts, as you will need to take steps to prevent damage to some plants in the garden. Conifers, in particular, are vulnerable to damage by heavy snowfalls, as the weight of the snow can bring branches down. Fruit cages can also suffer badly and be damaged by the weight of heavy snow.

Strong winds are a regular January feature and this is why it is important to make sure young trees and shrubs are well staked, especially in exposed areas. It's also why newly planted shrubs, especially evergreens, need some form of wind barrier. Cold winds can cause severe damage, particularly to evergreen leaves. These biting winds will scorch young foliage, which rarely recovers, so temporary shelter will certainly help preserve the investment you have made in new plants.

You may find that some parts of your yard seem to get much more heavily frosted than others, especially if the yard includes a slope or other change in level. Cold air is heavier than warm air and always finds the lowest level. This is an important point to bear in mind when you are planning where to position marginally hardy plants in the garden. You should also beware of planting fruit trees in low parts of the garden where there is a frost pocket, as the flowers may be damaged in the spring.

Time for some exercise

With the days just beginning to lengthen even shortly after New Year celebrations, it's a good time to work off the excesses of the holiday period. If you want to get warmed up on a cold winter's day, continue with winter-digging of borders and in the vegetable garden, as long as the soil is not waterlogged or frozen. If the ground is frozen, it is still a good time to cart out manure or garden compost and spread it on the ground.

Lawns will also benefit from some attention, even though it's still the middle of winter. Work done at this time of year will pay handsome dividends in creating a smooth green lawn in the summer. But keep off the grass when it is frosted over to avoid damaging it.

This is also a good month to go around the yard and catch up with repairs to fences and trellises and other clean-up jobs, which may not be very exciting but will make all the difference to the appearance of the garden in the summer months. Keep a notebook handy and take this with you when you are puttering around the yard in winter. This is a great help if you're planning any changes to the garden, especially to remind you of all the plants you want to acquire later!

A mixed winter border This gorgeous display of color includes *Prunus davidiana* 'Alba', *Erica carnea, Cornus alba* 'Sibirica', *Cornus stolonifera* 'Flaviramea', *Salix alba* 'Chermesina', *Erica erigena* 'Brightness' and *Carex montana*.

Weather watch

Winter temperatures vary widely, from coast to coast as well as from north to south. In the mild-winter areas along the West Coast and in the Southeast, winters tend to be cool and rainy, while Southwestern winters range between cool and dry to cold and dry in the higher altitudes. The Midwest and Eastern regions are universally cold in winter, often snowy, sometimes cold and dry (when winds whistle down across the prairies from the Arctic) with occasional and welcome warmer spells. But in general, no matter where you live, the coldest nights will occur when there is no wind, the skies are clear, and there is snow on the ground. The coldest air will be found on low ground. By comparison, cloudy winter nights can be surprisingly mild.

Biting winds

January is a month of freezing winds, with open prairies and areas of flat ground and mountainous regions experiencing the worst of all.

Sunshine and clouds

Southern regions overall have the most sunshine in winter, although moist air in the Southeast and Northwest can bring on days or weeks of cloudy weather. Enjoying warmer winter temperatures than other parts of the country, the coastal Southeast, Northwest, and Southwest rarely experience freezing lows.

Patchy rain

Rainfall also varies according to elevation and distance from the coasts. In the 19th century, before Russian immigrants brought winter wheat to the Midwest, making it "the breadbasket of America," this part of the country was known as "the great American desert," because it is in the interior of a vast country, as is Siberia, and its climate is similar, with extremes of cold in winter and heat, and periods of drought in summer.

Snow in places

Snow is common in areas where freezing temperatures combine with moist air, such as in the Mid-Atlantic and New England areas, around the Great Lakes, and at higher altitudes.

Plants to admire

Less strenuously, a walk around the yard on a January day can reveal surprises, with snowdrops and also carpets of the yellow winter aconite coming into flower. Another must for January (or February in colder areas) is the Christmas rose, *Helleborus niger*, which despite its name usually hangs back until this month—but the stunning white flowers are well worth waiting for. To achieve the purest flowers, protect the plants as the buds begin to open, to prevent rain and snow from spoiling the blooms.

We mustn't forget the tremendous amount of interest that can be created in the winter garden by using plants with attractive bark and colorful stems. Plants such as dogwoods (*Cornus* spp.) can be pruned back in spring to eye-catching bright winter stems in shades of red, green,

yellow, and even black. Evergreen shrubs and conifers in all shades from dark green to golden yellow also add life and luster to the winter scene. Scent is another bonus of many winter-flowering plants—chimonanthus (wintersweet), *Viburnum* x *bodnantense*, and sarcococca, another shrub that, despite its festive common name of Christmas box, will continue to pour out its stunning fragrance into the air through the New Year.

If the weather is just too cold and wet to venture outside, then there is plenty to get started on indoors. It's a good month for planning the rest of the gardening year. One job to do at this time, if you haven't already done so, is to put your feet up by the fireside with a glass of something to keep out the cold and browse through seed catalogs. Or, you can go down to the local garden

Winter treats Most winter-blooming shrubs, like this witch hazel, have the most intensely sweet-scented flowers.

center and pick the seeds you require. And although the first spring bulbs may have yet to open in the garden, it's time to choose summer-flowering bulbs.

Raising plants

It's not too soon to start thinking about sowing some early crops, always the most welcome, and of course the ones that will save you most money. Summer bedding plants that need an especially long growing season, such as geraniums and snapdragons (*Antirrhinum* spp.), can also be started off toward the end of the month. If you have a greenhouse or conservatory that can be heated sufficiently to keep out the frost, then you're off to a flying start, but even without a greenhouse, there is still plenty that can be done by raising plants on a windowsill.

Plants from seed

Raising your own plants from seed is a thrill that never leaves you, no matter how long you have been gardening. It's very easy to do, but there are a few items you will need, especially at this time of year, to provide a little extra heat. To heat a whole greenhouse is very expensive these days and many plants can be started off instead in a propagator. Plants such as tomatoes and the tender summer bedding plants all need a bit of extra heat, preferably from below the soil, to get the seeds to germinate, and this is where a propagator is so useful, gently warming the seed-starting medium from the base. There is quite a selection on the market; your choice will be based on cost, the space you have available, and the amount of seed you want to raise. You'll find even the cheapest and simplest models do a great job.

Always be careful with electrical appliances, especially where they will come into contact with moisture, and follow the manufacturer's instructions to the letter. If you have any doubts, be sure to contact the manufacturer or a qualified electrician.

So there you have it—almost as busy a month as in the summer. Bet you can't wait to get going now!

Early starters If you enjoy raising bedding plants from seed you can begin sowing them in January. Keep the young plants in a frost-free environment—a sunny windowsill inside the house is ideal.

Bold shapes Even under a dusting of frost, the strong outlines and textures of conifers such as silver fir (*Abies amabilis* 'Spreading Star') enhance the winter garden.

***Erica carnea* 'Springwood White'**
One of the many winter-flowering heathers (see p.282)

Garrya elliptica
Evergeen shrub that makes a good hedge in sheltered areas (see p.286)

***Hamamelis* x *intermedia* 'Arnold Promise'**
Scented flowers on bare branches (see p.288)

Galanthus plicatus* subsp. *byzantinus
Classic snowdrop with nodding, green-marked flowers (see p.286)

Betula papyrifera
The paper birch, with brilliant white peeling bark (see p.268)

Lonicera* x *purpusii
Shrubby honeysuckle with intensely fragrant flowers (see p.296)

Skimmia japonica
Tough evergreen shrub that does best in shade (see p.317)

Helleborus niger 'Potter's Wheel'
Small perennial for dappled shade (see p.289)

Sarcococca hookeriana var. humilis
Small but powerfully scented evergreen shrub (see p.316)

Cornus alba 'Sibirica'
This shrub has glossy, bright-red stems in winter (see p.276)

Prunus x subhirtella 'Autumnalis Rosea'
Winter-flowering cherry tree (see p.309)

Eranthis hyemalis
Woodland perennial forming mats of yellow stars (see p.282)

What to do in January

AROUND THE YARD

It's amazing how weed seedlings germinate during mild spells, even in the depths of winter. On any winter rambles around the yard, take a hoe with you so that these weed seedlings can be knocked out before they get too big. Gather up annual weeds and put them on the compost pile. Any perennial weeds should be dug up with as much root as possible and put in the trash.

There are few pests and diseases around at this time of year, but many are lurking in nooks and crannies, just waiting for the warmer spring weather to come along. So it is worth practicing good garden hygiene and clearing up any waste left that has been left lying around. Weeding is also a good idea.

Any decaying leaves should be collected and put on the compost or leafmold pile. Pay particular attention to clearing the crowns of herbaceous perennials and alpines, as these are vulnerable, especially the latter, to rot in prolonged damp conditions under fallen leaves. Leaves are best composted, not burned, as they can then contribute to the structure of the soil. Be careful when you are disturbing large piles of leaves as there may be toads or other small animals hibernating there.

Get to know your soil better. It can be disheartening to see plants struggle because the soil does not suit them. If you're not sure which plants and seeds to choose, testing your soil for its type and pH—its acidity or alkalinity—is always a good idea. Rub some soil between your fingers to get to know its structure: whether it contains a high proportion of clay, making it heavy and wet, or sand, making it light and dry—or something in between, the perfect balance being known as loam.

The pH of soil can be tested with commonly available kits stocked by garden centers; there are plenty to choose from and costs vary. Knowing more about your soil will help you select plants that will really do well in your garden. Regularly adding bulky organic matter to your soil—for example, digging-in compost or well-rotted manure, or mulching with leafmold—can do wonders to improve extreme soil types, keeping plants from drowning in heavy clay or drying out in free-draining sand. But it's better and easier not to try to change the pH of your soil in beds and borders, and just choose plants that like it as it is—you can always grow other plants in containers filled with tailor-made soil mixes.

Cart organic matter onto frozen ground. There isn't much to do outside when the soil is rock-hard, but an ideal job that will save you time later is spreading out well-rotted manure or garden compost. It's fine to walk on the soil if it is frozen hard. Carting muck or compost around can be a messy job, but in these conditions the cart can be wheeled over the ground with little effort. Don't, however, take the cart over a frozen lawn; if you can't avoid going over the lawn, put down planks. Spread the load evenly over the surface and the ground will soon thaw out when the weather improves.

Measuring soil pH Test kits are widely available, and easy to use. Soil is rarely uniform, so it's worth testing samples from different parts of the garden. Keep a record of where each sample comes from so that you can exploit any variation when it comes to choosing your plants; an acidic patch, for example, could be a prime site for camellias or heathers.

TREES AND SHRUBS

■ **Move deciduous shrubs or trees** that have been put in the wrong position. No matter how expert we like to think we are, it is all too easy to make mistakes when we are placing plants.

In milder climates, there is still time to move deciduous trees and shrubs if they are wrongly positioned or have outgrown their allotted space. You may need to enlist the help of another person to move larger ones. Never underestimate the effort that may be needed to move large plants, because you want to take as much of the root system, and the heavy soil around it, as you can. This is important for the plant to survive and grow well.

■ **Check tree ties and stakes.** Young trees and bushes that are being blown around by strong winds will never last long. It is therefore very important to check all the ties and stakes at regular intervals. When trees and bushes are planted too loosely, a sunken area may develop around the base of the main stem. This is caused by the continual rocking back and forth as the plant is blown around by the wind, and it is all too easy for puddles of excess water to collect in a pool. It is here that the plant will begin to rot and die off, so ties should be secure. However, they should not be so tight that they actually restrict the growth of the plant.

■ **To protect newly planted trees and shrubs,** especially evergreens, from wind damage, erect a windbreak to shelter the plant. The windbreak can be in the form of burlap, floating row cover, bubble wrap, or strong plastic sheeting, tied securely to a framework around the plants.

To increase the level of protection, some straw can be placed inside the windbreak framework, but make sure that the air can circulate and that light can get in, particularly for evergreens.

Planting

■ **Plant bare-root trees and shrubs,** but only if soil conditions allow. If the soil is frozen or very wet, heel in the plants temporarily in a corner of the yard until conditions are suitable. Dig a trench big enough to hold the root system and cover the roots with soil, firming gently. Plants can survive like this for quite some time.

If the soil is too frozen even to heel in the plants, then provided that their roots are wrapped in burlap, they can be kept in a porch, shed, or garage with some light. Unwrap the top growth if it is packed in straw so that some light can get in, and never let the roots dry out—keep the wrapping around the roots moist. With care, plants can last like this for a few weeks.

Pruning and training

■ **This is a good time of year to prune** trees to shape. Young trees often grow out in all directions into other plants in the border, throwing out shoots along the whole length of the trunk. You can prune out misplaced stems this month, always making sure that you cut to a junction or the main stem.

If you want to make a standard tree with a length of bare trunk, cut back some of the side growths now. But don't do this all at once—spread the process over two or three seasons, shortening some branches this year and removing them completely next year.

The extra leaves that are left on the main stem over the summer will help to encourage the vigor of the tree; cutting side branches off all at once would severely affect the tree's growth.

Seeds from berries

1 Separate the seeds by washing them in a fine mesh sieve. Or wrap the berries in a dish towel first and crush the pulp under running water.

2 Tap out the remains onto paper towels, pick out the seeds, and rinse them again.

3 Sow the seeds in trays or pots of peat-free medium and cover them lightly with coarse grit.

4 Place in a cold frame or by a sheltered wall, covering to keep off rain and protect from mice. Some seeds may take a long time to germinate.

Propagation

■ **Sow seeds of berrying shrubs** and trees such as cotoneaster, pernettya, and sorbus. Like alpines, seeds of these shrubs need a period of cold to break their dormancy.

■ **There is still plenty of time** to take hardwood cuttings from deciduous shrubs such as dogwoods (*Cornus*), willows, roses, forsythia, flowering currant (*Ribes*), and flowering quince (*Chaenomeles* spp.). Even if your garden is well stocked, it costs nothing to grow on a few of your favorites just in case some of the plants are lost in the future. And if do you end up with a surplus, young rooted shrubs are always a welcome contribution to garage sales or summer fairs.

Hedges

■ **Brush snow off evergreen hedges** before the weight of it splays out branches.

■ **Deciduous hedging plants** such as beech, hawthorn, and hornbeam can be planted now in well-prepared ground, if weather conditions permit. The cheapest way to buy hedging is in the form of young, bare-rooted plants known as whips, which are sold in bundles. If the soil is frozen or waterlogged, heel in the plants temporarily.

To prepare the ground, mark out a strip at least two spade-blades wide along the length of the proposed hedge. Start taking out a trench to one spade's depth at one end and cart the first load of soil to the other end. If the soil in the bottom of the trench is heavy, compacted clay, you may be able to loosen it up by using a garden fork, but be careful not to bring the poorer subsoil to the surface.

Incorporate as much organic matter as you can get into the soil at the bottom of the trench and then cover this with soil by digging the next section of the trench, repeating the process until you reach the end of the line, when the last part can be filled with the soil in your cart.

Space the young plants out along the trench, fill in, and firm with your foot. In exposed sites, a windbreak of, for example, plastic mesh stapled between posts, on the windward side of the hedge, will help the plants get established.

Preparing to plant a hedge

Even if the plants are small and slender, digging a trench for them is better than making individual holes.

Well-rotted farmyard manure worked into the bottom of the trench will give plants a good start.

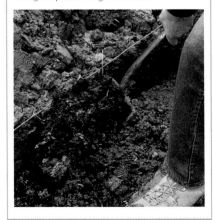

CLIMBERS

■ **Brush snow off dense evergreen** climbers and wall shrubs; when snow accumulates on these, it can break stems and put strain on ties and supports.

■ **Climbers to prune now** include wisteria (see below), ornamental vines, ivies, Virginia creeper and Boston ivy, and climbing hydrangea. These plants have a habit of working their way into window frames and doors, so cut them back as needed to prevent any expensive damage . And don't forget to prune them away from all gutters on house walls.

■ **Wisterias require pruning** twice during the year. In summer they need all the long new shoots cut back to 5–6 buds from the main stems. Now these same shoots should be shortened even more, to two or three buds from the main stems. You can do the same to any new sideshoots that have grown since the summer. The advantage of doing this pruning now is that with no leaves on the plant, you can see exactly what you are doing. It encourages the formation of flower buds to give a terrific show of color during the late spring and early summer.

Pruning wisteria In winter, shorten all of the sideshoots from the main framework of stems.

PERENNIALS

■ **There aren't many perennials** flowering this month, so hellebores are particularly welcome. The flowers can easily be damaged by winter rains splashing soil onto them, so it is a good idea to cover the plants with a cloche to protect them. This way you will be sure to have perfect flowers in the garden or to cut and take into the house.

■ **Continue to clear weeds** from around plants and cut down any dead stems left for winter interest that are by now looking shabby or diseased.

■ **Order herbaceous perennials** from nursery catalogs now for delivery and planting in the spring. Now is the time to look through bits of paper to find all those notes you made of "must-have" plants that you saw at shows and gardens last year. There is a bewildering array of plants to choose from these days and you can have plants in flower, if you choose them carefully, almost year-round.

For interest all season and a foil for the flowering plants, choose from some of the beautiful foliage plants that are for sale, especially the increasingly popular grasses, sedges, and ferns.

■ **Continue to lift and divide** overgrown clumps of herbaceous perennials when soil conditions allow—in other words, when the soil is not frozen or so wet that it sticks to your boots.

■ **Inspect dahlia tubers** that you are keeping in storage. Take a close look from time to time to see if there is any disease present. Any that are showing signs of rotting off should be carefully removed from the rest, or the disease may spread through the whole batch. Any individual tubers that seem to be infected can be cut from the main crown of the plant, retaining

the rest. Early stages of rotting can be controlled by cutting out the infected area and dusting with garden sulfur.

■ **Taking root cuttings** from perennials is an easy way of increasing your plants and doesn't require a lot of special equipment.

Plants that are ideal for this method of propagation are those with long fleshy roots, such as Japanese anemones, Oriental poppies, verbascums, and acanthus. Dig up the plant and wash off as much soil as you can to expose the roots. When taking cuttings, make a diagonal cut across the "bottom" (the end that was the farthest from the plant) so you remember which way up to plant them.

Plants with finer roots can also be used—for example, phlox, catmint, and primulas. Prepare the cuttings in the same way, but lay them flat on a tray of the

same seed-starting medium and cover lightly with medium. Provided that you haven't denuded it of roots, the parent should start growing again if it is carefully replanted and fertilized.

Alpines

■ **Alpine plants need protection** not from the cold, but from winter rains. If you haven't already done so, make them a shelter to keep off the worst of the wet.

■ **Sow alpine seeds** this month. By sowing now you can give the seeds the period of cold that they experience in the wild, which is essential for germination in spring.

Taking root cuttings

1 Cut off roots the thickness of a pencil and then cut these into sections about 2 in (5 cm) long, trimming off small fibrous roots. Make a slanting cut at the base.

2 Insert the cuttings, upright, in seed-starting mix with some vermiculite. Cover with grit and water well.

3 Put in a frost-free cold frame. You can use a heated propagator for faster rooting, but it is not essential.

4 New growth should appear in the spring, when you can separate the cuttings and put each in its own small pot of growing medium.

5 Grow on the young plants over the spring and summer, until they are large enough to plant out.

BULBS

■ **Order summer-flowering bulbs** now in plenty of time for planting in spring. Lilies are the most popular, but try some of the more unusual bulbs, such as *Galtonia candicans* (wood hyacinth) and *Ornithogalum* (star of Bethlehem). Even the frost-tender bulbs such as tigridias, which, like dahlias and gladioli, need to be lifted and stored in a dry, frost-free place over winter, are easy to grow.

■ **Forced bulbs.** Bring bulbs planted in pots and bowls last fall into the house in batches to give a prolonged flowering display. The time to bring them inside is when they have grown about an inch tall, so watch them carefully. It's best to bring them into a cool room for a week or two first of all; if it is too warm too quickly, they will grow fast, becoming leggy, and produce poor flowers. Water bulbs in bowls without drainage holes carefully or you may overwater them.

■ **Find a sheltered spot outdoors**, out of sight, but in the light, where you can put pots of bulbs as they finish flowering for you indoors. Remove the spent flower-heads to prevent the plants' energy from being focused on producing seeds. Feed them with a high-potash fertilizer to build

Galtonia candicans

up flower buds for next year. Continue fertilizing them regularly until the foliage dies back, and then in spring the bulbs can be planted in the garden. It is not a good idea to force the same bulbs year after year. Forcing takes a lot of energy out of the plants and they rarely flower well if forced more than once.

■ **Regularly check bulbs** being stored over the winter to see if there is any disease present. Any bulbs that have rotted should be removed immediately, otherwise the disease will spread to other bulbs.

ANNUALS AND BEDDING

■ **Sow summer-flowering** bedding plants that need a long season to grow: begonias (tuberous, fibrous-rooted, and semperflorens kinds), snapdragons, lobelias, geraniums, and gazanias. To raise bedding plants in any quantity, you will need a greenhouse or conservatory—especially when, like these, the young plants will be taking up space for months.

■ **Sow sweet peas now** unless you were able to sow them in the fall. They like a good root run, so it is best to sow them in long sweet pea tubes. Or, make your own with newspaper rolled into tubes and held together with tape—or keep the cardboard rolls from toilet paper or paper towels. Place the tubes side by side in a seed tray and fill with peat-free seed-starting mix. Some seeds, depending on the variety (check the packet), need to be soaked overnight to soften the seed coat. Another method is to chip the seed—to remove a sliver of the seed coat carefully with a garden or craft knife at the opposite end from the "eye," where the root will start growing. This allows water to penetrate the seeds more easily, hastening germination. Sweet peas don't need very high temperatures to germinate, so there is no need for a propagator—a cool, light room or sheltered cold frame is sufficient.

■ **Fall-sown sweet peas** sown several to a pot need potting on to make strong, healthy plants for putting out in May. Soak the soil and gently knock the plants out of the pot, and separate them carefully. Put each into a 3-in (9-cm) pot of peat-free medium and gently firm in. Water in gently to settle the soil and put in a light place. A high shelf in a greenhouse or conservatory is ideal; failing that, use the sunniest windowsill you've got. You should also pinch out the tip of the young shoots, either now or next month.

Ornithogalum umbellatum

Tigridia pavonia

CONTAINERS

■ **Deadhead** containers of winter-flowering pansies so that you can keep the display going into spring, and check whether they need water.

■ **Even in winter**, container plants may need watering, especially those that are growing at the base of house walls. Here they can be sheltered from rain by the overhang of the eaves of the house. It is surprising how dry plants can get when they are in this position.

■ **All container-grown shrubs** may need some protection as we enter the coldest part of the winter. It is not the hardiness of the plant that is the issue here; during very frosty weather, plants in pots are more vulnerable to damage from freezing because the roots in the pots are above ground. If you haven't already protected them, there are several ways to do it. The pots can be wrapped in bubble wrap or burlap. Extra protection can be given by wrapping straw or dry leaves around the pot and holding this in place with the bubble wrap or burlap. Grouping the pots together will give them further protection

Alternatively, if you've got the space, take the plants indoors during bad weather. Even a cold greenhouse, or a shed with windows, will provide enough protection from all but the severest frost. You can wrap the pots, too, to be on the safe side.

Remember that empty containers used for decoration in the garden, especially glazed pots and old terracotta, are also vulnerable to cracking by frost and may need protection too.

LAWNS

■ **Keep off icy grass.** Don't walk or work on the grass at all when it is frozen or frosted, otherwise when it thaws out, your footprints will show up as yellow patches.

■ **Improve drainage.** Improve the drainage of the lawn using a fork. Badly drained parts will be easily recognizable as lower patches where the water tends to collect. Wait until the surface of the lawn has thawed and dried out a bit and then push a garden fork 6 in (15 cm) into the ground and wiggle it around to open up the holes, at about 6-in (15-cm) intervals over the affected area. Immediately after aerating, spread sharp or horticultural sand (not builder's sand), or a sand and soil mixture, over the area and work this into the holes with a stiff broom. This prevents them from closing up too quickly and further improves the drainage.

■ **Repair hollows and bumps.** Even out bumpy lawns this month if the weather is mild and dry. Hollow areas where water collects can be raised level with the rest of the lawn quite easily. First make H-shaped cuts in the lawn with a spade or lawn-edging iron, and then carefully push a spade under the sod and roll each half back. Add soil to the exposed area, firm it well, and carefully roll back the sod. You

Spike lawns Use a garden fork to aerate grass. You can rent mechanical spikers for large lawns.

may have to add more soil to get the sod slightly higher than the surrounding lawn to allow for settling. After rolling back the sod, tamp down with the back of a rake. To repair bumps do exactly as for hollows, but when the sod is rolled back, scrape some soil from underneath to lower the sod.

■ **Disperse worm casts.** Worms may be active in lawns now and are most noticeable by their casts. These should be brushed off regularly; if they are left, they will be trampled into the surface of the lawn, looking unsightly and encouraging weed seeds to grow. However, worms do a lot of good in other parts of the garden. Use a flexible cane and swish it back and forth to scatter the casts. On small lawns, use a stiff broom. Do this when the surface is dry and the casts will spread easily.

New lawns

■ **Lay sod.** Sod can be laid on prepared ground only if the soil is not frozen or wet. Work from planks so that you do not make compacted dents in the leveled soil. While seed is economical, making a lawn from sod is more or less instant; you will have to keep off it for only a few weeks until it settles in. Sod costs more than seed, but if you can, buy the best-quality sod, guaranteed weed-free.

Bumps and hollows Lift a flap of sod and scoop out or fill in with soil to even them out.

VEGETABLES AND HERBS

■ **Complete winter-digging** of empty beds and new vegetable plots as soon as the weather allows. The sooner cultivation is completed, the better, to allow the winter weather to play its part in breaking down large clods of earth, improving the soil structure, and making it easier to work in the spring.

If you cannot dig at all this month, you can at least, if the ground is frozen hard, cart out manure or compost and spread it on top of the soil. When the soil is very wet, it is best to keep off it completely, or it will compact down and become a sea of mud that dries to a hard crust, and you will have great difficulty working it later on when you are trying to make seed beds.

One way of avoiding having to walk on the soil is to use the deep-bed method of growing vegetables. With this, beds only 4 ft (1.2 m) wide can be tended by reaching over them from the sides. Initially double-dig the beds, incorporating plenty of organic matter. Once this is done, you need never dig them again. Every winter, you simply add organic matter as a surface layer, and the healthy worm population that should exist will take it down into the soil for you. It will be possible to grow crops much closer together, the soil is not compacted in any way, and you'll get higher yields than on a conventional arrangement of rows.

■ **Plan your crop rotation.** In order to avoid the buildup of certain pests and diseases, and to make the best use of manures and fertilizers, it is best to practice crop rotation.

Vegetable crops can be divided into three main groups that share some vulnerability to the same plant problems, and also prefer different soil treatments before they are planted or sown. Vegetables within these groups should never be grown in the same place again until at least two years have gone by. The table set out below shows a simple crop

Maintaining deep beds Each year, spread organic matter over the beds, rather than digging it in. The level will fall over the season.

rotation, and it is meant to be a guide only. You may grow all the crops listed, or more, but the principles remain the same.

There are some vegetables that do not lend themselves to crop rotation and don't need it—the perennial crops, such as asparagus, globe artichokes, and sea kale. Asparagus needs its own bed, as it will be in place for many years, but the others are beautiful plants in their own right that make handsome additions to ornamental plantings. Sweet corn is an annual crop that does not fall into any particular group, so it can move around from year to year and be treated as a gap-filler.

■ **Cover ground with plastic sheeting.** When you have dug over an area, cover it with black plastic sheeting, anchored around the edges or tucked firmly into the soil. This will keep off the worst of the weather so that the soil can easily be raked down into seedbeds next month. It also helps to warm the soil for early setting out young plants sown now indoors, and also for earlier sowing outdoors. This way you'll get early vegetables.

Harvesting
■ **Continue to harvest** Brussels sprouts, leeks, parsnips, rutabagas, and turnips. If you haven't grown any winter greens,

Three-year crop rotation

YEAR ONE

Group one Add compost over winter and fertilizer before sowing.		**Group two** Rotted manure in winter and fertilizer before sowing.		**Group three** Add compost, lime and fertilizer.	
Grow:		Grow:		Grow:	
Beets	Carrots	Beans	Peas	Brussels sprouts	
Kohlrabi	Potatoes	Leeks	Lettuces	Cabbage	Cauliflower
Turnips	Rutabagas	Onions	Shallots	Broccoli	Kale
Celeriac		Radishes		Savoy	Spinach

YEAR TWO	Group two	Group three	Group one
YEAR THREE	Group three	Group one	Group two
YEAR FOUR	Group one	Group two	Group three

remember that turnip tops can be cooked and eaten as a green vegetable.

Sowing outdoors

■ **In sheltered southern parts** seeds may be sown under cloches on land that has already been covered for a few weeks. However, it is usually better to wait until February to sow under cloches, or March to sow direct. Seeds to sow include lettuce, salad onions, radishes, peas, fava beans, and spinach. Sow small amounts at 10- to 14-day intervals, and these crops will follow on from any sown under glass.

Sowing indoors

■ **Sow a few early crops,** either in seed trays or in cell packs. The advantage of growing in cells is that you need not disturb these young plants until you plant them out. The little rootballs can be transplanted intact, so the plants get off to a flying start. The plants will be ready to be put out under blankets of floating row cover from late February.

Sow small quantities of lettuce, summer cabbages and cauliflowers, radishes, carrots (choose round varieties for cell-pack sowing), spinach, salad onions, turnips, peas, and fava beans. None of

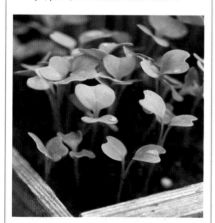

Baby salads Thin out seedlings sown in trays under cover to ensure that the strongest plants have enough space to develop.

these seeds requires high temperatures to germinate—about 55°F (13°C) is adequate, so a windowsill in a warm room will do, or, for faster results, use a propagator. Then grow them on in good light. If you sow in seed trays rather than cell packs, you will need to prick the seedlings out once they are large enough to handle safely.

■ **Sow onion seed this month.** To get the best onions they need a fairly long growing season. The easiest way to start off is to sow them in clusters in cell packs. Fill the cells with peat-free growing medium and water to settle it. Sow five or six seeds per cell and cover them with vermiculite. Put in a heated propagator or on a warm windowsill until the seeds germinate.

The onions will be ready to plant out in late March. There's no need to thin, just plant out the whole cluster.

Caring for crops

■ **In climates where freezes are rare,** bend leaves over cauliflowers to protect the developing curds, the plants' undeveloped flowerheads. When exposed to a prolonged period of light, the curds tend to turn green and flower buds develop, making them inedible. Bending a few leaves over the curd slows this process down, making the crops last a bit longer. Just snap leaves near the base of the midrib and tuck them in around the curd. You can tie the leaves up to keep the curds covered in windy weather.

Planning ahead

■ **Start early potatoes.** Freshly dug potatoes are in a class of their own when it comes to flavor. It's time to look for seed potatoes, as they need to be sprouted (started into growth) before planting in March. As well as advancing the date on which the potatoes will be harvested,

Sprouting seed potatoes An egg carton is ideal for this purpose, but the potatoes can rest against each other in a shallow box.

sprouting will also increase overall yield.

To start them off, lay the tubers in a tray with the "rose" end uppermost. Put them in a light, cool, frost-free place and after two or three weeks, shoots will begin to sprout. To get the best crop, thin the shoots to two or three per tuber. Plant out from March.

Beat the seasons

■ **Chicory forced for tightly** packed, blanched leaves is a good alternative when other salad crops are scarce in winter, but it can be eaten cooked as well. You need to have sown the seeds and raised plants outside over the summer. Now, lift the large taproots and pot them up. An 8-in (20-cm) pot will take about five roots. Any old potting mix will do for forcing. Once potted, invert another pot over the planted-up one and make sure you cover any drainage holes to keep out the light. Keep at a temperature of 50–55°F (10–13°C). Keep the roots moist, but not wet. If the growing medium was well watered to begin with, then little or no watering should be needed, provided the pot is not sitting in too warm a place. The chicory should be ready three or four weeks after potting up.

FRUIT

■ **Protect fruit cages** from damage by heavy snowfalls. Either roll the roof netting to the center supports and tie it in, or remove the roof netting entirely and drape it over trees and bushes that may be vulnerable to bird damage.

Picking and storing

■ **Inspect all fruits that are in storage** and remove any that are showing signs of rotting off. Disease can spread rapidly, so the sooner it is detected, the better. A place that is cool and dark is ideal for storage. Fruits that have been wrapped in paper are less likely to spread rot.

Caring for crops

■ **Protect fruit trees and gooseberries** with netting. Birds can cause a lot of damage, even in winter. Cedar waxwings, robins, and cardinals, in particular, love to eat plump, developing fruit buds. Larger free-standing trees can be difficult to protect, so you may have to accept some losses, but restricted forms of trees such as cordons and fans grown against a wall or fence are easily protected with netting. Make sure this is well secured so birds don't get trapped.

■ **Toward the end of the month** is a good time to apply an organic fertilizer to all fruit. Even in late January things are beginning to stir and sap is beginning to rise. An organic fertilizer such as blood, fish and bone, or seaweed meal is ideal, because organic fertilizers release their nutrients slowly over a long period; the plants don't get the sudden boost to growth as they would get with inorganic, or chemical, fertilizers. Too much soft growth early in the season is more susceptible to damage from frosts, pests, and diseases. Pull away any mulch around tree bases and bushes before fertilizing; water the ground and renew the mulch.

Inspect ties Look at all stakes and ties, especially on the growing stems of young trees.

■ **Check that all fruit tree ties** and stakes are sound. Older ties can break, so it is a good idea to check them regularly. Also, bear in mind that as a tree grows, the stem expands, so check that ties are not too tight on young trees.

■ **Examine apple trees** for signs of canker. The symptoms to look for are flattened areas of bark that show signs of splitting, causing the bark to flake off. The branch may also become swollen. During the winter, red fungal fruiting bodies can also be seen. Canker is caused by a fungus called *Neonectria galligena*; it is spread by windborne spores and attacks the tree through open wounds or pruning cuts. To control canker you may have to cut out whole branches or fruiting spurs. Make sure you remove all damaged bark and wood back to healthy tissue. Cut to a healthy-looking bud, a branch junction, or the main trunk. Look at the pruning cut: if the wood is white, you have pruned back to healthy wood and the cut should heal well. If it still shows brown staining, you should prune further back.

■ **Spray fruit trees and bushes** with a plant oil winter wash unless you did so last month. Many pests like to hibernate in little cracks and crevices in the bark. It is

important to spray really thoroughly with the wash to make sure any pests lurking there are killed. Be careful when using winter wash because it can damage evergreen plants and grass. If fruit trees are growing in grass, put plastic sheeting down to protect it. Protect other plants nearby by covering them with plastic sheeting. Black trash bags are ideal for small plants. Do the spraying on a frost-free, calm day, so that spray does not drift on the breeze onto other plants.

■ **Spray peaches against** peach leaf curl. This disease is quite noticeable in spring and summer. The foliage of the tree becomes puckered and turns red and purple, dropping off prematurely. It is not fatal for the tree; leaves produced later in the season usually remain healthy. But year by year, the disease will weaken the tree, and it is certainly unsightly and unpleasant.

Trees grown under glass are usually unaffected as the disease is spread by spores carried by wind and rain. Dwarf varieties are now available, and these are easily grown in large pots for the patio; they can be taken inside for the winter if you have the space.

A way of protecting outdoor fan-trained trees is to erect a temporary open-ended shelter of plastic sheeting. Put the shelter in position from midwinter until mid-

Peach leaf curl This is a fungus spread by wind and rain. Affected leaves pucker and blister.

spring. This keeps the tree dry and stops the fungus from infecting the emerging leaves. Spray with a copper fungicide at intervals from mid- to late winter, following the instructions carefully. Stop spraying as flower buds begin to open.

Pruning and training

■ **Continue to winter-prune apples,** pears, red and white currants, gooseberries, and black currants.

■ **Winter pruning of apples** and pears consists mainly of pruning back the leaders of trained fruit trees, whether they be fan-trained, espaliers, cordons, or bush trees. The main, or leading, shoots of main branches should be cut back by about one-third to half, depending on the vigor of the tree. The one basic rule to remember about pruning is that the harder you prune, the stronger will be the subsequent growth from the point of pruning. Also, thin out overcrowded fruiting spurs on trained trees. This allows better air circulation, reducing the risk of disease.

■ **Pruning of red- and whitecurrants** and gooseberries is similar. If fruiting shoots were summer-pruned, they can now be pruned further to a couple of buds from the main branches.

■ **Blackcurrants are pruned** in a slightly different way. Some people prune black currants just after the fruit has been picked, but in winter you can see better what you are doing without a lot of foliage on the plants. Blackcurrants fruit on new and old wood and they are grown as a stool plant (that is, branches grow in a clump from, or just under, ground level). Pruning is all about maintaining a balance between old and new wood. Around one-third of the bush should be removed each year to maintain the vigor of the

Long branches Shorten by a half or a third any branches that have grown too long. Cut them back to a side branch (lateral).

plant. Wherever possible, cut out older stems to the ground, leaving younger wood to fruit in the summer. It is inevitable that you will cut out some young growth. When finished, you should have a balance between old and new branches on a fairly open bush. Mulch, ideally with well-rotted farmyard manure, after pruning. Do not let the mulch touch the stems.

■ **Prune and train** summer-fruiting raspberries if this was not done in the fall. This is quite a good time of year to do the job, as it's easier to see what you are doing. The old canes that bore the fruit last year need to be cut from the wires to which they were tied last year, and cut to ground level. Tie in the new canes that grew last year, but did not fruit, about 4 in (10 cm) apart. Any stems that are taller than the support wires can be cut back to the top wire, or the tip of the shoot can be brought down and tied to the top wire. Whichever way you select, this will encourage the formation of fruit-bearing sideshoots in the summer.

■ **Prune outdoor grape vines**. Finish this task if you haven't already, as the sap will soon begin to rise, and if vines are pruned any later it will cause bleeding: the sap will seep badly out of the pruning cuts. All laterals should be pruned back to two or three buds and leading shoots pruned back to within the allotted space.

Planting

■ **Continue to plant** fruit trees and bushes, but only when the soil conditions are right. If trees are planted when the soil is too wet, first, the soil will get compacted with walking on it. Second, even if only the surface of the soil is frozen, it is not good practice to put frozen lumps of soil around plant roots. The ideal condition for soil to be in for planting is moist, but not sticking to your boots. If conditions are not right for planting, heel in the plants in a sheltered corner or put them in the shed for a day or two. They will be fine if you keep the roots moist.

Beat the seasons

■ **Begin to force strawberries** that were potted up last August, taking them under cover.

■ **Force rhubarb for tender** young delicious stems in the spring. Clear away all the dead foliage from the crown. If the winter has been mild, you may see fresh growth already starting at ground level; be careful not to damage it. Cover the plant with an old trash can or a large pot. Alternatively, you can buy special terracotta rhubarb forcers. These are upturned clay pots with a lid to check on the forced rhubarb, usually decorative. Place one of these over the crown of the plant, and if you can get it, cover the forcer with a pile of fresh horse manure. The heat generated by the manure as it rots will force the rhubarb on even quicker.

UNDER COVER

■ **Check that greenhouse heaters** are working properly. Electric heaters that are not functioning efficiently will waste electricity, costing more to run. With kerosene heaters, make sure the wick is trimmed regularly; if the flame does not burn properly, toxic fumes will be given off and these will harm the plants. Gas heaters should also be checked regularly by a qualified technician. Don't tinker with any appliance if you're not sure about what you are doing; call in a professional to do the job safely.

■ **Clean the greenhouse** or conservatory inside and out. Now is a good time to do it, before seed-sowing begins. You may have to move plants around or put them outside if the weather is not too cold. Cleaning the glass, inside and out, is the most important job, as plants need all the light they can get when the days are short. The inside should be scrubbed down with bleach solution— floors, walls, and benches. Pay particular attention to corners where glass meets frame and the roof meets the sides; these are the places where pests lurk and hibernate through winter.

■ **Ventilate on mild days.** Even in January, on the occasional sunny day, temperatures inside can rise dramatically. Open the ventilators for a few hours on such days, but close them well before sundown.

■ **Keep an eye out for fungal diseases** like botrytis, commonly called gray mold after its appearance on stems and leaves. It is difficult to control, as the spores are air-borne. It attacks plants through wounds and decaying stems, leaves, and flowers. The best way to control it when cold weather makes ventilation difficult is by practicing good hygiene. Remove any yellowing leaves or stems from plants before the fungus gets a chance to invade.

Clear any fallen leaves away promptly and put them in the trash, not on the compost pile, where the spores may survive. There are no fungicides available to amateur gardeners for the control of botrytis.

■ **Watch out for vine weevil** in heated greenhouses and conservatories, where the larvae of this pest may be active all year. Symptoms are a general lack of vigor or wilting, caused by damage to the roots by the grubs of the weevil: legless, creamy-white larvae, up to 3/8 in (10 mm) long, with curved bodies and a brown head. A wide variety of container-grown plants can be affected. In a heated greenhouse, you can use a biological control to combat vine weevil, even at this time of year.

■ **Clean pots and seed trays**, ready for seed sowing. Using clean containers, especially for seed sowing and rooting cuttings, will help cut down the incidence of pests and diseases, reducing the need for chemicals. Use bleach solution and rinse thoroughly. Keep the solution out of reach of children.

■ **Inspect any bulbs**, corms, and tubers stored in the greenhouse and throw away any that show signs of rot.

■ **Watering at this time of year** needs to be done with some care. Only water plants when they absolutely need it. The best way to gauge whether a plant needs water is to regularly lift the pot and feel the weight; the lighter the pot, the more water it will need, and the heavier it is the less water it will need. Plants that are almost dormant this month, such as overwintering fuchsias and geraniums resting in frost-free greenhouses, should be watered very sparingly; just enough to keep them alive. Too much water will make them grow too much. Actively growing plants like

winter-flowering azaleas, poinsettias, and bulbs will need more watering. It's best to do any watering early in the day in winter. This gives the greenhouse or conservatory time to dry out before the cold night.

■ **Prune established fuchsias** in heated greenhouses and conservatories. Fuchsias can be started into growth now by watering more often and moving them into the lightest position; indeed, they may already have started, with buds beginning to burst. To keep the plants bushy and healthy, prune them quite hard, pruning all the sideshoots back to one or two buds from the main framework of stems. The plants also need repotting at this time. Remove the plants from the pots and tease out as much of the old potting mix as you can. Then repot into the same-sized container with fresh peat-free potting mix and water in well to settle the soil around the roots. Spray the plants occasionally with a fine mist of clear water to encourage buds to swell.

Raising plants for outdoors

■ **Sow seeds** of those summer-flowering bedding plants that need a long growing season to produce flowers in time for summer—all kinds of begonias and antirrhinums, geraniums, lobelias, and gazanias. To germinate successfully, these seeds need to be grown in a propagator that can be maintained at a constant temperature of 68–70°C (21–22°C). Most propagators give a lift of about 20°F (10°C) above the ambient temperature, so on very cold nights some extra heating may be needed. At this time of year light is at a premium, so place the propagator on a south-facing bench.

The fine seeds of antirrhinums and begonias should not be covered. Even the lightest covering of soil is likely to be too deep for these very fine seeds. More

Sowing tender perennials

1 Fill a pot with peat-free medium and tap on the bench to settle it. Strike off the surplus and press lightly.

2 Water the growing medium thoroughly before sowing the seeds thinly over the surface.

3 Larger seeds like those of geraniums can be covered with sifted mix or vermiculite—just enough to cover the seeds.

4 Place a sheet of glass over the pot and place in a propagator until germination. Shade against sunlight to prevent drying out and scorching.

information about this can be found on the backs of seed packets. When the seeds are large enough, they can be pricked out into trays or potted up separately. Seeds sown in the warm, moist conditions in a propagator are prone to a disease called damping off. Avoid this by sowing the seeds thinly, to avoid overcrowding, and using clean trays and pots.

■ **Sow sweet peas** under cover in mild winter areas, or pot on and pinch out the tips of any sown in fall.

■ **Start off vegetables** and sow onions.

Glasshouse and house plants

■ **Keep winter-flowering houseplants,** such as azaleas and poinsettias, in a cool place in good light. If the air is too warm, the flowers will fade much more quickly. A light windowsill facing south, if you don't have a greenhouse or conservatory, is the ideal place. The plants will have to be turned every two or three days to prevent them from getting lopsided.

■ **Forced bulbs** Bring in pots of spring bulbs that were plunged outside in fall. A greenhouse or conservatory makes a good staging post on their way into the house, to get them used to warmer temperatures. Pots of bulbs that have finished flowering can be put outside now.

■ **Pot up some lily bulbs for early flowers indoors.** Lily bulbs are available in garden centers now and will be spectacular grown in containers indoors. Not only do you get the beautiful flowers, but the scent is terrific too. Put three or four bulbs into a 7-in (17 cm) pot containing peat-free multipurpose potting mix. Cover the bulbs with 3–4 in (7–10 cm) of mix and put in a light place. After a few weeks, the bulbs will come through, and in late spring, the

Lilium martagon

flowers will fill your home with color and with many wonderful scents. The bulbs can be planted in the garden when the flowers are finished.

Crops under glass

■ **Prune vines under glass** as soon as possible, because even in winter, the temperature under glass can rise considerably and the vines will start into growth very quickly. If they are pruned when the sap is rising they will bleed: sap will ooze out from the pruning cuts, weakening the plant.

To prune them, untie the fruited stems from the supports and cut back to one or two buds from the main stem, or rod, as it is called. Prune back the rod if it is growing beyond its allotted space. Check for pests by gently removing any flaking bark, and spray with a plant oil winter wash, as used on fruit trees. Don't spray if you see green buds starting to swell or they will be damaged; wait until next winter.

■ **Bring in strawberries** that were potted up last August to be forced. If you have enough plants, bring in half of them now and the rest next month, and the fruiting season will be extended. Remove any old, dead and diseased foliage and place the pot in as much light as possible, a high shelf being ideal.

The February garden

This month sees the sap beginning to rise, not only in plants but in the gardener too. It can actually be a colder month than January, but a few days of watery sunshine is all it takes to tempt us outside. Check over your tools, make sure your pots and seed trays are clean, and stock up on fresh potting mix and labels. It's time to get growing!

THINGS TO DO

Make sure backyard birds have enough food and water, particularly in cold snaps. This is a good time to apply organic-based fertilizers and check that plant supports are sound before they are concealed by the new season's growth.

Continue planting trees, shrubs, fruit trees, and bushes as the weather allows; firm in any newly planted trees and shrubs lifted by frost. Repot or top-dress shrubs in containers.

Prune winter-flowering shrubs—including winter heathers—when the flowers have faded, and summer-flowering shrubs that flower on new wood. Hardy evergreens and climbers, such as jasmine and late-flowering clematis, may also be pruned now.

Remove the old stems of herbaceous perennials, and start tender perennials into growth under cover. Divide and replant snowdrops, start dahlia tubers into growth, and bring in the last of the spring bulbs being forced.

Prepare seedbeds for vegetables, lime vegetable plots if necessary, and fertilize and mulch fruit trees. Prick out or pot up seedlings sown last month.

LAST CHANCE

Cut back overgrown shrubs and hedges before the nesting season starts, and finish pruning fruit.

GET AHEAD

Prune roses in southern regions. If you're planning a new lawn, prepare the ground in readiness for spring. Sow annuals under cover.

A winter border The Christmas rose, winter aconite, crocuses, and snowdrops make a delightful seasonal display.

New season approaching

This is the month of anticipation. Spring is on the doorstep, and new green shoots are preparing to burst into bloom. On the mildest days you can get on with winter-pruning jobs and cultivate the soil, but if you're huddled up indoors, why not fill the time with a spot of garden planning.

There is now a noticeable difference in the length of daylight and a feeling of anticipation, too, as a new season is just around the corner. It's a lovely month to just wander around the yard and look at the buds beginning to swell. Many buds are attractively colored at this time and they're packed with youthful energy, ready to burst forth. Toward the end of the month, early spring-flowering bulbs such as *Narcissus* 'February Gold' are in flower and the earliest primroses are also appearing. And in many parts of the country, early-flowering shrubs such as flowering quince and daphnes will start to bloom.

Promise of spring Daffodils such as *Narcissus* 'February Gold' burst into flower this month and mark the transition between winter and spring.

Winter wet

Weatherwise, however, February can be very cold, with heavy snow, severe frosts, and a lot of rain. Try to keep off the soil when it is excessively wet as you will do more harm than good. Walking on very wet soil compacts it, pushing out all the air and damaging the structure. Once this has happened, raking the soil down into a fine, crumbly tilth that will give seeds a good start becomes much more difficult. If you really must walk on soil in these conditions, work from a plank that will spread your weight evenly over the soil and reduce compaction.

Toward the end of the month, a fairly mild spell may often delude us into thinking that spring has sprung already. But beware; winter can often return with a

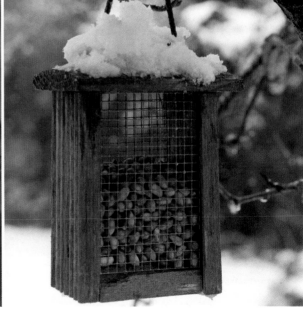

vengeance. Always be guided by your local weather conditions when you're considering planting, sowing, or doing any other work in the garden. You will find that from year to year, the timings of sowing and planting will vary quite considerably, depending on the weather conditions at the time. Don't get too frustrated if you are stuck indoors—take the opportunity to do some garden planning instead. A little bit of thought now about where plants should go in the garden will save you a lot of time in the busy spring season ahead.

Beat the blues

But it's not all doom and gloom outdoors and February can often be a good month for working off the winter blues. There is plenty to do as the garden begins to come to life. Check on any newly planted trees and shrubs to see if they have been loosened by frost and firm in gently where necessary, but don't be too heavy-handed about doing this, because if the soil is very wet you will drive out all the air from around the roots.

It's also an ideal time for planting bare-rooted deciduous trees and shrubs. The conventional wisdom on planting bare-rooted stock is that it can be planted at any time in the dormant season, from November until March. This still holds true, but current thinking now leans toward planting in February rather than in the fall. The reasoning for this is that often with fall planting, the trees and shrubs will just sit through winter in the cold, wet soil doing nothing, and they may be killed off in very cold spells. But if they are planted in February, then with spring just around the corner, they will get off to a much better start.

Another way to bring some cheer into the garden in late winter is to encourage the birds to visit. Keep your bird feeders well stocked and provide fresh water for them to drink and bathe in. This is also an ideal time to buy or build nest boxes in preparation for spring, when birds will be looking for homes for their new families. A simple wooden box that you can make or buy is sure to attract some feathered visitors to your yard this spring.

Winter rations Well-stocked feeders attract birds into the backyard, especially on wintry days when natural food is in scarce supply.

Weather watch

As far as temperatures are concerned, January and February are similar, and depending on where you live, this month can swing between winter and spring, with some warmer days and heavy rains in the south, and freezing rain and ice storms in the north. Hard freezes and snow are still common in the north, and frosts in the south, so continue to protect vulnerable plants.

Gusty winds

February can be windy, too, with gusts across the prairies, gales along coastal areas, and variations across the country, depending on topography.

Brighter days

Generally there is more sun in February compared to January. The days are getting appreciably longer, too. Sunny days make you want to get started on jobs such as seed sowing, but don't be in too much of a hurry—there can be a lot of bad weather to come. In some parts of the country, such as the Northeast, this can be the coldest month of the year, but southern gardeners can rejoice, because azalea season is near at hand.

Winter wet

Precipitation varies from one part of the country to another, but generally speaking this is a wet month. Winter is the wet season for western regions, and they will still be receiving winter rains. The Midwest and Eastern parts of the country will be pelted with what forecasters like to call a "wintry mix." But in the Deep South, gardeners will be enjoying the first spring rains.

Blankets of snow

A thick layer of snow can persist in high areas for most of the winter, and in some places for most of the year. But on lower ground the amount of snow will vary from east to west. Coastal areas, kept milder by warm ocean breezes, have very little snow, especially in the mild climate of the Pacific Northwest, which is considered a gardening Mecca because plants from warmer regions of the world, such as South Africa and Australia, thrive there. By stark comparison, the Northern prairies and mountainous regions of the country will still be blanketed with a thick layer of snow this time of year.

Recycling prunings

This is a month for pruning woody plants. Hardy shrubs that flower on new wood later in the summer, such as the butterfly bush (*Buddleja davidii*), can be cut right down, generating piles of twiggy prunings. You can recycle the sturdiest of these to make plant supports, but the rest of the debris is still too useful to burn. If you shred it, it can be added to the compost pile or used as a mulch. There are many types of shredders available to buy or rent.

Shredded prunings make a good home-grown mulch, but if you wait and apply it when the soil has warmed up a little, you will lock some of that warmth in under the mulch blanket. What you can do now is give the soil a dressing of an organic-based fertilizer, so that the nutrients it contains will be available to plants as they start into growth. Although this book is not specifically about organic gardening, organic fertilizers, such as blood, fish and bone, hoof and horn, fish and seaweed meals and pelleted chicken manure, deserve a few words. The synthetic or chemical fertilizers available today normally act as a quick tonic or quick fix to get plants off to a good start. But with these fertilizers plants often produce soft, weak growth, which is much more susceptible to attack from pests and diseases. The nutrients are used up more quickly and so they have to be applied more often. They also do little to improve the soil, whereas some organic fertilizers, especially those based on seaweed meal, do have soil-conditioning properties.

With organic fertilizers, the nutrients are released more slowly and are available to plants over a longer period. So instead of a rapid boost to growth, the plants grow more steadily and sturdily. They are also easier to use because quantities don't need to be as precise as when using artificial fertilizers. Because the nutrients of organic fertilizers are released slowly, they are best applied two or three weeks before sowing or planting, so they are available to the plants.

If you have a greenhouse or a conservatory, you'll be busy this month, but don't be in too much of a hurry to sow a lot of summer bedding plants yet. It's better to start them next month to reduce heating costs. If sowings are made too early, the plants will become leggy due to poorer light, and they also risk becoming starved from being in seed trays or pots for too long. Later sowings will produce much better-quality plants for planting out at the end of May and beginning of June. For now, be sure you have a good supply of seed-sowing medium, pots, and seed trays on hand for the busy sowing season ahead.

Sowing for early crops

This is a good time to sow some early vegetables for planting out under cloches next month: lettuce, radishes, beets, salad onions, peas, and fava beans. The easiest way of doing this is to sow the seeds in plastic cell packs. These seeds don't need heat, but they do need the lightest spot you can find for them. Once you've sown seeds inside, cover the piece of ground outdoors where the young vegetable plants are to be put out, using a sheet of plastic to protect the soil from further rain and snow and to warm it up. Then you will have the tastiest, freshest, and most welcome vegetables in the neighborhood.

Winter landscape Sumac trees are dramatic in snow, with chunky, felted, rust-colored seedheads.

Changing crops The tight florets of sprouting broccoli make a welcome change from leafy winter greens.

Helleborus orientalis
Evergreen perennial with variably colored flowers (see p.289)

Iris 'Harmony'
Dwarf bulb ideal for an alpine trough or raised bed (see p.292)

Narcissus cyclamineus
Short-stemmed, flowering earlier than larger daffodils (see p.299)

Cyclamen coum Pewter Group
Low, clump-forming perennial with marbled leaves (see p.279)

Euonymus fortunei 'Silver Queen'
Brightly variegated evergreen shrub (see p.284)

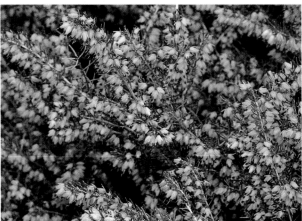

Erica x darleyensis 'Arthur Johnson'
Low-growing heather ideal for ground cover (see p.283)

***Clematis cirrhosa* 'Freckles'**
Small-flowered evergreen climber for very early spring (see p.274)

Viburnum tinus
Bushy evergreen shrub with perfumed flowers and black berries (see p.323)

***Chaenomeles speciosa* 'Phylis Moore'**
One of the first flowering quinces to come into bloom (see p.271)

Cornus mas
Deciduous shrub or small tree; the leaves color well in fall (see p.276)

Crocus tommasinianus
Carpeting bulb that naturalizes well in grass (see p.279)

***Camellia* x *williamsii* 'Anticipation'**
Evergreen, glossy-leaved shrub for acidic soil (see p.269)

What to do in February

AROUND THE YARD

If you use chemicals in the garden, even "organic" kinds, it is a good idea to go through them and see which have been lying around for a long time and can be discarded. There may be bags that have split open and the contents spilled on the floor or shelves, or bottles with only a few drops left in them, or others that have been left in the garage unused for years. Don't be tempted to pour them down the drain or scatter old fertilizer over the garden as you may cause a lot of harm. Take products like these to your municipal waste site and let them deal with disposal. Numbers will be in your local phone book or you can find them online.

Make sure backyard birds have plenty of food and water. February is a very hungry month for wildlife and putting food out may distract birds and small mammals from taking your buds and bulbs instead.

Put up bird boxes. Birds need a little time to get used to new boxes before they will select them to nest in.

Check that all tools and machines are in working order. Once the busy gardening season really gets under way, it is maddening to go to the tool rack and only then remember that your favorite spade has a broken handle, just when you want to start digging or planting a newly bought plant. Wiring of all electrical appliances should be checked for cuts, too, and if you are not sure what to do, contact a qualified electrician, or take the tool and cord to your nearest repair shop for advice.

Apply organic-based fertilizer to all borders. This is a good time of year to do this, as organic fertilizers release their nutrients more slowly than inorganic ones, so they will be available to the plants just as they start growing in the spring. A sprinkling of organic fertilizer like seaweed meal, blood, fish and bone, or pelleted chicken manure around the plants will do them a world of good after the long winter. Spread the fertilizer according to

Tool care Clean your tools after use: they last longer, and it reduces the risk of spreading diseases to other plants. Brush off dirt and sap, and give carbon steel blades a wipe with an oily rag to protect them against rust.

the maker's instructions and lightly stir it into the surface of the soil with a hoe or garden fork.

Buy plenty of potting mix, pots, and seed trays for the busy season ahead. Having a good supply on hand saves a lot of unnecessary trips to the garden center—time that you could spend gardening. Buying in bulk in partnership with your neighbors or as part of a local gardening society could save you a lot of money. The use of coir compost (which comes from coconut husks and is a renewable resource) and other peat substitutes is becoming more popular as we all become more environmentally aware. The less peat we use, the more we help to conserve the fast-disappearing peat bogs, where precious native flora and fauna exists.

TREES AND SHRUBS
Planting

■ **Bare-root trees and shrubs,** including roses, can be planted at any time during the dormant season from November to March, but recent research has shown that early spring can be the ideal time.

Provided the soil is not actually frozen, or so wet that it sticks to your boots, plants that you put in this month will get off to a really good start. The main reason for this is that the plants are not stuck in cold, wet soil all winter, when new roots will not grow much at all, especially so soon after they arrive from the nursery. But by planting during this month, it is not long before the soil begins to warm up and those new roots will get growing, quickly establishing the plant. Remember to care for plants well and water them thoroughly during any dry spells, especially as they are getting established in their first year.

■ **Deciduous shrubs** in the wrong place can be moved.

Pruning and training

■ **There may be quite a lot of pruning** to be done this month, especially if you haven't been able to brave the winter weather so far. Birds will soon be looking for nesting sites, so you should get pruning out of the way this month to avoid disturbing them later. Any overgrown or misshapen deciduous trees and shrubs can all be pruned to improve their health and shape. You can probably also start pruning roses this month in warm areas of the country. Many people start pruning roses in November, but in harsh northern winters this can cause dieback, and if the roses have already been pruned, this means you will have to go over them again in spring. For details of how to prune, see March, the traditional time to tackle roses and the safest in the north.

■ **Evergreens** that have become overgrown can be pruned now, provided they are completely hardy ; borderline hardy shrubs should be left until later in the year. Shoots that have become overcrowded or grown out awkwardly can be pruned back, to the main stems if necessary, to maintain the shape of the plant. Cutting back to ground level may be an option if the plant is one that tolerates drastic pruning—for example, *Prunus laurocerasus*, Japanese aucuba (*Aucuba japonica*) and *Viburnum tinus*. This will encourage strong growth from the base of the shrub. Fertilize after pruning, preferably with an organic fertilizer, and mulch with organic matter.

■ **In mild-winter areas,** trim winter-flowering heathers as they finish flowering. This job has to be done, otherwise the plants will become straggly and the center of the plant will become bare. The easiest way is to go over the plants with a pair of garden shears. Trim back to the base of the flower stalks: this will encourage sideshoots to grow, keeping the plant bushy and compact. Mulching the plants with a peat substitute and fertilizing a few weeks later will do a lot to encourage strong growth.

■ **Larger winter-flowering shrubs** such as witch hazel (*Hamamelis* spp.) don't as a rule need regular pruning, but at this time of year, once flowering is over, you can remove any stems that are rubbing or spoiling the shape of the plant.

■ **Late-flowering shrubs** can be pruned this month. These include *Buddleja davidii* (the butterfly bush), *Caryopteris clandonensis*, *Ceanothus burkwoodii* (the deciduous ceanothus), hardy fuchsias, santolina, ceratostigma, lavatera, and leycesteria (Himalayan honeysuckle). These shrubs flower best on growth made since the spring. It's a terrific job if you've had a bad day, as you can be quite brutal with them! Cut them back almost to the ground (see below), leaving one or two buds or shoots on each stem. You may feel you're cutting off far too much, but it is the right thing to do to get the best show of flowers. Where you want to increase the size of the shrubs, leave a few stems on and prune

Pruning summer shrubs

Pruning *Buddleja davidii* Use loppers to cut the thick stems back to a stubby framework.

Pruning caryopteris Cut back all of the whippy stems and a new crop will grow and flower.

these lightly. After pruning, feed with organic fertilizer and mulch with garden compost or farmyard manure to get them off to a flying start.

Hedges

■ **Brush snow off evergreen hedges** before the weight splays out branches.

■ **Overgrown or misshapen hedges** can be pruned now to improve their health and shape. Most deciduous hedges can be pruned back hard, as can broadleaf evergreens such as *Prunus laurocerasus* and laurel, but you must never cut conifers back into the bare wood, with the exception of yew. Yew is thought of as being slow-growing, but it is surprising how quickly it does grow, and even if it is regularly trimmed, it can gradually creep outward if it is not trimmed hard enough. Unlike other conifers such as Leyland cypress, yew will take very hard pruning: cut it back as much as you like and it will grow away again from the stumps. Other conifers must be lightly but regularly trimmed from the word go to keep them compact; never let them become overgrown.

■ **Conifers may need some attention.** If you didn't tie them in as a precaution, wind or snow may have bent branches down, spoiling the shape. If these are then pruned off it can leave an unsightly gap. So the thing to do is to tie them up again. Plastic-coated wire is fine as long as it is cushioned against the trunk with a piece of burlap or an old rag cut into strips and folded—otherwise the wire will cut into the trunk, eventually killing the tree.

CLIMBERS

■ **Brush any snow** off dense evergreen climbers and wall shrubs; when snow accumulates on these it can not only break stems but also puts strain on all the ties and supports.

■ **Prune late-flowering clematis.** Toward the end of the month, you can prune *Clematis orientalis*, *C. texensis*, *C. viticella* and its many varieties, such as 'Madame Julia Correvon' and 'Gravetye Beauty', and also the late large-flowered hybrids such as 'Ville de Lyon' and 'Jackmannii'. In some books these are all classed together as the "Group 3" clematis.

In sheltered parts of the country they may already be starting to produce shoots. These can be rather brittle, so you need to be careful when you are pruning and pulling away the old growth from last year. Apart from this, they are the easiest of all clematis to prune.

All you have to do is cut down all of the growth to 9–18 in (23–45 cm) from the ground, cutting each stem back to just above a healthy bud. These clematis are ideal for growing through other shrubs, because as they start afresh each year, they never become so overgrown that they swamp their host.

After pruning, feed with an organic fertilizer and mulch with organic matter, or put a large stone at the base of the plant. Clematis like their heads in the sun but their roots shaded and cool.

■ **Winter-flowering jasmine** can be pruned now that the flowers have faded. This lanky plant needs some attention to prevent it from becoming very untidy. First prune out any dead or damaged wood. Then tie in any stems that you need to extend the framework or coverage of the plant, and then shorten all the side growths from this main framework to 2 in (5 cm) from the main stems. This will

encourage plenty of new shoots for flowering next winter. Fertilize and mulch in the same way as for clematis.

■ **Summer-flowering jasmines** can also be pruned, but you must tackle this type by taking out an entire main stem or two to the ground. If you prune back all the side growths as with winter jasmine, they produce a mass of tangled, unproductive leafy growth.

■ **Plant new climbers** exactly as you would trees and shrubs (although they are more likely to be container-grown rather than bare-root), digging holes at least 9 in (22 cm) away from walls and fences so that the plant is not in a dry "rain shadow." Lean the plants into the support.

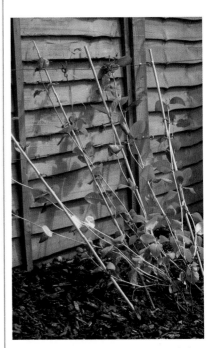

Planting new climbers To train a new climber along a wall or fence, put the wires in place before you plant. Guide the young stems up to their permanent framework using temporary supports such as bamboo canes.

PERENNIALS

■ **Finish weeding and digging over** the borders and new planting areas, incorporating organic matter if you can. Cut down any old, dead growth from plants such as sedums and acanthus that was left on for effect over the winter. The sooner this is done the better, as new shoots will already be emerging from some plants toward the end of the month and they are all too easily damaged.

■ **Toward the end of the month** herbaceous perennials will be starting into growth; now is a good time to feed them with an organic-based fertilizer.

■ **Continue taking root cuttings** from perennials.

■ **Check all the stakes and supports** that you removed in fall and stock up if you don't think you'll have enough for your plants later in the spring. One economical way of doing this is to keep the best of the prunings from shrubs pruned this and next month.

■ **Box up dahlia tubers** stored during the winter and they will produce shoots that make good cuttings. The tubers can be potted up singly, or several can be put into large trays. Place the tubers in good light and spray them occasionally with clear water to encourage the buds to grow.

New tubers bought from the garden center can be treated in exactly the same way. There are many different dahlias available from the smallest pom-pom blooms to showy decorative ones like the large cactus-flowered types.

BULBS

■ **Plant and divide snowdrops** and winter aconites after flowering, but while the foliage is still green. Both of these bulbs should be bought "in the green," as it is known. They often do not grow well when they are planted as dry bulbs in the fall. Look through gardening magazines and you will see plenty advertised by specialty nurseries, who will supply them in the green by mail order. Many garden centers also sell them in pots. It's best to buy snowdrops, in particular, from a reputable supplier, so you can be sure that they haven't been uprooted from the wild, an illegal practice which is causing great ecological damage.

Work in some compost or leafmold to enrich the soil before planting; a little bonemeal won't hurt. Put the plants in a little deeper than they were previously and water them in if the soil is dry. Overcrowded clumps in the garden can also be lifted carefully with a fork after flowering, and separated out. Replant them singly in informal drifts at the same depth as they were growing.

■ **Pot lilies for planting later.** Lilies are normally planted in fall in borders and

Planting snowdrops Unlike most other bulbs, snowdrops are planted while in leaf.

Iris reticulata

patio tubs, but if you didn't manage to do it then, you can still have lilies in flower this summer. Even if the soil is too wet for planting outside, you can pot up some lily bulbs and either move them or plant them out later in the spring. There should be plenty of lily bulbs in garden centers to choose from now. Look for good, plump bulbs, avoiding those that have become shriveled and dry in the sun.

Plant the bulbs three or four to a 7-in (18-cm) pot and keep them in a cool greenhouse or cold frame. Grow on inside, watering whenever the growing medium feels dry, to plant out later.

■ **Protect emerging bulbs** in the rock garden. Delightful dwarf bulbs like *Iris reticulata*, *I. histrioides* and *I. danfordiae* will all be coming into flower this month. If they are growing outside they will benefit from some overhead protection. Use a sheet of glass or acrylic on bricks, or a cloche, to prevent the flowers from being spoiled by rain and snow. Covering them brings them into flower a bit earlier too.

An ideal way of growing these wonderful bulbs is in pots or shallow pans. The containers can then be set on a table or on a low wall and you can enjoy the flowers without having to get down on your knees.

ANNUALS AND BEDDING

■ **Keep a watchful eye** on germinating seedlings sown last month to ensure that they get enough light.

■ **Sow hardy annuals in cell packs.** These cheerful plants are ideal to give a splash of color. And they are the perfect way to get children interested in gardening. It's very easy to sow hardy annuals outside next month, but if you want to get a head start and have earlier flowers, or if you want young plants to fill containers, then sow them in cell packs. The advantage is that the plants can be planted out without disturbing the root systems and so they get off to a flying start. Fill the trays with potting mix, give a sharp tap on the bench to settle it, brush off surplus, and gently firm with the bottom of another tray. Water the trays and then sow the seeds. Sow a small pinch of seed in each cell and cover with vermiculite. Place in a cold frame or sheltered area and they will germinate in a few days. Plant out when they are big enough to handle.

■ **Continue deadheading** winter pansies. The display will be prolonged. Although they are called "winter-flowering," they will continue to flower into early summer if you are assiduous about deadheading.

■ **Sweet peas can be sown** outside in warm regions of the country. Sow the seeds ½ in (1 cm) deep, and to speed up germination and protect the seedlings, cover each one with an improvised cloche, using the cut-off top half of a discarded plastic bottle. Pot up sweet peas sown in fall under cover if you didn't get around to doing it last month. These plants will be growing well by now, and if you want plenty of flowers, pinch out the growing tip to encourage sideshoots. If left unpinched the leading shoot often grows "blind."

CONTAINERS

■ **Check tubs, troughs, and pots** outside for water. Evergreen shrubs at high risk of drying out, as their foliage stops rain from getting into the potting medium.

■ **Plan now for summer planting** designs in containers. Time spent now planning what plants and how many to grow in containers is well spent. It's fun browsing through seed catalogs, dreaming up plant and color combinations. It's all a matter of personal choice and deciding which plants will suit particular situations, such as sunny or shady positions. If you have space, grow the plants from seed, or if you don't have space or time, buy young plants and grow them on under cover. You get a much wider choice by buying early.

■ **Top-dress container-grown shrubs.** Shrubs that have been growing in large tubs for many years benefit from top-dressing with fresh potting mix each year. Scrape away as much of the old soil from the surface as you can; about 1 in (2.5 cm) is ideal. Then add fresh potting mix with some slow-release fertilizer added. This will feed the plants over a period of several months, doing away with the chore of fertilizing them every week or month through the spring and summer.

Top-dressing Refreshing the soil makes more nutrients available to container plants.

LAWNS

■ **Keep off the grass** when it is frozen or frosted, otherwise later, when it thaws out, your footprints will show up as yellow patches on the lawn where the grass has been damaged.

■ **In mild areas**, start mowing. It may seem early, but in warm areas and mild spells, even in winter, the grass will continue to grow, albeit not a great deal. So it does no harm to give the lawn an occasional light trim, setting the blades of the mower at their highest setting. Don't do this if the lawn is soaking wet or frozen, or you'll do more harm than good. In colder regions of the country, don't mow until next month at the earliest.

■ **Disperse worm casts** Brush away worm casts on the lawn regularly. There are no chemicals currently available to amateur gardeners that can be watered onto the lawn to kill worms, but in any case, it is far better to preserve these creatures, which do so much good in the soil by breaking down organic matter and aerating the earth as they move through it.

A unappealing few worm casts are a small price to pay for having a healthy population of worms in your garden. Brushing the casts to disperse them is the best option.

Worm casts Exposed soil invites opportunistic weeds, so remove worm casts regularly.

A clean sweep Remove worm casts with a stiff broom; brush the loose soil into the border.

■ **Dig out lawn weeds.** If you have only a few weeds in the lawn, then the ideal way of removing them is individually. Weeds with fibrous root systems such as daisies and plantains are quite easy to deal with; dandelions, which have long taproots, are trickier. You have to make sure all of the root is removed, because any portion of the root left in the soil will grow again. If dandelions are too big to remove with a knife, or weeds are too extensive, use a selective lawn weedkiller or a spot-weeding treatment in the spring.

Making new lawns

■ **Lay sod.** Sod can be laid during this month on ground prepared earlier, provided that the soil is not frozen or so wet that it sticks to your boots.

■ **Prepare ground** for sowing grass seed in warm regions. If conditions allow, now is the time to get the work done for making a new lawn in the spring. By the end of March the soil will have warmed up enough to give grass seed a flying start. The ground should be dug over, incorporating organic matter to help retain moisture and removing all perennial weeds. Remove large stones as you see them. Now leave the ground to settle for a few weeks.

VEGETABLES AND HERBS

■ **Start preparing seedbeds** and cover them with cloches. Soil that has already been covered with plastic sheeting for a while should now be dry enough to make a start on preparing seedbeds ready for sowing next month. Rake down the soil until it is reasonably level, removing all the large stones. Apply an organic fertilizer now, about two weeks before sowing, and its nutrients will be available for the young seedlings as they germinate.

Put cloches or plastic sheeting over the prepared soil. This will keep off the worst of the winter rain and snow and also help to warm up the soil, allowing earlier sowing and planting outdoors. By making use of cloches you can probably gain about three weeks.

Kits to build cloches and, of course, ready-made cloches are available from mail-order companies. There are many types to choose from; the more decorative ones usually tending to be the more expensive. I think it's more satisfying to make them yourself if you have time.

The easiest way to do this is to put wire hoops into the soil at regular intervals and stretch a long sheet of clear plastic between them, burying or pegging the ends of the plastic in the ground at each end to anchor it firmly in place.

■ **Finish preparing deep beds.** Digging of new, deep beds and top-dressing of established ones should be finished now, before the busy seed-sowing time gets under way.

■ **Lime if necessary.** If you follow the crop rotation plan shown in January, about one-third of the vegetable plot may need to be limed every year, generally where the brassicas—Brussels sprouts, cabbages, and cauliflowers—are to be grown, as these all like alkaline soil. Lime should be added at least two months before planting, so if you do it now, the beds will be ready when you move transplants into them. But before applying any lime, always first check the existing pH (its acidity or alkalinity) of the soil with a soil-testing kit, as this will determine the amount of lime you need to put on. It may be that if you naturally have a very alkaline soil, you do not need to add lime at all.

The pH of the soil is a scale of 1–14, by which the alkalinity or acidity of the soil is determined. Around seven is neutral; values less than 7 are acid, and higher than 7, alkaline. Soil-testing kits are remarkably easy to use; most come with a numbered chart to which you match the color of your soil sample, after mixing it with the solutions provided.

Once you know your soil's pH, the instructions on the package will help you add the correct quantity of lime. Wear gloves, goggles, and a face mask, and choose a still day. It's safest to use ordinary garden lime, calcium carbonate—or the organic alternative, dolomitic limestone—rather than the caustic and hazardous quicklime or slaked lime.

Warm up seedbeds Make simple tunnel cloches with plastic sheeting and wire hoops.

Harvesting
■ Continue to harvest winter crops and check on any chicory being forced.

Sowing indoors
■ **Keep on sowing early crops** and take care of those sown earlier.

■ **Sow peas in gutter sections**. An ideal way of sowing peas is to sow them in a piece of plastic rain gutter, choosing an early variety such as 'Douce Provence'. You will have to drill drainage holes in the bottom of the gutter, then fill with a peat-free potting mix. Sow the seeds evenly in two rows 1–2 in (2.5–5 cm) apart and about 1 in (2.5 cm) deep, and water thoroughly. Keep them on a windowsill or in a greenhouse; it does not need to be heated, although bottom heat will speed up germination. When the seedlings have sprouted a few leaves, they can be planted out under a cloche by carefully sliding them out of the gutter section into a shallow trench already made in the soil.

Sowing and planting outdoors
■ **Sow seeds under cloches**—toward the end of the month in colder areas—as long as the soil has been covered for a few weeks to warm it up. Seeds to sow include lettuce, radishes, salad onions, peas, fava beans, beets, cabbage, and spinach.

To sow the seeds, rake the soil to a fine tilth, which should be easy if the soil has dried out under cover. Then scratch out shallow drills with a cane to the depth required and space the drills at the distance given on the seed packet. Water along the drills first, before you start sowing. If you water after sowing, the seeds may be washed deeper into the soil, making germination more difficult or even impossible. After watering, sow the seeds as thinly as possible and cover over carefully with dry soil. Firm down with

Sowing peas in gutter sections

Space out all the peas before pushing them in, so you don't lose track of where you are.

Once the seedlings have a few pairs of leaves, the whole batch can simply be slid into a trench.

your hand and the job is done. Put a cloche on top and wait for the seeds to germinate. Thin out the seedlings when they are large enough to handle; thinning instructions will be given on the back of the seed packets, too, so don't throw them away, but keep them somewhere safe.

■ **Plant shallots.** It may seem too early to be doing this, but now is the time in warmer regions. Prepare the ground thoroughly, if you have not done this earlier, incorporating plenty of organic matter. Add an organic fertilizer and rake the soil to a fine tilth. Plant the shallots 6– 7in (15–18 cm) apart, in rows the same distance apart. Don't just push them into the soil, or the new roots, as they form, will push the bulbs up and out again. Birds love to pull them out, too, if they see them. The best way to plant the shallots is with a trowel, with the bulb tips just beneath the surface of the soil.

■ **Plant Jerusalem artichokes.** These are difficult to site within a traditional vegetable plot because they grow enormously tall and cast a lot of shade. But they are ideal plants if you want a productive summer screen for a garden shed or the compost pile. Be aware, though, that they will spread rapidly, and keep an eye on them so they don't take over the garden. The tubers, which look like long, knobby potatoes, should be planted in a single row 6 in (15 cm) deep and 1 ft (30 cm) apart. They will grow quite tall in their first year, perhaps to 6 ft (2 m), and may need some staking, as the tall stems can be battered to the ground in wet weather. One way of supporting them is to drive four stakes into the ground, two at each end of the row, and run string or thin wire around them. The tubers are harvested from fall through winter.

Planning ahead
■ **Prepare a bed for planting asparagus.** This delicious vegetable is quite easy to grow in the garden, but it is a long-term crop, and will occupy a place of its own for several years, so you need to plan for this.

For planting the crowns, see April. This month, prepare the soil by digging thoroughly, removing perennial weeds completely and incorporating plenty of organic matter.

■ **Prepare trenches for runner beans.** If you want a delicious and heavy crop of runner beans, now is the time to make a bean trench. The better you prepare now, the better the crop will be later on. Dig a trench, to the depth of a spade and 18 in (45 cm) wide, and pile the soil up on either side. It need not be a straight trench—it could be a ring shape if you are planning to grow the beans up teepees. These are often easier to site than rows in a small garden, because they only cast a slim pointer of shade that moves around with the sun. Put as much organic matter as you can get into the bottom of the trench and fork it in. If you are short of organic matter, use old newspapers torn into strips. After digging in the organic matter, leave the trench open to allow the weather to break down the soil, improving its structure right up until it's time to sow or plant.

■ **Sprout early seed potatoes** if not this was not done last month.

Caring for crops

■ **Fertilize spring cabbages.** Cabbages that have been standing all winter in mild areas will benefit from being fertilized now. Use a general organic fertilizer to help boost the growth. As you harvest, cut every alternate plant in the row, leaving the others to grow on and form a head in late spring.

It is possible to get a second crop from cabbages that have already been cut. Leave the stem and root in the soil and make a cross-cut on the top of the stump. Fertilize the plant and in a few weeks "mini-cabbages" will grow from the cuts.

Preparing a runner bean trench

Because they grow so large, runner beans are notoriously hungry plants. A specially dug bean trench filled with compost or manure is the traditional way to create a super-rich bed to supply all the nutrients they need.

1 Mark out the position of your row and dig a trench about 2 ft (60 cm) wide. Loosen the soil in the base with a fork.

2 Put manure plus kitchen or garden waste into the trench, replace the soil, and scatter pelleted poultry manure over the top. Leave it all to rot down thoroughly.

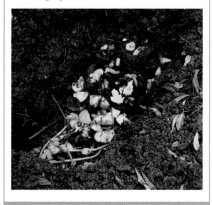

Herbs

■ **Cover parsley** and other overwintering herbs with floating row cover or cloches. This will protect the plants from pests and bring them into growth a bit earlier.

■ **Mint is an excellent herb** with the first of the early potatoes dug fresh from the garden. A few roots dug and potted up now will provide sprigs in the kitchen ready for the first vegetables of the new season. This is quite a good way to grow mint outside, as it can be very invasive, easily taking over parts of the garden. Grow it in a large pot and stand this on a deck or patio, or plunge the pot into the ground, leaving the top 2–4 in (5–10 cm) of the pot above the soil surface. This will usually prevent the mint from creeping over the rim into the soil, but keep an eye on it anyway.

■ **Top-dress shrubby herbs,** such as bay and rosemary, in containers.

Propagating mint suckers Cut above a leaf node into sections 3 in (8 cm) long and insert four or five into a pot so that at least one pair of young leaves is just above the surface.

FRUIT

Picking and storing

■ **Continue to check all fruit** you have in storage. Any that is showing signs of rotting should be removed immediately. If left, rot will quickly spread through the rest of the fruits. Put not-too-rotten fruits out for the birds to feed on.

Caring for crops

■ **Fertilize all fruit,** unless you did so toward the end of last month.

■ **Sprinkle sulfate of potash** around fruit trees—or use rock potash. To get good-quality crops, fruit trees need a high-potash fertilizer. Normal organic fertilizer is not especially high in any one nutrient, so supplementing it with a little extra potash will go a long way toward helping you produce good-quality fruit. Spread it below the trees or bushes in an area equal to the spread of the branches. Use fertilizers strictly according to the manufacturer's instructions.

■ **Mulch all fruit** with well-rotted manure or garden compost. It is well worth doing this after pruning and fertilizing has been done. Not only will a mulch help to keep down weeds, it will also hold in moisture. This cuts down watering in the warm summer months and will give you better-quality fruit. If the soil is dry, soak the ground first before applying the mulch. Mulch is as good at keeping water out as retaining it in the soil. You can lay soaker hose beneath the mulch to make watering in the summer simple.

■ **Complete spraying** with plant oil winter wash. This month is the last until next winter to use these washes, which can help avoid pests and diseases later on. Winter washes can only be used on trees and bushes that are fully dormant.

■ **Check that newly planted** fruits have not been lifted by frost. February can often bring the most severe weather of the winter, with hard, penetrating frosts.

When soil freezes, the water in the soil expands and this can push newly planted trees and shrubs up and out of the soil. This loosens the plant's grip on the soil, and if left, it will be rocked in windy conditions and eventually killed. So it is a good idea to check newly planted fruit when the frost has thawed and firm in as needed.

■ **Check tree ties and stakes**. Loosen any ties that are too tight or they will strangle the tree.

■ **Check fruit trees for signs** of canker. For details of symptoms and what to do, see January.

■ **Continue to protect** fruit trees and bushes from birds using netting, mesh, or webbing. If you didn't net the plants last month, do it now. Make sure coverings are supported off the plants, yet taut and held down firmly on the ground, otherwise the birds may get caught and be injured. An ideal way of growing gooseberries is to train them as cordons (one single stem) or as fans against a wall or fence. This way netting them against birds is a much easier task. If you have a lot of gooseberries and other fruits it may be worth investing in a fruit cage.

■ **Protect peaches and nectarines** against peach leaf curl if this was not done last month. This disease's symptoms show up as puckering and blistering of the leaves later in the year. The disease develops when spores lodged in the buds infect emerging leaves under wet conditions. The ideal way to prevent it is by covering the plants through the winter or by taking container-grown trees under cover. You will need to hand-pollinate the flowers. Using a soft brush, brush pollen from flower to flower all over the plant, at least twice while the flowers are open.

Pruning and training

■ **Finish winter-pruning fruit trees,** which will be starting into growth soon. If pruning is done as the trees come into growth, the rising sap will ooze out from any large cuts, weakening the tree. This may encourage disease to invade the wound. For details of pruning *see* January and November.

■ **Prune fall-fruiting** raspberries. There is a distinction to be made between the pruning times and methods for summer- and fall-fruiting raspberries. If you get it wrong, you lose the crop for that year. Fall-fruiting raspberries, which are pruned now, produce their fruit from August or September onward on long stems—canes—that grew during that summer. The best variety is called 'September'. Summer-fruiting raspberries will fruit on the canes that grew the previous year.

Prune fall raspberries Canes left over winter should be pruned right down to ground level now. New canes will soon grow.

Fall-fruiting raspberries should now have all their growth pruned to the ground. Sprinkle a high-potash organic fertilizer around the plants, and you should get strong canes growing that will produce a good crop of fruit. The stems of fall-fruiting raspberries are quite sturdy and they don't need tying in and training. You can wind twine along the rows and around posts at each end to keep them neat, but don't restrict them too much, to allow sun to reach all of the ripening fruits.

■ **Summer-fruiting raspberry** canes that have grown taller than their support frame can have the tips of the canes pruned back to one or two buds from the top wire. Alternatively, they can be arched over and tied down to the top wire. Either option encourages the formation of sideshoots along the length of the cane, so you will get a heavier crop of fruit.

Planting

■ **It's a good month** to plant bare-root fruit trees and bushes in moist-spring and summer areas (fall is best for wet-winter/dry summer areas). If the soil was not prepared during the winter, be sure to incorporate plenty of organic matter before planting. The best way to do this is to put well-rotted farmyard manure in the bottom of the planting hole. Fresh manure will scorch the roots. An application of general fertilizer will also help the trees get off to a good start. Always plant to the depth to which the plants were planted in the nursery. Look for the darker mark on the main stem. Insert a stake for trees, tying the tree to it with a tree tie, before refilling the hole, so you won't cut through any roots. Mulch with organic matter after planting and keep the young trees or bushes well watered in their first year until they get established.

■ **Plant raspberry, blackberry,** and hybrid berry canes. Toward the end of the month is the latest time for planting bare-root cane fruits. Have the soil thoroughly prepared by digging a trench all along the proposed row and working in plenty of organic matter, if not done during the winter. All except the fall-fruiting raspberries will need support for the fruiting canes. This is usually given by posts at either end of the row with at least three horizontal wires strained between the posts. Freestanding rows should be at least 5 ft (1.5 m) apart. If you are using a wall or fence for blackberries and hybrid berries, then you may be able to attach the wires to hooks in the wall. Plant raspberries about 18 in (45 cm) apart in the row. Blackberries and hybrid berries need to be at least 5 ft (1.5 m) apart, and some vigorous cultivars may need even more space: ask the nursery for advice. Prune the newly planted canes to about 9 in (22 cm) from the ground. This is essential to encourage the good, strong-fruiting canes from the base of the plant. Later in the summer you can cut it right out. Tie the canes to the wires as they grow through the season, but don't take a

Planting raspberries Plant new canes in trenches with plenty of organic matter and provide support such as three wires stretched between posts at each end of the row.

crop this year. The odd fruit is alright, but remove flowers if there are a lot of them. At this time you are trying to get the plants established. They will then give a good crop next year.

Beat the seasons

■ **Continue to force rhubarb.** If you didn't cover rhubarb last month, do it now, because it will soon be starting to grow.

■ **Cover strawberries with cloches** for an early crop. As well as forcing strawberries in pots in the greenhouse, a succession of fruits can be obtained by covering some plants outside with cloches. Any cloche will do, but once the strawberries are in flower, open the sides during the day to allow pollinating insects to get in. Keep an eye out for pests, especially aphids. Use an organic spray to control them.

UNDER COVER

■ **Clean out greenhouse** and conservatory gutters, as these may be full of leaves.

■ **Ventilate on good days.** With the lengthening days in February we often get sunny spells that can send temperatures under glass soaring rapidly. Open the ventilators when you can to maintain more even temperatures, but not so much that you let in cold drafts, which can affect growth. Remember to close the ventilators well before sundown.

The aim is to keep the temperature even. The less difference between day and night, the better for plants, otherwise they may produce spindly growth because of the warmth and the relative lack of light during the short days of winter. Keeping air circulating will also cut down diseases.

■ **Fuchsias in heated greenhouses** and conservatories can be sprayed with water to encourage growth. Those fuchsias that were started into growth and repotted last month will be showing signs of growing. Occasionally spraying with water helps buds to break and also keeps a humid atmosphere around the plants, which is ideal. Plants pruned early last month should now be producing new shoots and some can be used for making cuttings to increase your stock. Taking tip cuttings from a stock plant will also encourage more sideshoots, and therefore more flowers.

■ **Prune tender perennials** such as geraniums, fuchsias, argyranthemums, lantana, and salvias that have been overwintering, dormant, in greenhouses. These older plants can now be taken out of their pots or boxes. If they are not pruned now, they become very tall, with all the flowers at the top of the plant. Prune all the main stems back to two or three buds, or 2–3 in (5–8 cm) from their point of origin. Prune sideshoots quite hard to one or two buds from the main stems. Any prunings at least 3 in (8 cm) long can be made into cuttings, increasing your stock. At the same time, prune out dead or diseased material and any shoots crossing each other, to open up the center of the plant. Repot the plants into pots of fresh potting mix, gently firming around the roots, and water them in. After a few weeks new shoots will grow to give a stunning display over summer, inside or out.

■ **Make sure seedlings** get enough light, otherwise they will grow tall and leggy trying to reach the light—and then, being weak, they will be more susceptible to attack from diseases such as botrytis and damping off. Once germinated, move them to a high shelf, to get maximum light. If they are growing on a windowsill, turn them at least once a day.

■ **Watch for damping off** in seedlings. Warm, moist conditions encourage damping-off disease, causing rotting and collapse. A fungicidal treatment can be used, but the best prevention is always to sow seeds thinly so they have room to develop. Don't keep them too wet, either.

■ **Prick out seedlings.** If you sowed seed in small pots or trays in order to fit more into your propagator, then once they have developed two leaves, move them into more spacious surroundings to give them room to develop and reduce the risk of damping off. This is called "pricking out."

Replant the seedlings either 1 in (2.5 cm) apart in larger trays, or into the individual cells of a cell pack to grow on. Gently hold them by the leaves, but do not pull them; instead, lift them out from below. Drop them into holes dibbled in the growing medium and just nudge the soil back into the hole to fill. Don't be tempted to firm or press it.

Cuttings from fuchsias

1 The tips of shoots at least 1 in (2.5 cm) long can be rooted successfully. Remove the cutting by cutting just above a bud.

2 Trim the base of the cutting just below a bud and remove the lower leaves, making sure that there are at least two leaves left at the tip.

3 Dip the base of each cutting in hormone rooting solution and put each in a cell containing a mixture of equal parts peat-free potting mix and vermiculite.

4 Water the cuttings and put in a propagator at 65–70°F (18–21°C). The cuttings will root in three to four weeks and can then be moved onto a greenhouse bench or windowsill.

Prick out seedlings Carefully hold the seedling by its leaves, and use a dibber or pencil to gently ease it out of the pot from below.

Raising plants for outdoors

■ **Order plug plants.** With a greenhouse, you have the first choice of young bedding plants to raise under glass, so place your orders now.

■ **Sow hardy annuals** in modules.

■ **Sow seeds of** *Impatiens* (Busy Lizzies). This is a difficult plant to grow from seed, so if you're a beginner, it's probably not worth trying yet. But if you have a knack for raising seedlings, it will save you some money. The seed can be difficult because it needs light to germinate, so it can't be covered, and it also needs a constant warm temperature with a humid atmosphere. The easiest way to get seed to germinate is to draw shallow drills (grooves) with a pencil across the growing medium in a seed tray, sow the seeds in these drills, and lightly cover them with vermiculite.

The vermiculite holds moisture and still lets light through. Place the tray in a propagator, put a sheet of glass over the tray to hold in the moisture, and keep at a temperature of 70°F (21°C). The seeds should germinate in two to three weeks.

■ **Sow sweet peas** if not done last month, and pot up those sown in the fall.

■ **Sow early crops** in succession to those sown in January: for example, peas in gutter sections and fava beans in cell packs.

Greenhouse and houseplants

■ **Freesias and lachenalias** that have finished flowering can be rested. Bulbs planted last August will be coming to the end of their flowering period and will have to be fed to build up their reserves before resting for the summer. Feed them every week now for three or four weeks with a high-potash liquid fertilizer to build up the bulbs for next year and then gradually reduce watering until foliage dies back. The best way of resting the bulbs is to lay the pots on their sides under a bench, to be restarted into growth next fall.

■ **Start off begonia**, gloxinia, and achimenes tubers. All can be started into growth this month and through to March. Begonia and gloxinia tubers can be placed several to a seed tray, or potted individually into small pots and then potted into larger pots as they grow. The tubers of both are slightly hollow on one side and this hollow should be uppermost when the tubers are planted. Plant them so they are just covered with growing medium, as they form roots all over the surface of the tuber. Achimenes have small tubers about 1 in (2.5 cm) long, and these can be laid on their side several to a pot and potted on as necessary. Normal room temperature is quite sufficient. It is an easy way of growing these plants if you cannot maintain high enough temperatures to germinate their seed.

■ **Prune indoor climbers** such as plumbago and passionflowers. These popular climbers for heated greenhouses and conservatories are pruned in similar ways. The passion flower is a vigorous climbing plant and can be trained against a wall. Prune all the shoots to within two or three buds from where the previous year's growth started. Plumbago is best tied to a support. To prune it, shorten all sideshoots to 1–2 buds of the previous year's growth.

■ **Repot or top-dress** citrus trees. These will be putting on new growth, so they will need either potting on into larger pots— or larger, more mature plants can be top-dressed with fresh potting mix. To top-dress, scrape away as much of the old soil as you can without exposing and damaging roots, and replace it with a good-quality fresh loam-based potting mix.

■ **Plant out lily-of-the-valley** that was lifted and potted in the fall, to flower indoors over winter. Plant in fertile, humus-rich soil in full or partial shade. .

Crops under glass

■ **Continue to force strawberries.** The first batch brought in in January will be starting to grow, so a second batch brought in now will provide a succession of succulent fruits much earlier than outside. If you cover a few plants outdoors with cloches, this will continue the succession from those in the greenhouse, until uncovered plants fruit naturally.

Water and feed the indoor plants with a high-potash fertilizer to ensure good-quality fruits. Once they begin to grow, watch for aphids, which can become quite active. Once any flowers appear, they will need hand-pollination in the sheltered conditions of the greenhouse.

The March garden

The first month of spring has arrived at last in many parts of the country, and the garden really begins to come alive. But this can be a tricky month as far as the weather goes; it's possible to get mild sunshine one day, only to be followed by a hard frost the next, so be sure to make the most of bright spells. You can mulch and prune, take cuttings, reseed lawns, and sow hardy annuals.

THINGS TO DO

Start mowing lawns this month if necessary, and reseed any bare patches. Mulch bare soil in beds and borders. Take pumps out of storage and put them back into the pond, and begin feeding fish. As the weather warms up, make sure you water your indoor plants regularly.

Propagate shrubs by layering, and prune any with colorful winter stems. Bush and shrub roses will also need to be pruned during March, and evergreen shrubs can be moved.

Increase stocks of perennials by taking basal stem cuttings from the new shoots. Take cuttings from dahlia tubers, and split polyanthus after flowering. Sow sweet peas outdoors, or plant out young plants raised under cover, pinching out growing tips to encourage sideshoots. Sow hardy annuals where they are to flower.

Sow vegetables outside, and harden off young plants to set out. Plant early potatoes and asparagus, and make sure that you protect fruit blossoms against late frosts.

LAST CHANCE

Finish planting bare-root trees and shrubs and new fruit trees and bushes. This is the latest time to plant snowdrops and winter aconites.

GET AHEAD

Put growing bags in the greenhouse to warm up before planting. Put stakes and other plant supports in to support new growth around the garden before it really needs it.

Buds breaking on bare willow stems (*Salix*) to reveal silky, silver-gray catkins: a sure sign that spring is on the way.

Coming alive

Daylight saving time gives gardeners much-needed extra time for getting everything done—and there's quite a list. But the profusion of spring colors in flowering shrubs and blossoms will give plenty of encouragement. March can be cold, but you may get some bright days, too.

An abundance of spring flowers should now be brightening up the garden. Spring-flowering bulbs are coming into their own and toward the end of the month, those stalwart spring-flowering shrubs, the forsythias, bring forth their stunning show of bright yellow flowers in the North, while azaleas light up the South in shades of pink. Some early-flowering cherry trees herald the spectacular display of blossoms to come next month.

This is the month when daylight saving time begins, so there is no excuse for not using that extra time in the garden. Even at this time of year, there aren't enough hours in the day for all the gardening you want to do.

Take it easy at first

If you've been slumbering in an armchair all winter and have a sudden urge to get out and put the garden in order now that it's spring, then take it gently at first. But don't let me put you off! Gardening is great exercise and there is nothing better for clearing out mental cobwebs than working in the garden on a clear, warm spring day. Just go easy to begin with. Before starting any strenuous jobs such as digging, do some warm-up stretching exercises to ease yourself into the work. And jobs such as digging should be done in short spells—a whole day doing one job with repetitive movements may harm your back. So do about half an hour of digging at first, before switching to another job that does not involve too much bending.

Changeable weather

The weather can be fickle at this time of year, with one day having clear, blue skies and the next wintry showers. Make the best of good weather and move ahead with tasks such as making seed beds for sowing hardy annuals outside and in the vegetable garden, on the soil that was covered with plastic sheets or cloches earlier. Always bear in mind that there will still be sharp frosts in cold areas, so don't be tempted to buy bedding plants starting to appear at garden centers unless you have a greenhouse or frost-free place in which to keep them until all danger of frost has passed. And don't be in a hurry to remove protection from those frost-tender plants that were covered or wrapped up over winter. Plants can be uncovered during the day, but keep the protective material handy in case frost is forecast at night.

Deciding when to sow outside

Sowing seeds of hardy vegetables and annual flowers outside can begin in earnest this month in some areas, though in northerly parts, you'll have to wait until April or even early May. And if you have heavy clay soil, you may also have to delay sowing, unless you've had the ground covered during part of the winter. Remember that while books like this one can give general advice about when to do certain jobs, you should always be guided by local weather conditions before deciding to sow seeds or plant out young plants.

This year, try planting vegetables among flowers if your garden is small. Many urban backyards are too small to accommodate a separate kitchen garden, but fruit, vegetables, herbs, and ornamentals can be grown together very successfully. Many vegetables are attractive plants in their own right and they can make wonderful contrasts to other ornamental plants in the borders. The fine, feathery foliage of carrots contrasts well, for instance, with the bold leaves of hostas.

Deep-red new shoots *Paeonia lactiflora* 'Sante Fe' emerges against a blue background of *Chionodoxa forbesii*, creating a striking contrast.

Weather watch

Although March can be a cold month, on the whole, temperatures are rising and days are getting longer. However, in higher elevations and colder regions of the country, sharp frosts may descend on the land on clear nights, turning the ground hard, so don't put out tender plants yet. Cloud cover and wind will also have a direct effect on temperatures throughout each day, and in northern areas freezing rain and ice storms are as likely as snow to thwart gardening plans.

Bitter winds

March winds can be bitterly cold, but they do help to dry out the soil after winter rains and snow. Coastal areas can be subject to gales. All coastal areas, whether along the Atlantic, Pacific, Gulf Coast, or Great Lakes, are windy, and the ocean winds carry salt spray that can damage plants. On the Great Plains, this month signals the beginning of tornado season, which can bring rain and eerie periods of calm before storms send residents running for shelter.

Patchy sun

The longer days of spring bring longer hours of daylight each day. Clouds will, however cut down the amount of direct sunshine, along with their accompanying rains and snows. The northern states will still have fewer sunny days, on average, than the southern or western states.

Variable rain

The amount of rain falling around the country depends on how hilly or flat, or how far east or west of the Mississippi River, you live. Gardens along the West Coast will be enjoying some of the last of their winter rains this month.

Occasional snow

Heavy snowfalls can visit ski and other high-elevation areas, and snow can still be thick on the ground in most northern parts of the country. But the Deep South will be enjoying the first warm days of spring, accompanied by flowering shrubs and forced bulbs.

New shoots Salad leaves sown undercover will be ready to be planted outside in the vegetable patch.

Prevent weeds You can reduce weeding by planting through a permeable membrane. Clear perennial weeds, cultivate and level the soil, then lay the fabric. Cut small holes to plant into, and cover with a decorative mulch.

A decorative willow fence This has been created by pushing live willow wands into the soil. Bluebells emerge from the grass behind it.

Bright-colored bedding plants can be set against the rich foliage of beets and ruby chard. Globe artichokes and cardoons are striking architectural plants that stand out in any border. You can have great fun mixing and matching plants, and in addition to looking attractive, the garden will be productive, too. Sow or plant your vegetables in groups rather than the conventional rows, and they will blend in perfectly.

Watch out for weeds

Remember that many of the little jobs that keep the garden looking good can be done at the gentlest of paces. While taking a leisurely stroll around the yard, keep an eye out for germinating weed seedlings and slice them off with a hoe. The best time to do this is on a dry, sunny day, so that the weeds can be left on the surface of the soil to dry out and shrivel up in the warmth of the sun. Dig out any perennial weeds while they too are small, and they will be easier to control.

Weeding can become a bit of a chore, so to cut down on the time spent doing it, it is a good idea to mulch borders with a thick layer of organic matter after beds and borders have been tidied up. An effective way to prevent weeds from growing, mulching is also the perfect way to help conserve soil moisture, cutting down on the need to water as frequently during dry summer spells. Water is becoming a scarce commodity, owing to adverse changes in weather patterns worldwide caused by global warming and we must all do our best to conserve it.

The best time for applying mulch is early in spring while the soil is still moist; this way the moisture will not evaporate from the soil surface so rapidly. Water first if the weather has been dry. If a layer of mulch is applied to dry soil, it will be difficult for water to penetrate the soil.

Rose pruning

It's a traditional time for pruning bush and shrub roses. Some people prefer to prune them in fall, but there's a lot to be said for waiting until spring. Firstly, the more growth in general you can leave intact in the garden over winter, the more shelter you give to hibernating wildlife. Secondly, if your roses have taken a battering over winter—and pruned roses are not immune to this—then you can tailor your pruning to leave you with the best-shaped plants after removing the damage. Don't be shy about pruning bush roses hard. Modern bush roses tend to be grafted onto the roots of more vigorous species and are strong growers—they rise to the challenge of hard pruning by producing really good growth and flowers.

Pest patrol

Pests and diseases begin to make their presence felt in earnest from this month onward, particularly in the greenhouse or conservatory and in the house. Consider using biological controls, such as predators or tiny nematode worms that kill specific pests. These are regularly advertised in gardening magazines and you can order them by mail. Most are for use in the greenhouse, but there is one that can be watered onto open ground to control slugs. The sooner you can get on top of a slug or snail problem, the better—at this time of year, they're just as eager as we are to see all that tender new growth emerging from the soil.

Doronicum x excelsum 'Harpur Crewe'
One of the earliest-flowering perennials (see p.281)

Fritillaria imperialis
Striking bulb with clusters of bellflowers on tall stems (see p.285)

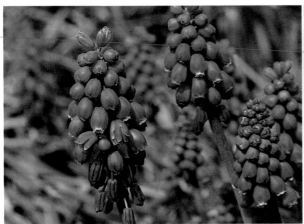

Muscari armeniacum
The grape hyacinth, with small but intensely colored flowers (see p.299)

Salix caprea 'Kilmarnock'
Small tree with drooping branches festooned with catkins (see p.315)

Iris danfordiae
Dwarf bulb ideal for an alpine trough or raised bed (see p.291)

Pulmonaria angustifolia subsp. _azurea_
Herbaceous ground-cover perennial for sun or shade (see p.309)

Narcissus 'Dutch Master'
Classic golden-yellow daffodil with trumpet flowers (see p.299)

Chionodoxa forbesii 'Pink Giant'
Small bulb, lovely planted under deciduous shrubs (see p.271)

Daphne mezereum
Exquisitely perfumed pink flowers clustered on bare branches (see p.280)

Hyacinthus orientalis 'City of Haarlem'
Bulb for indoor forcing or spring bedding (see p.290)

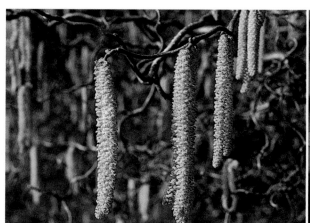

Corylus avellana 'Contorta'
Hazel bearing long catkins on contorted branches (see p.277)

Anemone blanda 'Violet Star'
Plant tubers in fall for a starry spring display (see p.265)

Lysichiton americanus
Perennial for damp ground or shallow water (see p.297)

Iris 'Katharine Hodgkin'
Dwarf bulb, ideal for an alpine trough or raised bed (see p.292)

Primula 'Miss Indigo'
Small but showy perennial for early spring display (see p.307)

Caltha palustris
Water-loving perennial for pond margins and boggy ground (see p.269)

Prunus sargentii
Flowering cherry tree with young leaves, to 60 ft (20 m) tall (see p.308)

Narcissus 'Cheerfulness'
Double-flowered narcissus with a powerful scent (see p.299)

Chaenomeles x superba 'Knap Hill Scarlet'
Stiff-branched shrub perfect for wall-training (see p.271)

Scilla siberica 'Spring Beauty'
Bulb, similar to but less invasive than bluebells (see p.317)

Forsythia x intermedia
Cheerful shrub tolerant of most soils and positions (see p.285)

Primula Gold-laced Group
Showy, unusual polyanthus-type primula (see p.307)

Crocus vernus 'Pickwick'
A spring favorite with attractively striped petals (see p.279)

Tulipa tarda
Small species tulip, short-stemmed, pretty in a rock garden (see p.321)

What to do in March

AROUND THE YARD

With warmer weather, pests are now on the increase, so keep an eye open for signs of infestation. If you pick or rub pests off as soon as they appear (or prune out badly infested shoots), you can keep them from multiplying and causing more trouble later on.

Mulch bare soil, having weeded and tidied it first, with organic matter—well-rotted farmyard manure, cocoa shells, garden compost, chipped bark, or spent mushroom compost (don't use the latter around acid-loving plants like rhododendrons, because it contains lime). Soil in borders left bare will very quickly lose water in dry spells. Covering with a thick layer of organic matter will cut down the rate at which water evaporates from the soil, reducing the need to water. This is especially important for young trees, shrubs, and perennials that have been recently planted. After spending your hard-earned cash on plants, never let them go without water in their first year. A mulch will also suppress weeds and it looks good, too. Never put a mulch on top of dry soil. If the soil is dry, water it first. A layer of compost is just as good at keeping water out as sealing it in.

Mulching Use a spade to spread a generous layer of organic matter over the soil; it should be at least 2 in (5 cm) deep.

TREES AND SHRUBS

■ **Move any evergreen shrubs**. Evergreens moved in winter are unable to replace water lost from their leaves through the action of frost and strong cold winds. Plants generally do not take up water from the soil until the temperature rises above 40°F (4–5°C). Now the soil is beginning to warm up and the shrubs will shortly begin to grow; they will therefore lose less water, helping them reestablish. When moving shrubs, take as large a rootball as you can manage. Provide protection from cold winds with a screen of burlap, keep the shrub well watered, and it should resume growing well.

■ **Feed winter-flowering heathers** pruned in February with a high-nitrogen fertilizer. For an organic option, choose dried blood, fishmeal, or pelleted poultry manure.

Planting

■ **Finish planting bare-root trees** and shrubs. This really is the last month, until fall, to get these plants in. With the leaves opening up they find it much more difficult to establish, because they are losing water rapidly from the foliage. Plants grown in containers can be planted year-round, although spring and fall, the traditional times, are best.

■ **Prune roses now** unless you got a head start last month. Prune bush and shrub roses now. Climbers are usually pruned in the fall, so that they can be tidied up and tied in before winter winds blow them around. Never prune ramblers in the spring unless you need to drastically renovate them, as you will lose this year's flowers. Prune them after flowering. The main reason for pruning roses is to build a healthy framework of shoots that will produce a good display of flowers. Thinning overcrowded growth allows in light and air, so there will be less chance of problems with pests and diseases, and also

Transplanting a shrub

1 Mark out a circle around the outer edge of the roots using a spade. Roots usually stay confined to the extent of the stems before they were pruned.

2 Dig a trench around the circle and use a fork to loosen the soil around the roots. With a spade, dig under the rootball so that it can be lifted.

3 Tilt the plant to one side and feed a piece of burlap or ground sheet under it. Then rock the shrub to the other side and pull the material through.

4 Get someone to help you carry the shrub to its new location. This is especially important if the rootball is large and heavy.

5 Dig a hole that is twice as wide and the same depth as the rootball at the new site. Carefully lower the shrub into the new hole and fill in with soil.

6 When you have filled the hole with soil, ensuring that there are no air gaps, firm the soil with your foot. Water in well and apply mulch.

encourages strong healthy growth. Cuts must be clean, not ragged or bruised, so use a good pair of sharp pruners. You may also need loppers for thicker shoots.

The first thing to do on any type of rose is to remove any dead or unhealthy wood. Leaving this on the plant can encourage diseases to invade. The next is to cut out any shoots that are crossing and rubbing against another.

Now, the flowering wood can be pruned, and here the method varies depending on the rose type. Always prune to outward-facing buds. The main rule to remember is that the harder you prune, the more vigorous the subsequent growth will be.

Clear up rose prunings carefully or they will ambush you later. It's best to dispose of or burn them, rather than shredding them for composting, as they can harbor disease. Then mulch around the roses, with well-rotted farmyard manure, or a bagged product such as shredded bark.

■ **Prune shrubby eucalyptus.** Not all of us have room to grow eucalyptus as a tree, but it responds well to hard pruning, making a lovely foliage shrub. Just prune all last year's growth to 6 in (15 cm) from the ground and you will be rewarded with the attractive, round juvenile leaves on a small bushy plant.

■ **Prune dogwoods** and shrubby willows grown for their ornamental colored stems. The best stem color from *Cornus* and *Salix* is produced by one-year-old shoots and this is the reason for pruning them in spring. Ornamental *Rubus,* with their white stems, should be pruned now too. Prune all these shrubs hard, to about one or two buds of last year's growth, to leave a stubby framework.

■ **Finish pruning late-flowering shrubs** such as *Buddleja davidii.*

Planning ahead

■ **Prepare for moving** large deciduous shrubs. You can still move them, but it's better to start preparing them for moving after the summer. Trees and shrubs often transplant more successfully when they have a good fibrous root system.

Many shrubs and trees don't produce very fibrous root systems, but this can be encouraged. Dig a narrow trench around the plant to be moved, to at least a spade's depth. This will cut through some of the roots and encourage the formation of new, fine roots within the circle. The trench can be refilled either with the soil taken out or with a compost mixture. Old potting mix is quite good, or fine, well-rotted garden compost mixed with the soil. In fall, when you dig around the shrub to move it, you will find that finer roots have formed and the shrub will have a much better chance of reestablishing well.

Propagation

■ **Layer shrubs to make new plants.** This is a good month to increase shrubs by layering. Many shrubs, like hydrangeas and philadelphus, will layer themselves, forming roots on shoots touching the ground.

■ **Layering** is quite easy. Usually, wounding the stem is enough to stimulate root growth, but if you want to encourage the process, you can also dust the wound with hormone rooting powder before pegging it down. The layered shoot will have formed roots by the following spring, when it can be cut from the parent plant and planted elsewhere.

Hedges

■ **This is your last chance** to plant bare-root hedging plants. From now until fall, only container-grown plants will generally be available, which can make buying in bulk for hedges expensive.

CLIMBERS

■ **Plant new climbers.** Install supports such as wires and trellis before you buy and plant. Wires may stand out at first, but are soon hidden by the plants.

■ **Finish pruning late-flowering** clematis.

■ **Prune climbing roses** now if you didn't do so in fall.

■ **Renovate climbers.** Tackle overgrown climbers: before they start into growth, yet with breaking buds so you can see where stems are dead. Climbers to cut hard back include honeysuckles, rambling roses, and winter jasmine.

Training up a pergola

1 Twist in four metal screw eyes at the top of each support and repeat this at the bottoms. Thread plastic-coated wire, secure, and pull taut.

2 Secure the climber to individual wires with soft garden twine. Twirling the plant around the support and tying it in ensures maximum coverage.

PERENNIALS

■ **Cut down all growth left over winter.** Even if seedheads and stems are still managing to look good, you need to get rid of them now to make way for new growth.

After a good tidy-up, if you didn't fertilize plants last month, you can dress the soil with a fertilizer now so that it is ready for a layer of mulch.

■ **In the south and in mild areas,** remove any cloches or protective blankets from plants susceptible to frost, or new shoots may be damaged. In colder regions it may be safer to wait until April. Fertilize the plants to get them going. You can also divide overgrown clumps.

■ **New shoots should now** be growing strongly from the crowns of plants and it is an ideal time to increase plants such as yarrow, Marguerite daisy, delphiniums, gypsophila, and lupines by a type of cutting called a "basal stem cutting." They are very easy to take, when the shoots are about 3–4 in (8–10 cm) high. Remove the shoots from as close to the plant as possible using a sharp knife. It's much like taking dahlia cuttings, except that the parent plant is in the ground. Insert the cuttings into a pot containing a mix of equal parts peat-free potting mix and perlite or vermiculite, cover with a plastic bag, and put on a shady windowsill or in a cold frame until they root in a few weeks.

Sometimes, you can take root cuttings with a small piece of root attached—especially from asters, and also lupines, campanulas, chrysanthemums, and sedums. These have a high success rate.

■ **Take cuttings from dahlia tubers.** Cuttings should be taken when the shoots have reached 3–4 in (8–10 cm) long, but before the stems become hollow (this is normal for dahlias as the stems mature).

■ **Trim the cuttings** below a leaf joint and remove the lower leaves. Dip the cuttings into fungicide (wear gloves for this) and then dip the bases into hormone rooting solution. Dibble the cuttings into pots containing equal parts peat-free potting mix and perlite or vermiculite. Put the pots in a propagator set at 50–55°F (10–13°C), with a plastic bag over them, to encourage a good root system. More shoots will grow from where the cuttings were taken, so you can take more later.

■ **Plant new plants.** Hardy perennials will grow quickly if they are planted now. Fertilize and mulch them after planting and keep well watered until they establish.

■ **Toward the end of the month** split up polyanthus-type primulas as the flowers fade. To divide them, dig up each clump with a fork. With very large clumps you will have to push two forks back to back into the center of the clump and push the fork handles apart. The sections can then be divided by hand. Trim off most of the old foliage, leaving about 2 in (5 cm). Apart from making the plants tidier, this reduces loss of water from the leaves: the plants establish quicker and new leaves soon grow. Either plant the divisions back *in situ*, after revitalizing the soil with garden compost or manure, or plant them in rows in a corner of the vegetable garden to grow through the summer and plant out again in the borders in the fall. The plants will then give a terrific splash of color in the spring.

■ **Lift and divide overgrown** clumps of summer-flowering herbaceous perennials. Most can be lifted and divided in spring, just as growth gets under way, and if the divisions are reasonably sized they should flower later in the year. Plants that need dividing are usually quite easy to see. As perennials age, the clumps push outward, with fresh, young growth to the edge of the clump, and the center dies out. This is the stage at which they should be divided. Lift each clump with a fork and insert two forks back to back and pry them apart; smaller pieces can then be pulled apart by hand. Add organic matter and fertilizer to revitalize the soil and plant the young divisions in groups of three, five or more, depending on the space you have. Water them in well if the soil is dry.

■ **Protect the young,** tender shoots of delphiniums and hostas from slug damage. Slugs and snails can do a lot of damage to young buds even when they've barely emerged from the soil, and you may not be aware of the damage until the leaves begin to open up. The tiny holes, at this stage perhaps the size of pinheads, expand with the leaves, and by the summer there may be a big hole, or series of holes, ruining the foliage. There are general measures you can take to combat slugs and snails, but it's worth taking extra precautions to protect individual plants. The best way to prevent slugs getting to your (and their!) favorites is to use a physical barrier that

Slug prevention A physical barrier such as copper tape helps prevent slugs away from the juicy young shoots of container-grown hostas.

the pests will not want to negotiate to get to the plants. The easiest barrier of all is coarse grit; slugs and snails really dislike moving over its rough surface. Put down a thick layer around the plants; the sooner you do it, the better.

■ **Support herbaceous perennials.**
Toward the end of the month, many herbaceous perennials will be growing quickly, and at the first sign of rain or a strong breeze, the shoots will be flattened. There is a wide variety of supports available today, and what you choose depends on the depth of your pocket. The easiest and cheapest are twiggy sticks pushed in around each clump; the plants soon grow up between them. Prunings from other shrubs, provided they are straight and strong enough, look rather unsightly to begin with, but the plants soon hide them completely. Supports you can buy include canes, plastic-coated stakes that link together, and mesh supports, which the plants grow through, some of which can be raised as the plant grows. The most important point about staking is to get it done early in the year so the plants will look natural as they grow. Don't wait until the plants flop over or

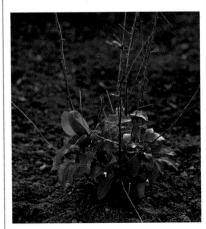
Plant supports Get stakes and supports in early so that plants grow up around them.

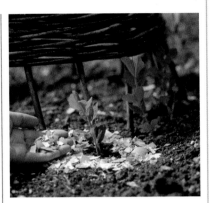
Gritty barriers Surround new plants with a thick layer of crushed eggshells or coarse grit to protect them from hungry slugs and snails.

are blown around; trying to stake stems that are growing in all directions can be problematic.

Alpines
■ **In the rock garden** weed seedlings will be growing in grit or gravel between the plants. Although a covering of gravel is fairly good at suppressing weeds, seeds of annual weeds like groundsel and annual grasses can germinate in the moist soil beneath and push through. They are easy to control by pulling them out or digging them up. Never use a sprayer in the rock garden to apply weedkiller; the plants are too close together for this and might be damaged. The best way to deal with perennial weeds is by spot-treating them with a weedkiller painted onto the foliage with a brush, usually built into the lid of the product. If the weed is growing up through the center of a plant, place a piece of wood or cardboard under the foliage of the weed to protect the plant, then carefully paint on the weedkiller.

After weeding, top off any bare patches where the gravel may have been washed away. This will give the rock garden a neat and tidy finish as the alpines come into their main flowering period in spring.

BULBS
■ **Deadhead daffodils** as the flowers fade, but leave the foliage alone. If the old flowers are left on, the plant's energy will be used for seed production. At this time the important thing is to build up the bulb's reserves so that a new flower bud forms inside it for flowering next spring.

■ **Plant snowdrops in the green** if this was not done last month. Snowdrops very rarely grow well from dry bulbs, so the best time to divide them or buy new ones is now, while they are still green. Overgrown clumps can be lifted and divided now, or new plants can be bought from specialty mail-order nurseries.

■ **Plant summer-flowering bulbs** this month and next month for a succession of flowers. They all enjoy a sunny position in well-drained soil. All summer-flowering bulbs, if planted at intervals over a period of a few weeks, will give a succession of flowers throughout the summer and into fall. However, in northern parts of the country, wait until next month before planting the frost-tender bulbs such as gladioli, eucomis, and tigridias.

Gladioli and other tender bulbs can be planted now in southern regions, but it is best to wait until mid-May in northern areas. They can be grown in several ways: in rows for cutting, in tubs, and in groups in borders. In ornamental borders, plant gladiolus bulbs (or, more correctly, corms) in groups of five or more. Plant the corms 4–6 in (10–15 cm) apart and 3–4 in (7–10 cm) deep. The deeper you plant, the less likely it is that you will need to stake the plants. In heavy clay, dig deeper and place the corms on a layer of coarse grit. Plant tigridias 2–3 in (5–8 cm) deep and 4–6 in (10–15 cm) apart. Plant galtonias 4–6 in (10–15 cm) deep and 9–12 in (22–30 cm) apart, and eucomis 6 in (15 cm) deep and 6–9 in (15–22 cm) apart.

Other bulbs to consider planting over the next few weeks include lilies and de Caen anemones. Lilies can be planted outside in well-prepared soil in groups in any mixed border. Plant the bulbs to three times their own depth and 3–4 in (7–10 cm) apart. In heavy clay soil, plant the bulbs on a layer of coarse grit to aid drainage. Lilies don't like to sit in damp soil. Plant de Caen anemones about 1 in (2.5 cm) deep and 4–6 in (10–15 cm) apart.

■ **Cannas for setting out** in June can be started into growth now.

■ **Bulbs that were forced** into flower inside can be planted out when the flowers are over, if this was not done earlier. Bulbs like narcissus, hyacinths, and dwarf irises will have finished flowering by now, so the best place for them is in the garden. Remove them from their containers and plant them without disturbing the roots. Feed them with a fertilizer high in potash to encourage the formation of next year's flower bud within the bulb. Don't try to force the same bulbs for a second year, as they rarely flower as well again. It's best to buy new ones in the fall.

Deadheading daffodils Pinch off the head behind the bulbous part, leaving the stem intact.

ANNUALS AND BEDDING

■ **Sow and plant sweet peas** outside in southern gardens. The easiest way to grow sweet peas is to sow them where they are to flower. There are many different ways of growing sweet peas, and they have many uses in the garden. The scented varieties are the best to grow. Erect a support first, if necessary. You can make teepees from canes or let them scramble up through shrubs.

Germination will be improved by soaking the seeds overnight to soften the seed coat. Then plant two seeds at 12-in (30-cm) intervals and $^1/_2$ in (1 cm) deep. When the seeds -germinate, the weaker of the two can be removed or moved to fill in any gaps. The young plants may need to be attached to the support with sweet pea rings initially, just to get them started. Soon the tendrils will twine themselves around the support. In mild areas, you can also plant out sweet peas sown last fall, in well-prepared soil.

■ **Sow hardy annuals outside.** Now it is safe to begin sowing hardy annuals outside in most areas. In northern areas you may have to wait until the end of the month or into early April.

■ **Hardy annuals look best** grown in informal drifts. If the soil has not been prepared, lightly fork it over, but don't add any manure or garden compost. If the soil is too rich, the plants will produce a lot of soft growth and very few flowers. All that needs to be done after forking over the soil is to apply a light dressing of a general fertilizer and rake the soil to a fine tilth. Now comes the fun part: marking out the informal drifts and sowing. The only rule to remember when planning an annual planting is that the taller plants, such as larkspur (*Consolida*) and cosmos, go to the back and the shortest, such as nemophila (or baby-blue-eyes), lobularia, and fried eggs (*Limnanthes douglasii*) at the front. You can spend time making elaborate color schemes, but from these plants all we really want is a good splash of color.

By sowing in drills rather than broadcasting the seed over each drift area, the young seedlings will be easier to tell apart from weeds. Once they grow together, you won't be able to tell that they are in rows. Varying the direction in which the drills cross neighboring drifts also helps avoid a regimented look. When the seedlings are large enough to handle, they will have to be thinned out.

■ **Any hardy annuals** sown under cover can be hardened off now to acclimatize them to outdoor conditions. Put the plants in a cold frame, top closed, for a few days. Then, gradually increase ventilation until the lid can be left off or up. This is usually done over a week or ten days. Keep some insulation like floating row cover to put over at night if a sharp frost is forecast.

■ **Sow seed under cover** of half-hardy annuals and tender perennials for summer bedding.

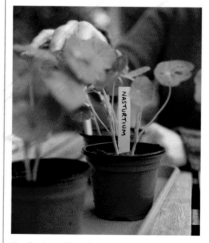

Hardening off Acclimatize seedlings by moving them outside during the day and back in at night.

CONTAINERS

■ **Plant up roses in pots.** Roses, particularly the "flowering carpet" varieties, miniature roses, and elegant standards, look excellent on the patio, in containers filled with a soil-based potting mix. Soil-based mixes are far better for shrubs in containers; they hold a supply of nutrients more easily than soilless ones and also retain moisture better, cutting down the need for watering. After planting, prune the roses hard to encourage plenty of new growth. After a couple of months, feed regularly with a high-potash fertilizer to encourage a profusion of flowers and you will be rewarded with a smashing display for weeks on end. Remember, though, that in dry weather, watering may have to be done once or even twice a day. The roses may fare better if they are moved into the shade in fiercely sunny weather.

■ **Many other plants** can be grown in containers: small trees, shrubs and climbers, herbaceous perennials, annuals, alpines, and ground-cover plants. Let your imagination run wild. The only real rule is to care for the plants well, watering, fertilizing, and deadheading regularly. Using slow-release fertilizers and the water-retentive crystals now available can save some work through the year.

Water storage Gel granules added at planting time expand and hold moisture, creating a built-in reservoir for container plants in dry spells.

LAWNS

■ **Get the lawnmower serviced** if you haven't already done so. This is usually a busy time of year for service centers. There is nothing worse than trying to mow a lawn with a blunt blade. The grass, rather than being cut cleanly, is more likely to be torn. It doesn't look good, and it harms the grass too.

■ **Start mowing regularly.** By this time in most regions, grass will be growing and needs to be cut regularly to keep it in good condition. A lawn will be much healthier and stay greener the less grass you remove every time it is cut. Now, for the first few cuts, set the blades at the highest setting. Even if you tend to leave clippings on the lawn in summer, keep the bagger on the mower in spring, so that air, rain, and fertilizer can penetrate the sod.

■ **Fertilize the lawn** toward the end of the month in southern parts. In the north or in cold springs, wait until next month: the grass needs to be actively growing in order to make the best use of the fertilizer.

■ **Remove thatch.** If you did not dethatch the lawn last fall, rake out the moss and dead grass, which inevitably accumulates in the grass over the course of a season. If moss is a problem in your lawn, dethatch it after applying any moss killer later on in the month. Don't be tempted to rake out the moss before you have applied a moss killer, as you will just spread the moss all over the lawn.

Moss in a lawn is a sign that all is not well. The application of a moss killer is a short-term answer, but to eradicate moss permanently you have to tackle the underlying likely causes; these could be compaction, poor drainage, shade, the grass being cut too short, or a combination of any of these. Raking out the thatch can be a backbreaking job if you're using the

Dethatching Vigorously pull a spring-tined rake across the lawn to remove thatch and dead moss; it also allows air to penetrate the surface.

traditional tool: a spring-tined rake. On a small lawn it will be fine, but on a larger area it may be best to use an electric dethatcher; these can be bought from most garden centers or you can rent one from a local rental center. Gasoline-powered dethatchers are available if you have a very large lawn, and these, too, an be rented very easily.

It's amazing how much material you will be able to remove from the lawn, and you may find that it actually looks worse for a while; you might wonder what you've done. But take heart: it will soon recover and look vastly improved.

■ **Repair damage to lawn edges.** Over the summer, lawn edges can be easily be damaged and often, especially with light sandy soil, edges can crumble away in places. To repair a broken edge, cut out the entire damaged portion of sod and turn it around so that the good side now becomes the edge. Fill in any hollow with soil and sow grass seed onto this. Water, and peg plastic sheeting over the top to encourage the grass seed to grow, and then you will have a perfect repair. You can reseed any other bare patches in the middle of the lawn in exactly the same way all through

Neat edges Take the opportunity to fix lawn edges and make repairs while perennials and bedding plants are confined to their borders.

the summer—by dethatching the bare patch first to roughen the surface and then spreading on a mix of potting mix and grass seed combined in equal proportions.

New lawns

■ **Finish preparations for sowing** a new lawn or laying sod. Soil that was dug over during the winter can now be leveled off and raked down to a fine tilth (a fine crumbly surface for sowing seeds).

Seed-sowing can be done at any time from the end of this month through until the fall, although sowing during the hot, dry summer months is probably not a good idea.

Although sod can be laid any time, it is better to carry out this task between fall and this month, so that it can benefit from the seasonal rain. When you are laying sod, always work outward from the laid sod, using boards to spread your weight. You will need to lay sod with the seams staggered—in a similar pattern to that of house bricks. The seams must never be in line. It is absolutely crucial to keep newly laid sod well watered. If it dries out at this stage, even slightly, the sections will shrink and leave persistent unsightly gaps in the lawn.

VEGETABLES AND HERBS

■ **Prepare seedbeds** for direct sowing. Even if it's been left exposed, soil should be starting to dry out now and will be in a better state for the making of good seedbeds for sowing. Getting the timing of this job right can be tricky sometimes. The soil doesn't need to be so wet that it sticks to your boots, nor so dry that it takes a lot of effort to break it up, but hopefully nature has given a helping hand and broken down the worst of the clods. If the soil is a little too moist to walk on, use planks to stand on. These will distribute your weight and prevent the ground from becoming too compacted.

Break larger lumps of soil down by hitting them with a fork, then use a rake to smooth out smaller lumps and create a fine tilth, pushing and pulling the rake back and forth to a depth of about 1 in (2.5 cm). Step down the soil to firm it, and apply an organic fertilizer, such as one based on seaweed, about two weeks before sowing. Rake that in and the seedbed is ready for the seed.

Sowing indoors

■ **Harden off early sowings** of vegetables. Those vegetables sown under cover in late January or February can be hardened off (put in a cooler environment) to acclimatize to cooler conditions. A week or ten days should be enough to acclimatize them before planting them out, under cloches that have ideally already been in place for a few weeks to warm up the soil.

■ **Lettuce, cabbage, and cauliflowers** can still be sown indoors to give a succession of crops from those sown earlier. The plants will get off to a better start if they are grown in cell packs. With no disturbance to the plants' roots when they are transplanted, there is less chance of growth being interrupted and there will therefore be less risk of the crops bolting,

Sowing cabbages

1 Fill a seed tray with potting mix and firm down, using either another tray or a board. Water the mix—a fine spray is best—and then allow to drain.

2 Scatter the seeds over the soil, distributing them evenly and sparingly so the emerging seedlings won't become overcrowded.

3 Cover the seeds with a fine layer of sifted potting mix so you don't introduce any lumps, then lightly firm the mix over the seeds.

Globe artichokes Sow these statuesque perennials now for one of the most beautiful edible plants.

or going to seed prematurely. Cauliflowers are particularly prone to bolting, or the heads not forming properly, if they experience the slightest stress.

■ **Sow globe artichokes** for planting out in May. These are quite large seeds and can be spaced out easily. Sow two seeds each in small pots, watering the potting mix first and cover with sifted mix. Place in a propagator at a temperature of around 65°F (18°C). When they germinate, move to a sunny bench or windowsill. Remove the weaker of the two young plants or transplant it to its own pot.

Sowing and planting outdoors

■ **Plant out young vegetable plants** hardening off in cold frames. Prepare the ground by raking it down to a tilth and spreading on an organic fertilizer before planting. Plant at the distances recommended for final spacing after thinning on the seed packets. Water in well after planting, and ideally, cover with a cloche. A good tip is to plant one half of a cloche with young plants and sow seeds in the other—this way you get a succession

of crops. On deep beds, the plants can go in much closer than would normally be the case. Because the soil is never compacted by being stepped on, plant roots tend to grow downward into the soil, rather than spreading out, so crops can be grown more closely together.

■ **Start sowing outside regularly.** This month seed-sowing outside can get under way in earnest. In northern parts, wait until late in the month or early next month before sowing outside. Sowings of lettuce, other salads such as endive, radishes, salad onions, peas, fava beans, spinach, cabbage, turnips, and beets can all be made now. Sow short rows at a time, at weekly or ten-day intervals; this way a succession of vegetables will become ready throughout the summer and fall. Many seeds are now sold in small vacuum-packed foil pouches within the main packet. When the foil pack is opened, the vacuum is broken and air gets in, so it's important to store the seeds between sowings in a cool, dry place—the refrigerator is ideal. Seeds not packed in foil pouches are also better kept in the refrigerator. These cool conditions ensure that the seeds remain viable (capable of germinating) for longer periods.

■ **To sow all of the fine-seeded vegetables,** slice out shallow drills with a cane. Water the drills before sowing if the soil is dry. Sow the seeds thinly along the drill and cover lightly with dry soil. Once the seedlings are large enough to handle, it is important to thin them.

With peas and fava beans, the technique is a little different. Take out a trench about 1 in (2.5 cm) deep with a spade and sow the seeds of peas about 1 in (2.5 cm) apart in the bottom of the trench and cover. With fava beans, space the seeds about 6 in (15 cm) apart in rows and cover with soil. Peas and fava beans will have to be

protected with netting or floating row cover to prevent rodents and birds from digging them up.

■ **Sow parsnips outside.** Sowing parsnips requires yet another, slightly different, technique, because parsnips are notoriously erratic at germinating. Take out a narrow drill as described above, but instead of sowing the seeds thinly along the drill, sow them in clusters of three or four seeds at 6-in (15-cm) intervals along the drill. This way, if some of the seeds don't germinate, there won't be any gaps in the row. Because germination can be slow and erratic, it's a good idea to sow a quick-maturing crop like radishes along the drill between the parsnip seeds; this way the row can be easily identified.

■ **Plant early potatoes.** Early potatoes can go in now. There are several ways to do this. In 4-ft- (1.2-m-) wide deep beds, potatoes are easily planted with a trowel. Plant about 12 in (30 cm) apart and as deep as you can get. Another way to get a really good crop is to mound up the soil into ridges about 24 in (60 cm) apart across the beds. Plant the tubers on the ridges, again, as deep as you can get with a trowel, spacing tubers about 12 in (30 cm) apart in the rows. After planting, cover the ridges with clear plastic sheeting, holding it in place between the ridges with planks of wood. After a few weeks, watch for the emerging shoots, and when you see them through the plastic, cut slits in the sheets to let them grow through. Keep row cover handy in case frost is forecast, as the young shoots are very prone to frost damage. The plastic helps to retain heat in the soil so the potatoes can be harvested early.

The traditional way of planting is to dig trenches to about a spade's depth and 24 in (60 cm) apart. Put some organic

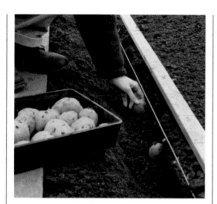

Planting seed potatoes Make a drill about 6 in (15 cm) deep, and plant seed potatoes, sprouts upward, at intervals of 12 in (30 cm).

matter in the trench and scatter an organic fertilizer along the bottom of the trench, or on the soil removed in making the trench. Plant the tubers in the trench 12 in (30 cm) apart and cover with the soil you dug out.

■ **Plant onion sets** from now onward. Prepare the ground as for preparing seedbeds—although the soil doesn't have to be as fine for onion sets—and apply an organic fertilizer. Plant the sets about 4–6 in (10–15 cm) apart in rows the same distance apart. Plant each set with a trowel: don't just push them into the soil, because as the roots form they will push the set up and out again. It is also worth trimming off the dry skin at the tip of the onion set, cutting straight across with a sharp knife, as birds use this to get hold of the sets and pull them out of the soil.

If growing onion sets in deep beds, plant them about 3 in (8 cm) apart. The eventual onions may be smaller, but you will achieve a higher overall yield.

■ **Plant asparagus crowns.** This is a good time to plant asparagus. If you haven't already prepared a bed, dig the soil deeply now, incorporating plenty of organic matter. If your soil is a heavy clay, add pea

gravel to improve the drainage. The beds should be about 4 ft (1.2 m) wide and as long as you like. Make the bed slightly higher than the surrounding soil to improve drainage. This should automatically happen if you are adding plenty of organic matter. Many firms sell asparagus crowns by mail. All-male varieties of asparagus, such as 'Jersey Giant', 'Jersey Knight', and 'Jersey Gem', produce the heaviest crops. When the crowns arrive, they may have to be soaked for a couple of hours. To plant them, dig out shallow trenches about 6 in (15 cm) deep and 18 in (45 cm) apart, mounding up the bottom of each trench to make a slight ridge. Place the crowns on top of the ridges 18 in (45 cm) apart, with the roots spread down each side of the ridge, and replace the soil. Keep well watered. Don't cut any asparagus the first year to allow the plants to get established.

Caring for crops

■ **Fertilize winter lettuces.** Plants sown to overwinter will benefit from an application of a general organic fertilizer after the long, dark days. Sprinkle it between the plants according to the manufacturer's instructions. Water it in well if the soil is dry. Cut every other lettuce when required and leave the others alone to grow on and head up.

■ **Watch out for pests and diseases.** Always try to prevent pests and diseases from becoming serious by taking preventive measures. If you want to use chemical sprays, do so in the evenings, when bees are not active.

Even so-called safe organic sprays contain substances that are harmful to a wide range of predators that do a lot of good controlling pests. It has been shown that by building up a diversity of plants and flowers in the garden and making beneficial predators, such as ladybugs,

welcome, the need for most spraying against pests is eliminated.

■ **Keep the hoe going** to keep weeds down. Now that spring is here, weeds seem to grow more vigorously than anything else. This is why it is important to hoe between rows of vegetables. Not only do weeds take valuable moisture and nutrients, they also act as host plants to pests and diseases. The more you can keep on top of them, the better for the garden.

Hoeing is best done on a dry day when the weeds can be left on the soil surface to dry out in the sun. A Dutch hoe is the tool to use for this job, walking backward with a pushing and pulling motion, slicing off the tops of the weeds. Perennial weeds will have to be dug out, because if any piece of root is left in the soil it will grow again.

Harvesting

■ **Harvest the last of the winter crops.** Put all the resulting debris on the compost pile, if it is not diseased. Spring greens should be cropping now.

■ **After harvesting** of forced chicory is completed, put all of the remains on the compost pile, and sow new plants for next winter later in the year.

Planning ahead

■ **Make a seedbed** for sowing winter crops. Toward the end of the month, prepare an area, perhaps a corner of the vegetable garden, for sowing crops such as Brussels sprouts, winter cauliflower, winter cabbage, broccoli, and kale. Prepare the soil in the usual way, raking it to a fine tilth, and apply a general fertilizer. Again, sowing the crops at intervals over a few weeks will ensure that they mature at different times, giving a succession of vegetables over winter when they are at their most scarce.

■ **Slice out shallow drills** with a cane about 6 in (15 cm) apart and sow each variety thinly in each row, watering beforehand if soil is dry. Cover the seeds with dry soil and label each row. Cover the seedbed with row cover to prevent damage from flea beetles. These tiny insects eat holes in the leaves. When the seedlings have two or three true leaves, they can be transplanted.

■ **Make runner bean trenches.** If this was not done at the end of winter, do it now. Take out a trench to a spade's depth, about 36 in (90 cm) wide and the length of the proposed row. Break up the bottom of the trench with a fork, but don't bring poorer subsoil to the surface. Put plenty of organic matter in the trench. Even shredded newspapers in a layer in the bottom are good at holding moisture, and they will have rotted down by the end of the summer. Just before planting the beans in early June, replace the soil taken out after mixing with general fertilizer.

■ **Add manure to celery trenches.** Celery requires plenty of water through the growing season, and to grow it well, good soil preparation is essential. Take out a trench to a spade's depth, about 24 in (60 cm) wide, and the length of the row. Put plenty of organic matter in the trench and lightly fork it into the soil, being careful not to bring the poorer subsoil to the surface. Then partly fill the trench with some of the soil taken out. Celery plants are not planted until early June, but the sooner preparation is done, the better.

Herbs
■ **Sow herbs outside** and buy young plants. Herbs that are hardy can be sown outside now. These include chervil, chives, dill, fennel, marjoram, cilantro, and parsley. Sow the seeds in exactly the same way as

for vegetables, in drills, and plant them out when they are large enough to handle without damaging.

Young plants of herbs that are more difficult to raise from seed can be bought now. These include mint, tarragon, and shrubby herbs such as thymes and rosemary. Choose French tarragon rather than the Russian kind, which has a coarser taste and is very invasive. So is mint in nearly all its forms: plant it in a pot and partially sink the pot in the ground to discourage it from taking over your entire garden.

A dedicated herb garden is one of the most attractive ways to grow these plants, but they also look wonderful growing in borders with other plants, so if your garden is too small for a separate herb feature, grow them in with other plants, or in pots on the patio.

■ **Divide chives now** that they are starting to grow. Lift each clump with a fork and divide them up. You can afford to be quite ruthless with them. Small clumps can be replanted in soil that has been revitalized with organic matter. Make sure you water them well after replanting. They make pretty edging for beds.

Fresh herbs Chives germinate quickly; you can start them under cover, or sow direct outside.

FRUIT
Caring for crops
■ **Check that fruits have water** in dry seasons, as fruits of all kinds need plenty of water to develop properly. Those growing in containers and trained against walls and fences should be checked from time to time in a dry spring. Trees trained against house walls are especially vulnerable, as the eaves often keep off a lot of rain.

■ **Protect open flowers** from frost damage. The buds and flowers of peaches, nectarines, and cherries open up early and are more prone to frost damage. Wall-trained trees can easily be protected using plastic sheets or floating row cover. The sheet can be fixed to two poles leaned against the trees at night and then taken off during the day. Free-standing trees are a bit trickier to protect, but draping floating row cover over small trees or bushes will give protection from all but the most severe frosts. Large trees just have to take their chances.

■ **Continue to protect peaches,** nectarines, and almonds against peach leaf curl. The symptoms of this disease show as puckering of the leaves during summer. Copper fungicides can be effective if applied the previous fall and again in January and February, but by March it is too late. Protecting the trees with a physical barrier from early January, as described above, is the best option. If you are plagued by this disease, grow dwarf varieties of peach and nectarine in large containers and keep them indoors until late spring or early summer.

■ **Hand-pollinate peach** and nectarine trees. During cooler spells in spring, there are few pollinating insects around, and if you cover your trees, or have container-grown trees under cover, you also reduce

Frost protection Cover young peach, nectarine, and cherry tree blossoms to reduce the risk of peach leaf curl, caused by winter rain and frost.

the chances of insects getting at them, so it is advisable to pollinate these trees by hand. Use a small, soft artist's paint brush and transfer the pollen from one flower to another, going over the whole tree. Do it two or three times over the course of a few days to ensure that all the flowers are pollinated. The best time of day to pollinate flowers is around midday, as the pollen is released freely at this time.

■ **Fertilize all fruit with potash** if you didn't do so last month. Most general fertilizers contain some potash, but it is a good idea to give a little extra to get really luscious fruits. Always follow manufacturers' application rates. Draw back any mulch before applying the potash and watering it in. Water in really well if the weather is dry at the moment. If the fertilizer is not watered in properly, it will not be available for the plants. Renew the mulch.

■ **Spray apples and pears** to prevent scab. If you use chemicals, then this is the time to start using a preventive spray against scab. Most garden centers supply a range of chemical controls. Look at the labels and follow the instructions carefully.

Spray firstly while the flower buds are tightly closed and again when they begin to burst and show color.

■ **Pears that have been attacked** by pear midge can be sprayed with a preventative spray containing pyrethrin. Spray when the buds are white, but still closed. Don't use sprays when flowers are open or you will kill off pollinating insects. Do any spraying in the evening when they are not around.

Pruning and training

■ **Tie in briar fruits** like blackberries and loganberries. These plants grow at an impressive rate from early spring, and if you don't tie them in at regular intervals you will end up with a mess. Briars produce fruit on the stems that grew the previous year, and the easiest way to train them is to tie in last year's canes on the supporting wires to one side of the plant, and the new growth made this year, which will produce next year's fruit, to the other side. This makes pruning them later on very straightforward and less painful.

■ **Prune fall-fruiting** raspberries if you have not already done so. All of the old fruited canes from last year should be cut down to ground level. Be careful now not to damage any emerging new shoot tips.

■ **Prune gooseberries** now if they were left unpruned over winter. If birds are eating the gooseberry buds, you can sometimes gain some protection by leaving the bushes unpruned until spring. This makes it more difficult for the birds to get at the buds. But now is the latest time to prune gooseberries to have any hope of getting fruit. All the sideshoots can be pruned to two or three buds from the main stems and the leading shoots pruned by one-third to half, depending on the vigor of the shoot (prune weaker shoots harder).

Treat the head of a trained standard gooseberry exactly as if it were a bush. Gooseberry cordons are also pruned similarly, shortening all of last year's shoots to only 1–2 buds. Occasionally, when a really knobby "spur system" has gotten very crowded, you can saw a portion of it off completely. After pruning the gooseberries, feed with a general fertilizer and mulch with organic matter.

Planting

■ **Complete planting of bare-rooted fruit** trees and bushes this month. This is the last month when these plants will be in a near-dormant state, and the sooner they are planted the better. If you have missed out on bare-rooted stock, there will be container-grown fruit for sale at garden centers that can be planted through the spring. Older plants may be in flower at this time and you may get a small crop of fruits this year. But if you plant young trees and bushes, it's best to pinch any flowers out this year, so that the plants' energies go into establishing a good root system over the summer.

Beat the seasons

■ **Cover some more strawberries** with a cloche, to give a succession of early fruits.

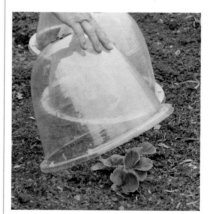

Protect strawberry plants Use clear plastic cloches to protect plants from the cold.

UNDER COVER

■ **Keep the glass** of greenhouses and conservatories clean to give seedlings maximum light. Long, thin, straggly seedlings rarely make good plants, and the cleaner the glass, the sturdier they grow. It is surprising how much dust and dirt accumulates on glass even in dry weather.

■ **Ventilate** whenever the weather is good. It is surprising how quickly the temperature rises even when the sun is out for a short time. Plants grow best without extremes of hot and cold, and ventilation is important in regulating the temperature inside. It can be a nuisance if you leave for work on a fine, sunny morning and later on it cools down, or vice versa, but there are many different types of automatic vent openers on the market. These can be set to open when the temperature reaches a certain level, closing again when it falls.

■ **Watch for pest damage.** Now that the temperatures are rising, all sorts of pests are on the move, enjoying the warm, still, humid atmosphere in the greenhouse or conservatory. By far the best way to control greenhouse pests is by using biological controls, very small living creatures that destroy pests. Many of the firms producing them advertise in gardening magazines, giving details of which are appropriate for which pests. These tiny organisms need a warm atmosphere to thrive. If you have a heated greenhouse, you can introduce them now. If your greenhouse is unheated, then order controls now for delivery next month, when temperatures have risen. If you are not sure which pests you have, or want an early-warning system for pest attacks, hang yellow sticky traps in the greenhouse. You will be able to examine what you catch and identify it more easily, and be alerted early to any problems.

Clean greenhouse windows The more light plants receive, the more strongly they will grow, so wash down the glass, inside and out.

■ **Fertilize plants and water** them regularly. By this time of year, most plants are growing actively, and we all have to keep up with the watering and fertilizing. On warm, sunny days, watering may have to be done several times as the temperature inside rises. Plants that have been growing in their pots for a few months will need regular fertilizing as most of the food reservoir in the potting mix will have been used up.

■ **Continue to take cuttings** from fuchsias.

■ **Prune and repot geraniums** and other tender perennials kept over winter if you didn't do so last month.

■ **Take cuttings** from overwintered tender perennials that started growing last month. Take cuttings about 3 in (8 cm) long, making a clean cut above a leaf joint with a sharp knife. Remove the lower leaves, trim the cutting just below a leaf joint, and dip the base of the cutting into

hormone rooting solution. There is no need to use hormone rooting solution on fuchsias, heliotrope, and geraniums as they all root very easily.

Put into a pot containing seed-starting medium (most multipurpose potting mixes, or any peat-free potting mix mixed with perlite, will do) and water in. Put a plastic bag or propagator cover over the pot and leave in a shaded area until the cuttings root in three or four weeks.

■ **Prick out and pot on cuttings,** seedlings and young plants. Seeds sown last month will need pricking out now, unless you used cell packs. Seedlings pricked out last month may be being planted out now, but those that have to stay indoors until all danger of frost has passed will be needing some more room, as will growing cuttings, and these can be potted up into their own small pots of multipurpose potting mix.

Watch out for damping-off on your seedlings. This disease causes seedlings to rot off and die. It is caused by several fungi, but can be largely prevented by sowing seeds thinly and not overwatering them. If it does become a problem, water the seedlings with a solution containing fungicide. It is difficult to control once it gets going, so prevention is the best course of action.

■ **Shade young seedlings** and cuttings on bright days. Plants lose water in the form of water vapor from their leaves, and on sunny, warm days this transpiration, as it is called, increases. Young seedlings and cuttings are less able to cope with this, so it is important to shade them on sunny days. There are several ways of providing shading, one being shades installed in the greenhouse or conservatory. But these can be rather expensive; the cheapest way to provide shade is to cover the young plants with sheets of newspaper.

Raising plants for outdoors

■ **Sow half-hardy annuals.** Most half-hardy annuals can be sown now, and with even a modest greenhouse you may find you have enough space to raise all the bedding and container plants you need. If they are sown too early, the plants will become leggy and useless for planting out when June comes.

Seeds to sow now include ageratum, alyssum, stocks, nicotiana, and marigolds. Don't forget to include "everlasting" flowers such as statice and strawflowers for dried arrangements—botanical names to look for include *Rhodanthe*, *Limonium*, and *Bracteantha*. Keep in a propagator at 61–65°F (16–18°C), at least until the seedlings have two true leaves, then you can move them to a bench, covered with a seed tray cover for extra warmth. Plants needing a minimum of 65°F (18°C) include lobelia, nemesia, phlox, and zinnias.

■ **Sow seeds of tender bedding** like salvias and gazanias. Sow the seeds thinly and cover lightly with vermiculite, as some of them need light to germinate. They need a minimum temperature of around 65°F (18°C). These plants can also be bought in as mini-plants or plugs for potting on. This is an easy way to grow them, as it cuts down the costs of heating to germinate the seeds. They will need at least frost-free conditions to grow on until threat of frost is past, in May or June.

Plants that need longer growing times as well as high germinating temperatures, like *semperflorens* begonias and busy Lizzies, are from now also better bought as young plug plants, as there isn't time for them to grow. You can, however, still sow seed of geraniums and have plants in flower this year provided you buy specially "primed" seed. It has been pretreated to germinate rapidly so that the seedlings will catch up with plants sown earlier.

■ **Lettuce, cabbage, and cauliflowers** can still be sown indoors to give a succession of crops to follow those sown earlier.

■ **Start cannas into growth** The fat rhizomes of these showy plants can now be brought out of storage and started into growth, for planting out in June. Split them up into short sections, each with a bud. Pot these up, each in its own small pot of peat-free potting mix, and keep in a light place at 61°F (16°C). Water sparingly at first. Once the roots fill the small pot, move each section into a bigger pot and grow on in good light, watering more regularly.

Greenhouse and house plants

■ **Fertilize and water amaryllis.** As the flowers fade, it is important to fertilize the bulb to build up next year's flower bud. Continue watering and feeding with a high-potash liquid fertilizer until the foliage begins to turn yellow and dies down. Then watering can be stopped and the plants allowed to rest for the summer.

■ **Sow seed of *Solanum capsicastrum*** (winter cherry) exactly as for tomatoes. These plants with their bright, ornamental fruits are a cheerful sight in winter.

Crops under glass

■ **Sow eggplants,** peppers, and tomatoes for the greenhouse. There is no point in sowing these too early: toward the end of the month is soon enough. Sow seed in small pots or trays of seed-starting mix. Water the mix before sowing, sow the seeds thinly on the surface, and cover with vermiculite or sifted potting mix until the seeds just disappear. Cover with a sheet of glass and paper to exclude the light and place in a propagator at 70°F (21°C). Germination takes two or three weeks. When you see the first signs of them coming through, remove the paper and

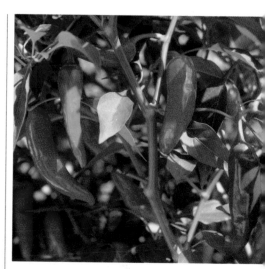

Fruiting vegetables Sow eggplants, tomatoes, and peppers this month to start indoors.

glass. When the seedlings are large enough to handle (usually when the seed leaves, or cotyledons, are fully expanded and you can just see the first leaves developing in the center), transplant into pots.

■ **Set out containers** to warm up before planting. Plants can sometimes stop growing if planted into a cold growing medium. Think how you'd feel plunging your feet into a bucket of cold water at this time of year!

■ **When forced strawberry plants** start coming into flower, you will have to pollinate the flowers for the fruits to set. This is easily done using a small paintbrush, such as those used for painting model aircraft—or a piece of cotton batting on the end of a cane. Dab pollen from one flower to the next, doing this a couple of times at intervals of a couple of days to ensure pollination. Water and feed with a high-potash fertilizer and wait for luscious, mouth-watering fruits.

The April garden

Now we are well and truly into spring. April is perhaps the most exciting month of the year. The garden suddenly begins to look green and vibrant and the warmer days and lighter evenings help to gladden the heart of every gardener. You can begin to prune early-flowering shrubs now and start dividing perennials. Regular weeding and deadheading will keep your garden in shape.

THINGS TO DO

Continue watering newly planted trees and shrubs if the weather is dry. Plant evergreen trees and shrubs; in cold, exposed positions, provide protection by putting up windbreaks.

Tie in the new shoots of climbers, and prune early-flowering shrubs as well as those grown for large or colorful foliage, such as smoke bush (Cotinus). Give gray-leaved shrubs a trim too, in order to keep them bushy. This is also the time to spray roses against black spot.

Divide perennials, stake the tall-growing ones, and protect young growth from slugs and snails. Pot up or transplant self-sown seedlings that you come across in beds and borders, and sow annual climbers and grasses.

Deadhead your daffodils and keep up with the weeding. You can pull up all annual weeds by hand, but always dig perennial weeds out with their roots. Seed or sod new lawns, if you need to, and fertilize established lawns during April.

Sow greenhouse crops such as tomatoes, and continue sowing and planting vegetables outdoors. Prick out or pot up seedlings before they get congested and grow leggy.

LAST CHANCE

Cut down any dead growth left over winter on perennials, especially grasses, before there is too much risk of damaging the new shoots. Plant summer-flowering bulbs and sow sweet peas.

GET AHEAD

Prepare trenches for runner beans, and plant hanging baskets if you have space under cover to shelter them for a few more weeks.

The days are lengthening The soil is warming up and apple blossoms (Braeburn is shown here) are now at their very best.

The exciting month

Typical April showers, which can sometimes be quite dramatic, are interspersed with both warm and cold snaps, so frost protection may still be needed. You'll feel inspired by color from flowers as well as foliage and a whole variety of delicious scents. Now's the time to start mowing the lawn regularly.

Gardens are now awash with a bright spring display of flowers. All the plants seem to start growing really fast this month, with April showers and warmer soil providing ideal growing conditions. Color and interest come not only from bright flowers but also from the unfolding foliage on trees and shrubs, as the plants fully wake from their winter rest. These opening buds come in all shades, from the palest green to deepest coppery bronze. The garden seems transformed into a place for all to enjoy—birds are building their nests and creatures such as toads are coming out of hibernation, looking to gobble up those

Spring perennials The bright pinks and yellows of early spring are now joined by the cooler tones of perennials such as pulmonarias, pulsatillas, and muscari.

pests that are also emerging, eager to attack your precious plants.

Walking around the yard on a warm spring day taking in the sights and smells of spring will really lift your spirits. But don't get too complacent; with all this exuberant growth around us, there is a tremendous amount of work to be done. So take this book out into the garden, if you must, but get out there—there's no time to sit indoors reading!

Sudden cold snaps

The month of April showers occasionally seems more like a month of deluges, with long spells of heavy rain. The weather can still be quite variable in all parts of the country, with sharp cold snaps and snow showers continuing in northern regions. Nights can still be very cold wherever you are, so keep an eye on the weather forecast and protect any tender plants on frosty nights with cloches or row cover—even a few sheets of newspaper can make all the difference, giving several degrees of frost protection. Or, if you have the space in your home, bring the plants inside for the night, but remember to put them out again during the day so that they don't grow tall and straggly due to lack of light.

Scented spring flowers

Scented plants are an absolute must in the garden at any time of the year, but particularly so in springtime. Many of the spring bulbs and shrubs, such as *Viburnum carlesii*,

Trays of vegetable seedlings Make sure these are acclimatized before you plant them out.

produce wonderful scents. One point to bear in mind with these plants is that they are best grown close to the house, or in pots so that they can be positioned near doors, windows, and pathways to get the maximum benefit of the fragrance. Hyacinths and lily-of-the-valley are easily grown in pots. Bring them into the house, where their sweet scent will fill the air in no time at all.

The short and the tall

Some of the most exquisite spring flowers are borne by those tiny jewels of the garden, the alpine plants. Carpets of pink and purple aubretia and furry-petaled pulsatillas will brighten up a free-draining spring border or alpine trough in April. It's also time to plant out hardy annuals, including climbers, such as sweet peas. A mainstay of cottage gardens, these sweetly scented plants would combine well with the rustic willow obelisk, which is a practical project (*see p.85*) featured this month. The obelisk is easy to construct and makes a decorative feature in itself, adding height and interest to a border before it disappears beneath a veil of flowers.

Get the mower out

The job that heralds the start of spring for many gardeners, mowing the lawn, will be a regular task from now on. For some people it's just a chore to get

Weather watch

On the whole, days are continuing to warm up, but in the colder regions, watch out for cold nights with sharp frosts. These can damage fruit tree blossoms. Clear, warm, balmy weather makes it tempting to put young plants out now, but slightly tender plants still need daytime protection. Some garden centers will have bedding plants for sale: If you live in a frost-prone area, snap up the pansies, but don't buy tender annuals yet unless you have a frost-free greenhouse.

Not so breezy

Winds are calmer now, but some parts, especially coastal areas and flat lands, can have gale-force winds, so give newly set-out plants some wind protection.

More sunlight

The amount of sunshine over the country as a whole is increasing, but rain and cloud cover on a day-to-day basis will have a dramatic effect on the amount of direct sunshine brightening each region.

Showers for flowers

April showers may well bring May flowers, but in the Midwest, South, and Northeast we sometimes wish the showers would ease off at some point. There is still a need to conserve water in the western states, where the water supply is directly linked to the amount of snow in the mountains during winter.

Rare snow

Heavy snowfalls are rare now, although snow storms can still cause Rocky Mountain gardeners to become temporarily housebound. As the saying goes, "If you don't like the weather, wait five minutes and it'll change."

Final frosts

Traditionally, planting times revolve around official "last-frost dates", which are generally trustworthy. Areas with April last-frost dates include the West Coast and inland from California into southern Arizona and New Mexico, the Gulf States, and the South East as far north as the upper reaches of Missouri, Kentucky, Virginia, and Southeastern Pennsylvania.

Cherry blossom time Spring-flowering cherries (*Prunus*), together with the crab apples (*Malus*), make beautifully shaped and manageably sized trees for small or medium-sized yards.

over and done with. For others, though, it's a deeply satisfying job, because once trimmed, the lawn sets off the rest of the garden so beautifully. A well-cared-for lawn, recently mown, with alternate light and dark stripes and the edges neatly trimmed, will really enhance the rest of your garden. Well-tended green lawns are admired by everyone—so why not get the mower out?

Vegetables to be sown

The vegetable garden is a hectic place to be now. There is plenty of seed-sowing to be done outside—all kinds of salad leaves, radishes, salad onions, peas, fava beans, and many more vegetables can be put in now. The point to bear in mind here is to sow little and often so you don't get a glut of produce reaching maturity all at once. Short rows of each type of vegetable sown at, say, seven- to ten-day intervals will give you a succession of crops that will keep your kitchen well supplied without being overwhelmed.

Plants under cover

Under cover, greenhouses and conservatories will be bursting at the seams with plants now. With all the rapidly developing plants, you will have to keep up with the watering: plants soon dry out as temperatures soar inside on sunny days. On warm, spring days, open ventilators or windows and doors to keep the maximum amount of air circulating, and splash water on the floor and under staging to increase the humidity levels. This not only helps to cool the atmosphere as the water evaporates, but will also reduce the likelihood that pests such as red spider mite will take hold, because they do not like humid conditions, preferring to be warm and dry.

Shade young seedlings and cuttings with newspaper on warm days to prevent them from being scorched by the sun, especially when they have just been watered. Droplets of water on the leaves act like miniature magnifying glasses and will burn the leaves in bright sun.

Catching problems early

Pests are also on the move outdoors now with the warmer weather. As the saying goes, prevention is always better than cure. By keeping the garden clean and tidy and plants in good health, there is less chance of pests and diseases causing much harm. A watchful eye can also alert you to problems early, so inspect plants regularly. Even though it's not a busy month in the fruit garden, don't forget to make regular checks on fruit trees and bushes and you may be able to take preventive action before your crops are affected. However, no matter how careful we try to be, it is inevitable that some problems will occur during the growing season. If you do not garden organically and feel that you must use a commercial spray, please read the packaging and follow the instructions to the letter. It's important to always try to spray when the weather is still and to do it in the evenings when there are fewer bees and syrphid flies around.

If, like me, you prefer to garden organically, then no spraying should be done at all. It is possible to rely on building up a wide diversity of plants in the garden, especially those that will encourage wildlife. Leave the odd corner here and there undisturbed, so that beneficial creatures such as frogs and toads can take shelter. It can take a few years to build up the natural balance between pests and predators that keeps problems under control, but be patient—it is a much healthier way of gardening.

So, life gets busier in the garden with each day that passes. Perfect!

Amelanchier lamarckii
Shrubby tree with pinky-bronze young leaves (see p.265)

Dicentra spectabilis
Tall, arching perennial with pretty foliage (see p.281)

Erythronium 'Pagoda'
Low-growing, clump-forming perennial for shade (see p.283)

Vinca minor
Creeping stems, studded with flowers in spring and summer (see p.323)

Bergenia 'Sunningdale'
Tough, leathery-leaved perennial, good ground cover (see p.268)

Corylopsis glabrescens
Large deciduous shrub that prefers acidic soil (see p.277)

Magnolia stellata
Compact, to 9 ft (3 m) tall, an ideal magnolia for a small yard (see p.297)

Epimedium x warleyense
Clump-forming perennial, good as ground cover (see p.282)

Fritillaria meleagris
The snakeshead fritillary; a small bulbous perennial (see p.286)

Euphorbia polychroma
Neat mound-forming perennial, very bright even in part shade (see p.284)

Prunus 'Kwanzan'
Double, deep-pink flowers, profusely borne in clusters (see p.308)

Clematis alpina 'Frances Rivis'
Bell-flowered climber needing little pruning (see p.273)

***Pieris* 'Flamingo'**
Large but rounded, compact evergreen shrub for acidic soil (see p.306)

***Cytisus* x *praecox* 'Warminster'**
Drought-tolerant shrub with arching branches (see p.280)

Pulsatilla vulgaris
Small perennial ideal for a rock garden, raised bed or paving (see p.309)

Convallaria majalis
Lily-of-the-valley, a sweet-smelling perennial that can be invasive (see p.275)

***Erysimum cheiri* Bedder Series**
Plant wallflowers in fall for bright spring bedding (see p.283)

Ribes sanguineum
Pinky-white flowering currant, a rounded upright shrub (see p.312)

Pyrus salicifolia 'Pendula'
Weeping ornamental pear tree with willowlike leaves (see p.309)

Malus x moerlandsii 'Liset'
Rounded tree with bronze-green leaves and dark purple-red fruit (see p.298)

Viburnum x juddii
Bushy deciduous shrub that often has good fall leaf color (see p.322)

Aubrieta 'J. S. Baker'
Creeping perennial, perfect tumbling over rocks or low walls (see p.267)

Jasminum mesnyi
Primrose jasmine; a twining climber with sweet-scented flowers (see p.293)

Rhododendron yakushimanum
Small mound-forming azalea covered in flowers (see p.311)

What to do in April

AROUND THE YARD

Pests are on the move now with warmer weather. Get on top of any problems as soon as you spot them and nine times out of ten you can keep them from taking hold.

Protect plants. The warmth and spring rains now will see huge increases in the populations of slugs and snails, which can cause enormous damage to plants. If you're not gardening organically, spread slug pellets that are nontoxic to pets or other animals around the plants affected. There are several organic ways to control slugs, including a biological control, a tiny nematode that attacks them, that can be watered onto the soil. Traps are also effective. One of the oldest and best known is the beer trap: a jar sunk into the ground with the lip just above the surface, filled with beer. Frogs, toads, and birds all prey on slugs and snails, so encourage them to visit your garden

Give borders a tidy-up. Set aside a morning or afternoon to go around the yard doing those small jobs that make all the difference to its appearance. Lightly fork over the soil, pulling out any weeds. Any plants

Thorough weeding Clear the ground before planting a border.

taking up too much space and growing into other plants can be lightly pruned into shape to keep them looking tidy. Don't be too harsh with the pruning or you may cut off all this year's flowers. Put in plant supports as you go.

Watch out for self-sown seedlings when working on the borders. It is amazing just how many plants seed themselves freely around the yard. A lot of hardy annuals seed quite prolifically and many shrubs and herbaceous perennials can, at times, almost become weeds. One group of plants particularly good at self-seeding are foxgloves (*see p.86*). They are quite happy to be moved at this time of year and will flower later, so it's a good time to "edit" their population. Sadly, seedlings from white foxgloves often turn out purple in flower—but they are beautiful nevertheless. Remember to water any seedlings you move.

Apply synthetic fertilizers now. If you didn't give plants an organic fertilizer earlier in the spring (see February), a chemical fertilizer will give them an instant boost now, just when they need it. Pull back any mulch, lightly fluff up the soil with a rake, and apply according to the maker's instructions. Replace the mulch.

All plants need nutrients to survive, but there is no need to fertilize absolutely everything every year. Trees and shrubs, for example, will grow quite happily for years provided that the initial preparation before planting has been done thoroughly. With these, all that may be necessary is to apply some fertilizer in the first two or three years after planting. After that, unless there is any obvious deficiency, they will cope well on their own. But do remember to water them well in dry weather in the early stages of getting established. The areas of the garden most in need of fertilizers every year are the vegetable and fruit garden, annual borders, and plants in containers, where the plants are taking more out of the soil. With all fertilizers, wash your hands well after use.

TREES AND SHRUBS

■ **Remove frost-damaged shoots** from any slightly tender evergreen shrubs like *Choisya ternata* (Mexican orange blossom). At the same time you can, if necessary, prune back any misplaced stems. In colder areas, pruning these shrubs is best left until next month, in case a late, hard frost causes more damage. Stems should always be cut back to a healthy leaf lower down the shoot, or to a stem junction.

■ **Spray roses** with a recommended fungicide to control black spot, which looks exactly as you might expect—black spots, or blotches, on the leaves. This will have to be done at regular intervals, as black spot is difficult to control. Follow the manufacturer's instructions for dosages and intervals between spraying.

Better still, try to grow only those varieties of roses that are resistant to black spot, such as 'Graham Thomas', 'François Juranville' or *Rosa mundi*—more correctly called *Rosa gallica* var. *officinalis* 'Versicolor'. Catalogs will highlight many more that are available. Rose breeders are constantly bringing out new varieties of roses that are more resistant to disease, therefore cutting down on the need to spray. A visit to a rose nursery's fields in summer is well worth the trip just to see for yourself which roses are more disease-resistant, but be aware that they may be sprayed for disease control.

■ **Check roses for aphids.** Rub or hose aphids off to avoid using sprays, or use one of the handheld sprays to direct the pesticide accurately. By doing this as soon as you spot them, you can help prevent colonies from building up.

Planting

■ **Plant container-grown trees and shrubs.** Bare-rooted deciduous stock will no longer be available, but all plants are

A good watering Give all plants grown in containers a good soak after planting.

now sold as container-grown specimens to plant at any time of the year, although spring and fall are best for the plants. Water the plant well in its pot an hour or two beforehand, then ease the rootball out of the pot. Set it firmly in a generously sized hole so that the top of the soil is level with the ground around it. Work soil down around the sides of the root ball with your fingers, water well again, and mulch

around the plant to lock in that precious moisture. For advice on sheltering evergreens in exposed sites, see Hedges.

Pruning and training

■ **Trim winter-flowering heathers** with shears if you didn't do it earlier in the year. The spent flowering stems will now be looking quite shabby, so remove them completely in order to show off the more attractive new growth.

■ **Prune shrubs** grown for their colorful foliage, such as elderberry (*Sambucus*) and cotinus (the smoke bush). The best colored foliage is produced by new stems, which is the reason for pruning hard now. If you want to increase the size of the plants, it is worth leaving two or three shoots unpruned, and these can grow on, making the plant larger without compromising on the colorful foliage. As always, after pruning, feed with a general fertilizer and water it in if the weather is dry.

■ **Prune forsythias** and flowering quince after flowering. These two shrubs put on a terrific show of color in the spring, on

Pruning early flowerers

Pruning forsythias Cut the flowered stems back to strong new leafy sideshoots, pointing upward and outward.

Pruning flowering quince Cutting sideshoots back to one or two buds encourages flowers. The shoot on the left was left unpruned.

wood made the previous summer, and now is the time to prune them for flowers next spring. Pruning for both shrubs is the same procedure. When the flowers have faded, cut back the flowered shoots to two or three buds from their base. On more established shrubs, cut out about a third of the older growth to the base of the plant. This will encourage new shoots to grow from the base.

These shrubs can also be trained to grow against walls or fences, and they look very attractive. Pruning in this situation is a slightly different procedure. After you have tied in any stems you need to fill gaps, prune all flowered shoots to one or two buds from their point of growing. You can do the same in summer to keep flowering quince, and also firethorns, flat where space is limited. Leading shoots can be pruned to keep the shrubs within their allocated place.

■ **Cut back lavender** once the plants approach the size you want them to grow to. If lavender plants are left unpruned, their centers grow sparse, which looks unattractive. and they don't like being pruned into older wood. So it is a good idea to prune them every spring to keep them bushy and compact.

Other silver-leaved shrubs to prune in the same way are *Helichrysum serotinum* (straw flower) and santolina (cotton lavender). Go over the whole plant, trimming off 1–2 in (2.5–5 cm) of growth. Use shears to speed things up if you have a lot of lavender—for example, a low hedge. It may seem a bit harsh, but doing this causes the plants stay compact and the center does not open up.

Propagation
■ **Increase conifers by taking cuttings.** This is a good time to propagate your favorite conifers and it is very easy to do.

Trim lavender In spring, prune the tips of all the shoots with pruners or shears.

Hedges
■ **Plant evergreen hedging plants.** This is a good time to plant evergreens; not only conifers but the many broadleaf plants that make excellent hedging. Most can be clipped to shape or grown informally, only being trimmed when they become overgrown.

By planting evergreens at this time of year there is less chance of their being damaged by cold winter winds, but they may still need some protection. It's not just winter winds that cause problems. Even in spring and summer, high winds can be just as damaging. The speed of the wind going over the surface of the leaf draws water from it more quickly than the plant can replace it from the soil, especially in summer if the ground is dry, and this causes withering.

If your plants are regularly scorched in this way, consider erecting more screens and windbreaks to shelter your garden—or research some more wind- and drought-tolerant shrubs to replace casualties.

CLIMBERS
■ **Climbing and rambling roses** should be tied in, training the shoots as near to horizontal as possible. By doing this, you restrict the flow of sap; this causes more sideshoots to develop along the whole length of the main stems and therefore more flowers are produced. If left to grow vertically, all the flowers are produced at the tips of the stems, where they are difficult to see. If you are growing roses on a post or pillar, wind the stems around the support in a spiral fashion and tie in, and this will have the same effect of restricting the flow of sap.

■ **Tie in shoots of twiners,** such as clematis, as they are growing fast now. With clematis, once they get a hold on their support, they can usually be left to themselves, especially if growing through other shrubs, but they may need guidance if encroaching too much on other plants.

■ **Plant container-grown climbers** as for trees and shrubs.

■ **Prune wall-trained forsythias and flowering quince.**

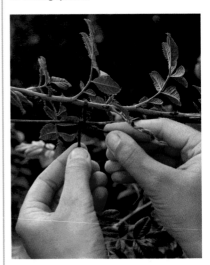
Training climbing roses Tie in shoots horizontally for more flowering sideshoots.

Make a willow obelisk

An obelisk is an attractive, rustic willow-wand structure that can be used for lightweight climbers such as sweet peas, late-flowering clematis, or runner and climbing French beans.

You will need

- Nine lengths of two-year-old (or older) willow, seven of roughly equal length for the uprights, and two for the main ribs of the horizontal bands
- six lengths of year-old willow for weaving
- a bundle of thin willow, less than one year old, for tying
- half-barrel or large tub
- pruners

1 You can make the obelisk *in situ*, but I find it convenient to use a tub as a guide. Insert the seven sturdiest of the two-year-old wands, evenly spaced so that they form a circle of uprights.

2 Make the lower band by twisting one of the remaining two-year-old wands around itself. Drop it over the uprights and adjust its size until they are slightly pulled together.

3 Using thin pieces of willow or twine, tie the band to each upright, about 12 in (30 cm) from the base.

4 Starting at one of the uprights, weave one of the year-old wands in and out and around the band and the uprights.

5 Finish the weave by pulling the tip of the wand sharply upward at one of the uprights to secure it.

6 Starting at different uprights, weave two more of the year-old wands around the band in exactly the same way (see steps 4–5).

7 Bind each of the joints with the flexible lengths of thin willow, winding each roughly around and threading it in between the willow joint until you have a stout, knobby "knot."

8 Trim off any protruding wand tips with pruners for a neat finish.

9 Make the upper band in exactly the same way as the lower one, but slightly smaller so that it draws the uprights together a little more.

10 Finish off the top by holding the uprights together and binding and tying them very firmly with your longest, most flexible, piece of thin willow. As with the bands, if you finish with a sharp pull upward between uprights, the pressure of the structure trying to spring apart should hold the end securely in place

11 The finished obelisk lets me use more vertical space for climbers, such as a clematis, in my border.

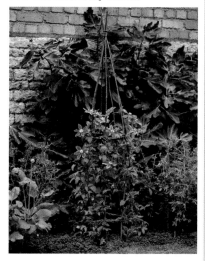

PERENNIALS

■ **Continue planting new plants.** Getting plants in by the end of the month will give the plants time to establish while the weather is still mild and wet, and grow well during the season.

■ **Continue taking basal cuttings.**

■ **Remove winter protection** from borderline hardy plants.

■ **Top off grit and gravel** around plants growing in a Mediterranean or scree-bed setting if it has been lost or shifted by winter weather. This will really smarten the area up before plants get going, to set them off perfectly when at their best.

■ **Finish dividing** and replanting summer-flowering perennials. This is the latest month for lifting and dividing if you want these to flower in the summer and fall. Whenever possible, revitalize the soil with well-rotted manure or compost before replanting perennials. Water in well after planting if the weather is dry.

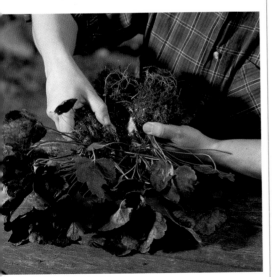

New plants Carefully separate congested clumps of herbaceous perennials.

Thinning shoots Some perennials flower better if you reduce the shoots at the base

■ **Thin shoots on perennials.** To get top-quality flowers from border plants, it is sometimes necessary to thin out overcrowded shoots. Plants most likely to need thinning include delphiniums and lupines, especially if you are growing these for showing at your local flower show. Phlox will also put on a bolder show if it is thinned. Remove about one in three or four of the shoots, depending on crowding.

■ **Dahlia tubers** can be planted in milder parts of the country. In other areas, wait until next month. Make sure the ground has been prepared well, as dahlias are heavy feeders; add plenty of organic matter and a good dressing of organic fertilizer before planting, and insert a stake into the ground to support the plants before you plant—then you will not damage the tubers. The tubers should be planted so that the crown of the tuber is at least 3 in (7.5 cm) deep.

Alpines

■ **Remove all winter protection** from alpine plants and beds.

■ **Plant new alpines** now. The cold rains they dislike so much should be tailing off.

Self-sown seedlings

1 Foxglove seedlings form a flat rosette of slightly coarse leaves, oval in shape, coming to a point.

2 Water the soil first if it is dry, then lift the seedlings gently with a trowel, taking a good ball of soil up around the fragile roots.

3 Plant the seedling in its new position, firming gently with your fingertips—do not press too hard. Water the young plant in very gently.

BULBS

■ **Deadhead the last of the daffodils** now that the flowers are fading. Snap the flowerhead off behind the swollen part; you can leave the stalk intact. If the spent flowers are left on, the plant's energy will be invested in the production of seeds. By removing the old flowers, the plant's energy is instead diverted into the formation of next year's flower bud within the bulb. For this to happen, the foliage must be left on the plant. For many years the practice was to allow the foliage of the bulbs to die back completely, to give the plants the longest time to build up that flower bud for next year. But recent research has shown that the foliage can be cut down six weeks after the flowers are done. You can choose which method you prefer. The old foliage of daffodils can look messy, but do not tie it up with raffia or elastic bands. The best way to hide it is to grow daffodils in among other plants such as hostas, which have large, bold leaves.

■ **Plant out all summer-flowering bulbs.** They should all be planted by the end of the month, in time to flower during the summer. Tender bulbs, such as gladioli, can

Carpets of gold Daffodils look superb naturalized in grass.

go out now, wherever you happen to live. These prefer a sunny spot in well-drained soil, so if you garden in heavy clay, put a layer of coarse grit in the hole and plant the corms on top to improve drainage.

■ **Divide nerines.** Overcrowded clumps of these beautiful fall-flowering bulbs can be split and replanted now. Put the spade or fork in the ground a little way out from the clump or you risk slicing through, or spearing, the bulbs. Do not replant any damaged bulbs, as they harbor rot that may spread through the rest.

ANNUALS AND BEDDING

■ **Continue sowing hardy annuals outside.** In colder parts of the country it is perhaps best to wait until this month before sowing outside, to give the soil a chance to warm up. Heavy clay soil, in particular, takes longer to warm up than light sandy soil.

■ **Plant out hardy annuals** raised in cell packs. Prepare the soil in the same way as for direct sowing and mark out drifts in the same way. Plant the young plants in the drifts and that's it. There is no need to thin out the plants and they will flower a little earlier than those sown outside.

■ **Sow half-hardy summer bedding plants.**

■ **Pot up cuttings** of tender perennials that you took last year. Keep them under cover until next month, when you can start hardening them off for planting out.

■ **Buy plug plants** of bedding if you have the room to grow them on in frost-free surroundings. Keep them inside until it is safe to plant them out.

Dividing nerines

1 Lift the clumps carefully and shake off as much soil as possible, then separate out individual bulbs. Retain as much root on each as you can.

2 Clean the bulbs and replant singly at the same depth as before, about 2 in (5 cm) apart. Peel off brown, flaky debris, but leave a layer of white, papery skin, or tunic, intact.

Lobelia plug plant Tiny plug plants are ideal if you are fortunate enough to have indoor space.

Ipomoea tricolor

Asarina procumbens

Tropaeolum peregrinum

■ **By the end of the month** spring bedding plants may start to look tired, but summer bedding cannot be planted out safely for a few weeks yet. So do what you can to keep plants neat, rather than pulling them out too early to leave bare ground that weeds will colonize.

■ **Sweet peas should** really have been sown earlier, but a late sowing now will still produce some flowers in late summer and fall.

■ **Plant out sweet peas** sown in fall. In cold areas, it's safe to do this toward the end of the month and into the next as long as they have been hardened off first for one or two weeks. Prepare the ground and sprinkle a little general fertilizer before planting—not too much or you will get a lot of growth and few flowers.

■ **Sow more unusual annual climbers.** Climbing plants have many practical uses: adding height to a border or hiding ugly buildings or other unsightly places like the compost pile. To use permanent perennial climbing plants such as roses and clematis can be a little expensive and many do take some time to get established and cover a given area.

For a cheap and quick way to cover an eyesore such as a compost pile, old shed, or unattractive wall, or to add height to a planting, annual climbers are really the ideal choice.

Another way to make use of annual climbers is to let them scramble through evergreen shrubs or through trees, extending their period of interest.

Like sweet peas, nasturtiums (*Tropaeolum majus*), in all shades from brilliant reds to yellows, can be sown directly into the soil now, but other more unusual climbers can be raised in pots and planted out in June. Many are tender

perennials grown in our climate as annuals. Lovely plants to try include *Ipomoea* (morning glory), with large blue or pink flowers; *Cobaea scandens*, with violet and purple flowers; *Canarina canariensis*, the Canary bellflower, with almost zucchini-like orangey flowers; *Eccremocarpus scaber*, or Chilean glory vine, with funnel-shaped red and yellow flowers; purple rhodochitons; black-eyed Susan, or *Thunbergia alata*; *Tropaeolum peregrinum*, and in small spaces, *Asarina procumbens*, which makes an effective trailing plant in a raised rock garden. Sow the seeds thinly and cover lightly with vermiculite as some of them need light to germinate. They will all need a temperature of around 65°F (18°C).

These plants can also be bought in as mini-plants or plugs for potting on. This is an easy way to grow them, as it cuts down on the cost of providing heating to germinate the seeds. They will need at least frost-free conditions to grow on until the threat of frost is passed, generally not until around the beginning of June.

■ **Sow annual grasses.** Their delicate foliage and attractive seedheads contrast well with broadleaf plants in the borders. It's an excellent, inexpensive way to try out

Hordeum jubatum

Briza maxima

the new way of growing perennials among grasses for a more "naturalistic" border look, and all of the seedheads can be dried and used in indoor flower arrangements.

Annual grasses to look for include *Briza maxima*, the quaking grass; *Lagurus ovatus*, hare's tail grass, and *Hordeum jubatum* or foxtail barley. They can be sown outside from now on.

You can sow them *in situ* in drifts as with annual flowers—in drills, so you can tell them from weed grasses when they germinate—or in drills on a spare piece of ground, to transplant in among plants in the border when they are big enough.

Sow the seeds in shallow drills that you have scratched out with a stick and water the drills if the soil seems dry. Cover the seeds lightly and label them. Thin out the young seedlings and transplant them if necessary when they have grown large enough to handle.

CONTAINERS

■ **Clean containers and pots** that are to be used for summer bedding displays. All pots should be cleaned thoroughly using a weak solution of ordinary household bleach. This is well worth doing as it will reduce trouble from pests and diseases.

You could also spruce up older, scruffy containers with some of the versatile paints that are now available, perhaps even experimenting with some more unusual shades to enhance summer color schemes.

■ **Plant up alpine troughs.** Whether you buy a trough or sink, or make your own, this is an ideal month for doing this job as many alpines are coming into flower now and you can get an instant effect when the job is done. The most important point to bear in mind when growing alpines is that they like good drainage, so make sure any container used for growing these plants has plenty of drainage holes in the bottom. Before filling the container with potting mix, put a 2-in (5-cm) layer of broken pot fragments or coarse gravel in the bottom to help with drainage.

The potting mix used for filling the container should be what is called an alpine mix, consisting of equal parts garden soil, garden compost or coir compost, and coarse grit.

After planting, spread a layer of coarse grit over the surface of the soil between the plants. This not only sets off the plants well, but also keeps down weeds and prevents the plants from being splashed with soil in rainy weather.

Alpine display This planter makes a natural-looking home for alpines. Use a range of plants that flower in different seasons for a long-lasting display.

LAWNS

■ **Mow your lawn regularly.** If grass is left to grow long and then cut short, it will turn yellow and be weakened, so regular mowing—by summer, once a week, or if you're really picky, twice a week—is the order of the day. Blades should be at their highest setting when you start mowing in spring—by the end of this month, start gradually lowering them each time.

■ **Continue to repair** and renovate established lawns, as described in January and February. It is especially important to level off lumps and bumps, as these cause the mower to scalp the grass, weakening it and encouraging weeds and moss to grow. Continue to remove weeds individually. Coarse grasses, which are extremely vigorous and look out of place on a finer lawn, can be removed by crisscrossing the clump with an old knife, then pulling out the tufts of grass. After this regular mowing will discourage coarser grasses from taking root.

■ **Fertilize established lawns** unless you did so late last month. Always use fertilizers according to the manufacturer's instructions. There is no point in putting on a little extra to "speed things up." Plants will only take up a certain amount and the excess leaches into the water table and into streams and rivers.

There are several methods of applying lawn fertilizer. One is to mark out the lawn into square yards (meters) with string and canes and measure out and scatter the fertilizer by hand, wearing gloves, in measured doses, as when you are sowing seed. This can be laborious if you have a large lawn, so use a fertilizer spreader. There are many types available and they can be bought or rented.

■ **You can treat moss** with moss killer now, but do bear in mind that this only treats the symptoms rather than the actual cause. The main causes of moss in lawns are usually poor drainage, weak grass, and compacted soil. The best way to remedy these faults is to aerate the lawn each year using a machine or fork to spike the lawn, and to rake out thatch: the moss and dead grass that accumulates. By doing this and fertilizing the lawn regularly the grass will be much healthier and moss and weeds less able to establish themselves in it.

New lawns

■ **Sow new lawns on prepared ground,** if this was not done last month. With the weather warming up, grass seed will germinate quickly now. The area for a new lawn should have been dug over during the winter, incorporating organic matter to retain moisture. You can still get away with this preparation now if you have light, sandy soil. After digging, the ground will have to be leveled off and the soil raked down to a fine tilth. Firm the soil well by stepping it down with your weight on your heels, rake the soil again, step it down at right angles to the previous direction, and finally rake it level. To sow the seed, first mark out the area in squares, as when spreading fertilizer, using canes and string. Weigh out the quantity of seed required per square yard, as recommended by the manufacturer on the packet, once on kitchen scales, and then put it into a cup and mark its level on the side.

Now you can either use the cup to measure out all the subsequent "doses" of seed, or pour a measure into your hand, see how it feels, and then take up similar-sized handfuls each time. This saves a lot of weighing. Scatter the seed evenly over each area; rake in and water with a fine spray or sprinkler. A quick alternative for a large area is to use a fertilizer spreader set at the seed-sowing setting.

After scattering grass seed, sprinkle a covering of straw over it that is light enough to admit light and water, yet heavy enough to keep the seeds from blowing away and birds from picking at them.

■ **Finish making new lawns** with sod before the weather becomes too dry. Newly sodded lawns should grow quite quickly now, and you may find that those laid earlier in the year are already in need of a trim.

Sowing grass seed

1 **Broadcast the seed** evenly over measured square yards. Scatter half one way and the rest the other until you become more confident.

2 **Rake very gently** to just cover the seed, using short strokes, so that you do not redistribute it unevenly.

VEGETABLES AND HERBS

Sowing under cover

■ **Sow tomatoes** for planting outdoors in May and June. Although you may have sown tomatoes for the greenhouse during the previous month, there is no point in sowing tomatoes to grow outdoors much more than six to eight weeks before you can plant them out.

Sow the seeds in trays or small pots containing seed-starting mix. Overfill the container, give a sharp tap on the bench to settle the soil, brush off the surplus, and firm gently with the base of a pot to level off. Water before sowing. Sow the seeds thinly and cover with vermiculite until the seeds just disappear.

Place in a propagator at a temperature of 70°F (22°C). Cover with a sheet of glass and paper, removing this when the seeds germinate in a couple of weeks. When the seedlings are large enough to handle, either prick out into trays or pot up into small pots.

There are many tomato varieties to choose from and which you grow is a matter of taste, from the small cherry tomatoes to the large, beefy slicing types. However, they do grow in different ways. Indeterminate tomatoes are the tall kind with a single central stem needing support, but there are bush varieties, many of which are relatively hardy, which do not need training and look very decorative, especially in containers on the patio. There are even trailing tomatoes that can be grown in hanging baskets.

Espaliers are the traditional choice for greenhouse growing because you can use the full height of the greenhouse to ripen a good crop, but the bush and trailing varieties look equally good on greenhouse benches and conservatories.

■ **Sow celery and celeriac** for planting outdoors in May and June, exactly as you would tomatoes.

■ **Sow sweet corn,** summer squash and zucchini, and pumpkins and winter squash toward the end of the month. If they are sown any earlier, they will get drawn and starved before it is safe to plant them out, at the beginning of June. Sow these two seeds per 3-in (8-cm) pot, pushing them into the potting mix on their edge. They don't need quite as high a temperature as tomatoes to germinate: 61°F (16°C) is sufficient. When the seeds have germinated, remove the weaker one and grow on the other. Pot up into larger pots if necessary before planting out in June.

■ **Sow leeks in modules.** You can sow leeks outside this month, but if you're growing vegetables on deep beds, the ideal way of growing leeks is to multi-sow them in cell packs. Fill a cell pack with seed-starting medium and firm gently. Put some leek seeds onto a piece of paper and, with the point of a knife, sow five or six seeds per cell. Cover the seeds with potting mix or vermiculite. When the seedlings are about 4 in (10 cm) high they can be planted out in clusters, 12 in (30 cm) apart each way. Although each leek will be smaller, you get more crop per square foot than when growing in conventional rows.

Sowing and planting outdoors

■ **Continue to plant asparagus crowns.**

■ **Carrots** sown late this month may need carrot fly protection.

■ **Plant maincrop potatoes.** This is the latest month for maincrops if you want to get a decent crop. To plant them, dig trenches 24 in (60 cm) apart to the depth of the spade, piling the soil to one side. If no organic matter was dug in earlier in the year, put some well-rotted manure or garden compost in the trench and set the tubers on this. Space the tubers about

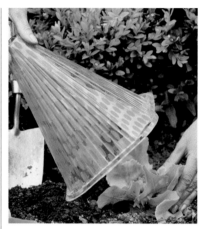

Young lettuces Protect your plants against frost with cone-shaped plastic cloches.

15 in (38 cm) apart. Sprinkle fertilizer in the gaps along the row before filling in. Cover the tubers with soil, leaving it slightly mounded up.

■ **Keep up with successional sowings** of vegetables like lettuce, radishes, beets, peas, fava beans, salad onions, and turnips. By sowing little and often, you will avoid having a glut of produce all at one time, which may be difficult to manage. Sow in shallow drills made with a stick, watering them before sowing if the soil is dry. Sow the seeds thinly, cover with soil, and label them. Thin out when the seedlings are large enough to handle.

■ **Plant out onions** sown earlier in the year. Rake in a general fertilizer before planting and don't grow on soil that had onions on it the previous year. Onions being grown as single plants can be planted 9 in (22 cm) apart, in rows 12 in (30 cm) apart. Those that were sown in modules and grown as multiple plants can be planted out in clusters on deep beds, 6 in (15 cm) apart each way. As these onions grow, they push each other apart. The individual onions may be smaller than when plants are grown singly, but the overall crop yield per square foot is greater because there are more plants.

■ **Sow dwarf French beans** under cloches in milder parts of the country. Take out a wide drill about 1 in (2.5 cm) deep and space the seeds 6 in (15 cm) apart in an arrangement of staggered rows. Water if the soil is dry and put cloches over the rows to protect them from the frost. Sprouts should emerge in a few days.

■ **Sow leeks.** It is now safe to sow leeks outside in a nursery bed (a spare piece of ground used to raise plants before transplanting them to their final cropping positions). Sow them in short rows by taking out narrow drills in the usual manner. Water the drills if the weather is dry and sow the seeds thinly along the drill. Cover with dry soil and label the row. When they are 4 in (10 cm) high they can be transplanted. The way to plant them is to make a hole with a large dibber. You can make one from an old spade handle or you can buy one and drop one plant into each hole. Water in, and some soil will be carried into the hole, anchoring the plant.

■ **Plant seakale.** This unusual vegetable is normally blanched for harvesting stems in winter and spring. It can be grown from seed, but for crops within the year it is far better to buy it as roots or "crowns." Plant them about 12 in (30 cm) apart, with the top of the root just below the surface of the soil. When the young shoots begin to grow, remove the weakest ones, leaving just one shoot on each root. By the fall the plants will have formed good crowns for forcing (see October).

■ **Sow kohlrabi** at intervals from now until August. It is the swollen part of the stem that is eaten; it has a turniplike flavor.

Kohlrabi Harvest the curious, swollen stem bases when they are small and tender and leave the central shoots on the plant.

Sow the seeds in narrow drills in the usual way and thin the resulting seedlings, leaving them 9 in (23 cm) apart each way.

■ **Sow Florence fennel** in drills 24 in (60 cm) apart and thin the seedlings to 15 in (38 cm), when they are large enough to handle. These are quite decorative plants with feathery foliage and they grow to a height of around 4–6 ft (1.25–2 m). It's the swollen stem bases, which have an aniseed flavor, that are eaten.

■ **Sow seeds of salsify** and scorzonera. These are two unusual root vegetables, rarely grown because they are slow to prepare, the roots being very long and thin. In countries such as France, where food preparation is seen as an art rather than a chore, they are very popular. Salsify tastes rather like oysters, and scorzonera has a nutty flavor, which, though difficult to describe, is delicious. Grow both in soil that has been manured for a previous crop, applying a general fertilizer before sowing. Rake the soil level and to a fine tilth and sow the seeds in narrow drills 12 in (30 cm) apart, watering the drills before sowing if the weather is dry. Thin the seedlings to 12 in (30 cm) apart. You can

use the roots in the fall or store them in boxes over the winter.

■ **Winter brassicas**—broccoli, cabbages, cauliflowers, and Brussels sprouts—can all be sown outside on a prepared seedbed early in the month, if this wasn't done last month. Those sown last month and ready for transplanting should be moved to their permanent bed before the plants get too large, the ideal time being when the plants have two or three true leaves. Spacing varies tremendously with the type and variety of crop, but instructions will be given on the seed packets. Water well after transplanting and place paper collars around the young plants to ward off cabbage root fly. Adult flies lay their eggs at the base of the plant and the resulting white larvae eat the plant's roots. Collars that fit snugly around the base of the stem prevent the adult flies from laying the eggs in the soil and they fail to hatch. There are no chemical controls available, so prevention is the only, and, of course, the organic way. Planting through mulching sheets and membranes also does the same job. You can even use old carpet, cut into 6-in (15-cm) squares.

Caring for crops

■ **Water regularly in dry weather.** All young vegetable plants need plenty of water to develop well.

■ **Thin out rows of seedlings** sown earlier. If seedlings are not thinned out, the plants will become straggly and not crop well at all. The distances to thin each type of vegetable will vary and it is best to check the back of the seed packet for details of individual plants. The thinnings of most vegetables, except root vegetables such as carrots, beets, and turnips, can be transplanted. The advantage of this is that these thinnings, having been disturbed, will

Thinning seedlings Be careful not to damage the remaining plants as you thin along the row.

mature a little bit later than the seedlings left in the row, thereby extending the succession of cropping. Water seedlings before and after thinning in dry weather. Seedlings being transplanted should also be watered gently but well after planting.

■ **If any shoots** of early potatoes are starting to show through, keep a sheet of floating row cover handy and cover them if frost is forecast, since the shoots are vulnerable to cold damage. If you have planted the potatoes under sheets of clear plastic, cut slits in it as soon as you see the shoots, to allow them to grow through.

■ **Watch out for flea beetles,** so called because when they are disturbed, they jump. These small insects attack brassicas, turnips, and radishes, nibbling small holes in the foliage. You can spray with an insecticide to control them, but one way you could try to keep the numbers down, or indeed if you want to confirm that flea beetles are the problem, is to make use of the fact that they hop up when disturbed. Get a small, square piece of wood or cardboard and smear one side of it with grease or petroleum jelly. Run this over the tops of the leaves and the beetles will jump up and get caught on the sticky surface.

■ **Support peas sown earlier.** Peas have rather straggly growth and if they are not supported some of the crop will be lost, because it will become spoiled lying on the soil. There are several ways to support peas. Plastic green support mesh, specially made for the purpose, can be bought from the garden center, or use twiggy sticks. One method that is useful is to use the prunings from other shrubs in the garden, provided they are strong enough and are reasonably straight. An ideal shrub for this is buddleja (the butterfly bush). It produces large purple or white flowers on long shoots made through the summer, and these shoots make ideal supports for peas, but any other shrubs with reasonably straight stems will do. Keep them to one side after you have pruned them from the shrub in spring. The tips with the old flower heads may have to be removed to make them look more presentable.

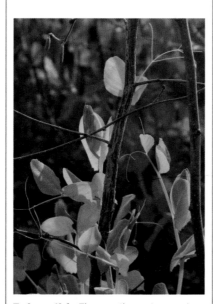

Twiggy sticks These are the most economic option for supporting young pea plants.

Planting herbs Water young plants regularly— even the drought-tolerant types such as thyme.

Herbs

■ **Divide chives,** if this was not done last month. With larger clumps, you may have to use two forks back to back to pry the clump apart, but otherwise they can be pulled apart by hand. Water well after replanting in soil that has been revitalized with garden compost.

■ **Propagate thyme by layering.** This method is very similar to that used on strawberry runners. Fill small pots with a mixture of equal parts of peat-free potting mix and sharp sand and sink the pots into the soil beneath the vigorous outer stems to be layered. Peg the stems into the pots and in a few weeks roots will have formed. The new plants can be cut from the parent and planted out into their permanent positions. Thymes require well-drained soil in a sunny spot.

■ **Continue sowing** and planting herbs. By now most herbs can be sown outside, and any sown earlier inside can be planted out from the end of the month, after hardening off in a cold frame. Many varieties of young herb plants are available. But it's a real treat to make a trip to a herb nursery, to see and, even better, smell all the different kinds of herbs for sale.

FRUIT

Harvesting

■ **Check under rhubarb forcers** regularly until the crop of young, pale stems is ready. When you have cut them all, leave the forcer off and fertilize the plants. Do not take a crop from the regrowth.

Caring for crops

■ **Feed blackcurrants,** blackberries, and hybrid berries with a high-nitrogen fertilizer. These plants grow a lot during the season and an extra dose of a high-nitrogen fertilizer will give them a welcome boost. Don't use too much—follow the directions on the package. Too much nitrogen will result in very soft growth, which is more susceptible to attack from pests and diseases.

■ **Control weeds around cane fruit.** Weeds take valuable moisture and nutrients from the soil and also act as hosts to pests and diseases. The easiest way to keep down weeds around fruit is to mulch with a thick layer of farmyard manure, garden compost, or straw.

■ **Keep frost protection** on early-flowering fruits; however mild the weather appears to be now compared to the earlier months of the year, night frosts are still common. Remember that this will also involve hand-pollinating the flowers.

■ **Keep an eye out for pests** and diseases by inspecting fruits regularly. If you feel you must use chemical sprays, then spray in the evenings when there are few pollinating insects around. Don't spray during the period when the flowers of any fruits are fully open—not even in the evenings—as you will harm pollinating insects. We have to do all we can to encourage a wide range of insects and mammals into the garden as their habitats in the countryside in general gradually

disappear. Even so-called "safe" organic sprays kill a wide variety of insects and will harm the beneficial ones.

By building up a diversity of plants in the garden you will attract beneficial insects, birds, and mammals and these will keep the pest problem to a minimum, and you may never have to spray at all. Sow or plant some annual flowers in the fruit garden, such as phacelia, as these will attract friendly pest predators like syrphid flies that will do your pest control for you.

■ **Watch out for gooseberry mildew** on gooseberries. This shows as a white powdery coating on the leaves. If you want to spray, use a fungicide recommended for the purpose, bought from the garden center. Read the instructions carefully. But it's better to grow varieties like 'Invicta', which are resistant to mildew, eliminating the need to spray at all. Winter-pruning, watering, and fertilizing also helps plants grow strong and more resistant to attack.

■ **Blackcurrants are often** affected by a mite that spreads a virus on its mouthparts: watch out for swollen buds in late winter and be aware of virus symptoms now. If the bush is affected by virus, the flowers will be red instead of pinkish-gray. There is no choice but to dig it up and burn it. There is no effective cure. Replace lost bushes with the mite-resistant cultivar 'Ben Hope'.

Pruning and training

■ **Prune fan-trained** stone fruits such as cherries, plums, and nectarines. First prune out any shoots that are growing either into the wall or directly away from the tree. Then thin out any overcrowded and crossing shoots, while at the same time removing any dead, diseased, or damaged shoots. The remaining shoots can be tied to the training wires.

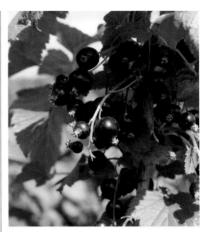

Pick blackcurrants Do this in sequence, selecting ripe berries individually.

The reason for pruning these trees now rather than during the winter months is that they are prone to the fungal diseases silver leaf and bacterial canker. These enter the plant through open wounds; by pruning now, when the plant is in growth, the pruning cuts heal over quickly, reducing the risk that disease will get in.

■ **Tie in vines.** Outdoor vines will be growing fast soon and the shoots will need tying in if they are not to get completely out of control. Vines grow extremely fast and can put on more than 10 ft (3 m) of growth in a season. So tying in, thinning, and stopping the shoots are important to encourage a good crop of grapes instead of a mass of leafy growth.

The easiest way to train grapes is to use a central, vertical main stem, or rod, that is kept pruned back to the height of the supporting system of wires. Each year, train selected sideshoots out sideways, to form an espalier shape. These shoots will carry the fruits, then in winter you can cut them back to within two or three buds of the main rod.

Planting

■ **Plant container-grown trained fruit trees.** By this month it is too late to plant bare-root fruit trees and bushes, but there are many different kinds, trained in attractive ways, available in containers. The advantage of container-grown plants is that they can be planted at any time of the year, because the root system is not disturbed. You can even buy them in flower and may get some fruit from them in the first year after planting, but don't take a lot of fruit in the first year. It's better to let the plants get established now and they'll fruit all the better in subsequent years. Lay soaker hose when you plant new fruit and mulch on top of it to water efficiently and conserve soil moisture.

Apples, pears, plums, red- and whitecurrants, and gooseberries can all be trained in several different ways; espaliers (tiers of horizontal branches), cordons (single-stemmed trees grown at an angle to save space) and fans (branches are trained to resemble the spokes of a fan). These are all both attractive and productive, and with modern dwarfing rootstocks they can be fitted into the smallest of spaces, so no garden need be without some fruit.

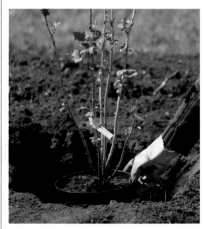

Planting a blackcurrant bush Ensure that the bush is planted deeper than it was in its pot.

UNDER COVER

■ **Ventilate well on sunny days.** It may be necessary to leave vents and doors open all day in warm weather, as the temperature can climb dramatically in a short time when the sun is out.

■ **Damp down on warm days.** On hot days the atmosphere indoors can become very dry—not the best conditions for plants. Damping down simply means splashing water onto the floor to increase the humidity of the atmosphere as this is much more conducive to plant growth.

Another advantage is that it reduces the incidence of red spider mite. This pest attacks the leaves of plants, causing them to become mottled and then die off. It thrives in warm, dry conditions, so damping down can reduce the problem without having to use sprays.

■ **Shade young plants** during sunny weather. As with newly pricked-out seedlings, cuttings will need to be shaded from strong sunlight too. Until new roots develop, the cuttings are continually losing water from their leaves, but in the meantime they have no roots to replace the water that has been lost. Shading them will reduce water loss from the leaves in hot weather. Temporary shading for young plants is easily provided with sheets of newspaper.

■ **Watch out for vine weevil.** This pest has become a serious problem in recent years, especially on container plants. The little creamy-white grubs live in the soil and eat roots, easily going unnoticed until you see the plants wilting.

There is a biological predator available to control them: a microscopic nematode worm that attacks the grubs. It is bought by mail order and watered into the pots. Alternatively, water container plants with products labeled for use on these pests.

■ **Introduce other biological controls** if this was not done earlier. In fact, this is perhaps a better time to introduce them, especially in unheated greenhouses, as they do not work in temperatures below 50°F (10°C). These controls are usually in the form of nematodes or small predatory insects or mites, and there are specific ones for specific pests—for example, the tiny wasp *Encarsia formosa*, which kills young whiteflies. Under cover, they do the job of friendly garden insects such as syrphid flies and ladybugs, which are encouraged by all good gardeners.

■ **Whiteflies can be a problem,** especially if you are growing tomatoes, which seem to attract every whitefly in the neighborhood.

Put up yellow sticky cards to catch them. Hang the cards on string near the tops of plants and raise them higher as the plants grow. It's amazing just how many will be caught on these traps. Whiteflies seem to be strongly attracted to the color yellow. Before an infestation becomes really severe, use a biological control as well. Growing some French marigolds in the greenhouse or conservatory is also believed to deter whiteflies.

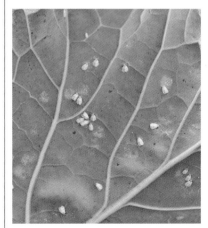

Whiteflies These pests lay their eggs on leaves and feed on the sap.

Raising plants for outdoors

■ **Buy bedding plants as plugs;** in the South and in sheltered areas they will grow on happily in an unheated greenhouse now. Buying bedding this way is growing in popularity among those who have space under glass to bring on the young plants. Many people don't have the time to sow seeds early on, then care for them until it's time to plant them out. Buying young plants also cuts out the time when seeds require the most heat to germinate, and it's easier than sowing tricky seed such as impatiens.

Most bedding plants are now available in this way. They come in small cell packs, one plant per cell. The advantage of this system is that the plants can be potted up with no disturbance to the root system, so that they grow away better. When the young plants arrive, pot them up into 4-in (9-cm) pots containing peat-free potting mix and grow them on in a cool greenhouse or conservatory. Don't give too much heat as the plants will grow too fast and become spindly. Harden off for a week or two before planting out.

Toward the end of the month, plant up hanging baskets. Although these cannot be hung outside until the threat of frost has passed, in early June, now, or early next month is a good time. This will allow the plants to fill out before being put outside.

■ **Complete sowing** of half-hardy annuals by the end of the month. Fast-growing half-hardy annuals like French marigolds can be sown as late as this, but others requiring a longer growing season to flower should have been sown by now.

■ **Continue pricking out** seedlings of half-hardy annuals sown earlier. Pricking out means spacing the seedlings about 1 in (2.5 cm) apart in trays, so that they have more space to develop. Water seedlings in well after pricking them out. On warm, sunny days they will benefit from shading from strong sunshine until they get established in the trays.

■ **Give young plants** more growing space. Continue to pot on growing young plants and cuttings. The ideal time to put plants into larger pots is just as the roots have filled the available soil, without becoming potbound. Generally, pot on to pots one or two sizes larger than the one the plant is already growing in.

■ **In mild regions** of the country, begin to harden off bedding plants toward the end of the month.

■ **Sow winter-flowering pansies.** These can be sown outside, but you will get better plants by sowing them in gentle heat now. Sow the seeds thinly in trays or in small pots, cover with a thin layer of potting mix, and put a sheet of glass and a piece of paper over the tray. Prick out the seedlings when they are large enough to handle, then pot up into cell packs with large cells or in small pots. They can sit outside in a sheltered, shady spot throughout the summer, provided you remember to water them regularly. Planted in fall, they will produce a terrific display right through the winter.

■ **Sow tomatoes, celery and celeriac** for planting outdoors in early June.

■ **Sow sweet corn,** summer squash, and zucchini toward the end of the month.

■ **Continue to take cuttings** from tender perennials like fuchsias and geraniums. Those which were taken earlier and have rooted can be potted up if you have not done this already. To encourage the plants to bush out, pinch out the growing tips. Fuchsias and geraniums being trained as standards should not have the growing tips removed. Instead, let the main stem grow to the height you want, tying it to a cane as it grows to keep the stem straight. Pinch out any sideshoots that form. When

Pot hydrangea cuttings

1 Take stem-tip cuttings by removing the top 3–4 in (8–10 cm) of young, healthy, nonflowering shoots.

2 Remove leaves at the base and tip, and cut the remaining leaves cleanly across in half.

3 Dibble the cuttings into a mixture of peat-free seed-starting mix and perlite, at the edges of the pot.

the stem reaches the required height, pinch out the tip and the sideshoots will grow to form the head. Pinch out the sideshoots to make a dense, bushy head full of flowers.

Greenhouse and house plants

■ **Take hydrangea cuttings** from container-grown plants. Mophead hydrangeas are increasingly popular as container plants, but they are difficult to keep going year after year. Remove stem-tip cuttings about 3–4 in (8–10 cm) long. Cut off the lower leaves and trim the base of the cutting. There is no need to trim immediately below a leaf joint as is normal practice with cuttings, as hydrangeas root perfectly well without. To reduce water loss from the large leaves, however, cut them in half. It may seem rather brutal, but it works. Put the cuttings into pots of seed-starting medium and place on a shady windowsill or on the greenhouse bench. No extra heat is needed. Pot up when they have rooted.

■ **Rest amaryllis after flowering.** Give the bulbs several applications of high-potash fertilizer to build up the flower bud inside the bulb for flowering next time. When the foliage begins to turn yellow, reduce the watering and dry off. Put the pots on their sides under a bench.

■ **Take leaf cuttings** of streptocarpus (Cape primrose). Remove a mature leaf from the plant, and cut it into 1-in (2.5-cm) sections. Bury the base of each section in a pot, or put several in a tray of equal parts peat-free potting mix and perlite or vermiculite. The part of the leaf that was closest to the plant should always face downward. Put in a warm, shady place and after a few months new plantlets will emerge from the base of each leaf section. These can be potted up individually. Another method is to take a mature leaf

Rest cyclamen Laying cyclamen on their sides prevents overwatering as they go dormant.

and cut it along the length of the midrib. Put in a tray with the midrib in the potting mix and plantlets will develop along the length of the midrib.

■ **Rest cyclamen** that have flowered in pots over the winter. This is done by gradually reducing the amount of watering until the foliage begins to die down. Place the pots on their sides under the greenhouse bench or in a cold frame until they are started into growth again.

■ **Pot up begonia** and gloxinia tubers that were started off last month, into 5-in (12.5-cm) pots. Water them after potting.

Crops under glass

■ **Tie in vine rods.** Vines growing inside will be galloping away now, and it is essential to keep up with tying in and pinching out growths, otherwise the vine will get out of hand. Fruiting stems should be pinched back to one or two buds beyond each flower truss and all sideshoots from these stems removed.

■ **Pot up tomato seedlings** sown last month. Tomato seedlings should be transplanted when you can see the first

true leaves beginning to emerge from between the two first, or seed, leaves (the cotyledons). Watering the seedlings an hour or two beforehand makes it easier to ease them out of the tray or pot. Pot up into 4-in (9 cm) pots, with the seed leaves almost level with the potting mix. Water in well and stand on the greenhouse bench or on a warm windowsill. If they are on a windowsill, turn them around every day, otherwise they will grow toward the light and bend over.

■ **Remove sideshoots** from older tomato plants. Those sown earlier will be growing strongly now and cordon varieties (those grown as a single stem) need to have any sideshoots growing from the leaf axils removed. If these are not removed, you will end up with a mass of growth and poor-quality fruits. The best time to remove sideshoots is when they are small; just large enough to handle. Take the shoot between your thumb and forefinger, push or pull the shoot to one side, and it should snap off cleanly. If the shoots have been left on and grown quite large, use a knife or pruners.

■ **Plant tomatoes in containers.** When earlier-sown tomatoes are potted up, they grow away quickly, and toward the end of the month they can go into containers or be potted into 8-in (20-cm) pots for cropping. Place large containers of potting mix in the greenhouse for a few days to warm up before planting. You can plant either two or three plants per container. Tie cordon plants to canes or support wires attached to the framework of the greenhouse. There are also support frames made specially for containers and these can be purchased from garden centers.

The May garden

Many gardeners regard May as one of the best months in the garden, with spring's freshness and the promise of summer. May's warmer weather makes gardening particularly engrossing, so you can enjoy getting your plot ready for summer and planning for the months ahead. It's also the month of outdoor plant sales and the opening of farmers' markets across the country.

THINGS TO DO

Take action to protect plants if you are expecting any night frosts, and water plants that need it regularly. If spring-flowering shrubs have finished flowering, now's the time to prune them and take softwood cuttings. You can lightly trim boxwood and other formal hedging and prune *Clematis montana* after it has flowered.

Take cuttings from herbaceous perennials and cut back and divide spring-flowering perennials. The end of the month is the right time to plant out dahlias. Don't forget to protect young plants from slugs and clear out spring bedding before beginning to harden off summer bedding plants. Thin out annuals and vegetables that you sowed outdoors earlier.

Fertilize and weed lawns during this month to encourage good growth, and be sure to mow them regularly—once a week is about right.

Sow and plant out tender vegetables at the end of the month and protect crops from carrot fly before continuing successional sowing of vegetables. Remove all frost protection from fruit trees and start pruning trained plums and cherries.

Ventilate any greenhouses or conservatories and think about permanent shading for summer. If you have any tender shrubs in containers, move them outside now for summer.

LAST CHANCE

Sow or sod new lawns before it gets too dry. Finish planting evergreen shrubs.

GET AHEAD

Sow biennials for next year's spring bedding plants. Inspect plants regularly for signs of pests and diseases and nip potential problems in the bud.

A mass of tall, pinky-mauve alliums
(*Allium hollandicum*), with blue Jacob's ladder (*Polemonium caeruleum*) in the foreground, stand out beautifully against fresh, green foliage.

The best month of all

Make the most of May's warmer weather to start getting ready for summer. Your garden should be looking its best at this time, with bright spring bedding in flower and trees in full leaf, and the flower-show season will give you even more ideas and inspiration for the coming months.

There are signs of summer everywhere, yet many spring-flowering bulbs, especially the tulips in colder parts of the country, are still at their best. Trees are leafing out and shrubs like rhododendrons are preparing to bloom in parts of the country during this month. There is a huge range of rhododendrons available, from dwarf shrubs only a few inches tall, which can be grown in pots and tubs, to treelike shrubs usually covered in large clusters of flowers. They are well worth growing if you have acidic soil. If your soil is alkaline, choose the smaller-growing

rhododendrons in pots or raised beds filled with acidic potting mix. With quite mature container-grown shrubs now available year-round, you could buy a rhododendron in flower and have it installed in a tub on the patio the same afternoon.

Change your bedding

While many plants are gearing themselves up for their summer display, the spring bedding plants will soon be over and it's time to think about their replacements.

A wide selection of summer bedding plants will be on display at nurseries and garden centers, but as in April, resist the temptation to buy these too early in the month unless you have a frost-free greenhouse, conservatory, or cold frame to keep them in. The majority of these plants are still quite tender and in northern regions it may not be safe to plant them out until the end of the month or into June. In southern areas of the country you may get away with planting summer bedding plants around the middle of the month, but do keep an eye on weather forecasts.

If you are new to an area, then a visit to a botanic garden or just a stroll around the area taking a look at some local gardens will tell you a lot about when to plant out summer bedding safely in your area. Talk to local gardeners—there may be a gardening club you can join, too—and find out as much as you can about the weather conditions. You'll most likely find that they are quite a friendly bunch and will be glad to give out hints and tips on how to grow all manner of plants—and they often swap plants between themselves, so you might get a few plants for nothing, as well as good advice!

Plants to protect

The weather in May is usually quite settled, but it can be changeable and there may still be the occasional sharp frost. So any tender plants being hardened off should be watched carefully and given protection with floating row cover or sheets of plastic, or put into a cold frame whenever required. The telltale sign of a night frost is a clear blue sky at the end of a sunny day.

Start of the shows

This is also the month when many communities, botanic gardens, garden clubs, and charitable organizations host spring plant sales and "plant tents." You can also find a wealth of bedding plants and vegetables for sale at farmers' markets and garden centers. There are, of course, many other flower shows throughout the summer, from large-scale national

Spring border Try a mixed planting of *Primula* 'Julia' syn. *pruhoniciana, Tulipa, Muscari, Saxifraga,* and *Hyacinthus.*

Weather watch

Spring, which began in the South sometime in February and has been traveling northward at a pace of about 15 miles per day, will by now have reached even the coldest parts of the North and upper elevations of the mountains. The days are warming up, but nights can be cold and we can still get sudden sharp frosts in the North and at high elevations. Late frosts are the scourge of fruit growers. Most varieties of fruit trees will be in flower now, and it only takes one sharp frost to destroy a potential crop for the whole year. Spraying fruit with water at sundown, as the Florida farmers do, can protect fruit. Ironically, as the water changes to ice, it releases a bit of heat that can make all the difference.

Wind and rain

In various parts of the country, May can be windy, especially along the northern Atlantic coast and over the flat lands of the Midwest. The major air masses that pass over North America originate in the Arctic and blow down through the central states and eastward through the Mid-Atlantic, and also sweep down through the Maritime Atlantic through New England. Meanwhile, tropical air masses travel upward from South America through the western states and along the Gulf States and upward toward the Mid-Atlantic. Where these masses collide with the colder ones coming down from the north, drastic weather changes occur, with thunderstorms and strong winds. But overall, May here tends to be a month of mild weather, gentle rains, and sunshine. Rain is plentiful in the Midwest and East. Although in recent years the Upper South has suffered summer-long droughts, things are looking up a bit for them. The West Coast tends to be cool and foggy.

Growth spurt

Although the sun is still at a fairly low angle, the days continue to lengthen and warm, causing a growth spurt in gardens everywhere. About this time ponds are filled with evening serenades from frogs that start to sing when temperatures reach about 50°F (10°C).

Waterside perennials Plants such as ferns, hostas, and the lovely candelabra primulas thrive in moist soil on the banks of streams and ponds. At this time of year, burgeoning new foliage still retains all the freshness of spring.

Intersowing lettuces and sweet corn This is good practice. Lettuces are fast-growing and will be ready to harvest before the sweet corn grows up and shades the ground.

delicious early vegetables planted out under cloches earlier in the year. To guarantee a succession of young vegetables throughout the summer, continue with regular sowing of all vegetables at seven- or ten-day intervals. Hoeing also becomes a regular chore among vegetables now, as weeds shoot up in the milder conditions. With the warmer, drier weather, watering may now become necessary, but don't use water indiscriminately, especially at this early stage in the season. Water only those plants that really need it—your precious young vegetables, developing fruits, and newly planted trees, shrubs, and perennials.

Getting warmer
Under glass, temperatures can get very high and it's vital from now on to shade young plants, open ventilators, windows, and doors whenever possible, and mist to prevent the air becoming too dry. Toward the end of the month it should be safe in all but the coldest regions to move pots containing tender shrubs and succulents such as agaves outdoors for the summer. Reducing crowding in the greenhouse will also help to improve air circulation in the hot months to come.

Outside, ornamental borders will be brimming with colorful displays of late spring flowers and fresh foliage, the sound of birdsong will fill the garden, and beneficial insects will be pollinating flowers. Herbaceous perennials are now growing fast and need to be staked, if this has not already been done. This is a job that often gets forgotten until it is too late and the plants begin to flop all over the place and look unsightly. By this stage, trying to tie up the stems is a hopeless task and it is often better to cut the plants back hard and let them grow back. The flowers may be later, but the plant will look much better for cutting back.

events down to small, local shows, and all of them are worth visiting. Here you will meet like-minded people who are fascinated by plants, and lifelong friendships can be forged at these events. Spring is also a good time of year to visit other gardens opening to the public for the season and to plan trips to those that are open for charity for a few days each summer. Here again there are many ideas to be gleaned that can be adapted to suit your own garden. Look out for the Open Days Directory, published since 1995 by the Garden Conservancy, a national nonprofit organization headquartered in Cold Spring, NY (to order a copy, visit the organization's website at www.gardenconservancy. org). It lists private gardens open to the public on certain days throughout the season.

Back to work
However, there is plenty to do in your own garden in between visiting flower shows and other people's gardens. In the vegetable plot you should now be harvesting

A word about water

One aspect of the famous British garden show at Chelsea that never fails to inspire most visitors is the wealth of water features on display. Water not only cools and refreshes the air around it, but it's also a real treat for wildlife, including frogs and dragonflies, which will be drawn to even the smallest pool. Small features, such as half-barrel ponds, also provide space for pretty aquatics, and they are quick and easy to make. Simply buy a half barrel, first making sure it has not been treated with preservative. Fill it with water and leave it to stand—the barrel will leak for a while until the wood swells and seals it. Or buy a special plastic insert for instant results. Then fill the barrel with water plants. Use aquatic potting mix and plant in baskets, setting marginal plants on bricks to raise their stems out of the water.

Laburnum x watereri 'Vossii'
Good small-to-medium tree with cascading yellow flowers (see p.293)

Clematis montana f. grandiflora
A vigorous climber for quick cover (see p.275)

Papaver orientale 'Cedric Morris'
Showy perennial poppy with dark-centered flowers (see p.303)

Aquilegia vulgaris 'Nora Barlow'
Cottage-garden perennial that will self-seed (see p.265)

Exochorda x macrantha 'The Bride'
Notably free-flowering deciduous shrub (see p.285)

Rhododendron 'Golden Torch'
Compact, upright evergreen shrub with salmon-pink blooms (see p.310)

Digitalis* x *mertonensis
Perennial foxglove that readily self-seeds (see p.281)

***Trollius* x *cultorum* 'Earliest of All'**
A lovely pondside perennial (see p.320)

***Wisteria floribunda* 'Multijuga'**
Woody-stemmed climber that needs twice-yearly pruning (see p.323)

***Tulipa* 'Spring Green'**
One of the green-flecked viridiflora tulips (see p.320)

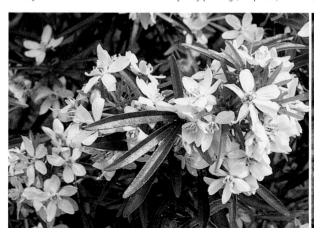

***Choisya* 'Aztec Pearl'**
Evergreen shrub with sweet-scented flowers (see p.272)

***Camassia cusickii* 'Zwanenburg'**
Bulb with tall conical spires of vivid flowers (see p.269)

Allium hollandicum
Drumstick seedheads look good long after the flowers fade (see p.264)

Euphorbia x martini
Bushy clump-forming perennial for a sunny site (see p.284)

Prunus padus 'Watereri'
Flowering cherry popular with backyard birds (see p.307)

Crataegus laevigata 'Rosea Flore Pleno'
Plant hawthorn as a tree or informal hedge (see p.278)

Kerria japonica 'Picta'
Clump-forming shrub with variegated foliage (see p.293)

Syringa vulgaris 'Madame Lemoine'
Bears large, double white flowers from creamy buds (see p.319)

Corydalis flexuosa
Low-growing perennial with ferny leaves (see p.277)

Viburnum sargentii 'Onondaga'
Deciduous shrub with lacecap clusters of flowers (see p.322)

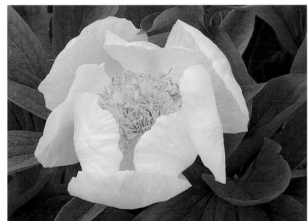

Paeonia mlokosewitschii
Herbaceous peony with lemon-yellow flowers (see p.303)

Hyacinthoides non-scripta
The English bluebell, spreads vigorously once established (see p.290)

Prunus 'Amanogawa'
Very slender flowering cherry tree for small yards (see p.308)

Clematis macropetala 'Markham's Pink'
Looks good climbing through trees and large shrubs (see p.274)

What to do in May

AROUND THE YARD

Now that the weather is warming up, you will have to watch for pests and diseases on a regular basis. It may be necessary to use chemical controls in severe cases, but be aware that long-term use of synthetic chemicals can actually cause problems to build up. These chemicals kill off not only the pests, but also the beneficial insects that prey on them, such as ladybugs and hoverfly larvae. If you feel it necessary to spray, carry out the task on a still day, as late in the evening as possible, when there are fewer beneficial insects around.

Keep plants in the garden growing strongly and they will be less susceptible to attack. Prepare the ground well to get them off to a good start. Keep new plants well watered during dry spells, so that they don't suffer stress. Mulch newly planted plants to retain valuable moisture in the soil. The mulch will slow the evaporation rate from the surface of the ground.

Keep the garden neat, especially now that it's time to clear spring bedding away and keep weeds, which often act as hosts to pests and diseases, under control. The most organic way of all to control pests is by using your fingers to squash them, but you have to be vigilant to keep on top of them this way. The memory of two days spent squashing cabbage white butterfly caterpillars on brassicas in a large garden remains with me.

Hoe bare ground to keep down weeds as they germinate. Weeds are more easily killed off at this stage, rather than leaving them until they get bigger. Then there is also no chance that they will be left too long and set seeds that will be spread around the yard. Hoe on dry, sunny days and the weed seedlings can be left on the surface of the ground to dry out and shrivel up in the sun. A mulch with organic matter will help to prevent the growth of further weeds. Water the soil first if it is dry, before applying the mulch. Alternatively, put some plants in the gap to add color to the border.

Night frosts Even though daytime temperatures should now be mild, night frosts are not uncommon in northern gardens this month, especially after clear, bright days. Keep a sheet of floating row cover or even some old newspapers handy to cover any plants that are vulnerable to frost if night temperatures are forecast to fall.

Water new plants Give newly installed plants a good soak regularly to help them establish.

TREES AND SHRUBS

■ **Water newly planted trees and shrubs** regularly if the weather is dry. A few days of sunny weather accompanied by drying winds now will dry out the soil surprisingly quickly. Watering may have to be done on a daily basis. It is important to water new woody plants well until they get established and their roots develop enough to be able to seek out moisture deep down. Any organic matter, such as rotted manure or garden compost, either dug into the soil or applied as a mulch, has good water-holding potential, which will help new, growing roots. Even grass clippings spread in a layer about 2–3 in (5–8 cm) thick around the plant (not touching the stems) will help to retain moisture.

Try to water in the evenings, when there is far less chance of the water evaporating from the soil, as it is certain to do in the heat of the day.

■ **Keep checking roses** for aphids.

■ **In milder regions,** tender shrubs in pots can be moved outside for the summer.

Pruning and training

■ **Prune evergreens** to remove any frost damage and tidy wayward shoots, unless you did so last month.

■ **Prune firethorns** trained against a wall or fence. Prune out shoots growing directly into the wall or directly away from it. Shorten the others to about 3 in (8 cm). This encourages formation of short spurs, which bear the flower buds and then the beautiful berries in fall.

■ **Prune early-flowering shrubs** like *Kerria japonica* and *Spiraea* 'Arguta', which will finish flowering about now on wood produced the previous year. For kerria, prune all the shoots that have produced flowers back to young sideshoots lower down. This shrub tends to spread out by underground suckers and these can also be removed if the plant seems to be encroaching on other plants. *Spiraea* 'Arguta' should similarly have its flowered shoots pruned back to buds or shoots lower down on the shrub and on older plants. In addition, cut out about one in three of the older stems right to the ground. This will encourage new, young growth from the base of the plant, keeping it vigorous and healthy.

■ **Take softwood cuttings** from shrubs. Most shrubs in the garden will now be producing plenty of young, fresh shoots, which are excellent for making softwood cuttings through until July, when the wood begins to ripen. Take a few shoots from any part of the shrub where their absence will not show. About half a dozen should ensure that you get at least one new shrub. It's always best to take more than you need as an insurance policy. Have a plastic bag at hand when you take the cuttings. Cut shoots about 3–4 in (8–10 cm) long from the plant, cutting just above a bud or leaf. Put the cuttings into the bag right away and keep it out of the sun. This prevents the cuttings from wilting.

Trim the cuttings below a leaf joint with a sharp knife and remove the lower leaves, leaving them about 2–3 in (5–8 cm) long. Immerse the cuttings in a fungicide solution, wearing gloves, and then dip the cut ends into hormone rooting solution. Five or six cuttings per 5 in (13 cm) pot, containing a 50:50 mix of peat-free potting mix and vermiculite, will be sufficient. Cover with plastic sheeting, making sure it is held off the foliage of the cuttings (you can use short sticks to support it) and secure in place with a rubber band. Place the pots in a shady part of the greenhouse or in a cold frame and the cuttings should take root within

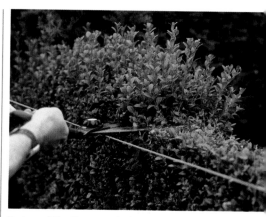

Hedge cutting You can make this task much easier if you use a guide (a length of taut garden twine or a cane) to keep lines straight.

six to eight weeks. They can then be potted up to be grown on.

Hedges

■ **Lightly trim formal evergreen hedging** such as boxwood (*Buxus sempervirens*), even if it has not yet grown to the desired size. Boxwood hedging does not take to being cut back hard, so the sooner it starts being trimmed to keep it in shape, the better. This is best done with hand shears rather than with a mechanical hedge trimmer, which can bruise rather than cut the leaves cleanly, making them turn brown and unsightly. It may take more time using the shears, but the overall appearance of the hedge will be much better.

You can make cuttings from shoots about 3 in (7.5 cm) long. Trim each cutting below a leaf joint, put into pots containing seed-starting medium, cover with a plastic bag and stand the pot in a shady part of the garden and in a few weeks the cuttings will root. You can then pot them into their own pots or space them out on a spare piece of ground until fall or next spring, when they can be put in their final positions.

CLIMBERS

■ **Prune *Clematis montana* after it has flowered.** The amount of pruning will depend on where it is growing. This is a very vigorous climber, so it's best to allow it to scramble through trees and large shrubs or up a fence or wall. In these situations, little pruning will be needed unless it is outgrowing its space. However, in more confined spaces some pruning will be necessary to prevent it from taking over the whole garden. Pruning is easy, although the untangling can be tricky; all you have to do is prune out any dead or diseased wood and prune the remaining stems back as far as you need to. This encourages young growth to take place and flowers to come next spring.

■ **Prune wall-trained** firethorn.

■ **Tie in climbers regularly.** Vigorous climbers such as clematis, roses, and vines need their shoots tied in at regular intervals, otherwise they may smother other plants in the border. Trying to untangle climbers from other plants is a tedious job, to be avoided if at all possible. Fixing wide-mesh wire netting to walls and fences is the easiest way to provide support for vigorous climbers. A trellis is more decorative, so choose lighter climbers for this so that the plants' growth does not hide it from view.

Tying in Make figure-eights with twine so that stems do not rub against supports.

PERENNIALS

■ **Continue staking** and tying in perennials, particularly tall-stemmed kinds such as delphiniums. These will need several bamboo canes placed around each plant, with string tied around the canes. Alternatively, you can tie each stem to an individual cane.

■ **Cut back and divide** clump-forming, spring-flowering perennials such as doronicums and pulmonarias. Doronicum just needs the old flower spikes cut off to neaten up the plant. But pulmonarias should have all the old foliage cut to the ground, as it will usually be covered in mildew by now and look shabby. It may seem like a drastic thing to do, but new, fresh foliage soon grows, transforming the appearance of the plants. At the same time, lift, divide, and replant overgrown clumps. After pruning and dividing, feed with an organic fertilizer, watering it in if the soil is dry.

■ **Cut back alyssum,** arabis, and aubretia. These spreading and trailing plants all tend to become bare and shabby, especially in the center of the plant, when the flowers have faded. Trim them back hard, almost to the ground, and fresh new growth will soon appear, producing a mass of flowers on a neat, compact plant next year. If you don't do this every year, then as the plant ages, it will be more reluctant to grow from the base when cut hard back. After pruning, feed with an organic fertilizer. Mulch with fresh gravel or grit if the plants are growing in an alpine setting.

■ **Divide early primulas** after flowering. With larger clumps you may have to use two forks back to back to pry them apart initially, but after that the clumps can generally be pulled apart by hand. Cut off most of the old foliage, leaving about 2 in (5 cm) on each division, and replant in the

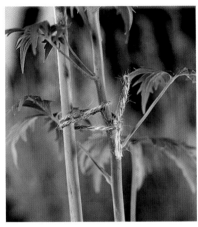

Staking delphiniums Tall plants need tall stakes. You must top them with corks or some other type of protector to prevent eye injuries when working in borders.

original position after revitalizing the soil with garden compost or manure. Water in well if the soil is dry. Alternatively, line out the small divisions in a corner of the vegetable garden and replant them in the border in the fall.

■ **Sow seed of perennials outside.** There is no cheaper and more satisfying way to grow perennials than from seed, especially collected from plants growing in the garden rather than from a packet. Most perennials can be grown this way: yarrows, alstroemerias, and cranesbills are especially easy examples. Take out shallow drills in the soil after raking it to a fine tilth. Water the drills if the soil is dry, allowing it to soak away before sowing the seeds as thinly as possible, then cover lightly with dry soil. Label each row. After a few weeks, when the seedlings are large enough to handle, they can be transplanted to a nursery area to grow on and bulk up. You can also sow the seed in pots to plant out in fall, just as for ornamental cabbages.

BULBS

■ **Continue deadheading** spring-flowering bulbs that are still going. Snap off tulip heads and leave the stalks. You must leave the foliage intact for at least six weeks after the last flower. If you must move them before this (for example, if they have been grown in among wallflowers and forget-me-nots for a spring display), you can move them temporarily, heeling them in in a corner of a border or in the vegetable garden. Lift the bulbs carefully with a fork. Dig a shallow trench where they are to be heeled in and put the bulbs in the trench with the foliage above ground. Cover the bulbs with some soil and lift them when the foliage has died down. Don't forget to label the row or—if you have a memory like mine—you'll forget where they are.

■ **Fertilize spring-flowering bulbs now,** whether they are still in place or heeled in, to encourage the development of the new flower bud in the bulb for next spring. A general organic fertilizer sprinkled around the bulbs according to the manufacturer's instructions is ideal. Water it in if the weather is dry.

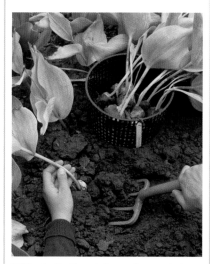

Lifting bulbs These tulips can be uprooted carefully and heeled in in a corner to die down.

ANNUALS AND BEDDING

■ **Clear spring-flowering** bedding plants and prepare the ground for summer bedding. Now that spring-flowering plants such as wallflowers, forget-me-nots, and winter-flowering pansies are coming to the end of their flowering time, they need to be cleared away and the ground prepared for summer bedding to go in. The old spring-flowering plants can be consigned to the compost pile to ensure a supply of valuable organic matter next year.

After the old plants have been removed, lightly fork over the soil, removing any weeds. At this time you can add a little organic fertilizer, as it breaks down slowly in the soil and will therefore be available to the plants when they are planted out. But don't apply too much or you will get a lot of soft growth at the expense of flowers. A light sprinkling is sufficient. Also, don't dig in organic matter at this time for the same reason. The time for digging in organic matter is in the fall.

■ **Most of the tender summer bedding** plants we grow originate in the warmer parts of the world like South Africa, where the soil is baked and very poor as far as the availability of nutrients is concerned, and this is why they don't require a lot of fertilizer to grow well.

■ **Harden off summer bedding plants.** Plants like petunias and French and African marigolds—whether bought now or raised from seed—need to be acclimatized to outdoor conditions before planting out at the end of the month and into early June. Do this by putting them into a cold frame and gradually opening the tops of the frames more each day until they can be left off altogether. Close the frame at night and keep something like row cover handy to throw over the frames, just in case a sharp frost is forecast. If you are bringing a lot of plants out in batches, then in mild areas

Frost protection If you can't resist buying frost-tender bedding, make sure you shelter it until the end of May.

the plants can be moved under a plastic cloche after a few days—but still be ready to give them extra protection at night.

■ **Take cuttings from tender perennials** like argyranthemums, geraniums, and fuchsias. You may have overwintered such plants from last year especially for the purpose of taking cuttings. Or, you may have some that have miraculously survived in sheltered spots, and taking cuttings from these will produce stronger, fresher plants that will flower better than the parent (as well as increasing your stock). Alternatively, you can now buy good-sized plants from garden centers, from which you can harvest several young shoots for cuttings without harming the parent unduly. Cuttings taken now will provide plants for flowering well into fall, but you must have somewhere frost-free to raise them until all danger of frost has passed. Shoots from all these plants can be removed when they are about 3–4 in (7.5–10 cm) long. Trim the cutting immediately below a leaf joint and dip the end in hormone rooting solution. Put the cuttings into pots containing seed-starting medium and water in well. Place a plastic bag over the pot and place it on a shady windowsill if you don't have a greenhouse.

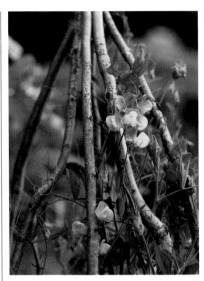

Support for annuals Twiggy sticks make informal supports for cottage-style annuals.

They will root in about three to four weeks, when they can be potted up ready to plant out in June.

■ **Thin out hardy annuals sown earlier.** If they are not thinned, the plants will become leggy and will not flower well. Thin out to leave one seedling at least every 6 in (15 cm). The taller the plants, the more space required. Check packets for details.

The easiest way to thin out seedlings is to choose the one you want to keep and pinch out the others. Measure the gap to the next one and do the same until the job is done. Most hardy annuals don't transplant well when they grow taller, so if you thin out as soon as the seedlings can be handled, they can be transplanted to fill gaps, or put them in other parts of the garden. Some of the very tall annuals need some support with twiggy sticks to prevent them from flopping over.

■ **Train sweet peas.** Sweet peas planted out earlier will be growing vigorously toward the end of the month and they may need a little steering in the right direction. If the plants are being grown for general display in the garden, tying them to the support initially will be all the help they need as the tendrils will then twine themselves around whatever they touch.

■ **Sow spring-flowering biennials.** These are the wallflowers, *Bellis perennis*, forget-me-nots, sweet Williams, and winter-flowering pansies that have just been cleared to make way for the summer bedding. The easiest way to remember the time for sowing these to flower next spring is to do it when the old ones are beginning to fade. Find a corner to sow the seeds. Try not to grow wallflowers in the same piece of ground year after year. They belong to the same family as cabbages and cauliflowers (brassicas) and are subject to the same diseases, such as clubroot, which is incurable and persists in the soil for many years. The preparation for sowing is the same for other seeds. Rake the soil to a fine tilth and level it off. Cut shallow drills with a stick or cane about 6 in (15 cm) apart and water them before sowing, if the soil is dry. Sow the seeds thinly along the row and cover lightly with dry soil and firm gently. Label each row. In a few weeks the seedlings will need to be thinned or transplanted to grow on with more space between them, before being planted in their final positions in fall.

■ **Sow ornamental cabbages** and kales. These handsome ornamental plants are grown for winter bedding displays. Their colored foliage comes in shades of red, green, and white. The colors are more intense when temperatures drop during fall. Sow the seeds in 3-in (8-cm) pots of seed-starting mix at a temperature of 65°F (18°C). Pot on when the plants are large enough to handle. They can be kept outside until planting time in fall.

CONTAINERS

■ **Clear out spring bedding plants** from containers to make way for summer bedding plants. It is worth removing some of the old soil if it has been in the container since last year. Some new potting mix will give the plants a fresh start. For containers, use soil-based potting mix, which does not dry out as quickly as soilless potting mix.

■ **In mild areas plant up** containers with frost-tender plants toward the end of the month. But remember not to plant out tender plants until at least the end of the month or early next month in more northerly parts. Keep row cover handy to drape over at night if frost is forecast.

■ **If you buy ready-planted** hanging baskets this month, harden them off to get them used to outdoor conditions. Leave them out for increasingly long periods until they can be left out at night.

■ **Water and fertilize all containers** regularly. As the weather warms up, watering containers can become a daily or twice-daily task. Hanging baskets, in

A beautiful display Blue and pink cultivars of *Nemesia* Karoo Series are shown to advantage.

particular, are prone to drying out quickly. Mixing up a fertilizer solution every time plants need feeding can be very time-consuming; the easiest way to fertilize lots of plants in containers is to make up a large quantity of solution. Fill a large tank with water, mixing in plant food according to the manufacturer's instructions. This solution can be fed at every watering. A high-potash fertilizer is best for the production of flowers. High-nitrogen fertilizers will result in a lot of leafy growth at the expense of flowers.

■ **Watch out for vine weevils** and make sure you don't introduce them into containers along with new plants. They can wreak havoc when they multiply within the closed confines of a tub or windowbox. Knock new plants out of their pots and look for the small white grubs, which eat at the roots. The adult weevils are rarely seen as they only come out at night; notched foliage is a telltale sign. However, it is the grubs that do the most damage. There are several products on the market now for controlling vine weevils. You can also control this pest with a fungus called *Beauveria bassiana*, which is a bio-control.

■ **Tender perennials in pots** and tender shrubs can be put out toward the end of the month in most parts. In northern areas wait until early June. The sooner these plants can be put outside, the better. They will benefit from the fresh air and rain after their prolonged period indoors . Larger-leaved shrubs, such as bay, can have their leaves wiped with a damp cloth. This will remove dust and dirt accumulated indoors. Be sure to keep up with watering and fertilizing because during warm weather pots can dry out very quickly. During hot spells you may have to water once or twice a day.

Plant a hardy annual border

Hardy annuals are terrific plants to have in the garden; they flower for weeks and are the easiest of plants to care for. They are also great for getting children interested in sowing and growing plants. Generally, the taller plants should be positioned nearer the back of the border, with shorter ones at the front. However, slight variations here and there, with taller, more open plants nearer the front or middle of the border, will make the display more interesting. The four plants suggested need no special treatment and prefer poorer soil to flower well. Too rich a soil produces more foliage than flowers. All prefer to be grown in full sun. Some will seed themselves around at the end of the season. For a minimal amount of care, hardy annuals will reward you with a splendid show all summer long.

Eschscholzia **'Single Mixed'** A low-growing annual for the front of the border, especially as the ferny foliage is also very attractive.

Limnanthes **'Scrambled Eggs'** A good variety of what is commonly called fried eggs or poached egg plant, excellent for attracting bees. They are suitable for the front of the border.

Nigella **'Allsorts'** Love-in-a-mist in a variety of soft pastel colors; both the flowers and the seedheads are good for cutting. They are suitable for the middle of the border.

Tropaeolum **'Peach Melba'** This nasturtium is more compact than some of the scrambling varieties, with an unusual flower coloration. It is suitable for the front of the border.

LAWNS

■ **Mow established lawns** once a week now that the grass is growing well. Each time you mow, lower the blades of the mower slightly, cutting the grass a little closer each time. Try not to lower the blades too much or the lawn will be "scalped." This will make the grass turn yellow and cause bare patches to develop, allowing weeds and moss to get established—and it looks unsightly too.

■ **Fertilize established lawns** if you haven't already done so. Follow the manufacturer's instructions carefully. Some modern fertilizers have anti-scorch properties, so it doesn't matter if you are a little heavy-handed when applying them—within reason, of course. But it is also wasteful to apply too much.

■ **Treat weeds in the lawn** with a selective weedkiller. This is a good month to do this, as weeds are now growing vigorously and the weedkiller will act more effectively on them. It is important always to use a selective lawn weedkiller on a lawn. This only affects the broadleaf weeds in the lawn. Any other sort of weedkiller will kill off the grass too. Again, follow instructions to the letter. Don't put on a bit extra for luck, as this may harm the grass. If your lawn has only a few weeds, such as dandelions, then you could use one of the "spot-treatment" weedkillers. These are painted or dabbed onto the leaves of individual weeds.

　Grass clippings taken from the lawn just after applying weedkiller should not be put on the compost pile, as traces of the herbicide will be in the clippings and could harm other plants in the garden. If you don't have time to apply fertilizer and selective weedkiller separately, there are several products on the market that combine a fertilizer, weedkiller, and moss killer all in one.

■ **Renovate damaged edges** and bare patches all through the summer until fall, as needed.

New lawns

■ **Finish sowing new lawns** before the weather becomes too warm. The best times to sow grass seed are spring and fall, when the soil is warm and generally moist.

■ **Roll newly sown lawns,** if you can, when the seed has germinated and the new grass is about 1 in (2.5 cm) high. The roller on the back of a cylinder mower is perfect for the job. Rolling encourages the grass shoots to grow from the base of the plant, ensuring a close-knit sward.

■ **Newly sown lawns** can have their first cut when the grass is 2 in (5 cm) high. Set mower blades at their highest setting. Gradually reduce the height of cut each time you mow, but don't cut new lawns from seed too close in their first year.

New grass Newly sown or sodded lawns may need their first cut this month, but don't cut too close in the lawn's first year.

VEGETABLES AND HERBS
Harvesting

■ **Harvest early crops,** such as radishes and salad leaves, as they mature.

Sowing indoors

■ **Vegetables can still be sown indoors** to shorten the growing period. Crops to sow now include zucchini, summer squash, runner beans, French beans, squashes, and sweet corn. This month, sow indoors and outside at the same time. The plants sown indoors will grow a little quicker than those outside, giving a continuity of crops rather than a glut all at once.

■ **Sow cardoons.** These are tall, handsome plants in their own right, often grown for ornamental value alone. But the stems can be blanched in the summer for cooking later. Sow two seeds to each small pot and cover lightly with potting mix. They don't need high temperatures to germinate: putting the pots on a warm windowsill is sufficient, but placing them in a heated propagator will hasten germination. Pull out the weakest seedlings when they are large enough to handle and plant out the one left in the pot in early to mid-June.

■ **Sow ridge cucumbers.** These can be sown early in the month for planting out at the beginning of June. Sow them in small pots containing a potting mix suitable for seed-sowing, placing two seeds in each pot. Push the seeds down into the soil to about 1 in (2 cm) deep and cover lightly with more potting mix. To achieve quick germination, use a propagator.

Sowing and planting outdoors

■ **Continue successional sowing** of beets, cabbage, carrots, salad onions, lettuce, peas, fava beans, radishes, and turnips. Sow in short rows to prevent a glut. Make shallow drills and water before sowing the seeds if the soil is dry. Sow the seeds thinly and cover with dry soil. When the seedlings are large enough, thin them out.

■ **Leeks sown earlier** can be planted out if not done last month. The method of planting will depend on the way the young plants were raised, but with all planting, apply a general organic fertilizer a few days beforehand. If the seeds were sown in seed trays and the plants left to grow on in the trays until 4–5 in (10–12 cm) high, they can be planted in individual holes. Make a hole about 6 in (15 cm) deep with a dibber and put one plant in each hole. Complete the row and water in. The plants should be about 12 in (30 cm) apart each way. Do not firm: watering them will automatically wash some soil down the hole to cover the roots. If seeds were multiple-sown in cell packs for deep beds, the small clumps of five or six plants can be planted in clusters, 6–9 in (15–22 cm) apart each way. This way you get more weight of crop per square yard (meter) than if they are grown in conventional straight rows.

■ **Plant out self-blanching celery** toward the end of the month. Make sure the ground has been prepared thoroughly, incorporating plenty of organic matter to retain moisture. Unlike blanching celery, there is no need to grow this type in a trench to blanch the stems. It is best,

Planting out celery Arranged in blocks, the plants will shade each other, aiding blanching.

though, to grow it in blocks rather than in straight rows.

■ **Globe artichokes sown** earlier under cover can be planted out toward the end of the month. Traditionally, globe artichokes are grown as perennials and planted at a distance of 3 ft (). You can grow them as biennials and plant them much closer together: 18 in (45 cm) apart. This year, pinch out flower buds from every other plant. After taking crops from the others this summer, remove them. The pinched-out plants will provide good crops next year, when you can also plant new plants between them, setting up a two-year cycle. Growing young plants each year also gives a continuity of crop throughout each season.

■ **Plant out summer squash and zucchini** at the end of the month. These plants are tender and prone to damage from frosts. Plant into soil that has been enriched with plenty of organic matter, as summer squash and zucchini require a lot of water during the growing season. They do take up quite a bit of room, so space them at 3 ft (90 cm) each way. Keep the plants well watered through the summer. If you do not have room in the vegetable garden to grow these plants, why not grow one or two in ornamental borders? The large leaves are bold and attractive and will provide a good contrast to other foliage plants in the garden—and the edible parts are a bonus. Trailing varieties can be grown up strong canes, bean poles, or other forms of support to make an attractive feature, which also saves space at ground level.

■ **Direct-sow runner beans,** French beans, and sweet corn. Although these are all tender, by sowing outside this month the seeds will germinate when the threat of frost has passed in most areas. Seeds of

runner beans can be sown two to the base of each bean pole or bamboo cane. The weaker seedling can be removed when the seeds have germinated. Sowing two seeds per "station" is an insurance policy should a seed fail to germinate.

Sow sweet corn in blocks, 24 in (60 cm) apart each way, again with two seeds in each hole. French beans can be sown in rows 24 in (60 cm) apart with the seeds 6–9 in (15–22 cm) apart in the rows.

Seedlings of all of these plants can be damaged by slugs as they germinate. To avoid this problem, after sowing the seeds cover them with plastic soda or water bottles that have had the bottom cut out, pushing them into the ground.

■ **Transplant Brussels sprouts** and other winter brassicas sown earlier. These plants can now be transplanted to their cropping positions. They do take up a fair amount of space over a long period of time. But other short-term crops such as lettuce, radishes, and turnips can be grown between the brassicas to use the space efficiently. All the brassicas to be planted out should be well watered beforehand, as they wilt very quickly. One point to bear in mind is that cauliflowers will not produce a proper curd if they receive even the slightest check to their growth. So watering before planting out and afterward is very important. The ideal stage at which to transplant the seedlings is when they have made two or three true leaves. The plants should be set out at a minimum of 24 in (60 cm) each way.

■ **Sow chard and leaf beet.** Swiss chard has large leaves and pure-white stems, both of which can be eaten, the leaves being used like spinach. There are also ruby and "rainbow" chards, with deep red and multicolored midribs, respectively, which look good among ornamentals. Leaf beets, or perpetual spinach, is also a good substitute for spinach as it, like chard, is less susceptible to bolting (running to seed) than spinach is. Often spinach will start bolting just a few weeks after the seeds germinate. Sow the seeds in drills, watering first if the soil seems dry. Thin out the seedlings when they are large enough to handle and keep them well watered during the summer.

■ **It's now too late to sow** tomato seeds, but garden centers will have a choice of plants. Try bush varieties 'Red Alert' and 'Beefsteak', and you won't have to stake them or pinch out sideshoots. Plant about 24 in (60 cm) apart and mulch with straw to prevent fruits from rotting on the soil.

Caring for crops

■ **Pinch out the tops of fava beans** when they flower to discourage aphids, which love the young, succulent tips of the plants. By removing the young tips when several trusses of flowers have developed, there should be less need to spray to control these aphids. Provide some support for

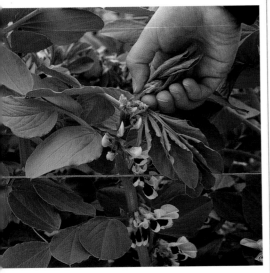

Pinching fava beans By removing the tender tip you take away the part aphids like best.

fava beans with string stretched between canes at either end of the row. The plants tend to flop over when the pods develop.

■ **Protect carrots from carrot fly.** The female of this pest flies around just above soil level seeking out juicy carrots by their smell and laying her eggs at the base of the foliage. The small larvae of the fly burrow into the root of the carrot, making holes in it, causing rot to set in. The carrots are then unappealing to eat and useless for storing over winter. This pest also attacks parsnips and parsley. The easiest way to protect the plants is to cover them with floating row cover, leaving it over the crop permanently as there is another generation of carrot fly later in August. Or you can erect a barrier made from floating row cover, fine mesh, or plastic sheeting supported on a wooden framework, preventing the carrot fly from getting to the crops.

To minimize the threat of carrot fly, sow seeds as thinly as possible to reduce the need for thinning the seedlings. Don't leave thinnings lying around, as the smell will attract any carrot fly that are around. You could also try growing alternate rows of onions and carrots, the theory being that the strong pungent aroma from the onions will mask the smell of the carrots, so confusing the carrot fly. Some varieties of carrots, 'Flyaway' and 'Resistafly', are less susceptible to attack.

■ **Hoe regularly to keep down weeds.** This job is well worth doing regularly, as it will save a lot of back-breaking work if the weeds are left to grow. Catch weed seedlings when they are small and they can be left on the surface to dry out.

■ **Earth up early potatoes,** drawing a little soil up over the emerging shoots. This not only protects them from any late frost,

Carrot fly barrier Fence carrots with fine mesh around canes to keep this pest away.

but also encourages the development of roots further up the stems, therefore increasing the yield. Keep earthing up potatoes at intervals to cover any developing potatoes in the soil, preventing them from turning green in the light. This is because when potatoes turn green they become poisonous.

■ **Tomatoes sown last month** need potting on now. Those being espaliered should have sideshoots, which form at the leaf axils removed. Do this when they are quite small, by rubbing them out with your forefinger and thumb and it won't be such a shock to the plant. Once the first truss of flowers has faded and fruits are setting, feed weekly with a high-potash fertilizer.

Herbs

■ **Lift and divide mint.** It can become invasive, so lift and divide it before it takes over the garden. Be sure to remove as many of the roots spreading out from the plant as possible, because if these are left in, they will continue to grow. New, small divisions can be replanted in the same place. To prevent mint from becoming too invasive, grow it in pots.

FRUIT
Caring for crops

■ **Control pests by putting up pheromone traps.** Many pests are very difficult to control because they are becoming immune to the chemicals we use to control them. An alternative way to control some pests is by using traps. Codling moth is a good example of a pest that responds well to this method. During May and June the moths mate and lay eggs on apples, and the eggs hatch into maggots, which tunnel into the fruits. Male codling moths are attracted to the females by a pheromone, or hormonal scent, which the females give off to attract the male when they are ready to mate. This pheromone is now produced artificially and can be purchased in a small container that is placed in a small plastic housing, rather like a bird house. In the house is a piece of sticky paper impregnated with this substance to capture males attracted by the scent. This reduces the mating success of the moths and so fewer viable eggs are laid. You will need one trap for every three to five trees.

■ **Tuck straw under strawberries** to protect the fruits from rotting. This also prevents the fruits being spoiled by rain-splashed soil and slugs. Garden centers may have special strawberry mats as an alternative to straw. As the fruits develop, cover the plants with netting to keep birds away from them. Make sure the netting is properly secured to prevent birds from getting ensnared in it. If you are concerned about birds being caught in netting, use floating row cover to cover the plants instead.

■ **Remove runners from strawberries** if they are not required for propagating new plants. If runners are allowed to develop, a great deal of the plants' energy will go into producing them. The crop of fruit will be poorer and the strawberry bed will end up

as a mass of tangled plants, which will be difficult to weed. Putting straw or strawberry mats down to protect the fruits from being splashed with soil will also be next to impossible. If you want to let a few plants develop runners for new plants, pick the flowers off and sacrifice their crop so that you get really strong young plantlets.

■ **Take off all covers** and protection from peach, nectarine, and cherry trees. But continue to protect late blossoms on fruit trees and bushes from late frosts. Sharp frosts can still occur at any time this month, especially in northern parts of the country. The easiest way to give protection in a hurry is to use floating row cover. This can be thrown over small trees or draped over trees trained against walls and fences and will help keep off a few degrees of frost. You might get fed up with hearing gardeners talking about late frosts at this time of year, when it seems so mild, but they do happen often, so it is always better to be aware of them and not allow them to ruin your crop of hard-earned fruit later in the summer.

■ **Keep newly planted fruit plants** well watered. Young plants need tender loving care to help them get established in their first year after planting. If they suffer stress due to lack of water at any time, it makes them more vulnerable to attack from pests and diseases and reduces the amount of growth and subsequently the amount of fruit produced. It is far better to give them a good soaking once a week rather than give smaller amounts on a daily basis during dry spells. Scant watering encourages the roots to develop closer to the surface of the soil in search of moisture, making them even more vulnerable in drought conditions. And they will be more easily damaged when weeding among the plants.

■ **Mulch all fruit,** if you have not already done so, to retain moisture in the soil. Use well-rotted farmyard manure, garden compost, spent mushroom compost, or any other organic matter you can get hold of. If the soil is dry, make sure it is watered well before applying a mulch, as mulches are just as good at keeping moisture out of the soil as keeping it in. If you have a sprinkler, leave it on one area at a time for at least

Protecting strawberries

Tuck straw under strawberries and the fruits will not be damaged by splashes of mud.

Strawberry mats are an alternative to straw. They may be available from garden centers.

two hours to give the area a good soaking, and then mulch. There is no point in giving small amounts of water every day. Instead, concentrate on watering small areas really well in rotation, or the water is wasted. Be sure there are no watering restrictions in your area before using a sprinkler.

Pruning and training

■ **Prune out unwanted shoots on all raspberries.** If too many new canes are allowed to develop them, as with strawberry runners, more energy will be put into developing these new canes than into fruit production. Thick, crowded rows are difficult to care for and the fruits will receive less ripening sunshine. Another important point is that the more congested the shoots are, the less air will circulate through the plants, making them more susceptible to fungal diseases such as botrytis. This fungal disease will attack the fruits, causing them to turn brown and rot off. The more air that can circulate around the plants, the less likelihood there is of their being attacked by disease. The canes that are left will also be all the more sturdy, because they have more light and room to develop.

'Warwickshire Drooper'

■ **Prune plums and cherries** trained against walls and fences. The pruning of these trees is done in spring and summer because they are vulnerable to silver leaf disease, the spores of which enter through wounds. By pruning at this time, wounds heal more quickly and the period of heaviest spore production is avoided. When this year's young shoots have six leaves, pinch out the growing tip. Once the fruit has been picked, prune back these shoots to about half their length, taking out any overcrowded and unhealthy-looking stems at the same time.

Trained sour cherries like 'Morello' are pruned slightly differently. These produce fruit on two-year-old wood and so you have to think about this when pruning. To start what is an ongoing process, tie in one shoot made last year to fruit this year and tie in a new one alongside it for fruiting the following year. Don't prune these shoots, but remove any surplus ones. When the fruit has been picked, prune out the fruited shoot altogether and the other one tied in alongside will be its fruiting replacement next year, when it, in turn, will have a new shoot tied in alongside it.

Propagation

■ **If strawberry runners** are required to make new strawberry plants, reduce runners to five or six per plant and peg them into small pots of peat-free potting mix sunk into the ground around the parent.

Beat the seasons

■ **Strawberry plants** that were covered with cloches to hasten fruiting should have them opened up for part of the day now, to allow pollinating insects in—otherwise, no fruits will develop. It may be worth going over a few plants with a small, soft paintbrush, transferring pollen from one flower to another to ensure pollination has taken place.

UNDER COVER

■ **Damp down regularly** in the greenhouse and conservatory, splashing water on the floor and under staging to increase the humidity levels, ideally two to three times a day by mid-summer. This is beneficial to plant growth and it also helps in the control of red spider mite. This microscopic pest can be detected by the mottled appearance it gives the foliage of affected plants. It can also be controlled chemically; alternatively, there is a tiny predatory mite that can be used as a biological control.

■ **Shade the greenhouse** or conservatory. It is best to try to avoid great fluctuations of temperatures under glass, and the best way to reduce the temperature is by using shading. The cheapest form of shading is a wash for the glass; it comes as a powder, which is mixed with water and painted or sprayed on. It can be wiped off with a duster at the end of the summer.

The one problem with this type of shading is that it is there even on dull days, reducing light inside. The alternative is to use roll-up shades. Ideally, they should be installed on the outside. A compromise is to use commercial shade cloth, which can be thrown over the structure on sunny days and taken off on dull days.

■ **Continue to prick out** and pot on seedlings, cuttings and young plants as they need it.

■ **Check all plants regularly** for signs of pests and diseases, which become more prevalent as the weather becomes warmer; be vigilant to keep them from building up into serious problems. Look on the undersides of leaves for whiteflies and the tips of shoots for aphids. Small infestations of pests can be picked off or may be caught on yellow sticky cards. Don't use these traps if you have plenty of predatory insects around, as these will be caught, too. Another way to keep pests at bay is with biological controls.

Raising plants for outdoors

■ **Plant hanging baskets** and other containers, provided you can keep them frost-free in the greenhouse to grow on, giving them a head start before putting them outside early next month.

■ **Harden off hanging baskets** that were planted up last month so that they can get used to the outdoor conditions. Leave them out for increasingly long periods until they can be left out at night—as long as frost is not forecast.

■ **Harden off bedding plants** for planting out at the end of the month and early next month. This means getting the plants used to growing in cooler conditions, without interrupting their growth. The usual way of doing this is to put the plants in cold frames and keep the lids closed for a few days. Then gradually open them, increasing ventilation over about a week until the lids can be left off—except on nights when frost is forecast. Or stand the plants outside for short periods, increasing the time they are left out.
　Don't be in too much of a hurry to plant out, even though space in the greenhouse and cold frame will be at a premium. If the plants have been in pots or trays longer than they should have been and are looking starved, apply liquid fertilizer.

■ **Sow half-hardy** and hardy annuals now for fall color. Some half-hardy annuals such as clarkia, calendula, and candytuft (*Iberis*) can still be sown early in the month to produce flowers in late summer and fall.

■ **Sow ornamental cabbages** and kales.

Cold frame Gradually extend the time you leave a cold frame open, to harden off your plants.

■ **Vegetables can still be sown indoors** to shorten the growing period.

Greenhouse and house plants

■ **Pot on begonias** and gloxinias that were potted into small pots earlier. Be sure to water the plants well beforehand, otherwise the root ball will remain dry and the roots will not grow into the new potting mix very well. Five- or six-inch (12–15-cm) pots are an adequate size for normal container plants. If you are growing them for exhibition, they will have to be potted on again into larger pots later in the summer. Leave a gap of about 1 in (2.5 cm) between the surface of the potting mix and the rim of the pot to allow room for watering. Water them in after potting to settle the potting mix around the roots.

■ **Sow half-hardy** and hardy annuals now for winter-flowering container plants. Some half-hardy annuals make excellent container plants in the winter—for example, browallia, calceolarias, cinerarias, and schizanthus. Sow them thinly in small pots or trays at a temperature of 65°F (18°C). Prick out the seedlings into small pots when they are large enough. Pot on into larger pots when the roots have filled

the smaller pots and you will have a glorious mix of color through winter and spring.

Crops under glass

■ **As forced strawberries** in pots finish cropping, discard the plants. They will not be capable of cropping well a second time. Pot up some runners from plants in the garden for next year.

■ **Plant up tomatoes,** peppers, and eggplants sown earlier. Young plants can be potted on into large pots to crop, or put into containers, or planted in the soil in the greenhouse border. Don't overcrowd them, as they will become drawn and leggy if they are planted too close together. Espaliered tomatoes have weak stems and they will need supporting all season. An alternative to canes or frames is to run baler twine under the plant's rootball when planting, tying the other end of the twine to wire supports strung across the greenhouse roof. The plants are wound around the string as they grow.

■ **Continue to remove sideshoots** from espaliered tomatoes. The smaller the shoots when this is done, the better. The best way to do it is to bend them to one side with your thumb and forefinger; they should snap off cleanly. If the shoots have grown too large to snap off, use a sharp knife, but have a weak bleach solution in a container with you and dip the knife into it each time a shoot is cut off. This sterilizes the knife and prevents the spread of viral diseases.

■ **Fertilize all tomatoes, peppers,** and eggplants with a high-potash fertilizer every week from now on through the season to achieve good crops.

The June garden

Summer is really here. There is still plenty to keep you occupied, such as cutting back and mowing, but this is a time of year when you can begin to enjoy the fruits of your labors. So above all else, take time to sit and savor the sensory delights of your garden and reward yourself for all the hard work you have put into it. Gardening shouldn't become a chore.

THINGS TO DO

Keep weeding and deadheading to maintain beds, borders, and container displays, and water new and young plants as necessary. Look out for pests and suckers on roses and prune spring-flowering shrubs. You can propagate climbers by layering them.

Cut back and tidy up spring-flowering perennials and take cuttings from pinks. Sow perennial seeds and cut down the faded foliage of bulbs, lifting and dividing any overgrown clumps as required. Plant out summer bedding in borders and containers, including hanging baskets, and sow plants for winter and spring color, such as polyanthus and pansies.

Mow the lawn and trim edges regularly. Give tired lawns a boost with a liquid fertilizer and water new lawns made in the spring.

Harvest vegetables as they come to maturity and plant winter brassicas, protecting them from pests. Keep fruit and vegetables well watered in dry spells and shade and ventilate all the plants in the greenhouse.

LAST CHANCE

Plant new plants before the summer really heats up and sow hardy annuals outside to flower this year. Plant out tender vegetables such as tomatoes and runner beans to get good crops this year.

GET AHEAD

Sow chicory to force in winter for salads and peg down strawberry runners to make new plants. Sow seed for a few container plants to flower in winter.

Annual poppies (*Papaver somniferum*) create a wonderful summer display of bright flowers, offset against marvelous blue-green leaves.

Time to relax and enjoy

Think of this month as the moment when things hit their peak—borders look perfect and summer vegetables and soft fruit are flourishing. You need to take time to admire the results of your hard work, but don't forget to keep an eye on pests and be alert to drier spells, when you will need to do plenty of watering.

Ornamental borders will soon be at the peak of perfection and there are plenty of early summer vegetables to be savored now. Toward the end of the month soft fruit will also be ripening, to provide a mouthwatering selection of berries during the rest of the summer. Also toward the end of the month, roses begin to flower in earnest in most parts of the country. Most have a wonderful scent and there is a terrific selection of flower colors and shapes available. Climbing and rambler roses look particularly good around doors and scrambling up through trees and large shrubs. At your local garden center there will be wonderful displays of roses in bloom; take some home and plant them out for instant color in the garden or in containers on the patio.

Most of the sowing, pricking out, and potting on will have been done, so you can now spend a little time

relaxing in the garden. The long summer evenings are pure joy and there is nothing better in the cool of a summer evening than to sit quietly in the backyard with a glass of something refreshing. Listen to the birds and insects and take in the scents (which are often stronger in the evening) and enjoy the sights and sounds of your own private piece of paradise. Pure bliss!

The start of dry spells

The weather in June is usually quite warm, with few days of rain. There may be thunderstorms followed by hot, dry spells, so keep a watchful eye on all newly planted plants and water them as and when required. With the sun now quite strong, it is time to shade greenhouses and conservatories throughout the day to prevent plants from being scorched in ovenlike temperatures. Good ventilation is also vital and the ventilators can usually be left open day and night through the summer. Thankfully, all tender plants can now be put outside as there should be little

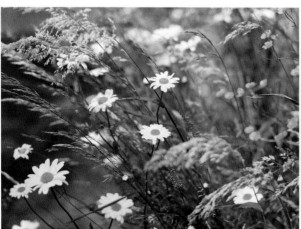

Meadow mood Grasses and wildflowers will attract bees and butterflies, but are also rich food resources for many other less conspicuous creatures.

risk of frost. Now is the time to plant up all those container, basket, and bedding designs you have been dreaming about. Cluttered greenhouse benches, conservatories, and windowsills can be cleared of all the young and tender plants sheltering indoors. If you haven't been growing on your own summer bedding plants, then get down to your garden center or nursery as soon as possible, before all the best plants are snapped up. Even if you don't think you're an "annual person," just take a look. You're bound to be tempted by some of the lovely new selections that have appeared in the last few years. Don't be afraid to plant closely, leaving much less space than when setting out hardy garden plants. After all, the plants only have to last a season. It's no bad thing to overestimate your needs when raising or buying bedding plants, as you'll always find gaps for any spares.

Pests on the march

Pests and diseases are now on the attack in full force in the warm conditions, both inside and outside. Biological controls are the answer, especially in the greenhouse. Conditions indoors are more favorable to biological controls because most need warm temperatures to be most effective.

Wherever possible, try to use organic means to control pests and diseases, rather than resorting instinctively to an arsenal of chemicals. Most problems with pests and diseases can be controlled by good garden hygiene and by good growing and gardening practices: not allowing plants to grow too closely together and fertilizing them to encourage strong growth—but not lush, soft growth, which is more susceptible to attack. If you follow these simple steps, the plants will be not only healthier but also more able to shrug off attacks from pests and diseases, thereby reducing the need for chemical controls.

The way ahead for the weather

There is considerable debate these days about climate change and how this will affect us in the future, but it is difficult to predict what may happen in the longer term.

A rain barrel is a great asset for gardeners. The stored water is suitable for all plants, except for young plants and seedlings.

Weather watch

The official start of summer is around June 21, but in northern areas summer arrives nearly a month later than in the South. The sun doesn't set until well into the evening, and days can be hot at times, with temperatures reaching into the 80s and 90s (25–35°C) throughout the South, Mid-Atlantic, Midwest, and Southwest, while the milder coastal areas of the Northeast and Northern states enjoy pleasant daytime temperatures in the 70s (20–25°C).

Hotter days

The beginning of summer also marks the beginning of weather challenges for gardeners. Sunny June days trend toward the hot days of July and August. Droughts drive gardeners to irrigate vegetable gardens in most parts of the country, and cause those in the driest areas of the West to garden in containers or focus on drought-tolerant perennials.

Thunderstorms

Cooling breezes from the poles collide with the sun-heated air across the continent, producing hail and thunderstorms accompanied by high winds, which come and go suddenly over broad expanses of open prairie and deserts. In the Rockies, cool mountain air clashes with warmer breezes from the valleys, making afternoon rains quite common. This is why wind farms with their huge windmills are seen on high ground, in the desert Southwest, and along the West Coast.

Summer solstice

Thankfully there are usually more sunny days than dull, overcast ones this month. The summer solstice is the longest day of the year, making it possible to garden from sunup to sundown, which can come as late as 9 pm. Many gardeners take full advantage of this in the short summers and long days of the northern regions of the country. But the heat causes evaporation, increasing humidity in the air, which can stress plants, which can in turn stall growth and fruit set, cause wilting, and make woolly-leaved plants susceptible to fungal infections.

Clearing the greenhouse By now, the greenhouse may be full to bursting point, but June nights should be reliably warm and all the plants here can be put outside.

Herb plantings Aromatic herbs such as chives, thyme, and sage will flourish in a sunny spot in the garden, yet survive cold winters. Alternatively, a hanging basket can be moved according to conditions.

If you don't already have one, install a rain barrel to catch valuable rainwater. Plants always grow much better when watered with rain water than with tap water, especially if you live in an area with hard water, which is alkaline. You can tell you've got hard water if you see lime deposits around your kitchen faucet. Plants like rhododendrons and azaleas growing in pots need acidic conditions and hard water doesn't do them much good. Keeping a rain barrel for rain water for these plants is very worthwhile.

The reason plants in general prefer rain water is that it lacks the chemicals routinely added to tap water to eradicate any harmful bacteria for human consumption. Plants don't have kidneys, as we do, to filter out these harsh chemicals.

The consensus of opinion seems to be that overall temperatures will continue to become warmer. Rising oceans will give rise to storms and damaging waves in some coastal areas, while the interior of the country will suffer droughts in some previously wet areas, such as the Southeast, while experiencing wetter and cooler summers in other areas.

Conserving water

With the effects of climate change becoming more apparent, we must do our best to conserve the natural resources of the planet. If you have not already done so earlier in the year, spread a mulch of organic matter over any bare soil after rain or watering to conserve as much moisture as possible. Another way to do this and to keep weeds at bay at the same time is to use ground-cover plants. There is a very wide choice of plants available from garden centers and nurseries that form a very effective green cover over the soil.

Keeping the garden looking good

Don't get too depressed about the climate, because nature always seems to balance things out in the end. There will be plenty of opportunities to enjoy the garden on warm, sunny June days and there are plenty of jobs to tackle. Spring-flowering plants may need some attention now that their main season of display is over. Pruning shrubs and trimming and dividing perennials will ensure that they give a good show next year and their neat appearance will set off your summer-flowering plants, rather than creating a shabby, overgrown distraction.

One task that is important but is often regarded as being rather tedious is deadheading—removing fading flowers to encourage a fresh crop of blooms. Some plants, such as pansies, may have a very short flowering period if they are not deadheaded. All of the repeat-flowering roses also benefit from being deadheaded as the flowers fade; it is the best way to encourage a further flush of blooms throughout the summer and into the fall.

Pack in more plants

Gardens are ablaze with color in June, but if yours is looking a little lackluster, now is the time to liven it up.

One way is to fill a few containers with annuals, providing an instant, if temporary, lift. Alternatively, make new flowerbeds, and plant them up with colorful perennials. An underused patch of lawn can be transformed into a blooming border in just a day or two, as outlined in this month's practical project (see p.135). Select plants that will suit your site and soil and leave gaps between them to allow for growth—many perennials will spread rapidly once they are established. If you want to keep some structure throughout the winter you can also work in a few flowering shrubs, such as cistus and choisya.

Nepeta x faassenii
Spreading perennial with a pungent scent (see p.300)

Cistus x cyprius
Sun-loving shrub that flowers over a long period (see p.272)

Achillea 'Fanal'
Perennial with flowers popular with beneficial insects (see p.263)

Astilbe 'Bronce Elegans'
Perennial, good for a shady spot that is not too dry (see p.267)

Genista aetnensis
The Mount Etna broom; a large, drought-tolerant shrub (see p.287)

Iris germanica
Bearded iris, often with several flowers on each stem (see p.292)

Geranium himalayense
Perennial that gives its best display in early to midsummer (see p.287)

***Potentilla fruticosa* Princess**
Small, bushy shrub that enjoys sun and dry soil (see p.306)

Dianthus 'Little Jock'
Small perennial forming flower-covered mounds (see p.280)

Crambe cordifolia
Statuesque perennial with huge sprays of flowers (see p.278)

***Santolina chamaecyparissus* 'Lemon Queen'**
Low-growing gray-leaved shrub (see p.316)

Geum 'Borisii'
Perennial that flowers over a long period in summer (see p.287)

Clematis 'Fireworks'
Large-flowered, deciduous climber with blue-mauve flowers (see p.273)

Philadelphus microphyllus
Free-flowering shrub with orange-blossom fragrance (see p.305)

Alchemilla mollis
Spreading perennial, good along path edges and as ground cover (see p.264)

Polemonium carneum
Jacob's ladder, a clump-forming perennial with pretty leaves (see p.306)

Lupinus 'The Page'
Clump-forming perennial with carmine-red flower spikes (see p.297)

Tamarix tetrandra
Arching shrub that grows well in coastal regions (see p.320)

Lonicera x heckrottii
Vividly colored honeysuckle for a sunny wall (see p.296)

Veronica gentianoides
Perennial with palest blue to white flower spikes (see p.321)

Viburnum plicatum 'Mariesii'
Large deciduous shrub with tiered branches (see p.322)

Buddleja globosa
Large shrub with honey-scented flowers (see p.269)

Paeonia lactiflora 'Sarah Bernhardt'
Herbaceous perennial with large double, rose-pink flowers (see p.302)

Lavandula angustifolia 'Munstead'
Compact, bushy lavender ideal for edging (see p.294)

What to do in June

AROUND THE YARD

In case frost is forecast, as it may still be in some northern parts, use floating row cover or old newspapers to give protection to bedding and vulnerable young vegetables, including the shoots of late-planted potatoes.

Apply and renew mulches over the soil. This is a good idea at any time of year, but especially now, to reduce water loss from the soil and suppress weeds. The most important point to bear in mind when putting down a mulch is to make sure the soil is moist beforehand. If the soil is dry, the mulch is just as good at keeping water out as it is at retaining it in the soil. Don't forget that you can also "mulch" newly planted containers; there is a wide range of decorative chips now for sale that will complement stone, terra-cotta, and glazed pots.

Water plants thoroughly during hot spells, concentrating on newly planted plants, young vegetables, and plants in containers, which need it most. If there's a lot to do, it is no good going out every night and splashing a little water everywhere. In drought periods, divide the garden into areas and every evening give a different one a good soaking, which should last for up to a week. This is more beneficial because the roots will go deeper into the soil in search of water. Smaller amounts of water encourage the roots to come to the surface of the soil, causing more harm in the long run; roots near the surface make the plants even more vulnerable in drier conditions.

Hoe or hand-pull annual weeds while they are still small. Choose a dry day and leave the weeds on the surface to wither. Perennial weeds have to be dug out, leaving no trace of the roots in the soil. If root is left, it will start to grow again, effectively propagating the weed.

Any gaps in borders are better filled with bedding plants for the summer now; more permanent plants can be put in in the fall. These gap-fillers will give instant color to what may have been a bare patch of earth.

Any annuals will do, whether hardy or half-hardy. If you need height among medium-sized plants, you can even drop in a whole pot of summer-display plants. Hardy annuals sown now will flower in late summer and fall, extending the flowering display in the borders.

Deadheading is a regular task in all parts of the garden as some flowers fade. With many plants—perennials, repeat-flowering roses and hardy and half-hardy annuals—the flowering period can be extended considerably if old flowers are removed as soon as they fade. This will prevent the plant's energy from going into seed production and channel it into new growth and flowers later in the summer and fall. Most deadheading can be done with pruners, cutting back to just above strong buds lower down the stems. Some plants, such as cranesbills, can be quickly trimmed back hard with a pair of garden shears when the flowers fade. It may seem rather drastic, but new foliage soon appears.

Deadheading This phlox is among many plants that will produce more flowers if deadheaded.

TREES AND SHRUBS

■ **Control aphids on roses** by hitting them with a strong stream of water, or use a solution of insecticidal soap according to package directions. Aphids are delicate insects, and once knocked off a plant they are usually unable to infest it again. Spray early in the morning so the leaves dry before sundown, when damp leaves are vulnerable to fungal infections. Also spray susceptible varieties against black spot with an appropriate fungicide. Avoid products containing insecticides unless pests are actually present.

■ **Watch out for leaf-rolling sawfly** on roses. This pest is easy to identify because the leaf edges roll tightly downward and inward. There is little detrimental effect to the plant other than the unsightly appearance. Minor infestations can be treated by picking off affected leaves and putting them in the trash. There are sprays that can be used, but by the time you see rolled-up leaves, it is too late. It's much better to be vigilant and remove leaves as soon as you notice a problem.

■ **Disbud hybrid tea roses** if larger blooms are required. These roses often produce several buds at the tip of each stem, making perfectly adequate blooms, albeit fairly small in size. If one show-stopping bloom per stem is needed, remove all the smaller buds, leaving the central, larger, bud to open up. This will also give a longer stem, ideal for arrangements.

■ **Remove fading flowers** from rhododendrons, camellias, and lilacs. By removing the fading blooms, the plant's energy is diverted from producing seeds into building up buds. Be careful when removing the spent flowers from rhododendrons (see right) and camellias, as the new shoots develop immediately below the old flowerheads. With lilacs,

Removing rhododendron flowers

Remove the faded flowers very carefully between finger and thumb.

With the flower removed, you will see why care is needed: new leaf buds lie just behind it.

cut back the flowered stem to just above a pair of leaves or buds lower down.

■ **Remove suckers from roses.** Most modern bush roses are grafted, or budded, onto a rootstock, which gives the plant the vigor it needs to produce all those beautiful blooms. One slight drawback with budded roses is that every so often the rootstock itself puts out the odd shoot. It is clearly identifiable because the foliage is generally lighter in color. It is better if suckers can be pulled off the plant at their point of origin on the roots rather than cut off. If they are cut off, the sucker is more likely to grow again.

Pruning and training

■ **Prune mature deciduous shrubs** that finish flowering. These include deutzia, kolkwitzia, philadelphus, and weigela. First, look over the whole plant and remove any dead or damaged growth, cutting to a stem joint or leaf. Then take a worm's-eye view through the thicket of stems at the base of the plant and cut out one in three quite low down, selecting the oldest and thickest for removal. Larger stems can be cut with loppers. Really tough old wood

will need a pruning saw. After pruning, feed with a general organic fertilizer and mulch with organic matter. The new growth produced over the summer will flower next year.

■ **If lilacs have become overgrown** and leggy, now is the best time for drastic action, just after you have enjoyed the flowers, but early enough to let the shrub produce new growth over the summer. Saw them right down to about 18 in (45 cm) from the base. New shoots will regrow; thin those growing inward across the center of the plant. The result will be a much bushier, better-shaped shrub.

Planting

■ **You may still plant container-grown** plants, but it isn't advisable now that the weather has started to heat up. A woody plant needs a lot of care and watering to get established in summer—it's better to use a stop-gap such as tall lilies and plant something more permanent in fall.

Propagation

■ **Continue taking softwood cuttings** from shrubs.

CLIMBERS

■ **Keep on top of training climbing and rambler roses.** These produce so much growth, at such a rate, that if you don't tie them in regularly, they trail over other plants and catch on clothing. Whenever possible, tie in the stems as close to horizontal as possible.

■ **Propagate climbers by layering.** Growing your own new plants is one of the most fascinating aspects of gardening. An easy way to propagate many climbers, including clematis, *Akebia quinata*, wisteria, and honeysuckle, is by layering. Many plants layer themselves when a branch or shoot touches the ground, forming roots at that point. If you spot any of these shoots with roots already forming, peg them directly into the soil or into a pot full of potting mix sunk into the ground as you would with strawberry runners. The young plants can been severed from their parent either in fall, over-wintering in a cold frame, or next spring.

■ **Prune** *Clematis montana* if you didn't do so last month. This is a vigorous clematis, but it only really needs pruning if it is getting out of control and smothering other plants. Thin out the growth and trim back to its allotted space.

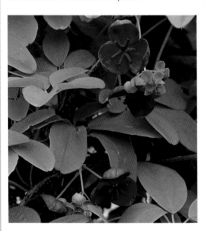

Akebia quinata

Layering a climber

Peg down a stem still attached to the plant at intervals along the ground. Roots should grow into the soil below the pegs.

1 In fall, or next spring, carefully uproot the stem and separate each rooted section.

2 Pot each up individually in a mixture of peat-free potting mix and vermiculite. Water thoroughly and place in a cold frame.

PERENNIALS

■ **Remove old leaves and flower stems of hellebores.** The old foliage looks shabby now and is often infected with leaf spot and other diseases. Remove the leaves at ground level and discard them. The new, young foliage can often be seen growing from the center of the plant. Applying a general fertilizer and a mulch with organic matter will also do no harm.

Hellebore seeds can be collected from the plants and you can sow them right away. If the seeds are left on the plants to ripen, this will inhibit germination. They don't require any special conditions to germinate. Sow the seeds in a tray or a small pot, cover them lightly with potting mix, and stand the container in a shady cold frame or at the base of a sheltered wall. When the seeds germinate, pot them on once they are large enough to handle.

■ **Cut back Oriental poppies** when they have finished flowering. This is good to do, since once the flowers fade these plants tend to look messy. It's one good reason for siting them in the middle or near the back of a border, so that when the flowers are finished, other plants will hide them. To make them look better, cut the foliage to near ground level. It may seem a bit drastic, but it is the right thing to do. Once cut back, sprinkle a little organic fertilizer around the plants and water it in thoroughly. This will encourage new growth to come and, if you are lucky, a few more flowers later in the summer.

■ *Euphorbia robbiae* and *E. characias* will look a lot tidier if the old flowerheads are removed when they are fading. Always be sure to wear gloves when you are pruning euphorbias, as the milky white sap can irritate sensitive skin. Remove the old growths to ground level. This will encourage new growth from the base of the plant and keep it bushy and healthy.

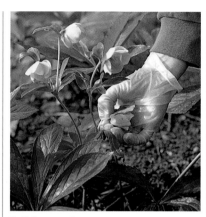
Hellebore seeds Wear gloves to collect the ripe capsules, which can irritate skin.

■ **Every year a new crop of seedlings** appears around the hellebore plants and these can be potted up and grown on as new plants. They will never come true to type—that is to say, if the seeds come from a pink flower, you may not necessarily get pink flowers from the new plants. But you never know—you may come across a stunning variation!

■ **Continue to stake tall-growing** perennials. Nothing looks more unsightly than plants that have been battered by rain and wind, lying all over other, smaller plants in the borders. Try to stake before this happens. The earlier it is done, the better, but it is still not too late to continue doing this task. There are many ways of supporting plants and many products readily available from garden centers. The types you use will largely depend on the depth of your pockets. Bamboo canes and string are cheap, but they have to be used carefully if they are not to look too rigid and prominent in the border, and you must remember to fit eye protectors on top of the canes. Twiggy sticks are another easy means of support. The advantage of these is that the plants can grow through and hide them.

■ **Deadhead lupines and delphiniums** as they finish flowering. If this is done as the flowers fade, there is a good chance that further blooms will be produced later in the summer. Cut the faded flower spires off at ground level or cut them back to strong new shoots.

■ **Take cuttings from pinks.** The cuttings taken from pinks (*Dianthus*) are called "pipings" and they are very easy to root. Look for healthy, young, nonflowering shoots. Hold the stem about four pairs of leaves from the tip and pull the cutting off. The cutting should come away quite cleanly. Put several cuttings around the edge of a 4-in (10-cm) pot in a mixture of peat-free potting mix and perlite, water them in, and place in a shady cold frame. The cuttings will start to root in three or four weeks, when they can be potted up individually into 3 in (8 cm) pots.

■ **Continue to pot up cuttings of** perennials taken earlier in the spring. As soon as the plants have made a good root system, pot them up. Otherwise, if there are several cuttings to a pot, the roots will become entangled and you will damage them as you try to separate them. Water the cuttings before and after you have potted them up. A shady, sheltered corner will be suitable over the summer; they can be planted out in fall.

■ **Sow seeds of hardy herbaceous** perennials outside. Perennials like lupines, delphiniums, and hollyhocks can be sown in shallow drills now in a corner of the garden. If space is limited, sow perennials in trays or small pots and place them in a cold frame or at the base of a sheltered wall. When the seedlings have become large enough, pot them on into individual pots, and grow on during the summer. Plant them out in the fall.

BULBS

■ **Cut down the foliage of bulbs** that have been naturalized in grass. By now at least six weeks should have elapsed since flowering and the bulb foliage and the grass can be trimmed. If you cut the leaves down too soon, the bulbs will be "blind" next year. Don't be too concerned about the grass turning yellow after it has been cut where the bulbs are planted. It will soon recover with watering and fertilizing.

■ **Plant out cannas,** and also lily bulbs that were potted up earlier in the year. Cannas started into growth in March and lily bulbs potted up when the weather was too cold outside to plant can be planted out in the borders. Or, simply put the whole pot in a gap in the border, either sinking it into the ground or, if the surrounding plants are tall enough to hide it, just setting it on the soil surface. Left in pots, they will need extra watering, so be sure to watch them carefully.

■ **Lift and divide bulbs** that have finished flowering. Bulbs can be lifted, dried, and stored when the foliage has died down, but if you tend to leave yours *in situ* year after year, lift overcrowded clumps now and divide them so that they can spend the summer reestablishing.

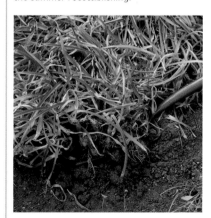
Dividing Clump of bulbs that have become overcrowded can be divided using a fork.

Anemone coronaria **'Lord Lieutenant'**

Anemone coronaria **De Caen Group**

■ **Plant anemones to flower in fall.**
Anemones generally flower about three months after planting, so timing the flowering can be quite accurate. By planting some now, the small tubers will give a delightful show of flowers just when other plants are beginning to fade. Plant some in pots at the same time to enjoy these wonderful flowers on the windowsill. The ones to look for are *Anemone coronaria* and the de Caen types, with flowers up to 3 in (8 cm) across in glowing colors. When planting late like this, it is best to soak the tubers overnight, to get them off to a good start. Plant them 2 in (5 cm) deep and 3–4 in (8–10 cm) apart. Incorporate organic matter and the plants will repay you with a glorious display.

ANNUALS AND BEDDING

■ **Plant out summer bedding plants.** By this time of year it is safe to plant out all bedding plants, including tender kinds like begonias, without fear of frost damage. Look out for plants like bidens, felicia, and brachyscome as well as old favorites such as geraniums, salvias, and lobelia. Make sure any old spring bedding is removed, if this was not done last month, and lightly fork over the soil. Spread a little general fertilizer before planting, but not too much, otherwise the plants will produce a lot of lush growth at the expense of flowers. Water the plants well an hour or so before planting them out. This is particularly important where young plants are growing together in a seed tray and the roots will be disturbed when they are planted out. And don't forget to give the plants a thorough watering after planting, too.

■ **Water bedding plants** regularly after planting. The plants will have to be watered at regular intervals during dry spells and for a few weeks after planting. The best way to do this and conserve water at the same time is by using a soaker hose. This is a hose that allows water to seep through its walls along its entire length. The advantage is that the water is concentrated at the plants' roots, instead of being sprayed through the air. The soaker hose can be buried under the surface or snaked between the plants. If you do have to water with a sprinkler, do so in the early morning or in the evening or the plants will get scorched.

■ **Thin out seedlings of hardy annuals** sown earlier (see also May). They should be thinned out as soon as they are large enough to handle, otherwise the plants will become too tall and leggy. Some of the taller-growing annuals may also benefit from some firm support from thin, twiggy sticks.

■ **Some hardy annuals sown directly** now will still have time to flower in late summer and fall, extending the flowering display. Choose fast-growing annuals such as clarkia, godetia, candytuft, and calendula. Sow them in shallow drills and thin them out when they are large enough to handle, and they will flower for you later.

■ **Continue to sow seeds of biennials** to flower next spring (see May). Seedlings sown last month can be transplanted to a spare piece of ground to grow on during the summer until planted in their flowering positions in the fall. If space is limited, then sow biennials in trays or small pots, and place in a cold frame or at the base of a sheltered wall. When the seedlings are large enough, pot them on and grow on during the summer. Plant them out into their flowering positions in the fall.

■ **Sow polyanthus for flowering** next spring. Unlike other biennials such as wallflowers and myosotis, polyanthus primulas need a little heat to germinate, 60°F (15°C) being about right. A sheltered cold frame should keep the temperature at the right level. Sow the seeds in trays on moist potting mix without covering them. It is all too easy to cover fine seed too deeply, inhibiting germination. Cover the container with clear plastic and place in a light cold frame. When the seedlings are large enough to handle, pot them up and grow on through the summer. Plant out into their flowering positions in the fall.

■ **Sow winter pansies.** These are sown in much the same way as polyanthus (see above) except that the seeds are covered to exclude light. After a couple of weeks, check to see if the seeds have germinated, and uncover them if they have. Grow on in exactly the same way as for polyanthus.

Make a new flowerbed

A passion for plants has one disadvantage—there is never enough room for all those you want to grow. One solution is to sacrifice an underused area of lawn to extend your planting area. A new bed against a background of other plants, a wall, or a fence will soon look settled in. Here, I added an area for sun-loving perennials to provide foreground to a dull shrub border and created a semicircular shape to give the extended bed a natural outline.

You will need

■ garden hose ■ half-moon edging tool
■ spade ■ fork ■ well-rotted garden compost or manure ■ trowel
■ selection of perennial plants

1 Make a temporary outline using the garden hose, keeping the curve simple. Group the plants that you want to include in your bed within it, at the correct planting distances. Stand back and look from all sides to make sure that you are happy with the effect.

2 Adjust the hose to even up the shape—for example, to line up with existing edges and corners in the garden—while trying not to enlarge the total area too much.

3 Cut along the edge of the hose, pushing a half-moon lawn edger (or a spade) into the soil to create what will become the new edge to the bed.

4 Strip off the sod from the entire area inside the hose, removing about 1 in (2.5 cm) of topsoil. Stack the sod, grass-side down, in a corner of the garden. In time it will rot down into a wonderfully fine compost.

5 Dig over the site to break up the soil to at least one, and preferably two, spade depths, forking over the bottom as you work to aerate farther down. Remove large stones, leaving smaller ones to assist drainage. Pull the soil away from the new lawn edge and check that you're happy with the bed's outline.

6 Once the soil is broken up, add organic matter, such as well-rotted manure or garden compost.

7 Fork the organic matter well into the dug-over soil. This will have been impoverished by the grass growing on it, so needs plenty of nourishing and conditioning.

8 Put in the new plants, planting as many as possible by reaching from the new lawn edge, so that you do not compact the soil. Keep the new plants well and regularly watered.

9 A new border, with late-summer flowering perennials in warm tones. The plants gave instant color in their first year and by next year will spread and look even better.

CONTAINERS

■ **Water all plants** in containers regularly during dry spells.

■ **Containers and hanging baskets** that were planted up earlier in the season and kept indoors to keep them from the threat of frost can now be placed outside for the summer months.

■ **Plant up half-hardy annuals** and tender perennials in tubs, troughs, and other containers outdoors now that any danger of frost has passed. If you have been raising half-hardy annuals and tender perennials indoors, either from seeds or cuttings, you can plant them out in safety from now on. If you haven't raised any plants yourself, then most garden centers will have a tempting selection of plants for sale now. Put as many plants as you can get into each container in order to get the best effect. Upright plants will give some height, and trailing and semi-trailing plants look most effective tumbling over the sides and softening the hard edges.

■ **Hanging baskets** are an effective way of showing off bedding plants and they are very easy to plant. Use one of the many types of liners available from garden centers. If you can avoid it, don't use sphagnum moss, as its collection can endanger rare wildlife habitats. You can put a disk of plastic sheeting in the bottom of the basket to help retain the moisture. Use taller plants in the center of it to give height to the display, and tuck in plenty of trailing plants around them and the outside of the basket. When the plants grow, the basket will be completely hidden and you will have a mass of flowers to enjoy all summer long.

Planting up a hanging basket

1 Set the basket in a pot or pail to keep it stable throughout the planting process. Put the liner (coir in this case) in position and trim it to fit along the rim. A circle of plastic sheeting placed at the bottom will help retain water.

2 Cut slits for trailing plants. Add a 2-in (5-cm) layer of soilless potting mix, mixed with controlled-release fertilizer and water-retaining gel.

3 Remove the trailing plants from their pots and thread them through the slits. Use a plastic bag to protect the stems and leaves.

4 Place a pot in the center to act as a reservoir and plant around it. Use upright plants centrally and trailers around the rim. Add more soil and build up the planting in tiers until the soil is just below the rim.

5 Firm the soil and water the basket thoroughly through the plastic pot. Use a watering wand so that the water doesn't puddle in one section.

6 Hang your basket in a sheltered spot at a height that you can reach easily to water it. Make sure the hook or hanger can support the weight of saturated potting mix.

LAWNS

■ **Mow lawns regularly.** By this time of year the lawn should be cut at least once a week and preferably twice a week if this is possible. The reason for this is that the less grass taken off at each cut, the healthier it will remain. It is also important to mow in a different direction each time, because if you mow in the same direction several times in a row, the grass begins to grow in that direction and the mower blades, especially those on a cylinder mower, will not cut it as well. By this time the mower blades should be at the lowest setting required; for most lawns, about 2 to 3 in (5–8 cm), or a little higher for a lawn that is heavily used. If there are dry spells, when the grass turns a bit brown, reduce the frequency of mowing and raise the blades a little so as not to cut it too close.

Now that grass is generating a lot of clippings, don't dump them in a mass on the compost pile or they will clump together and rot down into a slimy mess rather than good compost. This is because they are too dense to admit air. Keep the clippings separate until you have some looser material to mix in with them. Torn and crumpled newspaper will do if the garden is not generating much suitable debris at the moment.

Mowing direction Be sure to mow in a different direction each time so that the mower blades cut as efficiently as possible.

Long-handled shears These make edging the lawn a great deal less backbreaking.

■ **Don't forget edging.** Another job to bear in mind is to trim the lawn edges at the same time as the grass is cut. It makes all the difference to the appearance of the garden if the edges are cut regularly. And it's less work doing the edges once a week as the trimmings are few and don't have to be cleared up.

■ **Feed lawns with a liquid fertilizer.** These fast-acting fertilizers are the perfect thing to give a tired-looking lawn a quick tonic. Diluted in water, following the instructions on the bottle, they are easily applied with a watering can or sprayer. One advantage they have over dry fertilizers is that they don't have to be watered in if the weather remains dry.

New lawns

■ **Water new lawns** made in spring either from seed or sod. It is vitally important not to let newly laid sod dry out: it shrinks when it dries and it's almost impossible to get it back to how it was. One way to ensure that a sprinkler is watering the ground evenly is to place a number of empty jars around the lawn. You'll soon see, by the level of water collected, whether any areas are coming up short.

VEGETABLE AND HERBS

Harvesting

■ **Continue to harvest all crops as they mature.** Early peas will be ready to pick now. Cut down the top-growth of the plants (known as the "haulm") after harvesting, but leave the roots of the peas in the soil, as these will return valuable nitrogen to it. Nodules on the roots of peas and beans are able to fix and store atmospheric nitrogen in the soil. Follow peas with a leafy crop, such as cabbages, which requires a higher nitrogen content in the soil. This is one way, by practicing good crop rotation, of reducing the amount of artificial fertilizer we put on the soil.

■ **Japanese onions** that were sown last year will now be ready to harvest. The tops should have begun to fall over and the skins to harden. Lift them to break the roots in the soil and let them dry out in the sun. If it rains, put them in a greenhouse or cold frame to dry out.

■ **You may be able to start harvesting** early potatoes toward the end of the month. There is nothing like digging the first potatoes and taking them straight to the kitchen to be cooked. To harvest them, push a fork into the ground a little way from the base of the plant to reduce the chance of piercing any of the vegetables. Root around a bit to make sure you've got all the potatoes, as any left in the ground will grow again next year. They always seem to grow right in the middle of a row of seedlings, making it hard to get them out.

Sowing and planting outdoors

■ **In cooler climates,** plant celery in trenches prepared during winter or spring. Apply a general fertilizer before planting and put the plants in rows 12 in (30 cm) apart. Water the plants well after planting and keep them well watered throughout the growing season. Celery requires a lot of water to produce a good crop in the fall. The soil that was piled up on either side of the trench and will be used for blanching the celery in the fall and winter can be used in the summer for fast-maturing salad crops like lettuce, radishes, and salad onions. (The technique of growing quick-maturing crops on spare ground like this is known as "catch-cropping.") Self-blanching celery does not have to be planted in trenches, but is better planted in blocks 9 in (23 cm) apart, rather than rows, so that each plant blanches its neighbor.

■ **Plants of celeriac raised earlier** can also be planted out now.

■ **Sow radicchio (red chicory)** in rows 9 in (23 cm) apart. Sow in the usual manner, watering the seed drill if the weather is dry, before sowing the seeds. This is a leafy chicory, unlike the forcing type: the leaves are eaten fresh, and it makes a useful vegetable for fall and winter salads, being able to stand through cold weather in mild climates.

Cloches will protect the heads from weather damage. There are several varieties available with attractively colored foliage. They add a touch of color to any winter salad.

Pea seedlings When these are nearly ready to start climbing, they are vulnerable to attack by birds, so cover them up with netting.

Climbing frames These must be sturdy enough to support fully laden runner bean plants.

■ **Continue to sow peas** for maincrops later in the year.

■ **Plant out runner beans.** Now that the threat of frost has passed, these plants can go out into ground that was prepared during the winter. Put up whatever supports you require before planting, either making teepees or parallel avenues of canes with 24 in (60 cm) between the rows. Slugs love young runner-bean plants; the plants can be protected by surrounding them with a collar made from an old plastic soda bottle. To ensure that runner-bean flowers set and produce pods, spray them with water regularly and make sure they don't dry out at the roots.

Dwarf runner beans can also go out now. These don't require much support. It may be worth inserting a few twiggy sticks around the plants, as they do often flop over even though they are dwarf. This will prevent the pods from being splashed with soil when it rains. Dwarf and climbing French beans can be treated in exactly the same way as runner beans.

■ **Keep sowing salad vegetables** in small quantities at regular intervals of two or three weeks. This will provide a continuous supply of fresh salad over a long period,

rather than a glut all at once. One point to bear in mind now is that lettuce seed will not germinate in high temperatures, so if the weather is hot and dry, sow the seeds in a shady part of the garden, or sow them in seed trays and put these in a shady part of the garden. Transplant the seedlings when they are large enough to handle.

■ **Plant tomatoes outside.** Tomatoes can be planted in the soil at intervals of 18 in (45 cm), or planted two or three to a container. Tomatoes prefer a sunny spot against a south-facing wall if possible. Cordon plants will need staking with 4-ft (1.2-m) canes. When planting tomatoes outside, leave a slight depression in the soil. This helps to retain water around the roots of the plants when watering them in. It can be difficult to push canes into containers as there is insufficient soil to hold the canes upright. There are frames you can buy that hold canes especially for use in containers.

Feed all tomatoes with a high-potash fertilizer every week from now on through the season to get a good crop. Be careful not to let tomatoes, especially those in containers, go short of water. If they are neglected or watered irregularly, drying out in between, they will be prone to blossom end rot. This appears as a sunken brown area at the end of the fruit farthest from the plant. It is due to calcium deficiency, brought about by a lack of water, even for a very short period. Regular watering is the key to preventing this problem. Another problem that may be caused by irregular watering is splitting of the fruits.

■ **Plant out ridge cucumbers.** Although these are called "ridge" cucumbers, they do not actually have to be grown on ridges of soil. Plant out the young plants in early June, in soil that has been enriched with

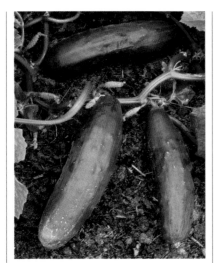

Plant ridge cucumbers The young plants will thrive in soil enriched with lots of organic matter.

plenty of organic matter to retain as much moisture as possible. Pinch out the growing tips of the plants when they have six pairs of leaves, to encourage sideshoots to form and produce the cucumbers. Fertilize and water regularly with a high-potash fertilizer through the summer and you'll get delicious cucumbers all summer long.

■ **Plant and sow marrows and zucchini,** and pumpkins and squashes, outside. Young plants should be spaced about 24 in (60 cm) apart in soil that has been enriched with plenty of organic matter to retain moisture. If plants were not raised earlier under glass, all is not lost. They can be sown directly outside now. Sow two seeds together in the place they are to crop. Pull out the weaker of the seedlings when they germinate, leaving the stronger one to grow on.

■ **Sow turnips for a fall crop.** Sow the seeds in rows 6 in (15 cm) apart. Thin the seedlings as soon as you can handle them without damaging the young plants. Thin them to leave one plant every 4 in (10 cm). The turnips are best harvested when they are young, before they get to the size of a tennis ball. You can leave some roots in for longer, as their leafy tops can be cooked for winter greens.

■ **Sow Witloof chicory** for forcing. Sow the seeds in rich, fertile soil to fatten up the roots for forcing in winter. Give a good dressing of a general fertilizer and sow the seeds in rows 12 in (30 cm) apart. Thin the seedlings to 6 in (15 cm) apart when they become large enough to handle. Keep them well watered during dry weather.

■ **Sow Chinese cabbage** and other Asian vegetables. These vegetables can be sown now at regular intervals until August. One way to get quick results is to sow the seeds under cloches. This way some of them will germinate in two or three days. These leafy vegetables are all excellent for stir-frying, making delicious meals fresh from the garden in a matter of minutes. Some are prone to attack from flea beetle and it may be worth growing them permanently under cloches or covered with floating row cover to stop the beetles getting at the plants.

■ **Plant out all winter brassicas** sown earlier. The young plants will need protection against cabbage root fly. These crops generally need plenty of room to grow—at least 24 in (60 cm) apart each way. But other, quicker-growing crops can be grown between the brassicas until they reach their maximum size. Salad crops like lettuce, radishes, and spinach can all be grown between the brassicas. This is known as "intercropping" and utilizes the space, fertilizers, and organic matter added to the soil to the best advantage.

Plant out sweet corn

Plant sweet corn in blocks, 12 in (30 cm) apart each way, rather than in rows. The reason for this is that sweet corn is pollinated by wind. The male flowers appear as the tassels at the tip of the plant and the pollen falls onto the female parts lower down. By growing the plants in blocks there is more chance of pollination being successful than if the plants are growing in conventional rows.

Use a marked plank to plant in blocks, the same distance each way.

Sweet corn flowering Planted in blocks, pollen will be blown onto other sweet corn flowers.

Herbs in containers For a space-saving alternative to an herb garden, plant a selection of herbs in a container. This example shows a yellow foliage combination of feverfew (*Tanacetum*), sage (*Salvia*) and thyme (*Thymus*).

don't grow many brassicas, it is worth covering them with row cover as a physical barrier to prevent the butterflies from laying their eggs in the first place.

■ Carrot fly is still a threat, so be sure to protect carrots with a barrier that the pest cannot penetrate.

■ **Fertilize asparagus after flowering.** You won't be cutting spears from young crowns, but once they are established and giving you a crop, stop cutting in late June to allow the crowns to build up strength for next year's crop. Apply a general organic fertilizer then to all plants, young and old, and let the foliage grow until it turns brown later in the summer, when it can be cut to the ground. Asparagus doesn't attract many pests, but asparagus beetle can be damaging, so keep on the lookout for it: it has a red body and black and yellow wings. To control it, use a spray labeled for asparagus, or pick off the adults and their grayish-cream grubs by hand.

Herbs

■ **Plant herbs in containers** for the patio or by the back door close to the kitchen. Most herbs are extremely effective grown in containers, but some are not very suitable; tall herbs like angelica and lovage can become top-heavy and also may look out of place in a pot—better to grow these in a border. All other herbs are suitable for containers and with many of them, particularly the sages, having attractively colored foliage, you can make stunning plant combinations by grouping pots together, or planting several different herbs in one large container.

Caring for crops

■ **Keep watering** young vegetable plants and hoe off weeds regularly.

■ **Protect young brassicas** against birds. Birds love to eat young brassicas as soon as they are planted out. In fact, birds often seem to sit and watch me planting, ready to pounce as soon as my back is turned. There are many bird-scarer products on the market, with varying degrees of effectiveness. Whichever you use, the birds sooner or later come to realize that it poses no actual danger. The only foolproof way of stopping birds from eating the plants is to grow them under cover. Support either netting or fine-weave mesh sheeting on stakes with strong twine or wire strung between them, so it is held above the plants like a tent. If it is left resting on the plants, the birds will peck through it. Always make sure netting is well anchored at ground level so that small garden birds do not get tangled in it. It's not a very pleasant job trying to untangle a bird from netting.

■ Cabbage white butterfly caterpillars will be hatching out now. A lot of damage can be prevented by going around inspecting the undersides of the leaves on all brassicas. You will usually find small clusters of yellow eggs here. The eggs can be squashed, but if you can't face doing that, use a spray labeled for brassicas. This will kill off any young caterpillars. If you

FRUIT

Harvesting

■ **Remove cloches** from strawberries and the fruits should ripen for picking.

■ **Harvest your rhubarb** until the end of the month.

Caring for crops

■ **Put up pheromone traps** for codling moth. One trap will protect up to five apple trees.

■ **Continue pruning and pinching out** shoots on wall-trained fruit. Get all the pruning of peaches, plums, and nectarines done through the summer. Wounds heal more quickly and the silver leaf disease fungus releases few spores in warmer, drier weather.

Remove unwanted shoots as soon as possible and tie in those that will be used to replace the current year's fruiting wood. Select two new shoots at the base of the fruiting shoot and retain these for tying in. One is just for insurance purposes in case the other is damaged. Cut out any other new shoots. Any sideshoots from the fruiting shoots can be pinched out to five or six leaves.

■ **Control gray mold on strawberries.** Spells of wet weather encourage the spread of gray mold (botrytis). Inspect fruits regularly and remove all the infected ones. Don't compost these, as they may spread the disease to other plants in the garden. Removing infected fruits early enough should help to keep the problem under control. There are no fungicides available to home gardeners to control gray mold. However, you can ensure that plenty of air circulates around the plants and keep developing fruits off the soil by putting straw or mats under them. This stops soil from being splashed on the fruits by rain, which can spread mold.

Gooseberries are borne on one-year-old wood. Prune sideshoots to encourage fruiting.

■ **Gooseberries can also be thinned** for larger fruits and the thinnings can be cooked. Look out for gooseberry sawfly caterpillars. They can attack right through the summer, and a bad infestation can completely defoliate a plant. The caterpillars are up to ¾ in (2 cm) long, pale green in color and marked with black spots. They rear up when disturbed. Inspect the plants regularly from spring onward, paying particular attention to the undersides of the leaves, and squash any eggs and caterpillars you see.

■ **Don't be tempted to thin out apples** and pears until the "June drop" (see previous entry) has happened. It is all too easy to plow ahead with thinning out the fruits, only to see that the ones you have left all fall off, leaving you with none at all.

■ **Blackcurrants can suffer** from a variety of problems. Aphids and spider mites are common, and can be controlled with a strong spray of water applied early in the day so that foliage can dry before sundown, when wet leaves are subject to fungal infections. Borers can invade stems, causing dieback. The best control is to take early action, cutting away affected foliage and burning it. The good news is that blackcurrant foliage is unattractive to deer.

■ **Keep all fruit well watered in dry spells** to ensure a good crop of quality fruits throughout the summer. Mulching with organic matter will help retain moisture and reduce the need to keep watering. It will also keep down weeds, which compete for water and nutrients in the soil; many weeds also act as hosts to pests and diseases.

■ **Heavy crops of plums** can be thinned early in the month to prevent the brittle branches of plum trees from breaking under the weight of the crop. Thin in two stages, removing only any damaged or diseased fruit first. Don't remove too many fruits to begin with as the trees will naturally shed some fruit around now. This is called the "June drop."

Wait until this has happened, then a second thinning out can be carried out if the fruits still appear to be overcrowded. You can also support heavy branches if you are worried that they will be damaged by the weight of fruit, especially if the trees are quite young.

Plentiful plums Heavy crops can break branches, so support them if necessary.

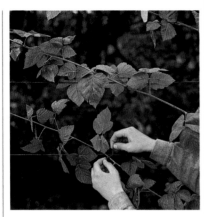

Tie in blackberries The long canes need to be secured regularly, or the thorns can be dangerous.

Pruning and training

■ **Continue tying in new canes of blackberries and hybrid berries.** Methods of training are many and varied, and some are unnecessarily complicated. The easiest is to train the shoots in the form of a fan, with the current year's fruiting canes spaced out to one side of the plant on the framework of wires and new canes tied in on the other side, completing the fan shape. After fruiting, the old canes are cut out and the process repeated next year.

■ **Prune excess growth on vines.** "Stop," or pinch out the tip, of the fruiting shoots to a leaf beyond three or four developing fruit clusters. Pinch back any sideshoots from these stems to one or two leaves. Vines grown outdoors in cool climates will only ripen a few decent bunches of grapes on each sideshoot from the main stem or rod, so it is counterproductive to allow any more to develop.

Propagation

■ **Strawberries will now be producing lots of runners.** These can either be removed or pegged down to make new plants, depending on your needs.

UNDER COVER

■ **Damp down regularly** to keep the atmosphere in the greenhouse or the conservatory humid. This will benefit plants enormously, especially if you can close the ventilators and doors for a short time after damping down, to allow the temperature and the humidity to rise and create a wonderful growing atmosphere. "Damping down" just means splashing or spraying water around. It will also help to keep down the incidence of greenhouse red spider mite.

■ **Water and fertilize all plants regularly** now that they are all growing fast. If soilless or peat-free potting medium dries out, it is almost impossible to rewet properly, so never let it dry out completely between waterings. If container plants have become dry at the roots, give them a good soaking by sitting them in water overnight, before applying fertilizer. If the fertilizer is applied to dry soil, it may scorch roots. Feeding flowering container plants and bedding plants with a fertilizer high in potash will ensure a continued display of good-quality flowers through the summer until the first frost. Be careful not to splash water on the foliage of plants in bright, sunny weather. The water droplets on the leaves act like small magnifying glasses, scorching the leaves. Watering is best done in the evenings, if possible, when there is less chance of the water evaporating than in the heat of the day.

■ **Shade the greenhouse or conservatory** with paint-on shading or blinds, as described last month. Ventilate whenever you can by opening windows, doors, and vents. Warm sunshine on a greenhouse can cause temperatures to rise to dramatic levels. It is best for the plants if the temperatures are kept as even as possible. Big fluctuations in temperature will not encourage good sturdy growth in the plants. There are many different automatic ventilator openers on the market, which take the guesswork out of whether to leave the vents open or closed when you leave for work in the morning. They can be set to open and close at a set temperature, and so give you peace of mind. Working in conjunction with shading, these should help to control the temperature on the hottest of days.

■ **Pot on all young plants and seedlings** as necessary. Plants that get potbound over a period of time rarely recover and grow well. The ideal time to pot on any plant is when, having knocked the plant from its pot, you can see a good tracery of roots around the sides of the root ball, without it looking congested with roots. Another good indication that plants really need potting on is roots growing out through the drainage holes in the bottom of the pot. Keep young plants well watered, and shade them from the sun if the roots have been disturbed when the plants were potted up (for example, when separating a pot full of cuttings). It takes a few days for the roots to take up water after they have been disturbed.

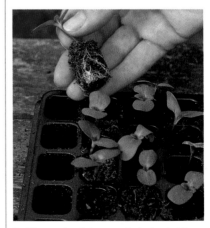

Potting on Gently tease each plant out of its individual cell.

Greenhouse and house plants

■ **Houseplants** that have been stuck in stuffy rooms can be moved to the greenhouse for a vacation. Even if houseplants are sitting on a sunny windowsill, they never really get all the light they need and the dry atmosphere in most houses is far from ideal for plant growth. So a spell in the greenhouse will be like a well-earned vacation for your plants. The foliage of large-leaved plants such as rubber plants will benefit from a sponge-over. The leaves will be shiny again and look a lot better, and the plants will be healthier, too; when that layer of dust has been removed, air can pass through the pores in the leaves much more easily.

■ **Sow seeds of** *Primula malacoides, P. sinensis*, cinerarias, and calceolarias (*Pericallis*) for container plants to flower in the winter and spring. Sow small batches of the seeds in small pots of seed-starting mix and place near a window. They don't need a lot of heat to germinate at this time of year. Pot on the seedlings, holding them by the seed leaves, when they are large enough to handle. Be aware that people with sensitive skin should handle primulas with gloves, as they can irritate the skin. If you are susceptible, you may find it almost impossible to grasp the little seed leaves to transplant them without wearing gardening gloves or latex gloves. Grow the plants on in a cool place—a shady cold frame is ideal—to get good, sturdy plants to take into the house in the fall and winter. Aphids can be a problem, particularly with cinerarias. Inspect the plants regularly and squash the aphids before they get out of control.

■ **Pot on cuttings taken earlier** from potted hydrangeas. Water the cuttings well before potting them on to larger pots. Knock the cuttings out of the pot and

Solanum capsicastrum

carefully tease the roots apart. Pot each cutting into a small 3-in (8-cm) pot, or for a really dramatic display, pot three cuttings into a 5-in (12.5-cm) pot and pot these together into a larger pot when the roots have filled this one. This way you get three plants bushing out in place of one, making a spectacular show later in the year. Grow the plants on outside and feed them regularly with a high-potash fertilizer to build up the flower buds. Bring the plants inside in the fall.

■ *Solanum capsicastrum* **plants** sown earlier in the spring will also benefit from being put outside for the summer. The plants will produce fine, sturdy growth, which will ripen over summer. Putting the plants outside also allows pollinating insects to get at the plants easily, ensuring that a good crop of attractive fruits appears in early fall.

Crops under glass

■ **Fruiting crops**—tomatoes, peppers, and eggplants—need watering regularly and a high-potash fertilizer every week to help the fruits swell and develop.

■ **Check the base of grape vines** to make sure they are not drying out. Traditionally, grape vines are planted outside the greenhouse and their stems trained in through a low hole in the wall. That way, the roots benefit from rainfall. Grape vines are completely hardy—improved ripening of the fruits is why gardeners with short summers grow them under glass. At this time, when the bunches are developing, check around the roots, whether outside or in, and give the plants a regular soak if they need it.

■ **Continue removing sideshoots** from tomatoes. The sooner the sideshoots are removed, the less of a shock it is to the plant. They are easily removed by bending them to one side with your thumb and forefinger. Larger sideshoots can be cut off with pruners. Dip the pruners in a weak solution of a bleach solution after each cut to avoid spreading virus among the plants. Tomatoes are very prone to picking up viruses—one reason why they are often used in plant research work.

Tomato sideshoots Pinching sideshoots needs to be done at regular intervals.

The July garden

Your garden will now be looking its very best and have reached its peak for the year. All your earlier sowing and planting will be paying dividends in the border and beds and in the vegetable garden too. There is always plenty to be done, but make the most of the long summer evenings after work and enjoy them to the fullest at weekends, relaxing and entertaining friends.

THINGS TO DO

Make sure that the birds have enough water during spells of dry weather, and be sure to keep new and young plants well watered during the summer. Regularly fertilize and water all plants that are growing in containers, but as a general rule, use water wisely and try not to waste it. Be on the alert for any pests and diseases.

Continue deadheading flowers as they fade and prune all those shrubs that flowered in early summer. Take semiripe cuttings from shrubs and trim conifer hedges and take cuttings from them. Now is the time to summer-prune wisteria and divide bearded irises.

Layer and take cuttings of carnations and pinks and disbud dahlias to get larger blooms. Plant fall-flowering bulbs, and transplant seedlings of biennials sown earlier.

Water vegetables regularly. Lift new potatoes, onions, and garlic and pinch out runner beans when they reach the top of their canes. You also need to pinch out outdoor tomatoes when four trusses have formed and remove all sideshoots. Pick raspberries and currants and harvest herbs. Keep greenhouses well ventilated and mist down regularly.

LAST CHANCE

Fill any gaps in beds and borders with bedding plants and sow the last vegetables for harvesting in fall. Plant out all winter brassicas.

GET AHEAD

Make plans to have your plants cared for if you are taking a vacation in July. Now's the time to order spring-flowering bulbs and prepare the ground for new lawns in fall. Sow salads under cover for fall and winter, and prepare new strawberry beds.

A favorite bloom It's not surprising that roses are so well loved; there is one to suit most gardens. A fine display of *Rosa* 'Perception' is shown here.

High-summer color

It's summertime; the garden is full of color, and the scent from flowers such as roses and sweet peas fills the air, especially at the end of the day. Gardening in hot weather needs to be leisurely, though you'll need to devote energy to keeping everything well watered in the morning and evening.

July is the month for taking time to enjoy the garden, having relaxing meals *al fresco*, appreciating the flowers, and watching the abundance of wildlife in residence.

Beat the heat

There is still plenty of routine work to be done, but by this time the work can be done at a more leisurely pace than in the hectic spring period. Care must be taken when working in the sun for long periods, even if you are taking it easy. Take plenty of breaks, wear a broad-brimmed hat, and use sunscreen to protect your skin from the harmful effects of sunlight. It's best to try not to work during the hottest part of the day. Wait until evening to do any strenuous work, if you won't be too busy with the barbecue grill. Hot days are often followed by thunderstorms and it's often a relief to do the gardening in the cool of the evening or in early morning.

If the weather is very hot you will have to pay careful attention to watering, especially trees and shrubs that were planted during the fall and winter. The most beneficial times to do your watering are also early morning or in the evenings, when it is cooler. By watering at these times, the precious moisture will not evaporate from the surface of the soil nearly as rapidly as in the heat of the day. Be aware, however, that in exceptionally dry periods there may be watering restrictions in your area and the use of garden hoses—even soaker hoses—may be banned. Check with your municipality if you are in doubt.

Use water wisely

During hot spells the lawn may begin to look rather brown and worn. At such times, it is all too tempting to water the lawn, but it really is not necessary, as grass has a remarkable ability to regenerate itself when the weather gets cooler. Whenever rain does fall, the grass will, as if by magic, be transformed back into a lush green carpet again. It's far better to use the water for plants that really need it: newly planted trees and shrubs, thirsty

Lavender is at its very best This long-stemmed fragrant, blue-purple flower sets off any mixed or herbaceous border.

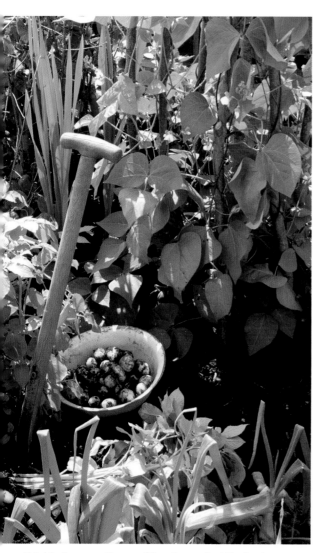

Height of summer So many different crops should be ripening that you could well be harvesting something every day.

vegetables, and other precious plants in the borders and containers, especially hanging baskets, which need water daily in midsummer.

Perfect your plantings

During your evening walks around the yard, take a notebook with you and look at your planting designs carefully to see which combinations of plants and colors have worked this year and which seem to be a bit of a

Weather watch

July is generally the hottest or second-hottest month of the year, with the highest temperatures occurring inland, away from the cooling influence of the oceans and Great Lakes and the breezes that blow down from the mountains. Temperatures can linger in the 90s (32–37°C) and occasionally hit or surpass the 100-degree mark (38°C) in the Southern states, Midwest, and Southwest.

Dog days of summer

Thunderstorms continue in July, pelting us with high winds, lightning, and rain. By August, these storms will give way to the so-called "dog days of summer," when heat and humidity hang on for days on end, rendering both dogs and their humans listless in the afternoon heat.

Light and heat

Because at this time of year the part of Earth that we live on is tilting toward the sun, the air around us is warmer than in other seasons. With longer days, the sun shines more hours during the day, seasoning summer with a taste of light and heat along with peak flowering in the garden and the first wave of vegetable harvests.

Droughts

Starting this month, a dry spell that lasts longer than a few weeks officially becomes a drought. Droughts are part of our normal summer in many parts of the country, and generally speaking, two weeks without rain in summer is enough to stress plants unless they are natives of arid regions. But in hot, wet climates like Florida, Louisiana, and southeast Texas, as little as a week without rain can signal a drought. To keep your plants going during water restrictions, stockpile water by attaching rain barrels to your house gutters, and if ordinances allow, recycle used household water, such a dish- or bathwater, which is popularly called gray water, for watering ornamentals (for health reasons, do not use gray water on edible plants).

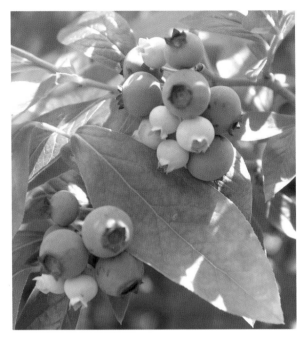

Blueberries Harvest your first blueberries now. Look for the plumpest, softest berries, with the darkest blue-black color.

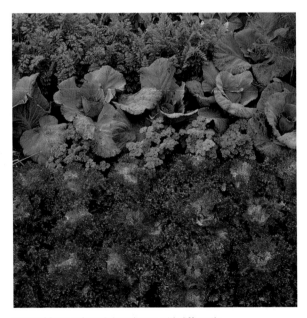

Vegetables on show Color schemes with differently colored vegetable, herb, and salad plants can be as attractive as a carpet of annual bedding plants—and of course, you can eat the results, too.

Beat the heat Make the most of shady areas in the garden, which will become welcome refuges in the heat of summer. Areas shaded from full sun will not get so dry, suiting many plants better.

disappointment. You can then plan to make changes in the fall or during the spring.

Earlier-flowering plants will now have to be deadheaded if you don't want to save seed from them. Many perennials will, if deadheaded regularly, produce further blooms through summer and into the fall. It's quite a pleasant and relaxing job to carry out on a warm summer evening.

Native flowers and grasses attract a host of birds, bees, and other beneficial insects to the garden. An attractive way to incorporate these plants in your plot is to create a small wildflower garden. Choose an open, sunny area where the soil has not been enriched with fertilizers; wildflowers tend to perform best in poor soil.

Summer symptoms

In the hot, humid weather that can be characteristic of this month, pests and diseases may spread all too rapidly. Keep a careful watch for them, as many can be controlled easily if they are caught early enough. Aphids, for instance, can be easily killed simply by squashing them, if they are not present in large numbers. If you have a heavy infestation of one particular pest and feel that you must use an insecticide, use an insecticide specific to that pest, where possible, so that it does not harm other, beneficial, insects. And do any spraying in the evening when the bees have gone for the night.

As for diseases, any parts of a plant that are showing signs of disease should be removed and either burned or put in the trash so that they are not able to infect other plants. Never compost diseased material or leave it lying around, as this increases the risk of spreading the disease to other plants in the garden.

For greenhouse plants, sun scorch and heat stress are the most common problems, so you need to pay particular attention to watering and ventilation. Another way of cooling the atmosphere is to mist several times during the day, splashing water on the floor to increase humidity.

Flavors to savor

You can continue to make regular sowings of salad crops that will carry you into the fall. Weeds continue to seed themselves too, so you still need to carry out regular hoeing and weeding in the vegetable garden. Crops will also benefit from a mulch of organic matter to retain the moisture in the soil. This is the month when your vegetable patch will be providing you with plenty of produce for the kitchen, along with the summery flavors of freshly-picked bunches of herbs.

Papaver rhoeas Shirley Series
Papery poppy that self-seeds freely in the garden (see p.303)

Nemesia strumosa 'KLM'
Bedding plant with unusual bicolored flowers (see p.300)

Hebe 'Gauntlettii'
Neat, bushy evergreen shrub that needs little pruning (see p.288)

Oenothera fruticosa 'Fyrverkeri'
Perennial evening primrose (see p.302)

Nymphaea 'Marliacea Chromatella'
Waterlilies with olive-to-bronze leaves and canary flowers (see p.301)

Diascia barberae 'Blackthorn Apricot'
Slightly tender perennial that may need winter shelter (see p.281)

***Verbascum* 'Cotswold Queen'**
Perennial bearing all flower spires (see p.321)

Campanula lactiflora
The milky bellflower; a tall perennial that may need support (see p.269)

***Phlox paniculata* 'Eva Cullum'**
Hardy perennial that will flower into fall (see p.305)

***Hemerocallis* 'Gentle Shepherd'**
Perennial: flowers last only a day, but keep on coming (see p.289)

Gunnera manicata
Perennial; by high summer the huge leaves are at their best (see p.287)

***Helianthemum* 'Raspberry Ripple'**
Sun-loving shrub with grayish leaves (see p.288)

Rosa 'Chinatown'
From summer to fall, scented double, deep yellow blooms (see p.313)

Centaurea hypoleuca 'John Coutts'
Pink cornflower; a nostalgic perennial (see p.270)

Solanum crispum 'Glasnevin'
Sprawling shrub, best trained on a warm wall (see p.318)

Nicotiana sylvestris
Very tall, elegant perennial tobacco plant, strongly fragrant (see p.301)

Clarkia amoena
The satin flower; a hardy annual that thrives in poor soil (see p.272)

Lilium 'Sun Ray'
Summer bulb that makes an elegant container plant (see p.295)

Antirrhinum majus 'Trumpet Serenade'
Cheery, cottage-style perennial grown as an annual (see p.265)

Borago officinalis
Borage, an annual herb with flowers in steel blue (see p.268)

Ipomoea tricolor 'Heavenly Blue'
Aptly named cultivar of the morning glory (see p.291)

Nicotiana x _sanderae_ Starship Series
Annual for evening fragrance (see p.300)

Artemisia alba 'Canescens'
Foliage plant that makes a lovely foil for summer flowers (see p.266)

Fremontodendron 'California Glory'
Lanky shrub to train on a sunny wall (see p.285)

Lychnis chalcedonica
Perennial popular with beneficial insects (see p.297)

***Cleome hassleriana* 'Color Fountain'**
Imposing annual, to 5 ft (1.5 m) tall (see p.275)

***Alcea rosea* Chater's Double Group**
Hollyhock with pompom flowers (see p.263)

***Matthiola* Brompton Group**
Strongly scented annuals, ideal for cutting (see p.298)

***Cosmos bipinnatus* Sensation Series**
Annual with flowers in pink and white (see p.277)

Eschscholzia californica
California poppies; annuals that will reappear every year (see p.283)

Astrantia major
Cottage-garden style perennial; the flowers dry well (see p.267)

Nigella damascena 'Miss Jekyll'
Love-in-a-mist, an old-fashioned hardy annual (see p.301)

Tagetes 'Naughty Marietta'
Small but striking plants for summer display (see p.319)

Verbena bonariensis
Tall, airy perennial with stiff, slender stems (see p.321)

Lobelia Waterfall Series
Half-hardy annual, a container classic (see p.296)

Helianthus annuus 'Teddy Bear'
Double sunflower with fluffy blooms (see p.288)

What to do in July

AROUND THE YARD

With warm weather, pests and diseases can multiply rapidly. Aphids breed especially fast and it can be hard to stay on top of the problem. If you can build up diversity in the garden by growing a great variety of plants, you will attract a lot of beneficial insects and other wildlife, and a healthy balance should develop between pests and predators. There may be a little bit of damage to some plants, but that is a small price to pay. There are many biological controls available now and these are widely available by mail order.

Plan for vacations The summer months are popular vacation times, and it is better to prepare the garden so that you don't come back to a jungle—or desert of dead plants. Ask a neighbor, family member, or a friend to take care of watering and fertilizing plants and mowing the lawn. Ask them to pick vegetables like beans and zucchini. If beans and also cutting flowers are picked regularly, they will continue to produce crops and blooms well into fall. Mow the lawn, but not too close or you'll encourage rapid growth. Most houseplants can be moved outside and you can plunge the pots in the soil to lessen water loss. Automatic drip irrigation systems are inexpensive and easy to install.

Save water If midsummer brings an extended period of dry weather, water may be in short supply, so it is wise to conserve as much water as you can.

■ Water can be diverted from rain gutters into a rain barrel. There are many types available, from plastic to genuine wooden casks; the latter are an attractive addition to the garden.

■ Mulch borders with any organic matter you can get your hands on, making sure the soil is moist before applying the mulch. Even old newspapers will reduce water loss from the surface of the soil.

■ Only water plants that really need it: newly planted trees, shrubs, and other plants. Newly sown or sodded lawns should be kept watered, but established lawns will recover when rain returns, even if they have turned brown.

■ Give plants a good soaking when you do water them. It is better to water a few at a time, giving them a thorough soak, than to give everything a little water each day.

■ The ideal, water-efficient way of watering plants in the border is to use a drip irrigation or soaker hose system. This lets the water seep out around the roots of the plant, just where it's wanted, thereby avoiding waste.

Irrigation hose Use one of these to make sure your plants have an even supply of water right through the summer.

TREES AND SHRUBS

■ **Deadhead roses** to prolong the display. Many people, when deadheading roses, just snap the old flowerheads off. But if you want to continue the display into fall, you have to prune back to a bud in a leaf axil lower down the stem, to encourage strong new shoots. Prune to an outward-facing leaf to keep the center of the rose bush open. Species roses should not be deadheaded as they produce attractive hips in the fall.

After deadheading, apply fertilizer to the roses to boost growth and encourage more flowers later in the summer. Use a fertilizer specific to roses, or one high in potash to encourage strong shoots. A fertilizer high in nitrogen will result in soft, weak growth that is more prone to attack from pests and diseases.

■ **Diseases like black spot, rust, and mildew** are more of a problem in summer, the first two especially if the weather has been damp. Mildew tends to appear when the weather is drier. To minimize the spread of diseases, gather up and burn all infected leaves that have fallen to the ground. Never put them on the compost pile, as this may spread the spores of the disease around the yard. If you spray for black spot, use a recommended fungicide, but do it early in the season before the disease takes hold. Once black spot is

Rust infection A leaf covered in a variety of rust-colored fungal infections.

Deadheading roses Cut through the stem well below the faded flowers, just above a leaf.

established, spraying is useless. Rust disease, the symptoms of which appear as orange spores on the undersides of the leaves, is more prevalent on plants that are deficient in potash, so feeding with a rose fertilizer, which is high in potash, will help to reduce the problem.

Mildew will attack plants that are under stress due to lack of water. Control mildew by keeping plants well watered and spray with an approved fungicide if it seems to be persistent. Shrubs growing in containers should be watered regularly and fed once a week with a high-potash fertilizer. Watering may have to be done twice a day in very hot weather.

Pruning and training

■ **Cut lavender for drying** just the same as you would everlasting flowers.

■ **Prune early-summer-flowering shrubs** such as philadelphus and weigela if not done last month.

■ **Remove unwanted growth** from the base or trunks of trees and shrubs. Many trees and shrubs often produce a mass of shoots at the base of the plant. One of the most common groups of plants with this

habit are the *Sorbus* species, such as rowan and mountain ash. These shoots need to be cut away cleanly to prevent them from sapping all the strength of the plant. At the same time, remove any shoots that have grown with plain green leaves on variegated plants.

Propagation

■ **Take semiripe cuttings** from shrubs. Semiripe cuttings are taken from growth produced in the current year once the stems have started to become woody at the base. It's a remarkably easy and successful way to take cuttings, increasing your stock of plants quickly.

Remove shoots about 4 in (10 cm) long with a sliver or heel of older bark from the main stem, or just trim them below a leaf joint. Trim the tail of the heel off, if there is one. Remove the lower leaves. Pinch out the tip of the cutting if growth is very soft. Dip the whole cutting in a fungicide solution (wear protective gloves). Then dip the base of the cutting in hormone rooting solution. Put the cuttings around the edge of a pot containing peat-free potting mix mixed with an equal amount of vermiculite. Put a clear plastic bag over the pot to create a humid atmosphere and put the pot in a shady part of the garden—in a cold frame or below a sheltered wall. The cuttings will root in about six to eight weeks, when they can be potted up and grown on.

■ **Take cuttings from hydrangeas.** These showy garden shrubs, a delight in late summer, can be propagated easily. Remove nonflowering shoots 3–4 in (8–10 cm) long, cutting just above a bud. Remove the lower leaves and trim the base of the cutting with a sharp knife. There is no need to trim the cutting immediately below a leaf joint, as the cuttings will root perfectly well if cut between buds.

Hydrangeas have quite large leaves, so to reduce water loss from them, cut the leaves across in half. Put into a pot of seed-starting medium, cover with a plastic bag, and stand in a shady corner. The cuttings will root in about four weeks, when they can be potted up.

■ **Take conifer cuttings.** After trimming your conifer hedge, make cuttings if you want to increase the number of plants to make another hedge. Pick out healthy shoots with sideshoots 2–3 in (5–8 cm) long and becoming woody at their base. Tear them off the larger shoot with a heel of older wood and treat them in exactly the same way as for semiripe shrub cuttings.

■ **Pot up or plant out softwood cuttings** taken earlier that have now rooted, watering them well before and after. If you have space, line them out in a corner of the vegetable garden, where they can grow on during the summer, forming excellent plants by fall. Otherwise, pot them into individual pots, but don't let them dry out.

Hedges
■ **Trim conifer hedges** to keep them under control. Conifer hedges have received quite bad press in recent years, due mainly to the notoriety of x *Cuprocyparis leylandii*. This is an excellent hedging plant, but as with all hedges it needs regular trimming to keep it under control. Admittedly, it does grow extremely fast, putting on 2–3 ft (60–90 cm) of growth in most years. As with all other conifer hedges, it needs trimming once a year, or even twice, to keep it in order. If you start doing this when the conifers are small, long before they reach the height and width you eventually require, you will build up a good, thick layer of leafy growth over the entire surface of the hedge.

CLIMBERS
■ **It is very easy to propagate** from clematis cuttings at this time of year. Try this easy method by taking "internodal" cuttings. Take a strong main stem and cut it into sections, midway between leaf joints, or nodes. Trim the stem below the node so that 1–2 in (2–5 cm) remains and trim the stem above the node to ½ in (1 cm) long. Dip the base in hormone rooting solution and put in pots containing seed-starting medium. Cover cuttings with thin plastic sheeting held off the foliage and tucked under the pot. Put in a shady frame and they will root in six to eight weeks. Pot them up and grow on.

■ **Try air-layering climbing plants** like clematis and akebia. Select a main shoot and make a cut at a sharp angle into the stem, without cutting it completely. Wrap sphagnum moss around the cut and hold it in place with clear plastic, tied top and bottom. When a good root system has formed in a few weeks, remove the young plant from the parent and pot it up.

■ **Prune wisteria by cutting back** the whippy growths made during the summer so that they are within five or six buds of the main stems.

Wisteria pruning This encourages the formation of flower buds for next year.

PERENNIALS
■ **Divide bearded and other rhizomatous irises** after the flowers are over. After several years these irises tend to lose vigor and need to be divided up. It's also a good opportunity to clear weeds from within iris clumps, as these are otherwise difficult to get out—a spot weedkiller is usually the only answer.

Once the flowers are over, lift the clump carefully with a fork and then separate out the younger pieces from around the outside of the clump. Cut off the younger pieces with a sharp knife. The older pieces can be thrown away. Cut off faded leaves and cut across the remaining foliage about 6 in (15 cm) from the root, leaving a fan shape of trimmed leaves. This helps reduce water loss from the leaves and stops the wind from catching the tall foliage like a sail and blowing the plant over.

Replant in groups of three, five, or more and water them in thoroughly. Irises must not be planted too deeply; on an exposed site, it may help to pin down the rhizomes with hoops of galvanized wire, removing these when the plants have developed their own anchoring roots.

■ **Disbud dahlias if you want larger** blooms and support the flowering stems with canes or stakes. If you've recently joined a local gardening society then dahlias are definitely one of the best plants with which to enter the cutthroat world of showing. Any club organizing a show will issue its own strict rules on how show flowers are presented, and for dahlias this nearly always means growing single, large blooms on long, sturdy stems. Rules for flower arrangements may not be so precise, but some stunning dahlias always make a good centerpiece for a display.

All disbudding means is removing some of the side buds at the apex of the stems, leaving the larger bud in the middle to flower. Remove sideshoots lower down the

Dividing irises

1 Lift the clump of old, knobby rhizomes and cut off small, healthy, young pieces that each have a clump of leaves attached.

2 Pull off dead foliage, then with a sharp knife cut across the fan of leaves. Replant the small divisions in a sunny spot, 4–6 in (8–15 cm) apart, the rhizome just below the surface.

stem, too, to get those long stems. Dahlias are normally supported with stakes, as there is a fair weight of top-growth on the plants. Use one stake at planting time, and later put three or four canes around the plants as well and tie twine around all the supports. In this way the whole plant will be supported.

■ **While borders are in full bloom** it is a good idea to take a walk around the yard and look carefully at the display and decide which plants look out of place—perhaps colors clash—and which just haven't performed very well. Look out, too, for those overgrown plants that may need dividing during the fall and winter. Dividing them may rejuvenate them, giving them a new lease on life. Take a notepad or gardening journal with you and note down all the things that need to be done, because by the fall, if you have a memory like mine, you'll have forgotten everything.

■ **Continue to cut back faded flowers** on perennials if seed is not required. This will encourage new growth and more flowers

later in the summer. Plants like Oriental poppies and hardy geraniums can be cut back to ground level with a pair of shears, and taller perennials such as delphiniums should have their faded flower spikes cut back, to encourage new shoots that, hopefully, will produce more flowers later in the summer. Aquilegias can have the old flowering stems removed if seed is not required from the plants. All the old growth can be discarded on the compost pile. Give the plants some fertilizer and a good watering if the weather is dry.

■ **Harvest seed from perennials.** Many perennials will be finishing flowering now and if they haven't been cut off, seed pods will be developing. A lot of seedheads will ripen toward the end of the month and must be gathered before they open up and scatter the seeds. You will have to be vigilant if you want to catch them.

Seeds are best collected on a dry, sunny day when there will be less chance of rot getting into them. When collecting the seeds, put the heads or pods into paper bags with the name of the plant written on

them. If the seeds are ripe and are beginning to come out of the seedhead, close the top of the bag and shake it to get all of the seeds out. If you cut off one corner of the bag, you should be able to trickle the seeds onto a sheet of paper, keeping most of the debris in the bag. If the heads aren't quite open, lay them out on a sheet of paper in a dry place until they begin to shed the seeds.

Carefully separate the seeds from any dirt and chaff using an old kitchen sieve, or by very gently blowing over them. The heavier seeds should stay in place while the chaff is blown away, but do it carefully.

Put the seeds into paper envelopes, seal, and label them. Store them somewhere cool and dry—the ideal place being in an air-tight container on the bottom shelf of the refrigerator.

■ **Herbaceous perennials in general,** and late-flowering ones like asters and chrysanthemums, in particular, will benefit from a sprinkling of a general organic fertilizer now to give a boost to their growth for the rest of the summer. Hoe or lightly rake it in and if the weather is dry, water it in as well.

■ **Layer pinks and carnations.** Border pinks and carnations are delightful cottage-garden plants to have in the borders. After three or four years they can become a bit straggly, but they are easy to propagate. You can layer them by pegging stems into the ground, so that roots form on the stems and become new young plantlets. This can be a bit tricky and sometimes not as successful as taking cuttings or "pipings," as they are called. However, the advantage of layering is that you need less space to grow on cuttings and young plants in pots, as the layers can be transplanted directly into their new site as soon as they have formed good roots, or even left in place until next spring, if you prefer. Some gardeners layer a few stems each summer, just to see what happens. You should get at least a new plant or two.

Alpines

■ **Save seeds from alpines** in exactly the same way as described for herbaceous perennials, though alpines require cold weather to break the seeds' dormancy, so they have to be left outside or in an unheated cold frame for the winter.

However, seeds of some alpines only remain viable for a relatively short time and these have to be sown now, right after harvesting. These include primulas, cyclamen, androsaces, dionysias, and meconopsis.

If you are not sure of the correct time for sowing a particular variety of seed, sow some as soon as the seed is ripe, or in the fall and then sow some in late winter or spring. This way you cover each period. Note down which seeds germinate best at which time for future seed sowing.

■ **Spot-treat any perennial weeds** that appear among alpines. If weeds grow between, or even through, alpines they can be difficult to uproot without disturbing the plants and impossible to spray with weedkiller, but all is not lost if this happens.

There are some weedkillers that come ready-prepared in the form of a gel, with a small brush built into the lid of the container. It is an easy matter to brush the weedkiller onto the foliage of the weed, using a piece of cardboard as a shield to protect the alpine plant.

■ **Some alpines with a carpeting habit** can die off in the center and look horrible. This problem can be remedied by filling the center of the plant with gritty alpine potting mix. This will encourage the plant to regrow, filling in the bare patch.

Layering pinks

1 **Find a shoot that can be bent** to touch the ground and remove all but the top few leaves.

2 **Wound the stems** to stimulate root formation, by nicking the shoot with a very sharp knife at a leaf joint.

3 Use hoops or staples of galvanized wire to peg the prepared shoot into the ground, at the point where you have made the wound.

BULBS

■ **Bulbs that were heeled** in in trenches for the foliage to die back can be dug up and stored until they are required for planting. Make sure they are dry and free from diseased material, so that they do not rot in storage. Remove all dead foliage and flowering stems. Inspect the bulbs for disease or rot, removing any that are affected. Lay the bulbs out in a single layer to dry off for a few days and then store in boxes or trays in a cool, dry, airy place.

■ **Plant fall-flowering** bulbs now. These bulbs will flower through September, October and, if the weather is reasonable, into November. The flowers appear without foliage because the leaves have died down during the summer. The leaves will appear in the spring. Bulbs to choose are fall-flowering crocus: *Crocus speciosus* with blue-purple and white flowers, *C. kotschyanus* with lilac-pink flowers, and *C. sativus*, with dark-veined lilac flowers. Plant them in full sun to a depth of 4 in (10 cm).

Nerines are wonderful plants from the warmer climes of South Africa. Like colchicums, the flowers appear before the leaves, with tall stems bearing up to nine blooms with pink, curling petals. They need a warm, sunny, sheltered spot, preferably at the base of a south-facing wall or fence, and well-drained soil. *Nerine bowdenii* is the most widely known and the easiest to grow, but even this will need some protection in colder areas. In northern parts and very exposed, chilly gardens it may be best to grow nerines under cover. Plant the bulb to at least twice its own depth.

■ **Lilies should be looking gorgeous** now, but it's easy to brush against the flowers inadvertently. Pollen on the large stamens can cause stains, so cut the stamens off to prevent this, as florists often do.

ANNUALS AND BEDDING

■ **Maintain annuals and tender perennials** to keep the display going well into the fall. Deadhead old flowers regularly to prevent the plants from setting seed unless, of course, you want to collect seeds from some plants. Do bear in mind, though, that hybrid plants such as F1 hybrids will not come true to type from seed. Plants such as pansies and petunias tend to get straggly now and picking off individual spent flowers from these plants can be tedious. An easy way to deadhead them is to cut them back with pruners or shears. Cut them back quite hard, give a quick boost with a high-potash fertilizer, and new growth will soon be produced with flowers later in the summer.

■ **Finish planting out summer bedding** plants in baskets, containers, and borders. The sooner this job is done, the better, as the plants will have time to settle in and flower for the rest of the summer.

■ **Continue to water plants** if the weather is dry. Give a good soaking once a week rather than a little each day. Regular feeding with a high-potash fertilizer will also help to prolong the flowering period. Hoe between plants, if they've not grown into each other, to keep down weeds.

July bedding planting Change plants and fill in any gaps in the border.

Cut flowers to dry

1 Cut everlasting flowers such as statice (*Limonium*) just as the flowers start to open. Cut low down to get the full length of stem.

2 Tie the flowers in small bunches and hang them upside down in an airy place, out of full sun, which will bleach the color.

■ **Transplant biennial seedlings** sown in May and June. Seedlings of wallflowers, forget-me-nots (*Myosotis*), English daisy, Canterbury bells (*Campanula medium*) and ornamental kales and cabbages can be transplanted to nursery rows, to grow into larger plants before planting in their flowering positions in the fall, when the summer bedding has finished. Water the seedlings an hour or so beforehand and lift them carefully. Replant about 6 in (15 cm) apart in rows in a corner. Water the seedlings well after transplanting to settle them in. Wallflowers tend to have one main, or tap, root with only a few fibrous roots, so to encourage more fibrous roots to grow, cut back the thicker taproot when transplanting. Water the young plants regularly, keep them weeded throughout the summer by regularly hoeing between the plants, and they should make fine plants to put in their final flowering positions in fall.

■ **Cut and dry everlasting flowers.** Flowers of plants like statice, bracteantha, and rhodanthe can be cut for drying and used for decorative displays in the home during the winter. They have to be picked just before they reach their peak, which is when they are almost fully open. They will open slightly more as they dry out. Tie them in bunches and hang them up in an airy place to dry out. Don't try to speed up the drying process by putting the flowers in a warm place—they will shrivel up.

■ **Disbud tuberous begonias** growing in pots or as bedding. These large-flowered begonias produce three flower buds at the top of the stems. The central bud is the male flower and this should be kept for its frilly petals. The smaller buds on either side are the less showy, single female flowers and these need to be removed to get a reasonable-sized double flower.

CONTAINERS

■ **Continue maintaining containers** to extend the colorful display well into fall. Water and fertilize the containers regularly and perhaps even do it twice a day during very hot spells of weather. Containers will still need plenty of water even when it rains. The mass of roots inside the container and the foliage on top make rain penetration almost impossible and so watering with a watering can or hose is the only answer. Deadhead the plants regularly to keep the plants looking good and prevent them from setting seed.

Plants crammed together in containers can sometimes begin to look a bit straggly toward late summer and it is a good idea to go over your containers occasionally, pruning off any straggly shoots and any that are crowding out other plants too much. You can always make some cuttings from the material you cut off.

Summer attention Water and fertilize your container plants regularly through the summer.

LAWNS

■ **Continue to mow** and trim edges once or twice a week to keep the lawn in good condition. During very dry weather, raise the blades of the mower and mow less often. The grass is best left a little longer during dry periods so that the plants retain more leaf area and can therefore cope better. The grass will also not be growing as vigorously, so the frequency of mowing can be reduced. Clippings left on the lawn act as a mulch, helping to retain moisture in the soil. When the grass gets going again in more moist conditions, the blades can be gradually lowered to normal height.

■ **Don't water unless absolutely necessary.** If you have to water the lawn, do it once a week, soaking it thoroughly. Established lawns will turn brown in hot weather, but it's not worth wasting water on them, as the grass will soon recover.

■ **Give the lawn a boost with a liquid** fertilizer unless you did so in June. Most lawns will benefit from a quick boost. There are many types of liquid fertilizers on the market.

New lawns

■ **Water new lawns** made in spring, either from seed or sod. It is vitally important not to let newly laid sod dry out: it shrinks when it dries and it's almost impossible to undo the damage when this happens.

■ **Get ahead.** If you are planning to make a new lawn, begin initial preparation now for sowing seed or laying sod in the fall. The more time you give the soil to settle, the easier it is to achieve a level surface. Dig over the whole site and remove all perennial weeds, leveling it roughly. If the ground is weed-free, use a rototiller over large areas. The final leveling-off and raking down can be done closer to the time of sowing or laying the sod.

VEGETABLE AND HERBS

■ **Water all vegetables regularly.** If this is not done they will bolt and start producing seeds, making them inedible. The easiest way to water is with a drip irrigation setup or soaker hose laid along the rows or buried. This directs the water where it's most needed, preventing splashing, especially from large-leaved plants. The most efficient time to water is at night. Keep down weeds by continuing to hoe between the rows. Hoe on a dry day and the weed seedlings will shrivel up in the warm sun. Mulching with a layer of dry grass mowings will also suppress weeds.

Harvesting

■ **Keep harvesting vegetables** as soon as they are ready. Most taste much better when they are young. Also, if you keep harvesting the young vegetables, you are more likely to get more crops than if all are left to grow to maturity.

■ **Early potatoes should be ready to** harvest. To see if they are, lift one plant and see how big the crop is. If there aren't many potatoes that are more than marble-sized, leave the rest of the plants to develop further. To encourage the tubers to swell, water the plants once a week, giving them a good soaking.

■ **Begin harvesting shallots.** Shallots need dry, sunny weather to ripen properly. Lift the bulbs carefully, levering them out of the ground with a fork when the leaves turn yellow. In sunny weather they can be left on the surface of the soil to dry out. Or, to allow plenty of air to circulate around the bulbs, erect a temporary support by driving four low stakes into the ground and stretching a piece of chicken wire between the posts to create a sort of "hammock." Put the shallots on this and they will dry out quickly. If rain is forecast, cover them with a piece of plastic sheeting.

If the weather is very wet, put the shallots under cover, in a cold frame with the lid on, or lay them out in a greenhouse or shed with good light.

■ **Harvest onions when the leaves** begin to turn yellow and flop. Ease the bulbs out of the soil and leave them on the surface for a few days if the weather is warm and dry. As with shallots, you can make a chicken wire support for them, allowing air to circulate freely. Once dry, onions can be stored in several ways. Tie them up to make an onion string, or put them into an old pair of pantyhose and hang them up— or just lay them in a single layer in boxes.

■ **Harvest globe artichokes before the** scales begin to open. This is a striking architectural plant that can be grown in ornamental borders as well as in the vegetable garden. The bold foliage makes a perfect contrast to other, finer-leaved plants in the garden. If the flower heads are left on, they open up to reveal the most beautiful thistlelike flowers.

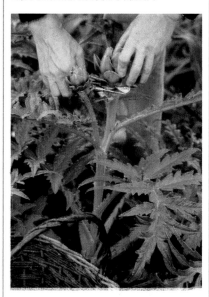

Fat, round artichoke globes Pick these promptly or the scales will open.

Lift garlic Spread the bulbs in the sun to dry before storing.

■ **Harvest garlic planted last year in** exactly the same way as for shallots. If the bulbs have been healthy and shown no sign of virus, then some of the cloves can be kept for replanting.

Sowing and planting outdoors

■ **It's not too late** to sow vegetables for fall harvesting. Whenever some ground becomes vacant, revitalize the soil with organic matter and sow vegetables such as lettuces, which will grow quickly as long as they don't dry out. An early variety, like 'Tom Thumb', is small and will mature quickly. Beets are another crop that can be sown now. 'Boltardy' is a good old reliable variety to try. Beets will be good for storing over winter. Carrots can still be sown, too, providing succulent young roots for immediate use and for storing. Turnips are very quick to mature and the leaves can also be used as greens.

■ **Sow fall and winter salads.** Corn salad and arugula can be sown now. Both are happy in most situations. Claytonia (winter purslane) prefers lighter, sandy soil. Sow the seeds thinly in drills 9 in (23 cm) apart. These crops don't need to be thinned out; they can be just cut as required and will grow away again.

Asian vegetables make an interesting addition to fall salads and these can be sown now too. They are all very attractive to look at and can therefore be grown in with ornamental plants in borders as well as in the vegetable garden. Ones to look for are Chinese radish, mizuna greens, bok choy, and spinach mustard. Sow in rows 12 in (30 cm) apart and thin to 6–12 in (15–30 cm) between the plants.

■ **Continue sowing peas** until the end of the month. Use an early variety such as 'Douce Provence', which will mature quickly. Dig a trench about 2 in (5 cm) deep with a spade or a draw hoe and space-sow the seeds about 1 in (2.5 cm) apart. Water the drill if the soil is dry. Cover the seeds and tap down the soil firmly with the back of a rake. Then cover the row with fine netting or floating row cover. Support the plants with twiggy sticks as they grow.

■ **Finish planting out winter brassicas** sown in April and May. To make watering the plants in easier, now that it is so dry, dig a deep drill with a draw hoe and put the plants in with a dibber or a trowel, planting in the drill. A watering can or hose can then be run along the rows, with the drill keeping the water where it is needed. Remember to put collars at the base of the stems to prevent the cabbage root fly from laying its eggs there. And grow them under row cover to protect them from the cabbage white butterfly, which lays its small, yellow eggs beneath the leaves

■ **Sow spring cabbages at intervals of** a week to ten days. This vegetable is particularly welcome when there is little else to be harvested from the vegetable garden. Sow the seeds thinly in drills 6 in (15 cm) apart, watering the drills before sowing if the soil is dry. Follow the directions on the seed packet. Cover them with row covers to stop birds from eating the seedlings and flea beetles from making small holes in the leaves. When the young plants have made two or three true leaves, transplant to their cropping places.

Caring for crops

■ **Stop outdoor espaliered tomatoes** when they have made four trusses of fruit. Outdoor tomatoes in temperate climates will not carry or ripen any more fruit than this because of relatively short summers. Pinch out the growing tip one leaf beyond the topmost flower truss. This allows plant foods to travel up the stem to the top truss, setting and ripening the fruit. Feed the plants with a high-potash fertilizer for a good crop and remove sideshoots from the leaf axils on cordon-grown varieties. Bush and trailing varieties can be left to their own devices; they fruit on sideshoots and there is no top truss of flowers.

■ **Endives can be blanched** to turn the foliage white and make it more palatable. Cover each plant with a plate, making sure you cover up any drainage holes in the bottom of pots so the plants are in total darkness. They should be ready to harvest after about ten days of blanching.

■ **Watch out for the tomato problems** blossom end rot and ghost spot. The symptoms of blossom end rot appear as a sunken brown patch on the fruit at the farthest end from the flower stalk. It is caused by a lack of calcium, brought on by even the briefest shortage of water. The way to prevent blossom end rot is to water the plants regularly and evenly, never allowing them to dry out.

Watering regularly will also prevent splitting, which happens after a dry spell if the plants are suddenly given a lot of water, the upsurge in water causing the skins of the fruits to split.

Ghost spot appears as small spots on the fruits, surrounded by a lighter ring. This fungal disease can usually be avoided by taking care not to splash the fruits with water when damping down or watering.

■ **Begin to earth up celery** growing in trenches. By now the stems should be about 12 in (30 cm) high and ready for blanching. This makes the stems more succulent. To stop soil from getting into the center of the plant and causing rot, make a newspaper collar, leaving the tuft of foliage exposed. The soil can be filled in from either side of the trench. Self-blanching celery does not

need earthing up and this type of celery can be left to grow in its blocks.

■ **Look out for potato and tomato blight.** Blight on these crops is caused by a funguslike pathogen whose spores are windblown and strike when conditions are wet. It causes rapid browning and collapse of leaves, brown blotches on fruit, and discoloration and rotting of tubers. Prompt removal and destruction of infected foliage may prevent spread to tubers. Regular sprays of copper fungicides will provide protection. The new potato variety 'Mira' and others from the 'Sarpo' range show promising resistance.

■ **Water runner beans regularly** at the roots to help the flowers set and form pods. Many gardeners also recommend spraying the flowers with water daily. Adding a small handful of hydrated lime to a full two-gallon watering can and applying along the row at the bases will also help the flowers to set and produce more pods.

■ **Stop climbing beans** when they reach the tops of their supports—that is, pinch out the tip of the leading shoot. This will encourage the plants to make more sideshoots lower down and therefore more beans will be produced. Be sure to pick beans regularly. If the pods are left on the plants too long they become tough and stringy. The more you pick them, the more you will get through the summer because plants will continue cropping for longer.

■ **Protect summer cauliflowers by** bending or snapping leaves over the flower heads. Keeping them in the dark by breaking leaves over them will keep them white and lengthen the time before they begin to open up.

Blanching endive

1 Put an overturned plate over the heart of the plant to exclude the light.

2 In a week or two, the inner leaves become pale and sweet to eat.

Herbs

■ **Pick herbs regularly** to maintain a supply of fresh, young shoots. It's almost like pruning the plant: the more you pick, the more young shoots, with the best flavor for cooking, will be produced. If herbs are not picked regularly they tend to become spindly. But if they have been neglected they can be brought back to bushiness again. Most herbs benefit from being trimmed to encourage new growth.

■ **Pick and dry herbs.** Sage, rosemary, and thyme can be cut now and hung up to dry. Do this in an airy place outdoors, where the herbs will be protected from the rain. Another easy way to store herbs is to freeze them.

■ **Take cuttings from herbs** such as lemon verbena, sage, and thyme—all the herbs that tend to become woody near the ground. To increase success, dip the bases of the cuttings in hormone rooting solution. The cuttings should root in four to six weeks, when they can be potted up individually. They can sit outside in a shady corner over the summer, provided you remember to water regularly, and planted in fall or overwintered in a cold frame.

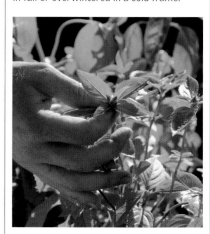

Pinching out basil Nip out the tips of the shoots to make the plant bush out lower down.

FRUIT
Picking and storing

■ **Summer-fruiting raspberries** should ripen this month. If you have a surplus, they freeze very well, either singly or cooked gently to reduce to a purée.

■ **Blackcurrant bushes can be partially** pruned, if you like, as the crop is harvested, so you can take some whole branches into the kitchen and pick the fruits off with ease. Remove about one-third of the bush each year, cutting from low down to encourage strong new shoots from the base of the plants. Pruning blackcurrants is a compromise between cutting out old wood and leaving enough new wood for fruiting the following year. It is inevitable that some new growth will be pruned out.

■ **Red- and whitecurrants are harvested** by pulling or snipping entire fruit clusters from the plant. Don't strip berries off individually until you have them indoors.

Pruning and training

■ **Prune red- and whitecurrants** and gooseberries late in the month. All sideshoots made this year should be trimmed back to three or four buds from their point of growth. Any crossing shoots and those growing into the middle of the bush can be removed at the same time. This allows air to circulate more freely around the bushes, lets more light in to ripen the fruits, and reduces of disease; it also encourages the formation of fruit buds for fruiting again next year.

■ **Prune summer-fruiting raspberries** after all of the fruit has been picked. The old fruited canes are easily identifiable as they should have been tied to the supporting wires. If not, the wood of these canes is more brown in color, there will be remains of fruit clusters, and the leaves tend to look a bit shabby by this time of

Summer-fruiting raspberries Prune out the fruited canes by cutting them at ground level.

year. By contrast, the younger canes that have been produced during the summer will have fresh, green foliage and the stems will still be green. First untie the old canes from the supporting wires and cut them out to ground level. The new canes can now be tied in, spacing them about 4 in (10 cm) apart. Only tie in good, strong canes; any weak ones should be pruned out completely. Any canes growing far out from the rows should be dug up or they will continue to creep outward.

■ **Continue training new canes of** blackberries and other hybrid berries. Most of the hybrid berries have vicious thorns and if you don't tie them in regularly they will become quite a problem, getting tangled up in other plants. There are some thornless hybrid berries as well as the blackberry variety 'Oregon Thornless', which are better for family gardens. As with raspberries, tie the new canes to the supports with twine, on the opposite side from the fruiting canes already there. There are many complicated ways of training hybrid berries, but this is the easiest way: fruiting canes to one side of the support, and new canes to the other, to form a fan.

■ **Continue training fan-trained fruits.**
Remove unwanted shoots that spoil the fan shape. Any shoots growing directly toward the wall or fence should also be pruned out. Young shoots growing at the base of each of this year's fruiting shoots should be retained and tied in. These will be used as replacements for the current year's growth, when these are pruned out after fruiting and will fruit next year.

■ **At the end of the** month, begin summer-pruning trained apples and pears.

Caring for crops

■ **Ripening fruit of peaches and nectarines** will need protection from birds and wasps. Trees trained against walls or fences are relatively easy to protect; you can easily drape floating row cover or commercial shade cloth over them. Make sure that it is secured to the wall and that there are no gaps where birds can get in. Free-standing trees are more difficult to protect, but row cover draped over will give some protection, particularly if it can be secured at ground level.

■ **Thin out fruit on apples and pears.**
Once the "June drop" is over (fruit trees naturally shed some fruit in June), it is safe to thin out any other fruits not required. Remove any very small, damaged, or diseased fruits in each cluster. To get apples and pears to grow to a reasonable size, thin the remaining fruits so that you leave one fruit every 4 in (10 cm) apart. It may seem disappointing to remove a lot of fruit from the tree at this stage, but the resulting crops in the fall will be of far superior quality than if a lot of fruits are left on the tree.

■ **Support heavily laden fruit tree** branches. The weight of fruit on trees can be considerable at this time and it makes

sense to support the branches of some trees. Plum branches, in particular, will break very easily. A stake with a "V"-shaped notch in the end can be put under any vulnerable-looking branch to prop it up. Smaller shoots on some trees can be tied up to a cane lashed to the tree's stake, or just to a more mature branch, to support the weight of the crop.

■ **Inspect apples for woolly aphids** and spray with a suitable insecticide. Woolly aphids appear as white fluff on the shoots and branches and their feeding causes lumpy growths to appear on the younger shoots. Aphids of all kinds can also spread virus diseases and so it is important to control them. Be sure to spray only in the late evening, when there are fewer pollinating and other beneficial insects around. Light infestations can be controlled by squashing the aphids by hand. Some of the organic insecticides will harm not only pests, but also beneficial wildlife too.

■ **Remove old foliage from strawberries** once fruiting has finished. Old leaves become diseased and are of little use to the plants. Remove them by going over the plants with a pair of shears. Any straw that was put around the plants to keep the fruits from being spoiled should be removed too. Lightly fork over the soil between the plants and take out any weeds. The plants will soon produce new foliage over the next few weeks. The old leaves and straw can be consigned to the compost pile.

Planning ahead

■ **Prepare the ground** for new strawberry plants. After three years, the yield from strawberry plants tends to decline and the plants sometimes get a viral disease. So it is better to replace plants after three cropping seasons. If the old plants have shown signs of viruses, buy new ones from reputable nurseries, where you will be able to get healthy new stock certified virus-free. Choose a new patch for the new strawberries. Prepare the ground well, incorporating organic matter to improve soil structure and retain soil moisture.

Strawberries after cropping

1 After the last fruits have been picked, trim all the leaves off the plants with shears and put them on the compost pile.

2 Remove straw mulches or strawberry mats, clear all debris from the crowns of the plants, and weed and gently fork over the soil.

UNDER COVER

■ **Keep the greenhouse** and conservatory well ventilated in hot weather. Ventilators can be left open almost all of the time now, to help avoid temperature fluctuations. Damping down paths regularly with water will also help to reduce the temperature.

If there is an occasional colder night, it is a good idea to make sure that the doors and ventilators are closed.

Greenhouse and house plants

■ **Start taking fuchsia cuttings.** Root them in exactly the same way as you would do for geranium cuttings. When the cuttings have rooted, pot them on.

■ **Train standard fuchsias from cuttings.** Growing standards is a very attractive way of growing these delightful plants. If you keep your greenhouse or conservatory heated over winter, then the young plants will continue to grow year-round, although growth will inevitably slow during winter.

Cuttings that have naturally developed with a single, definite, sturdy main stem are the best material to start with. As the cuttings grow, tie them to a cane to keep the stem straight. Remove any sideshoots as they develop from the leaf axils. Pot the young plant into progressively larger pots and keep it growing slowly over the winter in cool but frost-free conditions. You need only water very sparingly.

In spring, growth will pick up again. Once the plant has reached the height you want, pinch out the growing tip. The sideshoots that develop can be pinched out themselves when they have made three or four pairs of leaves. Do this another couple of times and you will have developed a good bushy head to the plant which will, in summer, be covered in flowers. Leaves on the clear stem should drop naturally, but remove any shoots.

■ **Take cuttings from regal geraniums.** These showy plants can be propagated by cuttings from now through the rest of the summer. Select nonflowering shoots about 4 in (10 cm) long and cut them from the plant. Remove the lower leaves, leaving two or three leaves at the tip of the cutting. In addition, remove the little scalelike structures at the base of the leaf stalks (stipules), as these may rot. They are particularly prominent on geraniums.

Trim the cuttings just below a leaf joint, so that each is about 3 in (8 cm) long. Dip the ends in hormone rooting solution and put into pots containing seed-starting mix. There is no need to cover them. Stand the pots on a well-lit bench or windowsill, but out of direct sunlight. The cuttings will take four weeks to root, when they can be potted up to grow on.

■ **Prick out seedlings of plants sown** earlier for winter-flowering container plants, such as cinerarias and calceolarias. Prick out the seedlings when they are large enough to handle. This can be a tricky job with calceolarias, as the seedlings are small, yet cannot be left in the seed tray too long. Either prick out into trays, spacing the seedlings about 2 in (5 cm) apart, or pot them up individually into small pots. More seed can be sown now to give a succession of flowers through the winter and into spring on plants that are kept in the warmth. Sow in trays or pots of seed-starting mix and water the container before sowing.

Seeds of cinerarias and calceolarias are very small and can be sown on the surface of the soil and left uncovered. You may find it easier to sow them by first mixing a little flour with the seeds. This makes it a little easier to see where you have sown the seeds and helps distribute them evenly.

Sweet peppers Support them with canes and twine. Leave a short stalk when harvesting.

Crops under glass

■ **Continue to maintain indoor fruits and vegetables.** Tomatoes need to have any sideshoots that grow from the leaf axils removed. Remove them before they get too large, to minimize the shock to the plant. Keep feeding all crops under cover with a high-potash fertilizer, applied weekly, and water regularly—every evening if possible. Eggplant and pepper plants may benefit from some support now that the fruits are forming. Like tomatoes, their stems are thick but fleshy and can snap easily.

■ **Start removing foliage from tomatoes** around the end of the month. This will allow more light to get to the ripening tomatoes and will also allow better circulation of air, reducing the incidence of diseases like leaf mold and botrytis. Start removing the older leaves at the bottom of the plants, some of which may be going yellow, especially around the first truss of tomatoes which will be starting to ripen. Don't remove too many all at once.

■ **Watch out for tomato disorders** like blossom end rot and ghost spot.

The August garden

August is a good month for a well-earned break, but whether you're going on vacation or just planning to put your feet up at home, make sure the garden can cope with the summer heat. Continue with all the usual deadheading and pruning activities, make preparations for fall-flowering bulbs, and don't forget to keep your vegetables well watered this month.

THINGS TO DO

Fertilize and water all plants that need it regularly during the summer, particularly new and young plants and those in containers, and watch out for pests and diseases. Make sure the birds in your yard have enough water to drink in dry weather.

Hedges grow quickly at this time of year, so trim them regularly. Prune rambling roses after flowering, and trim lavender plants once the flowers have faded to encourage sideshoots to grow.

Continue deadheading flowers as they fade. Take cuttings from tender perennials such as geraniums and fuchsias, and collect ripening seed from plants you wish to propagate. Layer pinks, rhododendrons, and clematis this month.

Water your vegetables regularly throughout August. Lift and dry onions, and cut and dry herbs for winter use. Tomato plants will need regular fertilizing and watering; remove any yellowing leaves at the same time. Prop up any heavily laden fruit tree branches, and summer-prune gooseberry and red currant plants. Your new strawberry plants should be planted now, and you will be able to harvest the first apples and pears.

LAST CHANCE

Finish summer-pruning apples and pears, and other trained fruit trees, and complete the summer pruning of wisteria. Plant colchicums for winter flowering.

GET AHEAD

Make a start planting spring bulbs, especially daffodils, and force hyacinths for Christmas. Divide perennials toward the end of the month, and prepare ground for making new lawns. You can also sow parsley and pot up herbs for later use.

The month of plenty Root vegetables, tomatoes, climbing beans, and peas will all be ready for harvesting—and eating.

Savoring the summer

You will certainly get some hot, sultry days this month, so be prepared to water your garden regularly and make preparations if you are going away. When you are at home, take the time to enjoy your garden, but don't forget to tackle a few jobs such as routine weeding, seed-saving, and deadheading.

This is traditionally a vacation month, but don't forget to make plans for the garden before you go away. Some preparation carried out beforehand will pay dividends when you come back. It's all too easy to leave the garden, hoping it will take care of itself while you're away, but at this time of year it can so quickly become overgrown. There's a risk of returning from your break to find weeds everywhere and much of the hard work you put in earlier in the year wasted.

Try to keep ahead with all the routine jobs, such as deadheading, weeding, and watering, which have to be done. The lawn may need mowing if there has been a lot of rain and it is growing fast, but resist the temptation to cut it shorter than you would normally do, as this will only encourage it to grow even faster while you are away.

Plants growing inside will need special attention. If you can, ask a neighbor or friend to stop in and water all of your indoor plants. If this cannot be arranged, then put as many plants as possible outside in a cool, shady corner of the garden. Even better, if you can, is to plunge the pots into the ground; this way they will not dry out as quickly as when the containers are fully exposed to the sun.

Automatic watering and ventilating systems for greenhouses and conservatories are not overly expensive to buy from garden centers or specialty suppliers. Some types are controlled by a small computer. There are similar systems that can be set up to water plants in containers outdoors as well and these are invaluable if you have a patio or courtyard garden, or even a roof terrace or balcony, and rely very heavily on pots and baskets filled with plants. These systems are no more complicated to operate than your average central heating system and can save you a lot of time even when you're

A cottage garden border The differing heights of delphinium, *Nepeta robinia* 'Frisia', and *Achillea* 'Ptarmigan' are used to advantage in this border.

not on vacation—and you can go away at any time, at a moment's notice, knowing that your precious plants won't go short of water.

Home and dry

If you're not jetting off to some far-flung corner of the globe, then take time to relax and enjoy the fruits of your labors earlier in the year. But make time, too, for some light summer maintenance in the garden to keep it looking its very best. As was the case in July, the early mornings and evenings are often the most comfortable and pleasant times to work.

The weather in August is often hot and sultry. In a prolonged dry spell, take care to conserve as much water as you possibly can, since some areas will have restrictions on the use of sprinklers. There are ways to economize on the use of water—by reusing dishwater on the soil around plants, for instance. This will do them no harm at all. Bathwater, as long as you haven't used lots of bubble bath or bath oil, can also be siphoned out of the tub, either directly onto the borders or into pails. The most needy plants—it can't be said often enough—are those that are growing in pots and hanging baskets and also trees and shrubs that were planted the previous winter and are still getting their roots established in the soil. Fruiting vegetables, such as tomatoes, are also thirsty for water at this time of the year, as they need a regular supply to help their fruits swell.

Topping off water features

Keep an eye on the level of water in ponds during prolonged dry spells, as the water can evaporate at an alarming rate in these conditions. Oxygen levels in the water will also become low in still, hot weather, so make sure that you top off the pond regularly and if you can, spray water on the surface to increase the oxygen levels. This is particularly important if you are keeping fish in the pond, but all aquatic life will benefit. Oxygenating plants also help keep the water clear and aerated, but at this time of year you are more likely to find that they are becoming overgrown and need thinning, rather than not having enough. One way to ensure that pond water remains well oxygenated for fish is to install a small

Weather watch

August temperatures often reach record highs throughout the country, ranging from the 80s (25–30°C) in coastal and northern areas and high altitudes, to the 90s (30–35°C) and even breaking the 100-degree (38°C) mark in the Midwest, South, and Southwest. Although the days are beginning to shorten and autumn is forecast by a few yellowing leaves, many summer vegetables and fruits, such as tomatoes, cucumbers, sweet corn, and watermelons, are reaching their peak of ripeness. Rural fairs and harvest festivals brighten late summer days.

Water rationing

With the heat and diminished rainfall, drought is common in much of the country, presenting a real challenge to anyone with a lawn and plants to care for. In most states, two weeks without rain signals an official drought. Western mountain vistas take on tawny hues and water rationing is a regular feature in many areas. As cooler mountain air clashes with warm air rising from flat lands, thunderstorms frequently result, and the threat of forest fires set off by lightning is a serious concern. Western coastal areas are enveloped in fogs as cooling ocean breezes carry moisture inland.

Wilting in the heat

In the East and South, ornamental gardens suffer in the heat and humidity; flowers and foliage fade, ferns turn crisp and brown, astilbes go dormant. Even with regular watering, perennials wilt and look tired, because they transpire faster than their roots can take up moisture. Deep-rooted plants cope best in water-challenged weather. At this time of year, gardeners try to restrict their outside work to the cooler morning and evening hours. In the Midwest, there is often a reprieve from the heat as a cool spell precedes the fall.

Ripening tomatoes These need plenty of
water, especially in hot weather.

fountain—this will help to move the water around. The
low, bubble-type fountains are by far the best for water
conservation as fine sprays will evaporate far too quickly.
You will need to run electricity outside to power the
pump. It's important to consult a professional if you
are not confident about installing electrical equipment
outdoors, especially where water is concerned. You could,
as an alternative, investigate self-contained solar-
powered fountains.

Weeding wisely

It's vital to keep up with the weeding in all parts of the
garden at this time of year. Weeds not only compete for
precious space in the borders, but they also take up
valuable moisture, which your plants need, from the
ground. The best tool for weeding is the Dutch hoe.

The technique is to slice off the tops of the weeds just below the surface of the soil and leave them on the surface to dry out in the sun. Therefore, a dry, sunny day is best for this job. Weeding is well worth doing, as it not only keeps the garden looking good, but by maintaining a loose, crumbly layer on the surface, you are also preventing the ground from cracking in hot weather, and are therefore conserving moisture in the deeper layers.

Saving seeds

Watch for seeds ripening on plants in the garden. Growing plants from seeds collected from your own garden is one of the most rewarding aspects of the gardening process. You will have to be vigilant, though; seed pods or heads may not look ready, but you can be sure that as soon as your back is turned the seeds will pop out and spread themselves over the border. This is no bad thing, of course, as many plants will freely seed themselves around the garden. But if there are some plants you particularly want seed from, then watch them carefully. Seed heads are usually ripe when they begin to turn brown; this is the time to cut them off and drop them into paper bags, to be cleaned and stored later on.

Enjoy the end of summer

This is the last month of summer and though it's hard to believe, with the abundance of flowers, fruits, and foliage around us, plant growth really starts to slow down from the end of August onward. So you can complete summer pruning of fruit trees and wisterias and trimming of hedges this month, without fear of too much regrowth—although fast-growing conifers may well need a final going-over in the fall. You can also look forward to spending less time weeding from the end of the month onwards as germination slows down. And if you want an even sharper reminder that the seasons are about to change, remember that however hot and sultry the weather is right now, this is the month to start forcing pots of bulbs to flower at Christmas!

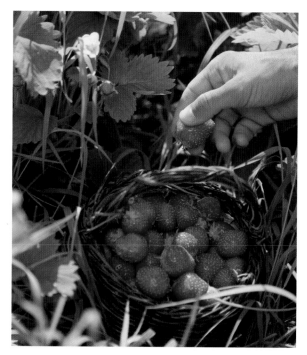

Picking strawberries Check your plants every day so that you can pick when the fruits are at their very best.

Dutch hoe Choose this tool for fast and efficient weeding. To save lots of work, simply slice the weeds and leave them on the surface of the soil to dry in the sun. This also helps to conserve moisture.

Cosmos atrosanguineus
Perennial with chocolate-scented flowers (see p.277)

Osteospermum jucundum
Sun-loving perennial with silvery leaves (see p.302)

Buddleja davidii 'Fascinating'
Shrub with enormous wildlife appeal (see p.268)

Hydrangea paniculata 'Grandiflora'
Huge flower clusters; a lovely shrub for shade (see p.290)

Begonia x tuberhybrida
Tender perennial with huge, showy flowers (see p.267)

Solenostemon 'Brightness'
Try these greenhouse favorites as annual bedding plants (see p.318)

Aconitum 'Bressingham Spire'
Lovely perennial, but toxic; site with care in a family garden (see p.263)

Phygelius x rectus 'Salmon Leap'
Slightly tender shrub for a sunny, sheltered spot (see p.305)

Monarda 'Mahogany'
One of the most popular perennials with bees (see p.299)

Penstemon 'Apple Blossom'
Narrow-leaved perennial bearing pale pink flowers (see p.304)

Lavatera 'Barnsley'
Reliable shrub, good even in poor, dry soil (see p.295)

Lobelia Fan Series
Dark-leaved perennial that enjoys damp soil (see p.296)

Clematis 'Ville de Lyon'
Large-flowered climber, which bears carmine-red flowers (see p.274)

Nemesia caerulea
Woody-based, slightly tender perennial, good in containers (see p.300)

Salvia coccinea 'Lady in Red'
Vivid perennial that needs some winter protection (see p.316)

Lantana camara
Frost-tender shrubs for multicolored summer display (see p.294)

Echinacea purpurea 'White Swan'
Hardy perennial; looks good well into fall (see p.282)

Lathyrus odoratus 'Colin Unwin'
Brick-red sweet pea; an annual climber (see p.294)

Argyranthemum foeniculaceum
Tender subshrub that forms a flower-covered bush (see p.266)

Rhodochiton atrosanguineus
Tender climber that can be grown annually for summer (see p.310)

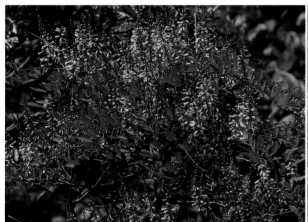

Indigofera amblyantha
Sun-loving shrub with pealike flowers and elegant foliage (see p.291)

Euryops pectinatus
Sun-loving perennial with cheerful daisy flowers (see p.284)

***Fuchsia* 'Auntie Jinks'**
A trailing variety of this popular shrub (see p.286)

***Scabiosa* 'Butterfly Blue'**
Cottage-garden perennial, popular with all flying insects (see p.316)

Pelargonium 'Apple Blossom Rosebud'
Lovely form of this summer favorite (see p.304)

Scaevola aemula
Trailing tender perennial; good in hanging baskets (see p.317)

Perovskia 'Blue Spire'
Dreamy subshrub with silvery stems and leaves (see p.305)

Tropaeolum speciosum
Exotic-looking climber that prefers acidic soil (see p.320)

Dierama pulcherrimum
Graceful perennial with wandlike flower spires (see p.281)

Heliotropium 'Marine'
Tender shrub, good in dry soil and in pots (see p.289)

Crocosmia x crocosmiiflora 'Jackanapes'
Clump-forming, nearly hardy perennial (see p.279)

Geranium psilostemon
Hardy perennial covered in flowers until late in the season (see p.287)

Abutilon 'Souvenir de Bonn'
Spindly, sun-loving shrub, good against a wall (see p.262)

Verbena 'Showtime'
Tender perennial; a popular bedding and container plant (see p.321)

Kniphofia 'Green Jade'
Cool-colored variant of a fiery perennial (see p.293)

Cotinus coggygria
The smoke bush, with clouds of tiny flowers in summer (see p.278)

What to do in August

AROUND THE YARD

Use water wisely, but during hot weather make sure that bird baths and other containers that wildlife drink from are refilled regularly.

Be vigilant in watching for pests and diseases.

Warm, dry weather encourages diseases such as mildew (a white powdery coating on stems and leaves). Preventive fungicidal sprays can be used, but by ensuring that the plants do not come under any stress—for instance, lack of water—the plants will stand up to problems much better. There will be the usual army of

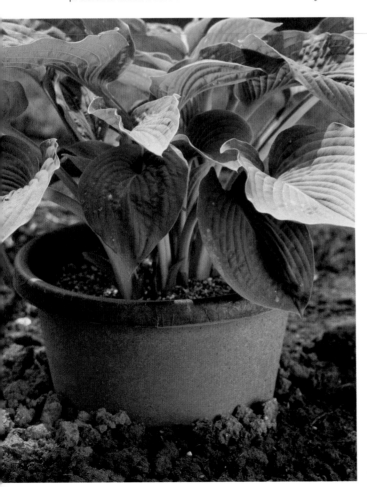

aphids around; these can be kept in check by squashing them by hand. If you have a bad infestation, control them by using a suitable pesticide that is available from garden centers; spray in the evening when fewer beneficial insects are around.

In damp summers, slug damage to plants in the garden can be rather dispiriting. The lusher and greener foliage is, the more they like it. But there are ways to combat the onslaught without resorting to pellets. First of all, birds, ground beetles, and toads all eat slugs, so the more they can be encouraged into the garden, the better. Put down pieces of slate or wood in the border for the slugs to creep under. They like dark, cool, moist hiding places. These traps can then be turned over, exposing the slugs to any birds in the vicinity—or pick them up and dispose of them. Other traps that work well include beer traps. You could also try inverted hollow grapefruit or orange halves placed around the border, or hollowed-out potatoes— these are often used as decoys by vegetable gardeners trying to protect a potato crop. Plants that are particularly prone to slug attack can be surrounded with a layer of crushed eggshells or grit. Slugs don't like the coarse surface and are less likely to reach the plants.

Continue weeding borders regularly, while watching for any self-sown seedlings. It is surprising what you can find. Most hybrids and many cultivars of plants will not reproduce true from seed, but the seedlings that do emerge can produce all sorts of variations in flower color, plant growth habit, and even leaf color. You never know when you might discover a winner of a plant in your own backyard.

Slugs and hostas Use a copper band around the rim of a terra-cotta pot to act as a barrier to slugs, which are particularly fond of hostas.

TREES AND SHRUBS

■ **Continue to deadhead roses** Remove the fading flowers to prevent plants from putting energy into producing seeds. Instead, that energy will go into new growth and more flowers. Even when deadheaded now, modern roses can still produce new shoots that will flower before the end of the season. It is not uncommon in mild-winter regions to see roses blooming into November or even later. Prune back to at least one or two leaves below the base of the flowered shoots, to a healthy, outward-facing bud. You may have to prune harder than this to find a good bud; the harder you prune, the more strongly the new shoot will grow.

Pruning and training

■ **Trim lavender lightly** At this time, you want to remove the old flower spikes. Go over the plants with a pair of hand shears, cutting off the old flower spikes and about 1 in (2.5 cm) of the leafy growth at the tips of the shoots. This will encourage sideshoots to grow, keeping the plants bushy and compact.

Lavender rarely grows again from old wood and if plants have become old and straggly, it is best to either take cuttings from them or remove the old plants altogether and buy in new plants. If your soil is on the heavy side, with a high clay content, incorporate plenty of coarse grit before planting new lavenders. This will improve drainage, which they will enjoy.

Propagation

■ **Continue to take semiripe cuttings** from shrubs. These cuttings are taken when the bases of the young shoots are beginning to turn woody or ripen. Take the cuttings in the early part of the day or in the evening, when it is cooler.

Almost all of the popular garden shrubs we grow can be increased by taking these cuttings, although you need patience while they grow to maturity. Plants to try include berberis, buddlejas, boxwood, ceanothus, choisya, cistus, cytisus, ericas, escallonia, hebes, lavenders, philadelphus, potentilla, firethorn, santolina, and viburnums.

■ **Layer rhododendrons and azaleas** These plants are difficult to root from cuttings, but they are easy to propagate by layering. Choose a flexible young shoot that is growing close to the ground, so that it can be bent easily into the surface of the soil. Then remove a few leaves 4–6 in (10–15 cm) from the tip of the shoot. Wound the shoot at the point that will be buried in the soil by cutting part of the way through it, or carefully twisting it until it just begins to crack.

Make a small depression in the soil and hold the shoot in place in the depression with a wire hoop. Cover up the stem with soil, insert a cane next to the shoot, and tie the shoot to the cane so that the tip of the shoot remains upright.

To conserve as much moisture as possible, place a brick or large stone over the stem in the soil. After about a year has gone by, the layer should have produced a good root system and it can be cut from the parent and planted out.

Hedges

■ **Most hedges** can be given their final trim toward the end of the month as they will not grow much after this, although conifers may need another once-over. If you want a level top to the hedge, put up a post at either end and tie twine between them at the required height. Trim the sides of the hedge first, working from the bottom up, whether using either a powered hedge trimmer or hand shears. The reason for working upward is that as you cut, the trimmings will fall away and you will be better able to see where you are going.

Make the hedge wider at the base and narrower at the top. This way it will stand up to the weather better. The top can be trimmed last, using the twine as a guide.

You may have trimmed conifer hedges last month; if not, do it now. It is often recommended that conifer hedges only be trimmed with shears, because powered hedge trimmers bruise the growth. This can happen, but damage is so minimal that it doesn't really make any difference. The key point with conifer hedges is never to let them get beyond the height and width you want, as none will regrow if cut back into hard, old wood. The only exception is yew. It can be cut back to very old wood and will still grow again.

Large-leaved hedges such as spotted laurel (*Aucuba*) cannot be trimmed with shears or hedge trimmers, however, because these would cut through the large leaves, causing the edges to go brown. The way to cut these hedges is with a pair of pruners. Put posts and string across the top, as described for other hedges, and trim the sides first in the same way, starting at the base and working up. It can be a tiresome task, especially if you have a large hedge, but it is well worth the effort, as the hedge will look so much better with no browned-off foliage.

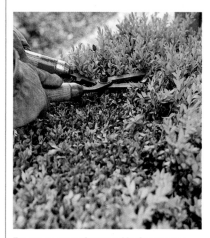

Encourage your boxwood hedge Create a good shape with regular light pruning. Shears are the tool of choice for this task.

CLIMBERS

■ **Prune rambling roses** after they have flowered. Pruning of woody plants, especially roses, can sometimes be portrayed as being very complicated, and this may make you hesitant when it comes to doing the job. But pruning rambling roses is, in fact, very easy. All you have to remember is that these roses produce flowers on wood produced the previous year. All sideshoots that have flowered can be pruned back to one or two buds from the main stems. Any new, strong growths can be tied in to replace older shoots and any very old stems can be pruned out to the ground, so encouraging more new shoots from the base of the plant.

■ **Propagate clematis by layering.** Select a shoot growing from near the base of the plant and lay it on the ground. To encourage the formation of roots, cut partway through the stem at each of the leaf joints, being careful not to sever it completely. If you want to, you can apply some hormone rooting solution to each cut, but it's not essential. Make some wire hoops and peg each leaf joint to the surface of the soil. Each can be covered with a little soil if you wish. After a few weeks, roots will begin to form and new growth will appear from each leaf joint.

Rambling roses Prune the flowered sideshoots hard to encourage more next year.

The new plants can then be separated from the parent plant, potted up individually and grown on.

■ **Complete the summer pruning of wisteria**, pruning all the long, whippy sideshoots to five or six buds from the main stems. This will encourage the plant to produce flower buds for next year's flowers. If you require any growth for tying in to extend the framework of the plant, you can leave it unpruned.

One of the most common questions put to gardening experts is, "Why does my wisteria not flower?" Lack of correct pruning is often the reason given, which rather puts the blame on the gardener. However, the main reason for wisterias not flowering is that they are not named hybrids and have not been grafted. To see if the plant has been grafted, look at the base of the stem to check that there is a slightly swollen area; the point where the plant was grafted. Always make sure you get a named variety. Often some garden centers and market stalls sell unnamed seedlings, which can take many years to flower, if at all.

Clematis 'Lady Londesborough'

PERENNIALS

■ **Chrysanthemums and dahlias** are terrific plants for displaying throughout late summer and fall until the first frost. They also last well as cut flowers. The more you cut dahlias (they make great arrangements in the house), the more flowers you get. But they both have one problem, and that is that the flowers are irresistible to earwigs.

The best way to control these is to put overturned pots filled with straw or shredded newspaper on the top of canes among the plants. Earwigs love to crawl into dark places during the day. In the morning you can empty the pots of earwigs and dispose of them.

■ **Continue collecting ripening seeds** of perennials. Collecting and sowing your own seed is most rewarding aspect of gardening. Collect the seedheads carefully in a paper bag. Spread the seeds on a sheet of paper and leave it to dry. Separate the chaff from the seeds and store them in labeled paper envelopes.

Some seeds can be sown right away, as they germinate best if they are fresh (such as meconopsis, cyclamen, *Aconitum,* and delphiniums), and kept in a cold frame over winter; others can be stored in a cool, dark place until spring.

Ripening cranesbill seeds The seed pods all too readily spring open to disperse the seeds.

Penstemon cuttings Propagate these attractive perennials by taking stem-tip cuttings.

■ **Take cuttings of penstemons,** which do not divide easily like other perennials. Take the cuttings in the same way as for geraniums.

■ **Cut back perennials** that have collapsed or spread over the lawn and other plants in the border. In wet weather, a lot of taller-growing perennials, especially yarrows, tend to flop over and smother other smaller plants. Trim them back from the smaller plants to give the latter a chance to recover and flower. The cut-back plants may also grow again and produce some flowers in the fall.

You may find that perennials that have spread over the lawn will have killed off the grass in that area. Trim the perennials back off the lawn. Give this bare patch of grass a good watering and a dose of lawn fertilizer and it will very quickly regrow.

■ **Cranesbills that were not cut** back earlier should be cut back now to make them look neater. Again, they will produce new growth, which may flower again later in the fall. Fertilize and water them to encourage growth.

■ **Continue to propagate carnations** and pinks by layering. Once the layers produce roots, usually in five to six weeks, they can be separated from the parent plant and planted in their flowering positions. There is no need to use hormone rooting solution as the stems root easily. If you find nicking the stems a little tricky, slightly twist the stem between your fingers until you feel that it is beginning to crack, and peg this part of the stem in the soil.

■ **Start dividing perennials** toward the end of the month. If the soil is dry, wait or water the plants thoroughly an hour or two before and afterward.

Alpines

■ **Take cuttings of alpines.** Many alpines, such as aubretia, *Phlox douglasii*, *P. subulata* and the dwarf helianthemums, can easily be propagated from cuttings. Take small nonflowering shoot tips about 2 in (5 cm) long, removing the lowest leaves, and insert them into gritty potting mix—equal parts peat-free potting mix and perlite or vermiculite, with a handful of horticultural grit added.

Put the cuttings in a warm propagator, spray them daily with clear water to maintain a humid atmosphere and shade in hot, sunny weather, and in five or six weeks they should have rooted. If you're not sure whether they have rooted, give the cuttings the gentlest tug; if there is resistance, roots have formed. The cuttings can then be potted up.

■ **Continue to weed between alpines,** and top off with fresh grit. Grit or gravel around the plants not only makes them look terrific; it also stops rain from splashing soil onto the plants, keeps down weeds, and retains moisture in the soil.

BULBS

■ **Plant daffodils and narcissi** before the end of next month. Daffodils look particularly good when they are planted in drifts, naturalized in grass. Bear in mind, though, that the grass will have to be left uncut for at least six weeks after the flowers are over, to allow the bulb to build up its flower bud for the following spring. Dwarf varieties also look good in rock gardens or in raised beds, where the flowers can be appreciated more easily.

If you are planting the bulbs in a border where you don't need to lift them, always mark them with a label; you may forget where they are after the flowers and foliage have died down, and it's all too easy to accidentally dig them up again.

The general rule for depth of planting for any bulb is to plant two to three times its own depth. If you're not sure, it's better to plant a little too deep than too shallow. If your soil happens to be a heavy clay, add some grit to the planting hole and set the bulbs on this. Bulb-planting tools make the job of planting large quantities of bulbs much easier. Leave tulip bulbs until late October or November before planting.

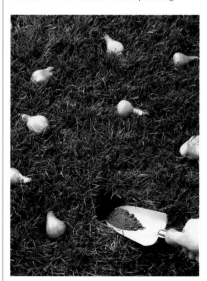

Use a trowel Place bone meal, mixed with a little soil, into each prepared bulb hole.

■ **Plant colchicums** (often misleadingly called the "fall crocus"). The flowers of this bulb appear before the leaves and it can look rather startling on its own, so plant it among other plants or naturalize in grass.

■ **Plant madonna lilies** (*Lilium candidum*). Most lilies are planted from November until the spring, but the madonna lily is best planted this month as it is dormant. It will start into growth next month. The most likely source of these exquisite bulbs is from a bulb specialist by mail order.

Plant the bulbs in a warm, sunny spot in well-drained soil. These lily bulbs must not be planted as deep as you would plant other lilies. Cover the bulbs with no more than 1–2 in (2.5–5 cm) of soil. Always fertilize them after flowering.

■ **Pot prepared hyacinths** and other bulbs such as 'Paper White' narcissi for flowers at Christmas. If you are planting them in bulb bowls with no drainage holes, use bulb fiber; otherwise, any potting mix will do.

Plant several bulbs in a bowl or pot, close enough together so that they are almost touching. Then cover them with potting mix, leaving just the noses of the bulbs uncovered. Next "plunge" the containers outside, covering them with soil, or, alternatively, put them in a cool, dark place. After six to eight weeks have gone by, start inspecting the bulbs every day and when they have made about 1 in (2.5 cm) of growth they can be brought inside into cool conditions.

ANNUALS AND BEDDING

■ **Continue to deadhead annuals** in borders, to prevent the plants' energies from going into producing seeds and extend the flowering period into fall. However, no matter how regularly you deadhead, some of the earlier-sown hardy annuals will be over later in the month. These can be cleared away and consigned to the compost pile. Gaps in borders can be filled with larger plants in pots, either planting or plunging them, to be lifted easily in the fall.

■ **This is the traditional month** for taking cuttings from geraniums, fuchsias, and other tender perennials. They can, of course, be taken at other times from spring through until fall. But if they are taken later than September, don't pot them up until the spring.

The cuttings are very easy to take, only those of geraniums differing in one or two ways. All cuttings should be removed from the parent plant by cutting off strong, nonflowering shoots just above a bud, leaving a cutting about 4 in (10 cm) long. Trim the lower leaves off and then trim the cutting immediately below a leaf joint. With all geraniums, remove the stipules— the little papery flaps—at the base of the leaf stalks. Geraniums do not need hormone rooting solution; they root perfectly well without it. All other kinds of cuttings will benefit from being dipped in hormone rooting solution. Insert the cuttings around the edge of small pots containing seed-starting medium (half peat-free potting soil, half perlite or vermiculite), and cover all kinds with plastic sheeting except geraniums; the fine hairs on the leaves will trap moisture and may cause the cuttings to rot. Place the pots on the windowsill or in a shady part of the greenhouse. The cuttings will root in about four weeks, when they can be potted on to overwinter under cover.

■ **Some hardy annuals can be sown** outside now and next month to overwinter and flower early in the summer next year.

■ **Collect seeds from hardy annuals.** Seed can be collected from most hardy annuals except the F1 hybrids, which will not come true to type. Harvest the seeds on a dry sunny day, into paper bags. Pour them onto a sheet of paper and sort them out from the chaff. This is well worth doing to get clean seeds. Any debris left in with the seeds may cause them to rot, so an old flour sifter can be useful. Store the seeds in labeled paper envelopes. Store in a cool, dry place; an airtight box in the bottom of the refrigerator is ideal.

Drying seeds Spread seedheads on newspaper to dry out before you sift and sort them.

CONTAINERS

■ **Continue watering and fertilizing** bedding plants in hanging baskets, tubs, and other containers. Watering may have to be done several times a day when the weather is very hot. Feed at least once a week with a high-potash fertilizer to encourage plants to bloom well into fall.

■ **Remember also to fertilize permanent** plants like shrubs, perennials, and trees in containers. These need to be cared for just as much as temporary summer bedding plants. They require regular fertilizing and watering, and again, especially with woody plants, feed with a high-potash fertilizer to encourage ripening of the wood rather than the production of soft, weak growth, which may be damaged in winter.

■ **Make sure containers will be cared for** if you are going on vacation. Before you go, group all the containers together in a shady spot, if this is possible. This will make it easier for the person watering, as well as benefiting the plants: a more humid atmosphere is maintained around the leaves where plants are clustered together. In normal circumstances this is not to be recommended, as crowded growth encourages diseases to spread. But it's fine for a week or two. Hanging baskets can be taken down and grouped with the others by perching them on pails or overturned pots.

Fertilizer Add fertilizer to a watering can before feeding container plants.

LAWNS

■ **Continue to mow the lawn regularly,** raising the blades if the weather is very hot and dry. The frequency of mowing can also be reduced in hot, dry weather, as the grass won't be growing much.

■ **Grass clippings can be left on the lawn** in dry weather. Nobody likes grass clippings tracked into the house, and this is easily done when they stick to your shoes in damp weather. But in dry spells, leave the bagger off the mower and the clippings will act as a mulch for the grass, helping to retain moisture in the soil and returning organic matter at the same time.

■ **Apply a fertilizer** with a high phosphate content. In late summer it is not advisable to apply a high-nitrogen fertilizer to a lawn as it will promote vigorous growth, which will not stand up to the rigors of the winter. Fertilizers high in phosphates will instead promote root growth, toughening up the grass for the winter ahead. Apply all fertilizers according to the manufacturer's instructions. A wheeled fertilizer spreader will take the guesswork out of applying the fertilizer and saves the chore of marking out the area to do it by hand. These wheeled applicators can be rented from your local rental center.

Fertilize your lawn If you mark out rectangular areas to treat one at a time, this may help achieve an even spread.

■ **Don't water unless absolutely necessary**. There is no point in watering established lawns, as they will soon recover whenever rain does come. Grass has remarkable powers of recovery.

New lawns

■ **Continue to water** new lawns regularly.

■ **Prepare for sowing seed or laying sod** next month. To create a good lawn from scratch takes a bit of work, but done properly, it is well worth the effort and you will be very happy with the results. Preparation is the key to success; this has been discussed earlier, but it is worth going over some of the points again, as fall is a good time for making a new lawn. There is usually more moisture in the ground, heavy fall dews making a contribution. New lawns need a lot of water. Seed must have water to germinate and grow, and if sod dries out it shrinks. It's impossible to get rid of the cracks along the seams. With the warm, moist weather of fall, you should not need to water new lawns as frequently as during late spring and summer, and the grass will establish before winter, ready to grow strongly in spring.

Dig over the area thoroughly, removing every trace of perennial weeds. Make sure all their roots are removed or they will grow again. Mowing keeps broadleaf perennial weeds down in lawns if you are not too fussy about their appearance, but some cause other problems: thistles, for example, can ruin a lawn as a play area. Leave the soil for a few weeks to allow annual weeds to germinate and then hoe these off, removing them to the compost pile. Preparing the ground a few weeks before you sow seed or lay sod will also allow the cultivated soil to settle, making it easier to level.

VEGETABLES AND HERBS

■ **Sow green manure crops** on vacant ground. If you find it difficult to obtain enough garden compost or farmyard manure to pile on beds, a good substitute is to grow a green manure crop on ground that is vacant. Rapeseed and mustard are fast-growing crops that can be dug in during the fall, before the plants begin to flower and are killed off by frost. Other green manures can be sown then to overwinter. These seeds are easily sown by broadcasting. Just lightly fork over the soil and rake it level, scatter the seeds and rake them into the soil surface. This is an easy way to add organic matter to the soil, improve soil structure and reduce the problem of nutrients being leached from bare ground. By covering the ground with a "living mulch" you also reduce the need to weed it.

Harvesting

■ **Harvest onions when the foliage** collapses, if they weren't ready last month. It is often recommended that you bend over the tops of onions to ripen them, but this happens naturally and there is no need to do it for the plants. Choosing a dry day if you can, gently ease the onions out of the soil to break the roots' hold. Leave the onions on the surface to dry. It's important that they are properly dry if they are to

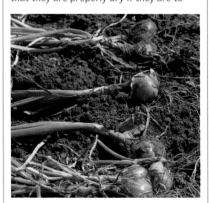
Dry shallots You can place shallots on soil or a chicken wire rack to allow the air to circulate.

Green manure This is a crop that is grown to be dug back into the soil.

store well. If the weather turns wet, cover them with a sheet of plastic or cloches, or lay them out in a shed or greenhouse.

■ **Keep harvesting crops** while they are young, as vegetables have a much better flavor when they are picked young. As they age, flavor and texture become coarser. If summer squash and zucchini are harvested regularly, the plants produce more flowers and fruits to continue the crop well into fall. Summer cabbages should be ready to eat too now; cut them before pests get to them first.

■ **Harvest beans and freeze them.** Fresh vegetables direct from the plant to the kitchen and cooked within a short time have the best flavor of all, but there are times when you get a glut of some crops and can't cope with them all. Freezing is one way around the problem, and most vegetables, including French and runner beans and podded fava beans, can be frozen. This is the perfect way to avoid wasting them. They will provide a welcome vegetable through the winter.

Sowing and planting outdoors

■ **Sow Japanese onions** to harvest in early summer next year. Japanese onions

are also available as onion sets. Before sowing seeds or planting sets, rake down the soil and incorporate a general organic fertilizer. For seeds, take out shallow drills 12 in (30 cm) apart and water the drills if the soil is dry. Sow the seeds thinly along the drills and cover with dry soil. Thin out to 3–6 in (8–15 cm) in the spring. In colder areas it may be useful to cover the young plants with cloches during severe winter weather. Japanese onion sets can be planted a little later than seeds, in October or November. Onions of both sets and seeds should be ready to harvest in July the following year, giving an early harvest before other onions are ready.

■ **Sow some salad crops now.** This is the last month for sowing salad crops outdoors, but it is worth trying a few. Not all of them will mature, but you will at least get some fresh, young salad material in the fall. Seeds to sow include lettuce, radishes, salad onions, red chicory, and spinach. It's even worth trying some peas, sowing an early variety such as 'Douce Provence'. You may be lucky with good weather in the fall. Don't expect to get a great crop, but even a few fresh peas are always welcome.

■ **Continue to sow spring cabbages** at intervals. Sow the seeds in wetted shallow drills, covering with dry soil. Transplant the seedlings when they are large enough to handle. Plant them 6 in (15 cm) apart in rows that are 12 in (30 cm) apart.

Caring for crops

■ **Continue watering and weeding** regularly. The weather can often be very dry in August and it is important to keep vegetables well watered if they are not to bolt and go to seed. Plants like celery and tomatoes need regular watering, or celery will bolt quickly and tomatoes will suffer problems such as blossom end rot (dark brown patches on the base of the tomatoes) due to a lack of water. Irregular watering will also cause tomato skins to split; after a dry spell, if they are given a lot of water, the upsurge of sap in the stems causes the skins to rupture.

Weeds rob valuable moisture from crops. They also act as host plants to pests and diseases, so by keeping them down, problems are reduced.

■ **Look out for pests,** and use a physical barrier to prevent them getting at crops. A second generation of carrot fly is about now, so make sure vulnerable crops are protected. Crops can be grown under floating row cover from sowing to harvesting, as it lets in light and water, but protects plants from insects. Make sure it is tucked into the soil or weighted down, or insects will crawl under it.

■ **Continue earthing up celery.** Blanching makes tough stems more palatable and easier to cook. Draw soil up from either side of the rows until only foliage is showing. Each time this is done, put a collar of paper around the plant to prevent the soil from getting into its heart, causing disease to set in. Self-blanching celery may be left to grow normally.

■ **Summer squash left to grow larger for** storing over winter are best raised off the ground slightly to expose them to the sun to ripen. This will also help to prevent rotting caused by the fruits sitting on damp ground. Support them on a block of wood or a couple of bricks. Remove some of the old leaves so that more sunlight can get at the fruits to ripen them. Harvest before the first frosts in fall.

■ **Stop outdoor tomatoes** when they have produced four trusses of fruits, if this was not done last month. Remove any

sideshoots growing from the leaf axils. Any old foliage can be removed at the same time. Foliage clustered around the trusses of fruit can be thinned too. This will allow more light to fall on to and ripen the fruits and improve air circulation, thus reducing the risk that diseases such as botrytis will take hold and spoil the fruits.

Herbs

■ **Make a sowing of parsley** to last through the winter in mild areas. Sow the seeds in shallow drills outside and thin the seedlings to about 6 in (15 cm) apart when they are large enough to handle. It is worth covering the seeds with row cover to protect them from the second generation of carrot flies, which will be around now. Parsley belongs to the same plant family as carrots and is therefore subject to the same range of pests. Cover the young plants with cloches later in the fall to protect them from the worst of the winter weather. Alternatively, lift a few seedlings and pot them up and grow on in a cool greenhouse or on the windowsill in the kitchen and you will have a supply of fresh parsley at hand through the winter.

■ **Pot up other herbs such as chives** for use during the winter. Lift a clump of chives from the garden; if it is fairly large, split it into smaller clumps. This way you may get several pieces to pot up. Put each piece into a pot with all-purpose potting mix, cut back the old foliage and water them in. Stand on the windowsill or in a cool greenhouse or conservatory and in a few weeks you will have a fresh supply of chives.

■ **Take semiripe cuttings from shrubby** herbs like bay, hyssop, rosemary, and sage.

Pot up chives

1 Dig up a clump of chives from the garden with a spade or fork. Shake off the soil.

2 Pull the clump apart into sections. Use a knife if necessary.

3 Pot up the small clumps individually in small pots of peat-free potting mix.

4 Cut back the leaves to about 2 in (5 cm) and water by standing the pot in a dish or tray of water.

FRUIT

Picking and storing

■ **Harvest early apples and pears.** You can tell when the fruit is ready to harvest as there will be one or two fruits on the ground. A more reliable way is to cup it in your hand and gently twist it. If it is ripe the fruit should part from the tree, stalk intact, with almost no effort at all. If it does not part from the tree, leave it there for a few more days.

Early-cropping apples and pears don't store for very long and they are best used soon after picking. Damaged fruits should be used first if damage is not too severe, otherwise put them on the compost pile.

Caring for crops

■ **Pay attention to fruit trees trained against walls.** The bases of walls can be very dry places indeed, especially if it is a house wall and there are overhanging eaves. So it is vital that these trees are watered regularly. It's amazing how quickly the soil dries out. After watering give the trees a thick mulch of organic matter to help retain the moisture.

Pruning and training

■ **Continue pruning summer-fruiting** raspberries. Cut out the old fruiting canes and tie in the new canes that have grown this year. Any that grow beyond the height of the topmost wire of the support can be pruned back to the top wire in the winter. Any weak canes should be pruned out rather than tied in as they will not bear much fruit. The old canes that have been pruned out can be shredded and then used as a mulch in other parts of the garden. If you don't have a shredder, look for one at your local rental center.

■ **Summer-prune trained fruit trees.** Summer pruning of cordon and espalier forms of fruit trees couldn't be easier; try to get it all finished this month.

Testing ripeness Cup the fruit in your palm and twist it gently. It should drop into your hand.

■ Cordon apple and pear trees should have the side growths from the main stem cut back to 3 in (8 cm). Those shoots that were pruned in the same way last year will have produced sideshoots of their own and these need to be pruned back to 1 in (2.5 cm). This encourages formation of fruit-bearing spurs for next year. When the leading shoot extending the height of the cordon has reached the limit of the support, prune it like the side growths.
■ Espalier and fan-trained trees should be pruned in the same way.
■ Trained forms of sour cherries, nectarines, and peaches need all the shoots growing from the main branches pruned to 4 in (10 cm), and sideshoots from these pruned to 2 in (5 cm).
■ For fan-trained plums, damsons, and sweet cherries, prune back by half all the shoots that have borne fruit.

■ **Finish off summer-pruning** cordon- and fan-trained gooseberries and red currants.

Planting

■ **Plant new strawberry plants** in ground prepared last month, provided you are not in the middle of a drought: if so, wait until September. If your old plants are healthy and show no signs of viral disease, use some of their runners, or plantlets, which you may have pegged down into pots. But if there are signs of virus, which usually shows up as streaks through the foliage, then start fresh with strawberries from a specialty fruit grower whose stock has been certified as being free from virus.

Grow the strawberries on ground that has not grown them for a few years. You can move a strawberry bed in stages—if you have, say, three rows of fruit growing in the vegetable garden, renew one row each year.

Plant the new row to one side of the existing rows and remove the last old row on the other side. Do this each year and you will gradually work your way down the vegetable plot, planting new strawberries in fresh ground each year.

Keep newly planted strawberries well watered. Planting them now enables the plants to build up and get well established before the winter, but if they go short of water this will not happen.

Propagation

■ **Strawberry runners** that were pegged down last month can be cut from the parent plant, either to be planted out or potted up to be forced inside during the winter to get early fruit in the spring. Pot these plants up into 7 in (18 cm) pots and leave them outside for the rest of the summer. In fall, lay the pots on their sides to protect them from the winter wet. After Christmas the pots can be taken inside in stages to provide a succession of fruits whenever they are scarce and expensive at the supermarket.

UNDER COVER

■ **Check that greenhouse heaters** are in working order. Winter may still seem a long way off, but the sooner this job is done, the better. It is better to have portable heaters sent off for a professional service. Permanent electric heating can be checked by a qualified electrician and gas systems should be checked by an engineer. Kerosene heaters need to have wicks trimmed or replaced as necessary and then be thoroughly cleaned.

■ **Damp down regularly during hot, dry** weather. It's been stated many times already, but it is a job that gives a good growing atmosphere to plants and helps to control pests like red spider mite. Soak the floor and under the staging and you will, almost immediately, feel the atmosphere cooling as the water evaporates. Do this several times a day in hot weather.

■ **Toward the end of the month the** nights can turn chilly, so it's worth closing ventilators and doors in the evening to maintain a little warmth. But remember to open up again early in the morning.

■ **At the end of the month,** remove shading. The days start to shorten at this time and plants under glass will need all the light they can get. Clean off shading wash with a dry duster, or remove mesh and shake it out and roll it up neatly for storage. Or consider investing in roller shades for next year. It's an ideal time to do some research.

■ **Continue taking cuttings** from geraniums, fuchsias, and other tender perennials.

Greenhouse and house plants

■ **Start cyclamen now.** Those cyclamen that were rested in their pots during the summer can be started into growth now. They may already be under way, and you will be able to see small buds growing. Start watering the plants now and scrape away some of the old soil from the surface, top-dressing with some new potting mix. This will give the plants a good start. Cyclamen don't require a lot of heat, so putting them in a cold frame for the rest of the summer is ideal; then bring them inside early next month. Occasionally they will produce an early flower or two, but these are best removed to allow the plant to build up strength before the main flowering period in the winter.

■ **Pot bulbs for flowers at Christmas**. The end of the month and early September are the latest times to plant prepared hyacinths and other bulbs to flower in time for Christmas. After about six to eight weeks, inspect the bulbs, and when they have about 1 in (2.5 cm) of growth, they can be brought inside to cool conditions. Then, after a few weeks bring them into the warmth to flower at Christmas.

■ **Start freesias and lachenalias** into growth. Freesias are beautifully scented flowers produced on wiry stems, ideal for winter flowering in a cool conservatory or greenhouse.

Corms of freesias can be planted from now at intervals over the next few weeks to provide a succession of blooms through the winter. Seven or eight corms can be planted in a 5 in (13 cm) pot containing all-purpose potting mix. Cover the corms with about 1 in (2.5 cm) of mix. Plunge the pots outside, and after about six weeks take them inside to flower. After flowering, fertilize the plants until the foliage begins to turn yellow and then rest the corms. Lachenalias are also good plants for cool greenhouses, grown like freesias.

■ **Continue to maintain house plants** by watering and fertilizing. Plants with large decorative leaves will benefit if the foliage is wiped over once in a while. It is amazing how much dust can settle on leaves, reducing the plant's capability to manufacture its foodstuffs from sunlight. This process of turning light into energy, photosynthesis, is essential for survival.

Crops under glass

■ **Continue to remove** old leaves from tomatoes and other greenhouse crops to aid ripening and air circulation. Yellowing leaves can be removed at the same time, otherwise they will encourage diseases like mildew and botrytis. All these leaves can be put on the compost pile. Tidiness in the greenhouse and conservatory will go a long way to reducing pests and diseases.

■ **Sow parsley for a winter crop.** Sow the seeds in pots or trays, watering potting mix before sowing and covering the seeds lightly with more mix. Put in a sunny spot. When seedlings emerge, pot them up individually when they are large enough to handle and you will get a good crop of parsley to see you through the winter.

Sowing seeds in pots Be sure to label your pots carefully, so that you can avoid later confusion.

The September garden

Throughout this month you will be gathering the harvest, and rich fall colors begin to appear—a hint of the glorious shades to come. There is a distinct chill in the morning air and northern regions will have their first frost. With winter approaching, you can start to think about shaping your garden for the year to come, planting new trees, shrubs, climbers, and perennials.

THINGS TO DO

Start clearing fall debris to prevent pests and diseases from overwintering; don't forget to net ponds to keep out falling leaves. Sow or sod new lawns, and dethatch and aerate established ones.

Move evergreen shrubs this month, and stop fertilizing trees and shrubs in containers. Take hardwood cuttings from roses that you wish to propagate for flowering next fall.

Begin dividing overgrown perennials, and make sure you support tall late-flowering ones. Plant spring-flowering bulbs, plant out spring-flowering biennials, and plant up containers with spring bedding plants. Lift tender plants and bring them under cover, or take cuttings.

Harvest your summer squash and the last of the zucchini, and lift the maincrop potatoes. September is the month to plant out spring cabbages and sow winter lettuce. Continue to harvest apples and pears and pick fall-fruiting raspberries. You can now reduce watering and ventilation levels in the greenhouse.

LAST CHANCE

Take the opportunity to force hyacinths for Christmas, plant onion sets and new strawberry plants, and sow spring cabbages.

GET AHEAD

Start to prune climbing roses when the flowers are done, and take time to clean the greenhouse in preparation for winter. Dig over heavy clay soil before the fall rains make it less workable, and sow hardy annuals to flower next year.

Fall is just beginning Crops are ripening now and the last of the early-season apples, such as 'Discovery' and the first of the mid-season crops, will be ready for picking.

A wonderful month

Shortening days are a sure sign that the year is moving on. After you've completed fall harvesting, storage tasks, and all the other jobs that need doing, why not think about putting up a greenhouse, if you have room? Now's the time to make a start so that you can enjoy using it throughout the winter.

September often brings dramatic contrasts to the garden. Its onset may be as sultry as the preceding summer months while its later days mark the official end of summer. The shifting angles of the sun alter summer's patterns of shadow and light, and clear sunny days often give way to cold nights that become frosty by month's end. There are apples, pears, and masses of vegetables to be harvested and stored over the winter. And after the (relative!) lull in activity in the garden during the heat of summer, there suddenly seems to be a lot to do.

Time to take cover

The effects of the shortening days are now quite noticeable. From now on, the climatic differences in the different regions of the country will become more obvious, with the north generally experiencing colder weather and frosts starting early this month. But even in the balmy south, frosts can also start quite early. In southern gardens, September hints at a respite from summer's heat and humidity. Now's the time to plant cool-weather crops like broccoli and kale.

August and September are the traditional months for taking cuttings from tender perennials, such as geraniums, fuchsias, and argyranthemums. The earlier in the month this is done the better, as the cuttings will form roots much more quickly before the cooler weather sets in. Normally these cuttings are first inserted around the edge of pots or in seed trays and then potted on when they have rooted, but if taken at this time of year it is better to leave them in their pots or seed trays over the winter. The plants will get a better start by being potted on when the days begin to lengthen again.

Some people prefer just to give the old plants shelter over winter—for example, in a cool utility room—and then take cuttings when the plants shoot again in spring.

Give yourself a treat

If you're forever trying to find space for overwintering plants, pots, and trays of cuttings and seedlings, maybe it's time to indulge yourself and choose a greenhouse. It may seem rather odd to advise buying a greenhouse at this time of year, right at the end of summer. But it is, in fact, far better to choose one now and have it erected and ready, rather than wait until spring and miss out on all the fun you will have raising your own plants. You could make a start right now by sowing a few winter lettuces. Once you have a greenhouse, you'll wonder how you ever managed without one.

Hyacinth bulbs Summer seems to be barely over before thoughts of next spring begin. Buy spring bulbs for the garden early to get the best choice of varieties.

Harvest your carrots As a rule, if you sow a mixture of early and maincrop varieties from May onward, you should be able to harvest them from June until the end of the year.

Plants for a cold greenhouse

It is surprising what you can grow in even an unheated greenhouse. Alpines, those fascinating plants native to mountain regions, are among the favorites for growing in cold greenhouse conditions. Although alpines endure harsh conditions in their lofty homes, they may languish in a garden. It's not the cold that bothers them, it's wet weather that often causes them to rot.

All the spring-flowering bulbs will flower earlier if grown inside in pots. Hellebores are terrific too; under cover in pots, the beautiful flowers won't be spoiled by rain. Hardy cyclamen also look good under glass. Winter-flowering shrubs can also be grown in a cold greenhouse, at least in their first year. Shrubs such as *Mahonia* x *media* 'Charity' and *Viburnum* x *bodnantense* 'Dawn' have

Weather watch

Summer heat gradually gives way to cooler fall temperatures across much of the country as September straddles the two seasons. The change may be barely perceptible to gardeners in the Deep South, while those in northern regions and higher elevations may see the gardening season's end as frosts arrive late in the month. Fall-blooming flowers such as asters and goldenrods reveal their colors; with ongoing good weather in September, their displays will accompany the fall foliage of deciduous trees and shrubs well into October.

Hurricane season

The Atlantic hurricane season reaches its peak in September, and stormy, unsettled weather may be the result throughout the eastern states. Tropical storms off the East Coast and in the Gulf of Mexico often bring drenching rains to coastal areas; with the right weather patterns in place, these may carry moisture thousands of miles inland. September rainfall, along with cooler temperatures, helps landscape plants recover from summer's relative heat and drought. On the West Coast, the Santa Ana winds keep things hot and dry and may contribute to the risk of wildfires.

Fickle sun

The sun may seem like a fickle friend this month, shining brightly one day and then disappearing behind the clouds for days on end. The gradual shrinking of the daylight hours becomes much more apparent as the month wears on and the angle at which the sunlight strikes Earth changes, too. Although the temperatures may seem like those of April or May, run in reverse, the quality and quantity of the light signals the end of summer and the arrival of fall. On clear days, take advantage of later sunrises and earlier sunsets to walk in your garden and admire the way the sunlight shines through shrubs and ornamental grasses rather than straight down on them.

Winter pansies Plants for winter color and spring bedding will now be available from garden centers in mild-winter regions.

in the garden. If it is left lying around it gives the spores of fungal diseases and other harmful organisms a chance to overwinter in the soil and thus cause more problems the following year. The same applies to pests: they love to crawl into a pile of leaves or into the cracks in tree trunks to hibernate over winter. Paradoxically, it is better if you can leave a small corner of the garden untidy for hibernating frogs, toads, and beneficial insects. A small pile of leaves makes a perfect home for these friendly creatures. Birds are friends, too. Robins feast on slugs and snails, while many birds eat caterpillars and grubs. Although fall is a time of plenty for the birds, winter is not far behind and they will need help to get them through these barren months. Keep bird feeders stocked up and buy (or make) a simple wooden bird table. They are available at many garden centers and nurseries.

In the greenhouse at this time of year, many biological controls will become less effective due to the cooler temperatures—most require a minimum of around 50°F (10°C)—and the best thing you can do to prevent pests from nestling down in the warmth of the greenhouse or conservatory is to give it a good cleaning before winter.

a terrific scent and you can enjoy this to the fullest under glass. Stand well-grown new plants in the garden, then bring them in during late fall and the flowers will soon open up. They can be planted out in spring.

The right greenhouse for you

The choice and size of greenhouse will depend on how deep your pockets are and how big your garden is. The staff of a greenhouse specialty business will be able to advise you on the best size for your garden, as well as the best placement on your property. But try to get the biggest one you can. It is amazing just how soon the space will fill up. Make sure there is good ventilation, with at least one roof ventilator and preferably one in the side. Most manufacturers will add more ventilators on request. It's also advisable to have a power outlet and a faucet put in at the same time as your greenhouse is built.

The manufacturer will arrange for your greenhouse to be erected, but there are some that are not so difficult to put up yourself. If you choose this option, then a greenhouse with a base will make the job much easier.

Don't forget the pests

Pests and diseases can still be a problem at this time of year and now is the time to clear up any diseased material

Plants to enjoy

There are still plenty of routine jobs, such as deadheading, in beds and borders, to be done. At this time of year deadheading is unlikely to extend the flowering performance of plants, but it will make the garden look neater, setting off plants such as dahlias and chrysanthemums, which start looking good now. Many asters will be in flower too. They make a stunning show, if the weather is not too harsh, but some of them are prone to attack from mildew. So keep an eye on them and spray with fungicide before mildew gets a grip.

By September most of the summer bedding plants are past their best and spring flowering plants and bulbs can be put in their place. If you haven't sown biennials earlier, there is usually a good selection available. The sooner they are in and settled, the better they will stand up to the winter—and also flower better in the spring.

It may be the end of summer and the days may be drawing in, but in fall there seems to be a special quality in the light. September mornings can be wonderful, with a clear blue sky and a freshness in the air. Put this together with beautiful fall-flowering plants and plenty of fruit and vegetables to harvest, and life doesn't get much better.

Continuing sunshine So many of the late summer and fall-flowering perennials seem to come in warm shades, as if in preparation for the blazing fall leaf color that deciduous trees will soon display.

***Caryopteris* x *clandonensis* 'Kew Blue'**
Small shrub that enjoys sun and shelter (see p.270)

***Solidago* 'Goldenmosa'**
Clump-forming perennial, good for cut flowers (see p.318)

***Viburnum opulus* 'Compactum'**
Shrub with clustered white flowers, then bright fruits (see p.322)

Eryngium* x *tripartitum
Prickly perennial with sea-green foliage (see p.283)

Clematis viticella
The easiest type of clematis to prune; in spring (see p.274)

***Dahlia* 'Bishop of Llandaff'**
Tender perennial with dark bronze-purple foliage (see p.280)

Plumbago auriculata
Sprawling shrub for a warm wall or conservatory (see p.306)

Stipa gigantea
Silvery, purplish spikelets, which turn gold when they are ripe (see p.319)

Sedum spectabile 'Brilliant'
Perennial, whose flowers are a late treat for wildlife (see p.317)

Agapanthus 'Blue Giant'
Tall bulbous perennial; perfect in a pot (see p.263)

Aster novi-belgii 'Peace'
Michaelmas daisy; a reliable, tall, clump-forming perennial (see p.266)

Rudbeckia 'Herbstsonne'
Perennial; the flowerheads still look good when faded (see p.315)

What to do in September

AROUND THE YARD

Buy or make a compost bin for all the fall debris. It is essential to add plenty of organic matter to the soil to keep it healthy and productive. Growing plants intensively, as we tend to do in small gardens, means that a lot of nutrients are taken out of the soil in a relatively small area. It is therefore essential to put something back in order to continue to get the best out of the garden. Making your own compost is the ideal way of doing this, and although there are plenty of bins to buy, you can make a simple one yourself. Remember to use a good mix of different materials, except woody and diseased material, to make the best compost. If you grow vegetables, they will generate quantities.

Damage from pests and diseases will be slowing down at this time of year, but it is still necessary to be on the lookout to prevent pests from overwintering and becoming a problem next year. Clear any debris in borders, putting it on the compost pile or burning it if it is diseased. Yellowing leaves on plants should be removed as they will encourage mildew and botrytis. Any pests, such as aphids, still around can be dealt with by squashing. Shoots tips heavily infected with mildew or overwhelmed by aphids can become distorted under the attack. Trim these back to healthy growth and burn the prunings.

Take a notebook on walks around the yard. Before the summer display is completely over for another year, it is a good idea to take a stroll around, assessing how plants have performed and deciding whether they need to be moved or removed completely. Sometimes you have to be tough, and if a plant just has not lived up to expectations, then it has to go. There is no point in spending a lot of time and effort in growing something, to find that no matter what you try, it just won't grow well. Or perhaps some colors have clashed and plants need to be moved. It can be fascinating thinking up new plant color themes and contrasts. Don't forget, too, that foliage plays an important part in any display and dramatic effects can be created by putting together a range of different leaf shapes, colors, and sizes. Variety and continuity can be created with foliage alone.

Cultivating clay soil. This type of soil can be difficult to cultivate, especially if it has not been worked for several years. Now is a good time to dig it, while the soil is reasonably dry. This will give the winter weather plenty of time to help break down lumps of soil, ready for making seed beds or planting out in spring. Roughly dig the soil, incorporating plenty of organic matter, and leave it rough for the winter. To permanently improve the drainage, dig in pea gravel. Combined with the organic matter, this will also raise the level of the soil slightly, making it drain more easily and helping it to warm up faster in spring.

Make your own bin Compost bins are easy to make and provide a great way to recycle kitchen and garden waste. Simply attach chicken wire to sturdy wooden posts, line the bin with thick cardboard to retain heat, and cover the contents with a piece of old carpet.

TREES AND SHRUBS

■ **Fall and early spring** are good times to move evergreen shrubs, while the soil is still relatively warm. Dig around the plant as far away from its base as you can and as deep as you can, to take as good a root system as possible. If it's a large shrub, you may have to enlist the help of a willing friend or family member.

Wrap the roots in burlap or plastic sheeting eased under the rootball to retain moisture. It may be necessary to rock the plant back and forth to work the sheeting under the roots, in which case you will certainly need to ask someone else to help you. Tie the sheet up and move the plant to its new location. Dig a hole big enough to take the root ball without having to cram the roots in. Be sure to plant to the same depth as before.

Put the plant in the hole, pull the wrapping out from under the roots, and gradually fill in the hole. Work the soil right in and gently firm with your foot as you go. Water in well and stake the plant if it is in an exposed place. If there are cold winds, it's worth erecting a windbreak of burlap or fine plastic mesh on stakes on the windward side of the plant. This will help to reduce evaporation from the leaves.

Planting

■ **Planting container-grown trees and shrubs** in the fall is beneficial in several ways. At this time of year, the soil is still warm and moist. This means that the roots can get established before winter sets in and the plants will get off to a flying start in the spring. Because the soil is relatively moist, there is no need to pay so much attention to watering in the early stages, saving on water and time. Plant them just as you would container-grown perennials, staking trees in addition. Planting of bare-root plants of deciduous trees and shrubs can be done from late fall to early spring, as long as the soil is not frozen.

Planting container-grown plants Check the height of the hole you have prepared against the tree or shrub by using a pole.

Propagation

■ **Take hardwood cuttings of roses.** Roses are normally propagated by budding—grafting a bud of the chosen variety onto a rootstock. This is an easy and quick commercial way of propagating roses. It does, however, have a downside. The rootstock will often produce suckers, which, if left unchecked, will take over the whole bush. Try to remove them when they are still small and can be torn from the plant quite easily. Tearing or pulling them off is better than cutting them out, which makes them regrow. It's just like pruning them. However, there is a way to produce roses that don't produce suckers, and that is by taking hardwood cuttings.

Select a shoot of about pencil-thickness and about 12 in (30 cm) long. Remove the soft growing tip and all but the top three sets of leaves. Trim the base of the cutting immediately below a leaf joint, making the cutting about 9 in (23 cm) long. Make a slit trench in the ground and, if your soil is heavy clay, put some sharp sand in the bottom of the trench to assist the drainage process. Set cuttings along the trench to two-thirds of their length and firm in. They will root and be ready to transplant to their flowering positions next fall.

CLIMBERS

■ **Plant new container-grown climbers.**

■ **Start pruning climbing roses.** Do this when the flowers start to fade. If they are still going strong, wait until next month. To prune (see below), first of all remove any dead or diseased wood. Then look for any new shoots, especially those growing from the base of the plant, for tying in. If there aren't many new basal shoots, prune all the sideshoots from the existing framework of branches to two or three buds. If possible, completely remove any very old stems, pruning them to near ground level. New shoots can be tied in to replace these.

Pruning climbing roses

First remove any dead, damaged, and unhealthy-looking stems and dispose of the prunings.

Tie in shoots that can extend the framework and prune others back to two or three leaves or buds.

PERENNIALS

■ **Plant new perennials.** This is a good time of year for planting new perennials. The soil is moist and still warm enough for the plants' roots to become established before the winter sets in. Garden centers should have a good selection of flowering and foliage herbaceous perennials available. It's fun going around deciding what plants to buy and taking them home. Perennials are generally inexpensive— and, of course, the plants can be lifted and divided and cuttings taken, in years to come, to produce more plants for free.

Choose plants carefully, making sure they are right for your garden and for the position they are intended for. It's a waste of money to buy something just because it is appealing, only to find it struggles or even dies because it was a bad choice. Look for plants with strong, healthy growth, with the rootballs showing plenty of roots, but not so packed that the plants are potbound. If you don't want to turn the plant out of its pot (though no good nursery should mind your doing this) then at least make sure that no roots are emerging from the drainage holes at the bottom. Water the plants well before and after planting. If they seem rather dry when you buy them, plunge them in a pail of water to thoroughly moisten the rootball.

■ **Keep collecting seeds from perennials** as they ripen. Be vigilant, otherwise the seeds will be spread as soon as your back is turned.

■ **Cut down and divide perennials** that have finished flowering and are not looking good. Most perennials look rather shabby when the flowers have faded, and the best thing to do is to cut them down and make the borders look tidier. At the same time, any clumps that are becoming old and bare in the center should be lifted and divided. Some plants, such as sedums, thrive on

Dividing perennials If you are using forks to pry tough clumps apart, push down on the metal hasps that form the lower part of the handle. This will avoid breaking the handle where the wood joins the hasp.

being divided every year, and others, like peonies, really resent being disturbed. It's very difficult to give general advice. There are so many thousands of perennials now available to gardeners that it is well worth treating yourself to a really good reference book on the subject—or perhaps putting one on your birthday list this year.

Clumps that need dividing can be lifted with a fork and placed on a sheet of plastic on the lawn. Divide large clumps with two forks back to back pushed into the center of the clump, prying them apart. Smaller pieces can be pulled apart by hand. Revitalize the soil with plenty of organic matter and plant the smaller pieces in groups of three, five, or even more, if you have the space.

If you don't have time to divide clumps of herbaceous perennials now, it can be done throughout the fall and into spring, as long as the soil conditions are good enough to work. But if you can't start the work, it is a good idea to go out and make notes about the plants to be divided or moved. Sometimes, no matter how expert we like to think we are, some plant associations just don't work. Color combinations are

easy to plan using photographs (though you can still occasionally miss getting the effect you were hoping for), but getting the heights and relative vigor of neighboring plants right can be more tricky. The one advantage of growing herbaceous perennials is that most are easily moved if this happens and they don't take many years to get reestablished.

■ **Tall-growing clumps of asters** will need support or they will be blown down in windy conditions. There are many different ways to support plants. The wire supports available from garden centers are popular and do a good job, but these have to be put in place while the plants are young and can grow through them. The easiest way to provide support now is by using canes and string. Put three or four canes around the plant and wind string around the canes to enclose all of the stems. If it's done carefully the canes and string will be almost hidden by the foliage of the plant.

Alpines

■ **Any plants that have outgrown their space** can be moved this month. This will give them plenty of time to settle in before the winter. Water the plants well before transplanting and lift them carefully, with a good ball of soil around the roots. Plant in the new position to the same depth as before, firm in well and water in to settle the roots. If the weather is dry, keep an eye on the plants and water them regularly (perhaps once a week) until they are established. Mulch the plants with grit to help winter rains drain away.

BULBS

■ **Continue planting spring-flowering bulbs.** This is the main month for planting spring-flowering bulbs, except for tulips. Look for chionodoxas, ornithogalum, scillas, puschkinia and *Iris histrioides*, as well as corms of the many varieties of *Anemone blanda*. Grape hyacinths (*Muscari*) are essentials too.

■ **This is the latest month for planting** bulbs to flower at Christmas. But continue planting spring-flowering bulbs in pots.

Dwarf bulbs in pots are particularly appealing. There are plenty of daffodils to choose from, among them *Narcissus tazetta*, with yellow and white scented flowers; 'Jack Snipe', with creamy yellow petals, and 'Minimus', with yellow flowers. Other dwarf bulbs to try include species tulips, such as *Tulipa tarda*; chionodoxas, crocus, and dwarf iris.

■ **Plant bulbs to naturalize in grass** Bulbs always look pleasing growing in lawns. All bulbs, with the exception of the tiniest alpines, can be used in this way. For smaller bulbs or corms like miniature daffodils and crocus, the easiest way to plant them is to lift a piece of sod and place the bulbs in groups on the soil, replacing the sod afterward. With larger bulbs, use a bulb planter rather than trying to dig individual holes. To get an informal drift of bulbs in grass, scatter a handful of bulbs over the area and plant them where they fall. The general rule is to plant them two to three times their own depth.

■ **Toward the end of the month, lift gladioli** When the leaves start to turn yellow, it is time to lift the corms before frost damages them. Lift them carefully, as the corms are usually surrounded by cormlets and these can be saved and grown on if you are intending to increase your stock. Leave the old foliage on until it

Scilla sibirica

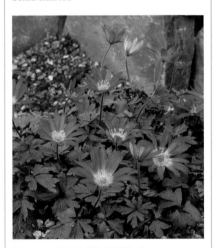
Anemone blanda **'Violet Star'**

has dried off and then cut it off 2–3 in (5–8 cm) above the new, main corm above the remains of the old one.

When the corms have dried, twist off the old corm, dust the base of the new one with sulfur to prevent the spread of disease, and store them in a cool, dry place. The cormlets can be separated out and stored in envelopes along with the other corms. These can be "sown" in trays in spring, just like seeds. It doesn't matter which way up they are; they are so small that the shoots will find their own way to the surface.

ANNUALS AND BEDDING

■ **Sow hardy annuals for flowering next year.** Some hardy annuals can be sown outside now for flowering next year. Sown now, the plants will flower from early May the following year. To sow, rake the soil to a fine tilth and mark out informal areas with a stick or sand poured out of a clean, dry wine bottle. Take out shallow drills within each marked area and water them if the soil is dry. Sow the seeds thinly and cover with dry soil. When the seedlings are about 1 in (2.5 cm) high, thin them out to about 4 in (10 cm). In spring you may have to thin them again. Look on the back of seed packets for those annuals that can be sown outside in August and September; they include *Calendula officinalis*, *Centaurea cyanus*, *Limnanthes douglasii*, California poppies (*Eschscholzia*), and *Papaver somniferum*. If your soil is heavy clay, seedlings may rot. Sow the seeds in cell packs and overwinter them in a cold frame, planting them out in the spring.

■ **Lift tender perennials** before fall frosts begin. Plants like argyranthemums, gazanias, lantanas, osteospermums, geraniums, and arctotis will have to be lifted and taken under cover for protection. Give the plants a trim, removing yellowing leaves and spent flowers; if they are a bit large for the space, don't be afraid to prune quite hard. If space is really limited, pack them closely into boxes and cover the roots with potting mix. Otherwise, pot them up and keep in a cool but frost-free place over winter. High temperatures will induce spindly growth. Keep them on the dry side, too, giving them just enough water to keep them alive until better weather and longer days come along. Some of the plants can be replanted next year just as they are. But others, like geraniums, are much better grown from cuttings each year. Cuttings can be taken either now or in the spring.

Clearing Bedding plants don't have time to root very deeply and are easy to rake out.

■ **Plant out spring-flowering biennials,** in nursery rows through the summer. Clear old summer bedding away when the flowers have faded. This is the time to incorporate organic matter into the soil. Afterward, rake the soil level and mark out informal drifts with a stick. Plant groups of each kind of plant in each drift for best effect. Make sure the crown of each plant is level with the soil and firm them in well. Water plants in to settle the soil around the roots. If you haven't been able to grow your own biennials, garden centers should have a selection available. Plants to look for are wallflowers, forget-me-nots (*Myosotis*), bellis, canterbury bells (*Campanula medium*), sweet Williams (*Dianthus barbatus*), foxgloves (*Digitalis purpurea*), anchusa, Iceland poppies (*Papaver nudicaule*), ornamental cabbages, and winter-flowering pansies.

Remember: don't grow wallflowers and ornamental cabbages in the same ground as last year. They belong to the brassica family and, like brassica crops, are subject to the disease called clubroot (a swelling of the root system), which is very infectious and persists in the soil. Rotate them just as you would brassica crops.

CONTAINERS

■ **Continue to care for bedding plants** by deadheading and fertilizing to extend the display until the first frosts.

■ **Stop fertilizing permanent plants** growing in containers. Plants like shrubs, trees, and fruit trees growing in containers will, if fed, produce soft growth now, which may be damaged in winter. So stop feeding them with general fertilizers now. One last application of sulfate of potash or rock potash will benefit them by ripening the wood, making it more able to stand up to the rigors of winter.

■ **Move pots of tender perennials** like fuchsias and geraniums under cover, to be kept over winter in a cool frost-free greenhouse or conservatory.

■ **Once summer bedding plants in containers** have come to the end of their time they can be cleared out and spring bedding plants planted in their place.

Remove some of the old soil and put in some fresh. The choice of plants and color schemes is entirely personal, so let your imagination run riot. If you haven't raised your own spring bedding like wallflowers, forget-me-nots, and bellis yourself, garden centers will have a wide range to choose from. Remember to plant bulbs in with the spring bedding too.

■ **Plant bulbs in containers** There is no need to renew the potting mix when summer bedding has been pulled out, as bulbs will thrive well in the old medium. The most important time to fertilize bulbs is after they have flowered, when they are building up to flower again the following year. Pack the bulbs in as close to each other as you can, planting them between two and three times their own depth. Use one kind, or color, of bulb for each container, to make a stunning show.

LAWNS

■ **Keep up with lawn mowing** as cooler temperatures and increased rainfall prompt new growth.

■ **Fall maintenance** Toward the end of the month, most gardeners start the annual round of work on the lawn to reinvigorate it. If you just have too much else to do in the fall, it is fine to do it in the new year.

■ **Remove thatch from the lawn** Over a period of time, a layer of dead grass and other debris accumulates in any lawn; this is called thatch. If it is left in the lawn over the years, it restricts air movement around the grass and can cause problems with surface drainage, encouraging moss and other weeds to colonize the lawn. From late August through the fall, begin to remove this thatch. It can be done in several ways, the most back-breaking method being to drag it out with a spring-tined rake. Use this tool to rake out the dead grass and moss. It can be very hard work and it is easier to use a powered dethatcher if you have a large lawn. These can be rented and you will find it relatively easy to remove all the thatch with little effort. Be warned, the lawn will be an absolute mess when dethatching has been done, but it will do it a world of good and it will soon recover.

■ **The next job to be done is aeration** Like any other plant, grass needs air, and the surface of the lawn gets very compacted over the summer, with constant use and cutting every week. To relieve this compaction, aerate the lawn with a fork pushed into the ground, to a depth of 6 in (15 cm), at 6–9-in (15–18-cm) intervals over the whole area. Again, if you have a large lawn, machines can be rented to do this job too. Some of these remove a small core of soil, which is of particular benefit if you have heavy clay soil.

■ **Top-dress immediately after aerating**
Top-dressing ensures that aerating holes stay open and revitalizes the upper layer of soil. A mix of three parts sifted garden soil, two parts of sharp sand, and one part sifted garden compost (or old potting mix, if you have some) is the best top-dressing to use. If your lawn is a bit worn, mix in some grass seed with the top-dressing mix. Spread a ½–1-in (1–2-cm) layer over the lawn and work it in with a stiff broom or with the back of a rake. It will look messy for a couple of weeks, but the grass will soon grow through again.

■ **Patches of broadleaf weeds** can be treated with a lawn weedkiller in fall or in spring. Make sure you use a selective weedkiller especially formulated for lawns,

otherwise you will damage the grass. Always use these chemicals strictly according to the manufacturer's instructions on the packaging.

■ **Established lawns can be fed now** unless you did so last month. Don't use up any high-nitrogen fertilizers that you were using earlier; at this time of year, it is better to use one of the low-nitrogen fertilizers sold as fall lawn treatments in garden centers, as you don't want to encourage soft, weak growth.

■ **Reseed worn patches on the lawn** Small bare patches can be easily repaired by sowing seed. Rake out any thatch and then roughen the surface slightly with a fork to make a fine tilth and level it. Put the

grass seed in a bucket and mix in an equal quantity of old potting mix or sifted garden compost. Spread this mix evenly over the bare patch and tamp it down with the back of a rake. To encourage quick germination, cover the area with plastic sheeting pegged into the ground. Keep the patch watered if it gets dry and the seed should germinate in two to three weeks. Remove the plastic sheeting as soon as the shoots begin to show.

New lawns

■ **Sow grass seed or lay sod** Although grass seed can be sown and sod laid at almost any time of the year, by far the best time is in early fall. If you have not already prepared the ground, do it as soon as you can now, digging over thoroughly and

Laying sod

1 Start from a definite edge, whether defined by a hard surface or a line. Butt the sod sections together tightly.

2 Lay the next row with staggered seams. Almost overlap the pieces and press them down with your fingers.

3 Once all of the pieces are laid, it is worth going over them, tamping down the joints with the back of a rake.

4 Cut edges as necessary with a half-moon edger. A garden hose or rope can be used to mark out curves.

5 Walking backward, brush up the grass with a stiff broom to stimulate its growth, especially across joints.

6 Water really thoroughly with cans or a sprinkler and keep the sod well watered until fall rains come.

removing all trace of weeds. After that, preparation up to a certain point is the same, whether you are sowing seed or laying sod:

■ Roughly level the soil with a rake to break down the lumps.

■ Then step down the ground with your weight on your heels, keeping your feet close together.

■ Rake over the soil and then step it down again, this time shuffling across it at right angles to the first time. Stand back and squat down to look across the soil surface and spot any hollows and bumps that should be taken out.

■ Finally, rake the soil to a fine tilth as if preparing any seedbed.

Now, either sow seed or lay sod:

■ Sow grass seed according to the specifications on the back of the packet. If you are sowing by hand you can mark out the area in square yards (meters) with string and canes to make it easier. Measuring the amount for each square into a small plastic cup once and using this as a guide will save a lot of time; you won't need to weigh out all the seeds each time. An even quicker way to sow is to use a fertilizer spreader. Detailed instructions for sowing seeds with this will come with the spreader.

■ Lay sod by rolling it out and butting it up close, so there are no gaps. Lay it in the same pattern house bricks are laid in, so that none of the seams line up. This ensures that a good bond is made when the sod knits together. Always work outward, from boards placed across the sod that has already been laid. Water well and keep it watered if necessary, but keep off the new sod as much as possible for four or five weeks, to allow it to establish.

VEGETABLES AND HERBS

■ **Cut down asparagus foliage** now that it is turning brown. Be careful, as there are sharp spines on the stems. Then give the plants a generous mulch of organic matter. This is also a good time to prepare a site for planting new asparagus crowns next spring. If your soil is heavy clay, it is worth ordering grit to incorporate into the soil to improve drainage, as asparagus likes well-drained soil.

Harvesting

■ **Harvest the last of the globe artichokes,** cutting only buds that have not started to open up.

■ **Pick summer squash, pumpkins, and squashes.** Leave them in the sun for a couple of weeks, or put them in a greenhouse to ripen and dry off before storing them in a cool, dark place. They should keep until well after Christmas. Clear the old plants away as soon as the fruits have been picked, as they will by now almost certainly be mildewed.

■ **Begin lifting root vegetables** for storing. Vegetables like beets, carrots, and turnips can be lifted and stored for use over the winter. Parsnips are best left in the ground as they taste better when they have had a bit of frost on them.

To store all the others, select only undamaged roots. Any damaged ones should be used right away and not stored, as they could spread disease. Lift the roots and twist or cut off the foliage, leaving an inch or two of stem. Put the roots in boxes between layers of sand or old potting mix. This precaution prevents them from drying out too quickly and keeps them in the dark, discouraging growth. Make sure they are in a frost-free place. Inspect them regularly and throw out any that are showing signs of rot.

Asparagus fern Female plants will produce bright berries among the ferny foliage.

■ **Lift maincrop potatoes** at the end of the month. Lift them on a warm, sunny day and leave them on the surface to dry out. Again, store only undamaged ones, in paper sacks tied at the neck, in a frost-free dark place. Potatoes must be kept dark, otherwise they turn green.

■ **Get onions under cover.** Lift and dry any still in the ground and bring them into a cool, dry storage area before damp fall weather sets in. In mild areas, if onions are left in the ground after the leaves have faded, they may start to regrow.

Sowing and planting outdoors

■ **Sow a winter variety of lettuce.** Sow in shallow drills in the usual manner and cover with cloches. The seeds will germinate quickly and when the seedlings are large enough to handle, thin them out to about 6 in (15 cm) apart. Harvest from January onward. A good old reliable favorite is 'Winter Density'.

■ **Plant garlic.** Fall is the traditional time for planting garlic as it needs a period of cold weather to grow well. To get good-quality crops, buy bulbs specially cultivated for planting. Plant in a sunny site in well-drained soil. In heavy soil, dig in some horticultural grit to aid drainage. Break each bulb into individual cloves and plant each one 3–4 in (8–10 cm) apart, with 12 in (30 cm) between rows. Plant so that the tips of the cloves are just below soil level.

To get the plants off to a quicker start, plant them in cell packs with large cells and keep these in a cold frame for the winter, or place them at the base of a sheltered wall. The plants can then be put in the ground in the spring.

■ **Plant out spring cabbages** sown last month. These can be planted 6 in (15 cm) apart in rows 12 in (30 cm) apart. Harvest every other plant as spring greens, leaving the others to head up.

There is still time to sow a fast-maturing variety like 'Duncan' or 'Pixie' under cover. To get them off to a good start, sow the seeds in modules, so that when it comes time to plant them out, the roots are not disturbed and the plants will get away without a check to their growth.

■ **Earth up trench-grown celery** for the final time, leaving just a tuft of foliage poking out at the top. Blanching has the effect of making the stems more tender. Keep some straw or row cover handy and throw it over the tops of the plants if severe frost is forecast over winter. Harvest the last of the self-blanching celery before the first frosts.

■ **Plant fall onion sets** In warm winter regions, plant short-day onion varieties in the garden now for late spring harvest. Plant them 3 in (8 cm) apart in drills deep enough to just cover the tip of the sets. Apply a general organic fertilizer in spring to boost growth.

Planting onion sets

Make a shallow drill 1 in (2.5 cm) deep and position sets 3 in (8 cm) apart.

Firm the soil around each set so that the tips are only just visible.

■ **Keep harvesting tomatoes and peppers** as they ripen. Use floating row covers or old sheets or blankets to protect tender plants from early, light frosts. Often warmer weather will follow an early cool period, and saving your plants from those first frosts will let you enjoy their fruits for a few more weeks. When ripening comes to a halt, and before a killing frost is expected, gather any fruits that have reached full size and bring them indoors to ripen. Let nature take its course with the plants and clean up the debris afterward.

FRUIT
PICKING AND STORING

■ **Toward the middle and end of the month,** fall-fruiting raspberries come into their own. These late-fruiting varieties are delicious, often more concentrated in flavor than their summer counterparts. Once the fruit is picked, leave the canes unpruned until late winter or early spring.

■ **Blackberries ripen in succession** over a much longer period than other soft fruits, and if you have only a few plants it can be frustrating trying to gather enough for a good meal. The trick is to freeze them in small batches until you have collected enough—raspberries, blackberries, and hybrid berries all freeze very well.

■ **Continue harvesting fruit** as it ripens. Cooking varieties of apples and pears will not be ready for picking until near the end of the month and into October. Handle all fruits as gently as possible as the skins are easily bruised and this can adversely affect their keeping qualities. Store only those that are unblemished. Fruits showing damage should be used right away or kept away from the main storage area. Large crops of apples should be individually wrapped in paper (old newspaper is handy

Conserving apples Wrap apples or leave them unwrapped, but make certain that the fruit are not touching—otherwise they will deteriorate.

for this purpose) and laid on trays in a single layer. Smaller quantities can be stored in plastic bags. Poke a few holes in the bags to let out gases given off by the fruits—this will hasten the ripening process. Pears are best left unwrapped, standing on slatted benches. Pick early dessert pears while they are still hard and let them ripen indoors.

Caring for crops

■ **Strawberries** that were planted last month need to be kept well watered.

■ **Protect ripening fruits** from birds and wasps, who like the sweet, ripening crops just as much as we do. Netting is the only way to keep birds off fruit trees, but it must be well secured to prevent them from getting trapped. If you can, grow all your fruit in a fruit cage made specially for the purpose. Be wary of wasps as you pick up spoiled windfalls and scatter them on bare ground in the vegetable garden for wildlife. Plums are a favorite with butterflies, who love to feed on the sugary juice.

■ **Prune off mildew-infected** shoots of apples and pears. Mildew often attacks

Fruit cages These are necessary to protect your crops from birds. You can buy cages in kit form or make your own by wiring sturdy stakes together and draping netting over.

trees at this time, and once it takes hold, spraying with a fungicide is next to useless. Fungicides should be used in the early part of the season before the mildew appears as a preventive measure. Now the only remedy is to prune off the infected shoots and burn them or put them in the trash. Don't shred them or throw them on the compost pile or the spores of the mildew will be spread around the yard.

Pruning and training

■ **Finish cutting out fruited canes** of summer-fruiting raspberries. Take care not to get them confused with the fall-fruiting raspberries, which will be ripening this month.

■ **Prune blackcurrants.** From now through the winter, blackcurrants can be pruned, if you wish. In the past the practice was to prune blackcurrants as soon as the fruits had been picked. But at that time the plants are still in full leaf, the foliage manufacturing plant foods. Early pruning takes off a lot of leaves, reducing the plants' capacity to manufacture this food; and it is also more difficult to see what you are doing. It is far better to leave the pruning until the leaves have begun to fall in the fall and in winter, when you can see what you are doing more clearly.

Planting

■ **Finish planting new strawberry plants** before the end of the month. This is the latest they can be planted to allow them to get established before winter sets in. The plants must have time to establish and form a good root system to crop successfully the following summer. However, if they get too little water, this will not happen and they will not be able to fruit very well next year, so if the weather is dry, they need plentiful watering. Plants

Trimming When planting strawberries avoid bending or constricting the roots by trimming them first to no less than 4 in (10 cm).

that are under stress due to lack of water are also more vulnerable to attack by pests and diseases.

Strawberries are not a permanent crop like other fruits, so if you can, grow them in the vegetable garden, where they can be rotated like the other crops.

■ **Plant container-grown peaches and nectarines** in a sheltered spot. Planting now, in the fall, will give the plants a good chance to become established before winter. Prepare the soil by digging it over and incorporate plenty of farmyard manure or garden compost.

Dig out a hole big enough to take the rootball and deep enough to plant it at the depth it is in the container. Make sure the point at which the tree is grafted (a swollen part of the stem near the base of the tree) is above ground level.

The rootstock onto which the tree is grafted controls the vigor of the tree. Gently replace the soil in stages, firming as you go. Water in if the soil is dry, and if the tree is being trained against a wall or fence, tie it to its supports.

UNDER COVER

■ **Remove shading** Clean off shading washes, give blinds a shake or brush before rolling them back, or fold and store shading curtains. From now on, plants under cover need all the light they can get.

■ **Check the glass and putty** in the greenhouse to see if repairs are needed. Replace broken panes of glass. It is surprising how much heat can be lost through cracks.

■ **Start preparing the greenhouse for winter** Toward the end of the month, but before tender perennials are brought inside for the winter, take all the plants outside and thoroughly clean the place. Get it done this month, so that if it takes more than a day, the plants can be left outside overnight without fear of their being harmed by frosts. Make sure you get into every little corner, where pests hibernate and lay eggs. A hose-down with a jet of water, inside and out, is ideal initially; then, wash down with a weak solution of household bleach. Then rinse down again. Be sure to cover power outlets and remove appliances. Switch off the electricity completely. If there are any problems, call an electrician before turning it on again.

■ **Reduce watering and ventilation** Now that the nights are getting cooler, reduce watering and water early in the day. This allows the greenhouse to dry out before the cooler evenings, reducing the chance that diseases such as mildew and botrytis will take hold. Ventilators should be closed now at night, but opening them on mild days to keep air circulating will help reduce disease infection.

■ **Bring in tender plants** to overwinter. Plants like geraniums, argyranthemums and lantanas should all be brought inside now. With these plants inside, the greenhouse can seem as packed as it was in the spring, but most will be quite happy under the staging, where it is cool. Be careful when watering, giving just enough to keep the plants alive until the spring. Inspect them regularly and remove yellowing or diseased leaves before infection spreads.

Raising plants for outdoors

■ **Sow the last spring cabbages** There is still time to sow fast-maturing spring cabbage varieties like 'Duncan' or 'Pixie'. They are best sown in modules.

Greenhouse and house plants

■ **Bring houseplants indoors** that have been standing on the patio or on greenhouse shelves for the summer.

■ **Continue planting winter- and spring-flowering** bulbs in pots. Get prepared hyacinths and other bulbs in before the end of the month if they are to flower at Christmas, but non-prepared hyacinths and plenty of other bulbs will provide a continuity of blooms until spring. Plunge them outside under compost or leafmold, or put them in cool, dark place to form roots. The formation of a good root system first is the key to getting a good display from forced bulbs.

■ **Sow hardy annuals in pots** to flower under cover during spring. Sow your own seeds collected in the summer. Sow a few seeds thinly in each 5-in (13-cm) pot and cover with a thin layer of potting mix. The seeds will germinate fairly quickly and can be kept in a cool greenhouse over winter. Don't give them too much warmth or they will produce weak growth with the lack of light. Just keep them watered. If you sow at two-week intervals you will have plants in flower for longer.

Pick tomatoes Wait until your tomatoes separate easily from the truss before you harvest them.

Crops under glass

■ **Pick tomatoes, peppers, and eggplants** Continue harvesting tomatoes as they color up. Removing some of the leaves from around the trusses will let more light in, hastening ripening. This will also increase air circulation around the plants, reducing the risk of botrytis. The leaves are removed easily: snap them off by putting your thumb under the leaf stalk close to the main stem and pushing upward. Then give a sharp push down and the leaf will come away cleanly. Fertilize and water regularly or some fruits may split.

Harvest peppers regularly. They can be harvested green, so don't worry if they don't color up. If you are growing the chili type, the riper they get, the hotter they will be. If there are fruits still to ripen at the end of the month, remove the plants from the pots, shake the soil off the roots, and hang them in a warm place with fruits still attached; they will soon ripen.

Eggplants should be picked when the fruits are well colored, but the skin still taut. If they are left longer and the skin begins to wrinkle, they will taste bitter. They are harvested by cutting the stalk at least 1 in (2.5 cm) away from the fruits. They don't keep for long.

The October garden

Fall colors are at their best this month; be sure to make the most of them, since they pass very quickly, and before you know it, it's winter again. Enjoy observing the garden birds that will be attracted to the bright fruits and berries displayed by your trees and shrubs. Make sure you keep your garden as neat as possible, and you'll be ready for the winter months ahead.

THINGS TO DO

Rake up fallen leaves and pile them up to make leafmold. Continue clearing up the garden, and burn or discard any debris that shows signs of fungal infection. Dig over empty areas of soil, and make new lawns from sod. Clear fallen leaves out of ponds and remove pumps for the winter.

Finish planting evergreen shrubs, and take hardwood cuttings from all the shrubs and fruit bushes you wish to propagate. Now is the time to collect berries from trees and shrubs for seed-sowing. You can give conifer hedges a last trim if necessary.

Plant new climbers, perennials, and lily and tulip bulbs. Divide any perennials that have become overgrown. Protect alpines from winter rain and lift and store dahlias, gladioli, and summer-flowering bulbs, making sure you label them first.

Cut down the dying tops of perennial vegetables; you can also lift and divide rhubarb this month. Fixing sticky bands to apple and pear tree trunks will catch pests that crawl up them. Don't forget to insulate the greenhouse and check that your greenhouse heaters are in good working order.

LAST CHANCE

Sow grass seed and finish planting spring bedding; lift and store tender perennials. Harvest apples and pears before they are damaged, and lift and store your potatoes and carrots.

GET AHEAD

Prepare the ground for planting bare-root stock next month. Make early sowings of fava beans for next year; you can also sow sweet peas under cover, to be potted up in spring.

A rich show The brilliantly colored berries of *Cotoneaster salicifolius* 'Gnom' set against the shrub's dark-green foliage make a rich display in the garden.

Fall richness

The nights are growing longer and temperatures are dropping, but the garden still has much to keep us occupied. Now is the time to plant trees and shrubs, gather the harvest of fruits and vegetables, and collect and store seeds. And don't forget to clean and maintain your greenhouse.

October can bring a richness of color to the garden, with the multitude of different hues displayed by fall foliage. Frosty nights and clear sunny days are typical of this month; these conditions bring out the intensity of the colors in the leaves of deciduous trees and shrubs. "Leaf peepers" take weekend jaunts to follow the dramatic foliage display as it gradually spreads from north to south.

Seeds and fruits The fluffy seedheads give clematis its common name of "old man's beard." Both the seeds and these succulent rose hips are a treat for garden birds.

Sharing with friends

Fruits and berries are an added attraction now, not only to us but to the birds as well. Shrubs such as cotoneaster and trees like the mountain ashes and crab apples are often covered in fruits. But the birds love them so much that often a whole tree can be stripped of berries quite literally overnight. I, for one, don't feel too aggrieved about sharing with these garden friends—though ask me that again in the spring when they've stripped an unprotected fruit tree of buds! Overall, though, garden birds are a joy, not only when they eat pests for us, but also when you witness their feeding and bathing antics and especially when they honor our own green sanctuary by raising their young in it.

Because frosts are quite common now, any tender plants in the borders that you want to keep over winter must now be lifted, potted up, and put into a frost-free greenhouse or conservatory—or if you have room, overwinter cuttings taken from them on the windowsill.

Shortening days

There is less time to garden in the evenings now, so for most people, that means most of the work outdoors must be done on weekends. This leaves little time to get things done, depending on the size of your garden, of course. With some jobs, the earlier they are done in fall, the better. One such is winter digging, especially if you have heavy clay soil. The more time this type of soil gets for the winter weather to break it down, the better, so dig it as early as you can. Don't underestimate the effect wind, rain, frost, and snow will have in improving this type of soil. After a winter of pounding by the elements,

Pumpkin time Whether destined for the table, for show, or for Halloween jack-o'-lanterns, pumpkins benefit from being harvested in advance. Leave them in the sun for a few days to harden, or "cure," the skins and dry off the fleshy stalks.

in spring you will be able to break down the clods easily to make good seed beds. Incorporate as much organic matter as you can into the soil, as this will also help to improve its structure. If you don't have a compost pile of your own, look in the phone book for riding stables and see if you can buy a load of horse manure. It's wonderful stuff and most stables will either charge a very small fee or be only too glad to have you take it away for free.

Time for planting

This is a good month to start planting trees, shrubs, and herbaceous plants, while the soil is still warm enough for the roots to take hold before winter sets in. Any plants that are on the borderline of hardiness are better bought and planted in spring, when they will have a greater chance of survival.

Choose hardy plants that give a good show right now, such as asters, with their daisy-shaped blooms, and crocosmia, which has strappy leaves and tall stems of bright red, orange, or yellow flowers. Mix these with evergreen grasses, such as bronze carex, to inject color throughout the fall and winter. These plants not only give the garden an instant fall lift, but will continue to perform year after year.

Weather watch

Cooler temperatures rule in most regions in October, giving southern gardeners fair conditions for tending fall-planted crops. Crisp, sunny days are on tap in northern regions, with clear blue skies that set off fall foliage to perfection. Clear days also allow for clear nights and accompanying frosts that bring an end to summer's crops of tomatoes, peppers, eggplants, and summer squashes, as well as tender annuals like impatiens. The angle of the sun sinks lower too, so that even brilliantly sunny days remain cooler than the sunny days of midsummer. Sites in your garden that enjoyed full sun in June and July may now be shaded much of the day.

Days shorten

The length of the days continues to shrink noticeably throughout the month, reducing the amount of time children have after school and adults have after work for enjoying the outdoors. As a result, gardening tasks wind up relegated to the weekends and must be strictly prioritized to ensure that essential chores take precedence in the limited amount of daylight available.

Moderate rainfall

With the exception of lingering effects from tropical storms, rainfall in October tends to be moderate in most regions of the country. When rain does fall, however, it brings down a shower of colorful leaves, ready to be raked and added to the compost bin or set aside to break down into leafmold.

Early snow

Snow is not unheard of in mountain regions and across the Upper Midwest and New England; it may arrive early in the month in those parts. By late October a few flakes may swirl as far south as Washington, DC, although rain and almost summer-like warmth are just as likely at that latitude.

Give your greenhouse a good, thorough scrub-down. Tackle all surfaces, particularly any wooden benches. Use a good disinfectant diluted as stated on the packaging, before rinsing down with a hose. Your efforts will help discourage pests.

Bringing in the harvest

Now is the time to gather any remaining fruits, such as apples and pears, before they are damaged by frost. It is easy to tell if a fruit is ripe and ready for picking. Carefully cup the fruit in your hand and, with a gentle upward movement, the fruit should part from the tree easily; if it's not ripe, leave it for a few days and try again. Only store fruit that is not damaged in any way. Storing damaged or diseased fruit will only encourage diseases to spread through the other fruits more quickly, reducing the time they will keep over the winter.

Elbow grease in the greenhouse

Now is a good time to get the greenhouse and conservatory thoroughly cleaned out before the onset of winter. Most plants can still be left outside for the day

and this will make the process of cleaning much easier. Thoroughly clean the glass inside and out to admit the maximum amount of light during the shorter days of winter. Scrub down benches with a disinfectant and, finally, hose the whole place down, paying particular attention to all the corners where pests can lurk and hibernate for the winter.

You may have frost-tender plants that will need some heat at night, so check now to see that all your heaters are in working order. Be careful with electrical heaters; if you are unsure about anything or you suspect there is a problem with your heater, call an electrician. And always use a GFCI (ground fault circuit interrupter). This will cut the current in a fraction of a second if there is a problem with the electrical supply and could save your life.

Seedheads to save

Keep watching for ripening seeds to propagate, and collect them before they are shed. Dry the seeds off and put them in paper envelopes, storing these in turn in an airtight container, which you can place on the bottom shelf of the refrigerator. If you're not sure when to sow the seeds you've collected, it's a good idea to sow half of them now, but store the other half and sow those when spring arrives.

Even if you're not on the lookout for seeds to collect, many plants now have seedheads and pods as beautiful as their flowers. While fall is a time for tidying up the borders, it's also perfectly possible to clear up at ground level without cutting down the tall stems of plants like yarrow and acanthus. If bad weather threatens to knock them down, you can always cut the stems for drying and displaying indoors. But if the weather holds, October can be a lovely month in the garden—so savor it before the onset of winter.

Maple in fall color The maples provide some of the most brilliant foliage tints in fall—from burning yellows through rich reds to bronze-purple.

Nerine bowdenii
Springlike flowers at the end of the season (see p.300)

Sorbus commixta
Deciduous tree with white flowers followed by heavy clusters (see p.318)

Prunus sargentii
Flowering cherry tree with fine fall color (see p.308)

Colchicum cilicicum
Perennial whose funnel-shaped flowers appear before the leaves (see p.275)

Malus 'John Downie'
Narrow, conical tree bearing orange and red fruit (see p.298)

Rhus typhina
The staghorn sumac; a spreading deciduous tree (see p.311)

Acer palmatum 'Corallinum'
A slow-growing tree with long, brilliant pink leaves in spring (see p.262)

Schizostylis coccinea 'Sunrise'
The kaffir lily; an exotic but hardy perennial (see p.317)

Anemone x hybrida 'Max Vogel'
Perennial with pink flowers that fade to white (see p.265)

Amelanchier lamarckii
Shrub or small tree with spring and fall interest (see p.265)

Cotinus 'Grace'
Smoke bush with brilliant fall color (see p.278)

Rosa rugosa
Shrub rose with purple-pink flowers and large hips (see p.315)

What to do in October

AROUND THE YARD

Pests are generally on the decline now that the weather is turning cooler, but diseases such as botrytis and mildew are still quite prevalent with the more moist weather in fall. Practicing good garden hygiene will go a long way toward avoiding problems. Don't leave waste lying around; either compost it or discard it. Diseased material should be burned or put in the trash, never composted. Clear weeds, as they harbor many pests and diseases.

It's not worth using chemical sprays for mildew and botrytis at this time; they are more effective as a preventive measure early in the year. Plants like zucchini and summer squash are particularly prone to both at this time of year. Burn the infected parts as they come to the end of their cropping time.

Rake up fallen leaves at regular intervals from the lawn and among plants in the borders. If leaves are left in a thick layer on the lawn they will kill off the grass. Fallen leaves left lying over and around plants can encourage slugs and snails.

Make a container for fallen leaves Autumn leaves piled up and left to decompose for a year or two will make the most wonderful organic matter to use as a mulch or a soil conditioner, known as leafmold. Leaves can, of course, be mixed with other material and put on the compost pile, but if you want leafmold, then they will need a pile of their own. Make a container with four stakes and chicken wire. Drive the four posts into the ground to make a square and nail the netting around the posts to form the container. The netting helps to keep the leaves in one place. Larger leaves take longer to rot down, but after about 18 months to two years you should have good friable leafmold. Use it as a mulch or dig it in to the soil as you would do with garden compost.

Dig empty areas of soil Digging sounds like hard work and so it can be if you do it all day long, day after day. But it needn't be like that. By this time of year the soil is moist but not too sticky and the weather, generally, is not too warm or too cold—perfect for some exercise. The first point to make about digging is not to rush at it. Take it easy and work at a steady, but not hectic, pace. Work for short periods, perhaps for half an hour at a time, and then take a break or do something else that does not involve bending. Then go back to the digging for another half hour and so on.

Use a good spade that is well balanced. Always pick tools up and handle them for a while before buying. If you can afford it, choose a stainless-steel spade, as it should last a lifetime with little need for maintenance. Don't lift too much soil at a time as this will only cause a backache.

You can sow green manure crops to cover and condition soil that otherwise will be bare over winter. Green manures that will stand through winter, to be dug in in spring, include winter rye, Austrian peas, and hairy vetch.

Raking up Use a rake with long tines to gather up all the fallen leaves. Raking will help improve the lawn as well.

TREES AND SHRUBS

■ **Move evergreen shrubs** This is still a good time to move evergreens, while the soil retains some warmth. At this time of year there will be less need to water plants that have been moved than there would be in hot weather. In exposed areas it is worth erecting a wind barrier on the windward side of the transplanted shrub, as winter winds can cause evaporation from the leaves. This can cause browning, known as "scorch." Deciduous trees and shrubs should be moved when dormant.

■ **Rake up fallen leaves from roses** to prevent black spot spores from over-wintering in them. Do this regularly and burn the leaves or put them in the trash. Don't add them to the compost pile, as the heat may not be sufficient to kill off the black spot spores.

Pruning and training

■ **Tall shrubs such as lavateras** and *Buddleja davidii*, which will be pruned hard in the spring, can be cut back now by about a half their height to prevent wind rock. If plants have a lot of top-growth to catch the wind, they can be blown around and rocked back and forth. When this happens, a hole forms in the soil at the base of the stem, where water collects, causing the stem to rot. In cold weather, the water can

Lavatera **'Barnsley'**

freeze, damaging roots further. Check all newly planted trees, shrubs, and hedging plants and if they are loose, firm them in again and, if necessary, provide a stake.

Planning ahead

■ **Prepare ground for planting** bare-root trees and shrubs next month. If you want long-lasting plants, it is worth preparing the ground well.

If you are planting a border of shrubs and trees, dig over the entire area, removing roots of perennial weeds. Don't leave even tiny portions of roots behind as they will grow again. Dig in plenty of organic matter. If the soil has not been cultivated before, "double-dig" it. Dig a trench at one end of the area and cart the soil to the other end. Then break up the soil in the bottom of the trench with a fork, without bringing the poorer subsoil to the surface. Put organic matter into the trench and mix it in. To make the next trench, throw the soil forward onto the first trench covering the organic matter. Continue the process until the area has been dug. The soil you carted to the end when you began goes in the last trench.

For planting trees and shrubs in an existing border, take out a hole big enough to take the roots without cramping them. Drive a stake into the hole before planting, so as not to damage the roots. Fork over the bottom of the hole to break up the subsoil and mix in organic matter. Plant the tree or shrub to the same depth. Work soil back in among the roots and gradually fill in, firming as you go. Then rake the soil level and water in. Finally, tie the trunk to the stake using an adjustable tree tie.

Propagation

■ **Take hardwood cuttings of deciduous shrubs.** Dig a slit trench by pushing a spade into the soil and then pushing and pulling the handle back and forth. If your

soil is heavy clay, trickle in some sharp sand to improve drainage. Remove shoots of the current season's growth, about 12 in (30 cm) long. For each, trim off the soft growing tip and trim the base of the cutting below a bud. Dip the base into hormone rooting solution. Place the cuttings in the trench to about two-thirds of their length and firm in gently. Label the row and the cuttings will root and be ready to plant out next fall.

Plants to try from hardwood cuttings include buddleja, cornus, escallonia, forsythia, leycesteria, philadelphus, roses (see also September) and weigela.

■ **Collect berries from trees and shrubs.** They generally don't need warm conditions to germinate and most need to go through a period of cold weather to break the seed dormancy. This is called "stratification."

First remove the seeds. Separate the seeds, dry them off, and store in a cool place. Sow the seeds in trays or small pots of multipurpose potting mix, covering the seeds with grit. Place the container outside in a cold frame, or in a sheltered place covered with a sheet of glass or plastic to keep excessive rain out. Alternatively the seeds can be stratified, or given an artificial chilling period. Mix the seed with moistened vermiculite or sharp sand in a plastic bag and place it in a refrigerator. Generally, up to six weeks will be required. Check the seeds regularly, and when you see signs of germination, take them out and sow in trays or pots. Some trees and shrubs to grow from berries: cotoneasters, *Rosa rugosa*, gaultheria, and all sorbus.

Hedges

■ **Trim conifers again if necessary.** Leyland cypress can regrow after trimming in late summer, but can now be trimmed again. Be sure not to cut into old wood, as most conifers will not regenerate.

Planting a mixed hedge Informal hedges can combine flowering and berry-producing, evergreen and deciduous shrubs planted close together. They need little or no pruning.

■ **Plant hedges of evergreen and deciduous plants.** Evergreen plants for hedging should be put in as soon as possible this month; if not, wait until spring. Deciduous hedging can be planted all through the winter if soil conditions allow. Prepare a trench 3 ft (90 cm) wide along the length of the proposed hedge. Dig in generous amounts of organic matter and add a dressing of bonemeal, according to the instructions on the package. Peg out a line along the trench to plant to. Deciduous hedging, such as beech, is usually planted at around 18 in (45 cm) apart and conifers about 3 ft (90 cm) apart. Plant firmly to the same depth as they were previously planted and water them in well if the soil is dry.

If you live in a cold area, protect conifers with a screen of plastic mesh stapled between strong posts for the first year after planting. Make sure new hedges are watered regularly during their first year, while they get established, and feed them with an organic fertilizer in the spring.

CLIMBERS

■ **Prune climbing roses** and get them tied in before harsh weather arrives. Rose stems are stiff compared to those of other climbers and can be snapped by high winds. Clear up all fallen leaves around them carefully and also any leaves that ramblers have dropped. Rose leaves can harbor diseases such as black spot: it is safer to discard them rather than putting them on the compost pile.

■ **Plant container-grown climbers,** provided they are hardy plants that will stand up to their first winter when young. All are planted in the same way as container-grown trees and shrubs, then tied into their support to get going. Dig a deep hole and work some organic matter into the bottom—leafmold and a sprinkle of bonemeal is ideal, as it will condition the soil without adding too much nitrogen at this time of year.

Climbers should be planted so that the surface of the root ball is level with the soil's surface, with the exception of clematis.

Most clematis varieties are prone to a disease called "clematis wilt," which is noticeable when a plant suddenly begins to wilt for no apparent reason. To overcome this problem, it is advisable to plant clematis deeper than is normally suggested for most plants, with part of the stems below the surface of the soil. Plant so that the top of the root ball is up to 6 in (15 cm) below soil level.

If the plant is then affected by wilt, cut it down completely. The portion of stem below ground will have unaffected buds that may send up new shoots from the base of the plant, giving it a better chance of survival.

PERENNIALS

■ **Cut back perennials** that have finished flowering. This will make the garden look much tidier and discourage diseases from attacking old growth. If on some plants the flowers have finished, but the foliage is still quite green and attractive, leave it until it is really blackened by frost. Cutting everything down can leave unsightly gaps in the borders and this should be avoided until as late in the fall as possible. Any soft growth you cut down, such as that of cranesbills, can be consigned to the compost pile. Other growth that is semi-woody will take longer to break down on its own. But the process can be speeded up by shredding the material (rather than burning it, which is the more usual practice). Shredded material can be added to the compost pile to rot down further, or used as a mulch on the borders in spring.

■ **Plant new herbaceous perennials** while the soil is still warm and moist. Prepare the soil well by incorporating plenty of organic matter and adding some bonemeal. There is a wide range of perennials to choose from and attractive displays can be created inexpensively. Perennials will last for many years if they are propagated regularly, by dividing them up and replanting, collecting seed and sowing it, and by taking cuttings and growing them on.

Perennials always look best when they are planted in groups of three or more plants, but if your budget is limited, buy one of each of the varieties you want and then propagate them yourself using whichever methods are most appropriate, so building up the numbers over two or three years.

■ **Lift and divide overgrown clumps of perennials.** Older clumps are easily spotted, as all the young, vigorous growth is toward the outside of the clump and the center is bare. Dividing can be done from now through until spring as long as soil conditions allow. If the soil is so wet that it sticks to your boots, keep off it; likewise later on if it is frozen. Late-flowering perennials like asters are best left until the spring before being divided.

Lift the clumps and separate larger ones with two forks pushed into the center of the clump back to back, pushing the handles apart to separate the roots. Smaller pieces can be separated out by hand. Replant the new pieces after revitalizing the soil with organic matter. Water in well after planting.

■ **Dahlia tubers** will have to be lifted and stored now. Cut the plants from their supports and cut the stems back to about 4 in (10 cm) from ground level. Label each plant before you lift it and forget which variety it is. Use a garden fork to dig carefully around the plant so as not to damage the tubers. Shake off as much of the old soil as you can and then use a hose to rinse off the rest.

The stems of dahlias are hollow and if moisture collects at the base of the stems while the tubers are in storage it will cause them to rot. So the tubers and stems must be turned upside down and left like this for a couple of weeks in a cool, dry place so that any moisture drains from the stems.

After that, box up the tubers in peat-free potting mix, making sure the crowns of the tubers (the point where the stems meet the tubers) are not buried. Small embryo buds are located here and if they are buried they may rot off. You can cover the surface of the potting mix with something loose and dry, such as bark chips, as an extra precaution. Keep them in a cool frost-free place over winter. They can be started back into growth in the spring and will provide cuttings for you to increase your stock before they are planted out.

Lifting and storing dahlias

1 Cut down all of the top growth from the plants (here blackened by an early frost). Lift the tubers and shake or rinse off all soil.

2 Stand them upside-down in wooden trays in a cool, dry place so that they dry off thoroughly.

3 Store them for winter in boxes of dry, peat-free potting mix. To save space, they can be packed more tightly. Make sure the stem is above the surface and space out in spring.

Alpines

■ **Clear leaves from around alpines.** Leaves collecting in among alpines will encourage rots and other diseases to affect the plants. Pick out leaves from around the plants at regular intervals during the fall. Plants that are particularly susceptible to rotting are those with gray woolly foliage, but it's best to keep all plants clear of leaves. A layer of leaves on plants will also exclude any light, making the plants turn yellow and eventually killing them. Don't let leaves lie on top of any plants for any length of time.

■ **Protect alpines from wet.** This is the time of year when alpines will appreciate protection from the wet weather. It's not the cold alpine plants mind but the damp. This is why some alpines are grown in cold greenhouses, where there is no heat in the winter and plenty of ventilation. Specialty alpine houses have extra ventilators fitted to keep a good through-flow of air at all times, but an ordinary unheated greenhouse, or even a cold frame, will make a perfectly good home for alpines.

Of course not all alpines have to be grown in a greenhouse and those growing outside can be protected from the rain quite easily by using a cloche, with the ends left open for ventilation, or a piece of glass or rigid clear plastic supported on bricks. Then weight the sheet down with extra bricks to prevent it from being lifted off by winds. If you have a raised alpine bed, with a little improvisation you can make a mini-greenhouse with open sides to protect the plants through the winter.

BULBS

■ Plant tulip bulbs toward the end of this month and next month. Tulips are more prone to disease than other bulbs and are planted later. The depth of planting for tulips is about twice to three times their own depth. In heavy clay soil, put a layer of grit in the bottom of the hole and set the bulbs on this.

■ **Lift and store tender summer-flowering bulbs.** In sheltered gardens and warm regions, slightly tender bulbs like galtonias may survive *in situ*, but in cold areas bulbs such as these and eucomis, and certainly tigridias, should be lifted, dried, and stored in pots or boxes of dry sand. Lift, clean up, and dry the bulbs just as you would spring-flowering bulbs.

■ **Finish planting all spring-flowering** bulbs now. The bulbs will start to send out roots. Planting them late just means they will flower a bit later than others—perhaps no bad thing to give continuity.

■ **Examine bulbs being forced** in darkness to see if any top-growth is emerging. If so, bring the bulbs into the light in a cool place. But first knock them out of their containers to see the root system. If there aren't many roots, put them back in the dark for a few more weeks.

■ **Plant lily bulbs** this and next month. Plant them in well-prepared soil in sun or partial shade. If your soil is heavy, set the bulbs on a layer of coarse grit to aid drainage. Plant the bulbs at two and a half times their own depth. Lilies can also be planted in pots, in all-purpose potting mix and on a layer of grit, from now until late winter. Leave the pots outside to allow a good root system to form. When new growth emerges, take some pots inside and the lilies will flower early. After flowering, these bulbs can be planted out.

ANNUALS AND BEDDING

■ **Finish lifting any tender perennials** in order to protect them from frost. If you don't have anywhere suitable to keep them, cuttings can still be taken. Those taken earlier than this may need potting up now, but don't pot up any cuttings you take now until the spring.

■ **Half-hardy fuchsias** need a rest period over winter and should be potted up, if necessary, and taken under cover, either storing them with other tender perennials, or keeping them on benches in gently heated greenhouses or cool rooms. The leaves will still drop off now, but these plants will start into growth and produce the earliest shoots for cuttings.
   The plants should be kept cool and on the dry side, but don't let them dry out completely. Just give them enough water from time to time to keep them alive. It's difficult to say how often plants kept over winter should be watered, as it depends on how warm the plants are kept. It really is a matter of experience and practice.

■ **Finish planting spring bedding plants** this month. It is important to get this job done, especially if you have heavy clay soil, before the ground cools down too much. In some regions, summer bedding plants may still be flowering, but you will have to take the bull by the horns and get them out if you want to put spring bedding in.
   In light, sandy soil you may get away with planting spring bedding later, as the soil warms up much quicker in the spring. If planting late, add a little fertilizer that is high in phosphates such as bonemeal, seaweed meal, or fish emulsion to the soil rather than a general fertilizer. This encourages root growth, which is what we are aiming for at this time of year. Soft growth made now will be more easily damaged during winter.

Sowing hardy annuals

1 Use a bamboo cane to create some straight drills for the seed—press the cane lightly into the soil.

2 Transfer a little seed to the palm of your hand and gently tap it with your finger to trickle the seed into the drill.

3 Water well, using a watering can with a fine spray. A sprinkling is less likely to disturb the seed.

■ **Sow overwintering hardy annuals** outside if this was not done last month. If you act fast, there is still time to do this in milder parts of the country.

CONTAINERS

■ **Continue planting containers** with spring-bedding plants and bulbs in order to achieve a worthwhile display in the spring. The sooner this job is completed, the sooner the plants will establish before the winter sets in.

■ **Don't forget perennials and shrubs for winter color.** You don't have to limit your choice of plants for containers to bedding plants. Many evergreen shrubs will provide color and interest year-round. Variegated shrubs are particularly useful and will brighten up a dull or bare corner at any time of the year. There are many to choose from, but look out for *Euonymus japonicus* 'Marieke' and 'Aureopictus'.

There are also varieties of variegated boxwood and dwarf conifers in a wide variety of shapes and colors.

Other plants to brighten up containers throughout the winter include hardy cyclamen and heathers, which also have a wide range of foliage hues. In mild-winter regions, winter-flowering pansies will give a bright, cheerful display from now right into the early summer.

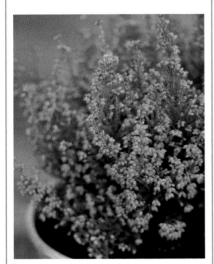

Versatile plant Heather makes a colorful display, whether you choose to grow it in a bed or container.

LAWNS

■ **Reduce the frequency of mowing now.** Established lawns should be mown less frequently now as growth slows down. In addition to this, raise the height of the cutting blades in the mower. Grass that is cut too short over the winter will not stand up to the poorer weather conditions and will be more likely to become infested with moss and weeds, since it is weaker.

■ **Rake out thatch, aerate, and top-dress lawns.** This fall overhaul of your lawn will make a great difference to the grass after a summer of hard use. If you have larger lawns to deal with, machines can be bought or rented to help with these jobs.

■ **Reseed any bare or worn patches**.

New lawns

■ **Make new lawns.** Sod can be laid from early to mid-month, as long as the soil is not frozen or waterlogged. Be sure to keep the new sod rolls well watered until you get the chance to lay them.

There is still time to sow grass seed if it is done early enough in the month. The soil is still reasonably warm and moist and germination should be fairly quick. If you have doubts about the weather and the area sown is not too big, cover it up with plastic sheeting; this will encourage even more rapid germination. Remove the plastic as soon as you spot the first seedlings coming through.

■ **New lawns made earlier** may need cutting, but again, don't cut them too short. About 1 in (2.5 cm) is the closest to cut newly sown lawns and newly laid sod for the last cut before winter.

VEGETABLES AND HERBS

■ **Cut down the tops of Jerusalem artichokes.** It is the swollen roots, rather like potatoes, of these plants that are eaten. The tops can grow to over 6 ft (2 m), making this an excellent plant to use for screening ugly structures such as the shed or the compost pile in summer; occasionally they produce quite attractive yellow flowers. But by this time of year, the plants will be dying back and looking messy. Cut them down to ground level. Shred the old stems and use them for mulching borders, or mix them in with other garden compost. Although it makes a good screen, Jerusalem artichokes can be invasive, so keep a close check on them and harvest the swollen roots regularly. As with potatoes, even the smallest tuber left in the ground will regrow.

■ **Cut down asparagus fern** now that it has turned yellow, if you didn't do it last month. After cutting down the foliage, top-dress over the crowns with garden compost or well-rotted farmyard manure.

■ **Empty compost bins** of well-rotted compost and use it for mulching and digging in to improve the soil. Well-made garden compost will do the soil a world of good and using it up will free the compost bin for more material. If you don't have much compost, it is better to give adequate amounts to a smaller area, rather than trying to spread it too thinly over all of the ground. With a good crop-rotation system , you should plan to incorporate organic matter into at least a third of the vegetable garden each year.

■ **As soon as ground is cleared, dig it over if necessary.** The sooner soil cultivation in the vegetable garden can be done, the better. Heavy clay soil, in particular, will benefit from being broken up and exposed to winter weather conditions for as long as possible. Rain, snow, and frost all play a vital part in breaking down soil particles, enabling us to make good seed and planting beds in the spring. Dig for short periods at a time and do other jobs in between to prevent injury to your back.

The easiest way to dig a large area of the vegetable garden is to take out a trench at one end of the plot and cart the soil to the other end. Put organic matter into the bottom of the trench. Then take out the next trench with your spade and throw the soil forward into the first one, covering the organic matter. Carry this out over the whole area and fill in the last trench with the soil taken out at the start of the process.

■ **Dig in green manure crops** sown earlier in the fall. Green manure crops are a good substitute for well-rotted garden compost or farmyard manure if you cannot get a good supply of organic matter. They will condition the soil, and some, like clover and vetch, also "fix" nitrogen for use by the plants that follow.

To dig them in, dig a trench and skim the surface of the neighboring soil, scraping the tops of the plants into the bottom of the trench. Throw the soil containing the roots forward into this first trench to cover them, so that you make the next trench in the process. Repeat until the job is done. You can also sow green manures now to overwinter.

■ **Cover some ground with plastic** to keep the worst of the rain off. Hold the plastic in place with bricks or long pieces of scrap lumber. It is surprising just how much water will be kept off the land by covering it and how early you can start planting and sowing by replacing the plastic sheeting with cloches in late winter and early spring.

Harvesting and storing

■ **Pick the last of the runner beans** No matter how quickly you pick runner beans, there comes a point when they seem never-ending. If they are not too big they can be frozen; overgrown pods can be composted, as they will be old and stringy. If you want to collect your own seed, leave some pods on the old plants until they turn brown. Otherwise, cut the plants from their supports and compost them, but leave the roots in the ground. Runner beans, like fava beans and peas, return valuable nitrogen to the soil. In the crop-rotation system, beans can be followed by leafy crops such as brassicas that have a high demand for nitrogen and less will have to be applied to the soil in the form of synthetic fertilizers.

■ **Finish lifting potatoes** Leave them on the surface of the soil for a couple of hours to dry out. If it is a damp day, put them in a cold frame or a greenhouse to dry. They must be dry before you put them into storage. Store only undamaged potatoes, using those that are damaged first. Store them in paper or burlap sacks, ensuring that no light gets to them, as this will turn them green.

Potatoes Be careful how you dig; above-ground stems give no indication of how many you'll find.

■ **Continue lifting carrots and beets** for storing and only store sound produce. Any that is damaged should be used first and not stored. Store these crops in boxes in layers separated with moist sand or old potting mix. Store all root crops in a cool, dark, dry, and frost-free place. Check through at regular intervals during winter. If any show signs of rot, discard them.

■ **Make a clamp to store root vegetables** This is an old method of storing root crops, ideal if you don't have much room indoors. You will have to get some straw. Put a thick layer on the ground and start laying the dry roots on it. Build up the crops in a cone shape, tapering toward the top. Next put a layer of straw around the mound of roots, building it up to the top and making sure it goes right over the top. Then start covering the straw with soil, digging it from around the mound and again building it up to the top until the entire mound is covered, except at the very tip. Leave some straw poking out, to let air in.

Sowing and planting outdoors

■ **Finish planting fall onion sets** Plant them 3 in (8 cm) apart in well-prepared soil. Japanese onion sets can also be planted, a little later than seeds are sown, in October or November. Japanese onions from both sets and seeds should be ready to harvest in June the following year, giving an early harvest before other onions are ready.

■ **Plant garlic** if you didn't do it last month. Like spring-flowering bulbs, garlic may be planted throughout the fall, as long as the soil is not frozen. If the soil is too wet to plant outside, grow the cloves in modules and plant out in late winter or early spring. Put one clove in each cell, with the tip of each clove just sticking out of the soil. They don't need any warmth, so keep them in a well-ventilated cold frame or outside under the shelter of a wall, just to keep the heaviest of the rain off them.

■ **Many leafy crops appreciate** the milder temperatures late fall brings to southern gardens. Now is the time to sow seeds of cool-loving greens such as kale, mustard, turnips, and spinach.

Planting garlic

1 Break up the head to separate the individual cloves.

2 Make holes with a dibber—roughly twice the depth of the cloves and 7 in (18 cm) apart.

3 Plant cloves individually, pointed end uppermost.

Caring for crops

■ **Earth up celery** for the last time, if not done last month. Leave a tuft of foliage at the top uncovered. If hard frost is forecast keep some straw or row cover handy to cover the plants. Straw can be held in place with chicken wire or plastic netting pegged into the ground; row cover is easily kept in place with a few bricks. Start harvesting the celery as needed.

■ **Remove yellowing leaves from Brussels sprouts** and other winter brassicas such as cabbages, cauliflowers, and broccoli. Old yellowing leaves are of no use to the plants; they will just encourage diseases such as botrytis and gray mold to invade, reducing the overall crop yield. These crops will remain productive until hard freezes bring their season to an end.

Planning ahead

■ **Prepare a bed for planting asparagus** in the spring. Asparagus likes well-prepared soil enriched with plenty of organic matter, but drainage must be good. Drainage can be improved permanently, especially in heavy soil, by double-digging and incorporating generous amounts of organic matter. This will raise the level of the bed, but this is no bad thing as a raised bed will also help to improve drainage. If your soil is very heavy clay, which asparagus really doesn't thrive on, there is still a way of growing it; in high raised beds with strong sides to retain the soil. Make sturdy wooden frames with planks and posts, about 24 in (60 cm) deep and as long and wide as you want, but 4 x 4 ft (1.2 x 1.2 m) is a good size. Make up a compost mix to fill the beds, ideally of equal parts garden compost and grit; if you don't have enough compost, buy bagged products.

Beat the seasons

■ **Force chicory.** Chicory, such as Witloof, which has been growing through the summer, can be lifted in batches and forced for a succession of pointed, tight-leaved "chicons." The roots can be potted up in old potting mix. Cover the pot with another upturned pot, ensuring you cover drainage holes. To get the best chicons, place the pots in a minimum temperature of 50°F (10°C).

Herbs

■ **Lift parsley and mint** for winter use. A few pots of herbs will provide you with valuable additions to winter meals. Dig up a few roots of each and remove yellowing leaves. Put each piece in a small pot of potting mix, water them in, and set on a bright kitchen windowsill. You will then have fresh herbs at your fingertips all through the winter.

■ **Basil needs more warmth** than the average outdoor temperatures of October. This tender herb is among the first to wither at a hint of frost and needs a warm greenhouse to keep it growing over the winter. Sow seeds in containers to grow on a sunny windowsill or under lights during the cold months, in order to have a few fresh leaves for sauces, salads, and soups. Or harvest every last leaf from the plants in your garden in advance of frost and freeze them in ice cube trays topped with water.

FRUIT
Picking and storing

■ **Finish picking apples.** Varieties like 'Jonathan' and 'Liberty' and the cooking apples will be ready for harvesting around now. Pick them when they are ripe and only store sound fruit. Damaged fruit can be used right after picking, if it is ripe. If fruits are ripe they should part from the tree easily. If they don't, leave them for a little longer. If stored properly they will last most of the winter. Apples can be eaten straight from storage, but pears may need a few days in a warm room to ripen.

Caring for crops

■ **Clean up strawberry beds.** Remove yellowing foliage and old runners that were overlooked and generally weed the area to tidy up and lessen the risk of pest and disease problems next year. Older plants showing signs of virus infection should be taken out and put in the trash. New plants can be bought in and planted in the spring. Young plants put in during the spring should not be cropped in the first summer as they need time to build up a crown to produce good crops in subsequent years.

■ **Mulch dormant strawberries** with a 2–3-in (5–8-cm) layer of mulch to protect the crowns from cold injury and prevent plants from heaving through the winter. Choose a weed-free organic mulch such as straw or pine needles that won't pack down too heavily on the crowns, and spread it over the top of the bed. A double layer of floating row cover may be used in place of organic mulch; be sure to secure the edges to keep it from blowing away in winter winds.

■ **Keep newly planted strawberries well watered.** Planting strawberries now in southern gardens enables them to get established before winter so that plants develop well, but if they don't get enough

Pruning blackberries Untie all the fruited canes and cut them to the ground.

water, this will not happen and they will not fruit well next year.

■ **Spray peaches and nectarines** against peach leaf curl. Trees that were sprayed with copper fungicide earlier in the year to prevent peach leaf curl need another application now, just as the leaves begin to fall. When the leaves have fallen, covering the trees with plastic sheeting supported on a wooden framework will also reduce the incidence of peach leaf curl disease, as its spores need water to infect.

Pruning and training

■ **Blackberries and hybrid berry fruits** should be pruned after fruit is harvested. Cut out the old fruited canes and tie in the new ones. It is easier to cope with training these fruits if the new canes are tied to one side of the support, and the canes that will grow next year and fruit the following one can be trained to the other side.

■ **Prune blackcurrants.** These shrubs can be pruned now, but it is better to wait until winter.

Planning ahead

■ **Order new fruit trees.** As you enjoy the wares at local farmer's markets, you may find a variety or two that you'd like to grow This is a good time to choose fruit trees. There will be a selection of varieties available, on different rootstocks. This means that the top part of the tree that bears the fruit has been grafted onto the roots of a different tree. The rootstock will affect the eventual size of your fruit tree, and also the age at which it bears fruit.

■ **Prepare the ground for new fruit trees.** Although a reputable nursery will ship your trees at the appropriate planting time for your region, it's a very good idea to do prepare in advance. If you're planting several trees, dig over the whole area, incorporating plenty of organic matter. If just one or two trees are being planted, prepare generously sized individual holes. Break up the bottom of the hole to loosen the subsoil, without bringing any subsoil to the surface. Put plenty of manure in the hole and work it into the bottom.

Order new fruit trees Dwarf trees like these young pears are perfect in small gardens.

UNDER COVER

■ **Thoroughly clean** the greenhouse or conservatory if you didn't do so last month.

■ **Continue ventilating** on warm days, but close the vents in mid-afternoon to conserve heat. It is important to keep air circulating indoors to keep diseases such as mildew and botrytis at bay, as they flourish in warm, moist, still conditions.

■ **Buy bubble wrap** to insulate the greenhouse or conservatory. You can do a lot to keep bills down by lining the structure with bubble wrap. Although it may cut down on some of the light getting in, it is well worth installing it for the warmth it keeps in. It can be taken down again in the spring.

■ **Take more care with watering** at this time of the year. With the shorter days and cooler temperatures, watering has to be done with much more care now. If diseases such as botrytis are not to thrive, it is better to get watering done as early as possible in the day, so that the plants have a chance to dry out before nightfall. Watering in early morning is preferable. Try to avoid getting water on the plants' leaves too, as this can take time to dry out. Most plant growth will have slowed down now, so only water plants when you can see they really need it.

■ **Check plants over regularly** and remove any yellowing leaves and fading flowers. Don't leave these lying around as they will encourage diseases to set in and attack your cherished plants. A look around the greenhouse once a week is quite a pleasant job when the weather is bad outside. It also gives you an opportunity to spot pests that may be lurking and deal with them quickly and easily. It is surprising how many pests you can find overwintering in the warm conditions inside.

Raising plants for outdoors

■ **Sow sweet peas for next spring.** With the luxury of space in a greenhouse, you can sow sweet peas now, though a cool, light windowsill will accommodate a few pots too. Sow as you would in spring, but sowing five or six seeds to a 5 in (13 cm) pot rather than using long tubes, and the young plants can be potted up individually in spring.

Greenhouse and house plants

■ **Lift a few herbaceous perennials** for some early flowers inside. Naturally early-flowering plants like hellebores, doronicum, and pulmonarias can be potted up and they will flower even earlier. You can do this when dividing them. Pot them in pots containing soil-based potting mix and water them in. Stand them outside and bring them in from January onward. They make unusual container plants and can be planted out afterward.

■ **Citrus fruit trees** and any other tender shrubs in pots, such as bay and oleander, which have been outside for the summer should be brought in now. Keep them in cool but frost-free conditions, opening ventilators or a window whenever the weather is mild to give them some fresh air. Fertilizing and watering will have to be done carefully, as citrus trees will be coming into flower. Some will already have fruits on them as well and these should ripen over the winter.

Crops under glass

■ **Clear out old tomato,** eggplant, and pepper plants and all their debris as they finish cropping. Any green tomatoes can be brought indoors to ripen on the windowsill, clearing the space so you can give the greenhouse a clean before winter.

■ **Grow radishes, mustard, and cress for winter salads in containers** used previously for tomatoes and other crops. Some lettuces (see below) will also do well. Give them a liquid fertilizer regularly, as the previous plants will have used up the nutrients in the soil. It is a good way of making full use of these containers. And when these crops have finished, the growing medium can be used again, to improve the soil in the garden. Don't, however, add the soil from tomato containers to beds where you will be growing potatoes or outdoor tomatoes next year, as diseases common to both may be passed on.

■ **Sow a few winter lettuces** in a cold greenhouse, or grow a few in pots on the kitchen windowsill. Sow the seeds in small pots or trays and place them in a propagator, maintaining a temperature of 61°F (16°C). The seeds will germinate in a few days, when they can be either potted up in small pots of peat-free potting mix, or planted in the border soil of a greenhouse or in used containers. Water the lettuces carefully as they are very prone to botrytis and rotting off. Always err on the cautious side when watering in the winter. The lettuces will be ready to harvest in early spring.

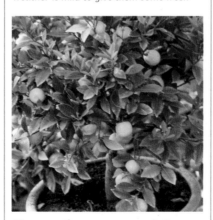

Citrus crop You can grow oranges in the greenhouse very successfully.

The November garden

November can be a damp, raw month. Flowers may be scarce in the garden, but there are many berries, evergreen foliage, and trees with decorative bark to add interest on the dullest of days. You can warm yourself up by tidying up the yard and preparing for the winter ahead. It's also a good time to check your tools, catch up on greenhouse maintenance, and begin planning your spring display.

THINGS TO DO

Clean or discard any old pots and trays that you're not intending to reuse. Clean out nesting boxes and put food out for the birds on a regular basis. If you have a late fall bonfire, check the pile for hibernating creatures before you set it alight.

Check your tools, and get the lawnmower serviced and sharpened. You don't need to do much to the lawn itself, but stay off it in frosty weather. If you have a pond or a greenhouse, you may need to install heaters—and don't forget to insulate the greenhouse properly too.

Press on with winter digging. This is the time to plant bare-root trees and shrubs as well as new roses, and to get the tulip bulbs in. Protect all tender and newly planted shrubs from frost and wind, and the alpines from winter rain. Insulate any pots that will remain outside during winter, otherwise both plants and pots will suffer.

Plant fruit trees and bushes, and winter-prune established plants. Lift and divide rhubarb crowns. If you have grown your own leeks, heel in a winter supply by the back door, ready to use when needed.

LAST CHANCE

Protect tender plants from the winter weather. Lift and store your dahlias and start amaryllis bulbs so that they will flower at Christmas time.

GET AHEAD

Now is the time to order seed catalogs. Begin winter-pruning deciduous trees and shrubs, start renovating hedges, and prune greenhouse vines.

Vibrant shades *Acer palmatum* 'Sango-kaku' displays a startling range of fall foliage colors, which are sure to brighten up your yard at this time of year.

Last days of fall

Make the most of any late fall foliage color in the yard this month. There is quite a bit of seasonal variation, so rich displays may go on and the weather may well stay good for while. Take advantage of this by moving ahead with winter-preparation tasks while there's still a chance.

By this month there may still be some color in the garden, especially from the asters if the weather has been reasonable. Nerines will also be in flower, and if you are lucky there will still be a few roses to pick. You may also still have some late fall foliage color. The main period for autumn color is usually in October, but due to seasonal variations, the peak of the fall display can vary by several weeks from year to year. So there are may well be public parks and gardens to visit where you can still enjoy the richness of colorful foliage.

Where leaves have fallen, clear them up. A blanket of sodden leaves on lawns and around the bases of plants will do no good at all, and wet leaves on paths and steps are a real safety hazard. Fallen leaves will rot down into a really good soil conditioner—leafmold—over time, so pile them up or make a chicken-wire container for them to keep them from blowing away. If you don't have enough leaves to make a good pile, either put them on the compost pile or stuff them into a plastic trash bag with some holes pierced in it. If you choose the latter option, remember that the leaves must be wet to rot down, so either bag them on a damp day or pour in some water.

Prickly, green fruits The horse chestnut (*Aesculus hippocastanum*) splits to reveal shiny, brown seeds, known as conkers, a familiar sight in large gardens and parks.

Make leafmold You don't need a compost bin or lots of space. Pierce plastic bags, fill them with wet leaves, and give them plenty of time to rot down.

Use the warm spells

The northern third of the country is now experiencing genuinely wintry conditions, and cold snaps have put an end to the growing season for most gardeners in the middle as well. Snow is not unexpected in the North and at elevations, although lingering warmth in the soil may keep it from lasting too long on the ground. Cold, gray rainy stretches are common in November, but the month can still produce the occasional sparkling fall day. Before the real winter weather sets in, take advantage of any warm spells to get going on your work so that you don't fall behind in the spring. Many people regard this as the end of the gardening season, but it is really the beginning. Work done now can save a lot of time and effort when spring comes around.

Revamp the vegetable plot

The earlier any winter digging is done, the better, as this will allow rain, snow, and frost to break down the clods of soil, improving its structure and making it much easier to cultivate in the spring. One major project, which if done now will save you lots of work, not only next spring but in many years to come, is to convert your vegetable plot to the deep-bed system. This is a way of growing vegetables that acknowledges the "no-dig" approach to gardening, popular with many organic gardeners. The theory is that if you cultivate and improve the soil once, really thoroughly, you will encourage a population of soil-dwelling creatures, especially earthworms, that in subsequent years will take a mulch of organic matter down into the soil for you, aided by the ongoing processes of planting and harvesting. So there's no need for digging and turning to interfere with the soil's structure and, because beds are made small, there's never a need to step on the soil and compact it. You'll have to sacrifice some of your plot to create more paths from which you can work and weed, but on the other hand, you'll find that with this system you can plant much more closely, so it shouldn't affect yields.

You can make beds long and narrow, or create a checkerboard effect with small, square beds intersected by paths, a design that shows off the ornamental potential of many of the crops.

Weather watch

Some November days can be damp and raw, especially with low cloud cover. In all but the Deep South, frosts are expected at night, particularly in the wake of clear, calm days. Temperatures across the country are trending lower, and damp conditions typically make it seem even colder than it really is.

Rain and wind

Steady, drenching rains and accompanying blustery winds conspire to strip deciduous trees of any remaining foliage that still clings to their branches. When temperatures hover around the freezing point, November's moisture can turn from liquid to solid and may arrive as wet, heavy snowfall in New England and the upper Midwest.

Tropical storms

The weather this month is generally unsettled—intense cold may begin creeping down from the Arctic, while the oceans still harbor enough warmth to send the remnants of warm, wet tropical storms up the East Coast or northward from the Gulf of Mexico.

Reduced sunlight

If we're lucky, a few days in November will be bright and pleasant. The amount of sunshine is considerably reduced compared with summer for all parts of the country, but it is all the more welcome for its limited supply. We're still a month away from the shortest day of the year and the hours of daylight continue to wane.

A welcome display *Viburnum* x *bodnantense* 'Charles Lamont' sports a welcome display of bright-pink blossoms from as early as late fall into spring.

Routine tasks

Tidying up borders by clearing away old stems and dead foliage and lightly forking over the ground around plants will transform the appearance of the garden, making it neat for the rest of the winter. Leave a few plants like

Sedum spectabile and ornamental grasses such as *Carex pendula* and miscanthus uncut, as frost on these plants looks extremely decorative.

During all this clearing up you will inevitably generate a lot of material, most of which can be composted, but some of the woody and semiwoody material will take a long time to rot down. One way to get rid of this woody material is by burning it, but although a bonfire can be cheery and satisfying, it's a terrible waste of material that can be recycled in the garden. If you can, invest in a garden shredder instead. There are many different models available, powered by gasoline or electricity. These machines will shred all woody material into fine pieces that can then be used as a mulch—or they can be mixed with other composted material to make the best compost you'll ever have. And, of course, these machines can also be rented if you don't want to buy one.

Planting and transplanting

Where the soil is not frozen, November is a good time to plant new trees, shrubs, and roses. And if you have been walking around the yard with your notebook in hand earlier in the year, making notes of any changes to be made, then this is a good month to move plants, because there is still some warmth in the soil left from the summer. Larger plants are best moved first, with as much soil around the roots as possible. And if they are large trees or shrubs, remember to stake them again if you garden in an exposed place. Water plants well after moving them and mulch with a thick layer of organic matter; keep watering them through the next season.

Stars among the sleepers

This is the month when most plants become dormant and everything, as far as plant growth goes, shuts down for the winter; but there are some plants that begin to flower around now in mild regions and carry their blooms throughout the winter months. Plants such as *Viburnum x bodnantense* will produce exquisite pink flowers from as early as October right through the season. The flowers borne by this shrub are also powerfully and sweetly scented, and will fill the air around them with fragrance even on the coldest and dullest November days. The

Miscanthus sinensis **'Graziella'** This perennial grass, makes a delightful autumnal display, with its arching leaves and graceful spikelets.

winter-flowering autumn cherry, *Prunus subhirtella* 'Autumnalis' produces its white blossoms intermittently throughout the winter. For a change in color, try the pink-flowering variety, 'Autumnalis Rosea'.

Ordering early

When the weather makes it difficult to do any work outside, taking a look through seed catalogs is not just a pleasurable occupation for a dreary late fall day. If you get your seed order in early, you are less likely to be disappointed, because the seed companies often quickly run out of popular lines of seeds. This applies especially to any plants highlighted at gardening expos, on TV shows, and in gardening magazines. And you'll receive your seeds earlier, too, and can therefore get a head start in the spring.

Vitis coignetiae
Clinging, very vigorous climber; at its finest in fall (see p.323)

Cimicifuga simplex 'White Pearl'
Fall-flowering herbaceous perennial (see p.272)

Libertia ixioides
Slightly tender perennial with brown-edged white flowers (see p.295)

Pyracantha 'Golden Charmer'
Spiny shrub ideal for wall training (see p.309)

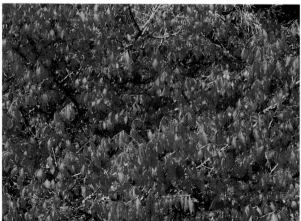

Euonymus alatus
Dense, bushy deciduous shrub with bright fruits and leaves (see p.284)

Lonicera fragrantissima
Shrubby honeysuckle with richly scented flowers (see p.296)

Chrysanthemum 'Glowing Lynn'
Hardy perennial; can be left in the garden all winter (see p.272)

Chelone obliqua
Herbaceous perennial that enjoys heavy, damp soil (see p.271)

Clematis GOLDEN TIARA
One of the last clematis of the year to flower (see p.275)

Rosa moyesii
Shrub rose with distinctive bullet-shaped hips (see p.314)

Cortaderia selloana 'Sunningdale Silver'
Pampas grass; an old favorite back in vogue (see p.276)

Iris foetidissima
The stinking iris, with insignificant flowers but vivid fruits (see p.292)

What to do in November

AROUND THE YARD

There will be few pests around now, but it is best to be on guard as some will be hiding in corners. The best way to avoid problems is to practice good hygiene, and this includes keeping sheds and equipment clean and tidy as well as the borders. Any dirty pots and seed trays should be thrown out or recycled: washed in a weak solution of garden disinfectant and stored for the winter. Clean the ends of stakes and canes before storing as pests often lurk there.

Clean out bird houses of old nesting material, which can harbor parasites. Clearing them out will encourage birds to nest in them again next year. Do this as soon as possible, as birds will soon be looking for winter roosts. If they are already familiar with a house by spring, they are much more likely to select it as a nesting site.

Protect young plants from rabbits. Rabbits can do an enormous amount of damage, but a few simple precautions will prevent some of it. Surrounding young plants with chicken wire will give them some protection. Tree trunks can be surrounded similarly, or there are special rabbit guards that wrap directly around the trunks to stop rabbits from eating the bark. If you can afford it, putting chicken wire around the perimeter of the garden, sinking it at least 6 in (15 cm) into the ground, is the best deterrent of all. Bend another few inches at the base of the netting in the trench outward, to prevent the rabbits from digging down and then underneath.

Continue to gather up fallen leaves. This job can be made much easier by using a vacuum, either bought from the garden center or rented from your local hardware store. There are both electric and gas-driven models available. Some have a blowing function so that leaves can be easily blown out from around the base of plants.

Continue sowing green manure crops on bare ground, especially in the vegetable garden. Winter rye can be sown well into November. These crops can be dug in during the spring and they will return valuable organic matter to the soil, improving the soil structure and its organic content.

Cold frames are endlessly useful unheated, but they can also be insulated for warmth and even heated, either with small heaters or with heating cables on the base and around the sides on the inside. However, to install any electrical wiring, especially outdoors, call in a qualified electrician to do the job.

Bubble wrap can be used to insulate the top of the frame and polystyrene slabs cut to size for the sides. Insulation alone will help to keep out several degrees of frost, enabling some tender plants to be overwintered there in mild regions if space in the greenhouse is limited. More protection can be given on very cold nights by covering the cold frame with a piece of old carpet or another sheet of polystyrene held in place with bricks.

Have a bird house Attracting birds into your yard is an important way to help replace disappearing wildlife habitats.

TREES AND SHRUBS

■ **Protect tender and newly planted trees and shrubs** from frost and cold winds. Strong winds damage foliage by dehydrating it and winds in freezing temperatures can cause more harm to plants than a severe frost on its own. Use a windbreak made from netting supported by posts. Evergreen shrubs and hedging plants are more prone to wind damage than deciduous ones, so these are the more important ones to give protection to. Smaller shrubs and those that are newly planted can be protected from the frost by packing straw around them and holding it in place with netting. Clear plastic can also be used for temporary protection, but it must not touch the foliage of evergreen plants, as any moisture condensing out on the plastic will freeze and damage the foliage. Support the plastic by nailing it onto a framework of canes or onto wooden battens.

■ **Check tree ties and stakes** These should be checked regularly to see that the stakes are sound and that ties are not cutting into the trunks of the plants; if they are, they will eventually strangle the plant as the trunk expands outward.

■ **Clear any snow off conifers** and other shrubs. Heavy snow lying on branches will

Staking trees These angled stakes give support low down, where it is needed, and can be inserted without damaging the rootball of container-grown plants.

weigh them down, spoiling the shape of the plants. Although it looks very pretty, shake the snow off the plants as soon as you can to avoid branches being broken under the weight of snow. It is surprising just how heavy a layer of snow can be.

Planting

■ **At this time of year** bare-rooted stock of most deciduous trees and shrubs will become available and can be planted throughout the dormant season (that is, from now until at the latest, March), whenever soil conditions allow. They are cheaper than container-grown plants, but do take a look at the root systems before you buy, to ensure that they have been lifted with care and are not dried out. Make sure they are well wrapped before transporting them and plant as soon as possible. If the plants are shipped to you, call the supplier right away if the plants do not seem satisfactory.

To plant (see right), prepare the ground well, incorporating plenty of organic matter. Dig a hole large enough to hold the root system without cramping the roots. Put a stake in first for trees and tall shrubs, on the windward side so that the plant is blown away from the stake (this prevents rubbing). Then plant the tree or shrub to the same depth as it was planted before at the nursery (you can see this easily—the darker part of the stem near the roots), fill in the hole, and firm in gently with your foot.

Make sure all newly planted trees and shrubs are well staked and tied. The stake should come at most about one-third of the way up the trunk, and often even shorter stakes are recommended. The only exception is when staking top-grafted standards, such as dwarf, weeping trees, when the stake should reach the graft point. But for all other trees, a low stake allows the top of the tree to flex in the

Planting bare-root roses

1 **Dig a generous hole** so as not to cramp the root system. Incorporate organic matter into the hole and add a small handful of bonemeal.

2 **Place the rose** in the hole with the roots well spread out. Lay a cane across the hole to check that the graft union will be below soil level.

3 **Fill in the hole** by gradually working soil in around the roots with your hands and pressing down firmly. Lightly firm the soil and water well.

wind, strengthening the trunk. Make sure the tree is secured to the stake using a tree tie. Check as the tree grows and loosen ties as the trunk expands.

Container-grown trees and shrubs can also be planted all through the year. The soil will require the same thorough preparation as for bare-root trees and shrubs. If container-grown plants look a little potbound, it is a good idea to tease out some roots, otherwise they will continue to grow around in circles, forming a weak root system.

■ **Plant new roses**. Bare-root roses may be available from this month through to March. They are slightly cheaper than container-grown plants and they do establish better. For roses to perform their best, thorough preparation of the soil is essential. Cultivate as large an area as you can or dig as large a hole as possible and work in plenty of organic matter.

Never allow the roots to dry out, and if the roses have arrived by mail order and the roots are dry, put them in a pail of water. Plant the rose deep enough so that the point at which it was grafted is about 2 in (5 cm) below ground level. Work soil in among the roots well and firm as you go. Mulch the surface with well-rotted garden compost or manure.

If you are planting new roses to replace old ones, you may have problems. New roses planted in soil that has grown roses for a number of years are prone to a disease known as "rose sickness." Take out as much of the old soil as possible and replace it with fresh soil from another part of the garden that has not grown roses.

Pruning and training
■ **Begin winter pruning deciduous trees and shrubs**. Don't prune unnecessarily, though, however satisfying a job it is hacking away at woody growth.

Unnecessary pruning weakens growth, and the fewer wounds you make the better, as each is a potential entry point for disease. Ornamental cherries (*Prunus* species) are susceptible to the same disease, silver leaf, that is so dangerous to plum and cherry trees if pruned in winter and it may be wise to delay pruning of ornamental cherries until the summer.

However, on most deciduous trees, dead, diseased, and damaged wood should be removed now, as although the pruning will create wounds, these are less risky than leaving the unhealthy wood on the plant. Any further cuts you make will probably be more cosmetic, but consider the effect before removing anything substantial— it's not only the effect of removing growth that you must envision, but also the direction in which the new growth that will come from the point of pruning will grow.

Propagation
■ **Continue sowing seeds of berried shrubs and trees**.

■ **Hardwood cuttings taken last fall** should have rooted by now and these can be lifted and planted in permanent positions. Hardwood cuttings are an easy way to propagate plants, as they don't require special conditions, being happy outside unprotected. There is still plenty of time to take more hardwood cuttings.

Hedges
■ **Continue planting hedging plants**.

■ **Carry out renovation of deciduous hedges.** From now until spring, major renovation in the form of hard pruning can be carried out on deciduous hedges. Evergreen hedges should be left unpruned until spring.

CLIMBERS
■ **Tie in long, whippy shoots** of climbers and wall shrubs to prevent them from being blown around and possibly damaged during any bad weather. If there doesn't seem to be a suitable gap in the framework to secure the shoot to, try pruning it back to five or six buds.

■ **Continue planting** new climbers in the same way as for other container-grown woody plants.

■ **Complete fall planting** of hardy climbing plants so that they can establish their roots before the onset of winter. Plants that were propagated from semiripe or hardwood cuttings earlier in the year can also be planted out now. It is worth preparing the planting site well before you start.

Mix well-rotted organic matter with the soil that you have removed to make the hole. Water the plant thoroughly before you remove the plant from the pot.

Add a good dusting of bonemeal and plant the climber so that the top of the rootball comes level with the surface of the soil and firm it in well (use a stake to assess depth). Water well after you have completed planting and apply a mulch with a 2–3-in (5–8-cm) layer of organic matter.

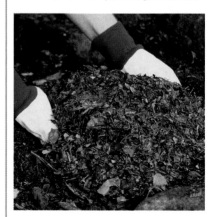

Protecting marginally hardy plants Blanket them with a mulch of leafmold.

PERENNIALS

■ **Pot up some lily-of-the-valley** rhizomes to force them into flower early. A cool, frost-free greenhouse or conservatory will allow the plants to grow at their own pace, but if you want to hurry them up a bit, it's a good idea to give them warmer conditions. The plants can be put back in the garden after flowering and will flower again the following year.

■ **Protect kniphofias (red-hot pokers)** from frost. In parts of the country where kniphofias are marginally hardy, especially when young, they can easily be given some protection. Gather up the foliage and tie it together quite firmly. This will protect the crown of the plant, so if the foliage is damaged by a hard freeze, the crown should be unaffected.

Protect other slightly tender herbaceous plants like penstemons too. Straw placed over the plants and held in place with netting, or a layer of a dry loose mulch such as leafmold or bark chips, will give a good degree of protection from hard frost. Check the plants from time to time through the winter to make sure that no diseases have set in.

■ **Clear leaves that have accumulated** on top of clumps of perennials. If the leaves are left there for any length of time, the plants will suffer through lack of light and the dark, moist conditions will attract slugs and snails. Don't burn the fallen leaves; either add them to the compost pile or make a separate leaf pile to make leafmold later on.

■ **Take root cuttings** of perennials from now until late winter.

■ **If dahlias have not yet been lifted,** do this when the foliage has been blackened by frost. Dry and pack them into boxes and fill in with old potting soil, leaving the crown uncovered, and keep them in a frost-free place. Cuttings can be taken from the tubers in the spring.

■ **Continue lifting and dividing** herbaceous perennials as the weather and soil conditions allow. The earlier this is done in the month, the better, as the newly divided plants will have time to settle in before the harsher winter weather.

■ **The routine job of cutting down old growth** can continue, but if you live in a colder area, it may be better to leave some of the old growth on now so that it can provide protection for the plants during severe weather. Some of the more attractive or architectural dead stems can look quite stunning when covered with frost or snow.

■ *Helleborus niger*, the Christmas rose, rarely actually flowers in time for Christmas, but it can be encouraged to flower a little earlier if you cover it with a cloche. Covering it will also help prevent the flowers from being splashed with soil in heavy winter rain. Also, you could try lifting one or two plants and potting them up and forcing them in gentle heat, or just in a cold greenhouse. Then the full beauty

Helleborus niger

Cutting back bamboo Use long-handled loppers to do a really efficient job.

of the flowers can be enjoyed no matter how cold the weather gets.

■ **Cut back ornamental grasses** and bamboos. Those that are not ornamental in winter are best cut back now, as they can often look messy in winter. Some bamboos, if their canes are thick enough, can be cut, cleaned up, and stored and used for supporting plants next season.

Alpines

■ **Continue to remove fallen leaves** from around alpines. If the leaves are left, they will keep light off the plants and encourage slugs and snails. At the same time, clear any weeds growing in between the plants, and give the rock garden a general tidying-up before winter.

■ **Cover vulnerable alpines** to protect the crowns of the plants from the rain, or take alpines in containers indoors. Plants that are most susceptible to winter wet are those with gray, woolly leaves, such as erinus, lewisias, and edelweiss.

BULBS

■ **Continue planting lilies until the spring** if soil conditions allow.

■ **Remember to examine bulbs** that are being forced for early flowering. When they are about 1 in (2.5 cm) high, move them into a cool greenhouse or a cold frame. If you have a cool windowsill, this would also be an ideal spot. When hyacinths and narcissi, such as 'Paper White' and 'Soleil d'Or', begin to form flower buds, bring them into warmer conditions so that they flower in time for Christmas.

■ **Continue to check** all stored bulbs, corms, and tubers. Any that are showing signs of rotting should be thrown away. If only small parts of the bulb, corm, or tuber are affected, you may get away with cutting out the infected part with a sharp knife and dusting the cut surface with garden sulfur.

However, it's important to keep them separate from the others in store, just in case any infection is spread.

■ **Protect slightly tender bulbs** left in the ground, such as nerines and agapanthus, with a thick mulch of garden compost. If possible, grow them in a sheltered part of the garden, at the base of a south-facing wall or fence.

■ **If you want hippeastrums (amaryllis) in flower at Christmas,** start them growing at the beginning of the month. Pot up and water the bulbs and put them in a warm place to get them going quickly. Some people start them off on top of the refrigerator; over a radiator or a heat register (a place most houseplants hate) is also ideal.

■ **Plant tulips this month.** By planting tulips late, after the other spring-flowering bulbs are in, there is a better chance of preventing the bulbs from being infected with the fungal disease tulip fire. Try to get them in before the end of the month.

Tulips flower better in a sunny situation, and if your soil is heavy clay, lighten it by digging in coarse grit. You can of course grow tulips in containers as well as other spring-flowering bulbs. One advantage of growing them in containers is that they can be planted, pot and all, in any part of the garden lacking color in the spring and then are easily lifted out again when the flowers are finished. Plant tulips in borders and pots just as you would other bulbs, at two to three times their own depth. Plant the bulbs on a layer of coarse grit to prevent them from rotting off. It is always better to plant tulips a little more deeply than too near the surface.

Tulipa 'Dreamboat'

Tulipa 'Giuseppe Verdi'

Overwintering dahlia tubers Label individual tubers with tags.

Tulipa 'Spring Green'

Tulipa 'Dreaming Maid'

ANNUALS AND BEDDING

■ **Protect seedlings of hardy annuals**
Keep an eye on the weather forecast and if it turns very cold, protect those hardy annuals sown earlier in the fall. Cover them with cloches, or have some floating row cover handy to throw over the plants. It would be rare indeed for these plants to be killed by frost, but it does no harm to have some protection on hand for really severe weather.

■ **Tuberous begonias** that were bedded out for the summer should be lifted and brought inside before the frost gets at them. Allow them to dry out under a greenhouse bench or other frost-free place. Once the old stems have parted from the tubers, clean these up and store them in boxes in a cool place.

■ **Finish planting spring bedding plants.**
If the planting of wallflowers, forget-me-nots, English daisy, and sweet Williams has not been completed by now, get it done as soon as possible so that the plants have a little time to become established before the winter sets in.

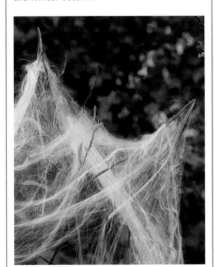

Wispy protection Hang floating row cover between stems to protect the plant from frost.

CONTAINERS

■ **Insulate pots that are too large to take indoors.** The roots of plants growing in containers outside tend to be more prone to suffering from frost damage than plants that are growing in the open ground, and they need some protection from hard freezes. Insulate them by wrapping bubble wrap or burlap securely around the pots.

Tie up the leaves of plants such as cordylines to protect the growing tip from excess winter moisture, which will rot it, and wrap in row cover.

Containers can be moved together for mutual protection. Modern plastic or terra-cotta containers are generally frost-proof, but older terra-cotta pots may not be, so even if they are empty, wrap them or take them indoors for the cold winter months. Ensure that containers are lifted off the ground slightly to improve their drainage. There are decorative "feet" that you can buy from garden centers designed for this very purpose.

■ **Finish planting containers** with spring bedding plants.

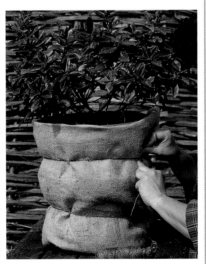

Insulate pots Even if the plant is hardy, the root system exposed above ground may be vulnerable.

LAWNS

■ **Keep off the lawn during wet weather.**
If you have to walk over the lawn to reach borders when it is extremely wet, put down some planks to walk on, but ideally try to keep off the grass altogether. Don't walk on the lawn when it is frosted, either, otherwise you may leave marks.

■ **In dry weather, rake up fallen leaves**
on the lawn. Don't just burn them or throw these away—instead, use them to make leafmold, which makes an excellent soil conditioner, mulch, and ingredient in potting mixes.

■ **Take the lawn mower in for sharpening and servicing.** All machines do a far better job if they are maintained properly. Service centers are relatively quiet at this time of year because a lot of people leave it until the last moment in spring to have mowers serviced, and this causes a rush.

Don't forget, though, to give the lawn an occasional light trim through the winter, if you live in an area with year-round grass growth, so that you can keep it looking neat. Just take the tops off and don't do it if the lawn is very wet or frozen.

New lawns
■ **Continue to dig over areas for new lawns and to lay sod** on prepared ground when the soil is not excessively wet or frozen. This month may be the last chance you have to lay sod in the current year, as the weather may turn bad next month. The one advantage of laying sod at this time of the year is that it won't have a chance to dry out. Always work from boards when you are laying sod so that you don't compact the soil in places and make the lawn uneven.

VEGETABLES AND HERBS

■ **Press on with winter digging** as the weather allows. The soil should not be so wet that it actually sticks to your boots when you walk on it. You can cover ground with clear plastic sheeting to keep off the worst of the rain. Pull it back on a fine day to dig and cover the soil again when you are finished.

■ **Check all stored crops** for signs of disease. It is better to do this regularly so that any rot doesn't get a chance to spread. It's a good job to do when it is too wet to work outside.

Harvesting

■ **Lift parsnips** Parsnips taste better when they have had a touch of frost on them, but they can be lifted and stored in the same way as carrots. Pack them in boxes of sand and they will keep through the winter. An alternative, if you don't have much room available for storing crops, is to pile them up outside the back door and cover them with a thick layer of straw. Hold this in place with some netting pegged into the ground.

■ **Heel in a supply of leeks** by the back door. Hard freezes will make it impossible to dig up crops for the kitchen, so lift a supply and re-bury them horizontally with the tops sticking out, close to the house in a sheltered part of the yard.

■ **Begin harvesting Brussels sprouts** Start harvesting from the bottom of the plant upward, since the largest sprouts form at the base of the plant first of all. Very tall plants that look as if they might blow over in high winds can be staked and tied to a cane.

Sowing and planting outdoors

■ **Finish planting garlic** by the end of the month. The sooner it is in, the better it will

Stand on a plank Spread your weight evenly over beds while you are digging.

grow. If the weather is too wet to plant outside, start the cloves off in modular trays and overwinter these in a cold frame.

■ **Fava beans and peas** can still be sown outside this month, covered with cloches, but the difference between the cropping times of these and sowings made in the spring is negligible. These sowings will, however, be greatly appreciated by all the mice in the neighborhood, so make sure the cloches are firmly in place and the ends closed properly so there are no gaps.

To make some cheap, improvised cloches, get a length of clear plastic sheeting and some galvanized fencing wire. Cut the wire to make hoops and stick these, at intervals, into the ground. Stretch the plastic over the hoops and bury it in the soil at both ends. These cloches will also be useful for protecting crops sown and planted early in the spring.

Caring for crops

■ **Net all brassicas** if you haven't done this by now. As the weather gets colder and there is less food around, birds will be increasingly attracted to the winter crops in your garden. There are many different types of bird scarers on the market, but by

far the best way to protect the crops is by covering them. Make sure traditional netting is properly secured at ground level so that small birds don't get caught up in it; a safer alternative for birds is the very fine mesh sheeting used as a barrier to pests like carrot fly, or even spare pieces of floating row cover. Whatever you use as a cover, you must hold it up off the plants with cane supports or the birds will peck through it. Remember to shake it after any heavy falls of snow, or the weight may bring supports down or rip the netting, making it useless.

■ **Protect the curds of cauliflowers** to keep them white and delay the time when the flowers will open. The inner leaves can be tied or snapped and bent over the curd.

Beat the seasons
■ **Force chicory and seakale**.

Herbs
■ **Terra-cotta pots containing herbs** may have to be wrapped with insulating material if it is impossible to move the pots indoors.

■ **Lift clumps of chives** and grow them in pots on a windowsill.

Medium-gauge netting This will keep birds off brassicas. A finer mesh will prevent cabbage moths and butterflies from laying eggs.

Deep beds for vegetables

Deep beds can be any length, as long as they are no more than about 4 ft (1.2 m) wide, so that they can be tended from each side without stepping on them. However, here we suggest a design using square beds intersected by paths that makes a really good-looking, as well as productive, kitchen garden, combining potager-style traditional formality with an up-to-date, labor-saving way of producing your crops.

The design uses an herb garden with a bay tree as the centerpiece, and all of the vegetable beds are built in exactly the same way. First, dig and turn the soil thoroughly and then make timber-framed square-raised beds. Finally, add a top layer of soil mixed with compost or potting mix. This is the last time you will need to dig these beds. The soil will sink and settle over time, making room for a good top-dressing of well-rotted manure or

garden compost and a feed with an organic fertilizer every winter—and that's it!

Remember to rotate crops around the beds just as you would in old-fashioned rows. Path materials are up to you. Beaten earth is serviceable (and free), although it can become muddy. A thick layer of straw with planks laid on top for the wheelbarrow is traditional and clean. Old, mucky straw can go onto the compost pile in spring.

Bed 1 Beets and carrots
Bed 2 Turnips, celeriac, and a teepee of runner beans
Bed 3 Kohlrabi and parsnips
Bed 4 Brussels sprouts and broccoli,

with a teepee of peas and sweet peas
Bed 5 (central bed) Bay tree, sage, thyme, chives, and basil
Bed 6 Lettuce and radishes, with a teepee of peas and sweet peas

Bed 7 Onions, shallots, and salad onions
Bed 8 Cabbages and cauliflowers, with a teepee of runner beans
Bed 9 Dwarf runner beans and broad beans

Crop rotation

Move crops to different beds each year on a four-year rotation (right). Crops that do not fall into traditional rotation groups, such as salad greens, corn, and also potatoes and tomatoes (as long as ground has not been recently manured) can replace any crop in any year (do not follow potatoes with tomatoes, or vice versa). Strawberries and perennial vegetables could also occupy beds on a longer-term basis.

Year 1	1, 2	3, 4	6, 7	8, 9
Year 2	8, 9	1, 2	3, 4	6, 7
Year 3	6, 7	8, 9	1, 2	3, 4
Year 4	3, 4	6, 7	8, 9	1, 2
Year 5	1, 2	3, 4	6, 7	8, 9

FRUIT

Picking and storing

■ Check fruits in storage regularly and remove any showing deterioration.

Pruning and training

■ **Start winter pruning** established apple and pear trees. Winter pruning of established trees consists mainly of pruning back the leaders by about one-third. Long sideshoots can be pruned to two or three buds to form fruiting spurs on spur-bearing trees. Tip-bearing apples produce fruiting buds on spurs and on the tips of branches, so limit spur-pruning. Short shoots, of about 9 in (23 cm) or less, should be left unpruned, and longer shoots can be spur-pruned. The leading shoots of the branches can be tipped, pruning off the top three or four buds, to encourage them to produce more sideshoots. Older branches that are crossing and rubbing should be cut out to prevent damage and keep the center open.

■ **Blackcurrants** produce shoots from the base and you will have to cut out older shoots to ground level every year to stimulate new shoots from the base. Aim to remove about a third of the bush each year. You will remove some current-year growth when pruning, but it is necessary to encourage new shoots from the base.

Hard prune Established black currant bushes need pruning to take out unproductive stems.

When pruning, make your cuts clean Trim any torn or ragged edges. In winter, when the tree is dormant, wounds should heal without becoming infected.

■ **Prune gooseberries and redcurrants** in much the same way as apples and pears. The intention with pruning young bushes is to build up a framework of four or five main branches, each with plenty of fruiting spurs to produce a lot of succulent fruits.

On established frameworks, any shoots not summer-pruned in late summer should be pruned back to two or three buds from the previous year's growth. Leading shoots can be pruned by one-third to half. Dead, crossing, or diseased wood can be cut out. Opening up the center of the bush to allow air to circulate helps to prevent disease.

Planting

■ **Plant fruit trees and bushes** whenever the soil is not frozen or too wet. Bare-root trees and bushes are planted during the dormant season, from now until March. Container-grown plants can be planted at any time. Make sure the ground has been well prepared by incorporating plenty of organic matter. If just one or two trees are

being planted, the preparation can be done at planting time. Dig a generous hole to accommodate the roots. Break up the bottom of the hole to loosen the subsoil, without bringing it to the surface. Add plenty of organic matter and work it into the bottom of the hole.

The planting technique is the same for all trees and shrubs, with the fruits always being planted at the same depth as previously. With grafted fruit trees, the point of grafting should always be kept above ground level. Otherwise the variety part of the tree will begin to root into the soil and control over the vigor of the tree will be lost. So, never plant deeply: put the tree in at the same level as before. Gradually fill in, working the soil between the roots, and firm gently. Level off and water in thoroughly and tie to the stake with a tree tie. Then mulch with a thick layer of organic matter. Garden compost or well-rotted manure is ideal; straw is also good in sheltered spots.

■ **Blackcurrants are a slight exception** to the planting rules above in that they should be set lower in the planting hole, with 3–4 in (8–10 cm) of stem below ground level. This encourages new growth from the base of the plant. The newly planted bushes should then be pruned to 4 in (10 cm) from the ground to produce strong growth for future fruiting.

■ **Prune newly planted young apple and pear bushes and trees.** Trees bought when three years old or more should not need pruning, but young trees that are to be freestanding will benefit from pruning to form a good shape. Crossing branches or those that make the tree misshapen should be pruned out first. What you do then depends on the age of the tree.

■ Maiden (one-year-old) trees should have the main stem pruned back to 30 in

(75 cm) from the ground, cutting to a bud. This will encourage branches to form lower down.

■ For a two-year-old tree, prune the sideshoots to half of their length. These will form the primary branches. Cut the main stem back to the topmost sideshoot, keeping the center of the tree open.

■ In the third year, prune the leaders to form the main branches by about half again, cutting to a bud facing in the direction you wish the branch to extend. Any sideshoots growing from these branches should be pruned to one or two buds to form fruiting spurs. In the fourth year, formative pruning should be finished and the tree will be cropping.

Propagation

■ **Propagate rhubarb.** Lift a large root and split smaller pieces, with each piece having at least one bud. Plant the divided portions 3 ft (90 cm) apart in soil that has been enriched with organic matter.

■ **Young strawberry runners** that were potted up for forcing and left outside should be put on their sides to prevent them from getting too wet. Or put them in a cold frame, but keep it well ventilated so as not to start them into growth too early.

■ **Take hardwood cuttings** of red-, white-, and blackcurrants, and gooseberrries.

■ **Take cuttings from vines.** Now is a good time to propagate vines from eye cuttings. Make each cutting about 1½ in (3 cm) long, with each having one bud or "eye." On the opposite side, make a shallow sloping cut just underneath the bud and dip the cut part into hormone rooting solution. Put the cutting horizontally, bud facing upward, into a small pot of potting mix, lightly covered. Keep in a propagator at 75°F (24°C).

UNDER COVER

■ **Some heating will be required now** if you are keeping frost-tender plants inside. The most convenient heaters are thermostatically controlled electric ones, although there are gas and kerosene heaters as well. Heating large greenhouses can be expensive. To save on heating bills:
■ Separate off a smaller part of the greenhouse with bubble wrap.
■ Insulate the greenhouse with bubble wrap to reduce the heating costs.
■ If your greenhouse has glass to the ground, the lower half can be insulated with bubble wrap plus polystyrene.

■ **Ventilate whenever possible.** It is vital to keep air circulating. Good circulation, without drafts, is vital to keep down diseases, such as botrytis. Close the ventilators in the early afternoon to conserve precious heat.

■ **Clean pots and seed trays.** If this job is done now, it will save a lot of rushing around trying to find clean containers for seed-sowing and taking cuttings in spring. Also, trays left lying around with bits of dead plants and old soil in them will harbor

Seed trays and pots When you have cleaned them thoroughly, group pots according to size, ready for sowing seeds under cover.

pests and diseases, making propagation less successful. Using clean containers is an important step toward success in propagating plants.

■ **Water all plants more carefully now.** With shorter days and cooler temperatures, plant growth will be slowing down. So it is important to be more careful with watering. Wait until plants look as if they really need watering.

Glasshouse and house plants
■ **Pot up some lily-of-the-valley** rhizomes for an unusual and fragrant houseplant.

■ **Sow cyclamen now** to give the plants a long growing period before flowering, not this coming Christmas, but the following one, giving them 14 months to make good plants with plenty of flowers. Soak the seeds prior to sowing to soften the seed coat, then sow in a pot or tray filled with seed-starting mix and cover lightly with mix or vermiculite. A temperature of 54–60°F (12–15°C) is required for germination. When the seedlings are large enough to handle, prick out into small pots and water in well. A winter temperature of 50°F (10°C) is needed to keep the young plants growing. A final potting into a 5–6-in (12–15-cm) pot will be required in the summer. The plants can go outside once the threat of frost has passed. Fertilize and water the plants regularly. Bring them inside again in September.

Crops under glass
■ **Begin pruning indoor vines** by cutting all the fruited shoots back to one or two buds from the main stem. Vines can be pruned through to late winter, but those under glass are best pruned early to admit light for other plants under cover. Cuttings can be made from the prunings.

The December Garden

Any sunshine there is in December will be weak, but sunny days can be quite pleasant, and if you wrap up well, you can have a good day in the garden, catching up with cleanup tasks or just taking a stroll. Now's your chance to carry out any repairs and maintenance jobs that have been piling up during the year, and make the most of any good weather by pruning and protecting plants for the winter.

THINGS TO DO

Feed birds in cold weather, and do not allow ponds, water features, and bird baths to freeze over. Continue winter digging, incorporating organic matter into the soil, and repair lawns, sheds, and fences if weather conditions allow.

Prune woody ornamental plants and fruit trees and bushes, shredding the prunings if possible; also prune ornamental vines and grapevines. Shake heavy snow off trees, shrubs, and hedges to avoid damage.

Water plants that are overwintering under cover sparingly now that they are dormant, to avoid the risk of rotting. Take care of container plants to get the best of their winter display. You can sow seed of alpine plants now too.

Lift and heel in celery so that you have plenty of winter supplies, and earth up tall Brussels sprout stems to support them. Spray your fruit trees and roses with a plant oil winter wash to reduce pest and disease problems.

LAST CHANCE

Protect plants and containers that are vulnerable to frost damage, and either insulate outside faucets or shut off their water supply and drain them. Prune tall bush roses to guard against wind rock, and bring in Christmas bulbs for flowering.

GET AHEAD

Sow geranium seeds under cover for next year's plants. Sow some early crops under cover for the first plants to put out in the new year.

Witch hazel (*Hamamelis* x *intermedia* 'John')
makes a lovely display to enliven a winter garden.

Cold, crisp, clear days

Clear skies can mean cold, sunny days—so time in the garden can be enjoyable and worthwhile. Color can be found, too, to cheer up the short winter days. Look for bright berries, subtle heathers, and the vivid red feathers of cardinals. There are plenty of tasks to be done—especially winter pruning.

December can be a wonderful month in the garden. The days may be short, but on the occasional clear, frosty, sunny day, it can be a pleasure to be outside. It really is much better for you than snoozing in front of the fire! Make the most of these days, since they may be few and far between.

Plants can look charming with a light covering of snow on them and the bare stems of trees and shrubs can be transformed with a shimmer of sharp frost. But be aware, overly heavy falls of snow will damage trees and shrubs, so thick layers will have to be knocked off before they cause any harm.

The winter scene

It's not a completely bleak month for color in the garden. Plants such as the winter-flowering heathers and *Jasminum nudiflorum* should be in flower throughout the month. There should still be berries on trees and shrubs, too, if the birds haven't eaten them all during spells of bad weather when other food is scarce.

There is still plenty to do outside, although the pace of work will be more gentle now. There is no need for the urgency with which things have to be done in the spring and summer. Pay close attention to any new plantings you've installed earlier in the fall. If the soil is not frozen, they may need watering during periods of dry weather. Evergreens, in particular, are prone to drying out in cold, dry conditions when their roots can't take up enough water to make up for what's being lost through their foliage. Consider applying an anti-transpirant spray to any evergreens, needled or broad-leaved, that might be at risk through the winter months.

Check mulch around newly installed plants, too. Once the soil is frozen, mulch helps to keep it that way, protecting plants from the effects of alternate freezing and thawing that can literally heave them right out of the ground, especially if they haven't gotten fully established in a new location.

Winter-pruning of fruit trees is a satisfying job to be undertaken now. And it's a good time to do any major pruning of ornamental deciduous trees and shrubs, not only because the plants are now in their dormant period,

Winter stems Dogwood underplanted with winter creeper (*Cornus alba* 'Sibirica' and *Euonymus fortunei* 'Silver Queen') gives the garden a festive glow.

but also, with the leaves now off the plants, it's much easier to see what you are doing. It's also much easier to identify dead and diseased wood, which can then be cut out. Of course, shrubs such as the dogwoods (*Cornus*) and willows grown for their ornamental bark should be left until spring. If you prune them now you will lose the colorful stems—the very reason why they are grown.

Company in the garden

Winter digging can continue this month whenever weather conditions allow—that is, when the soil is not excessively wet or frozen. While you're outdoors, take the opportunity to observe the birds that are visiting your yard. You may notice that new species have taken the place of the feathered friends that sang to you during the summer months. It's time to set out your bird feeders, preferably before the arrival of harsh winter weather. A varied selection of food put out regularly from now on will help see birds through the winter and keep them in the neighborhood of your garden, rather than trying their luck elsewhere. If you have decided to replant part of the garden, you can do much to encourage birds by including

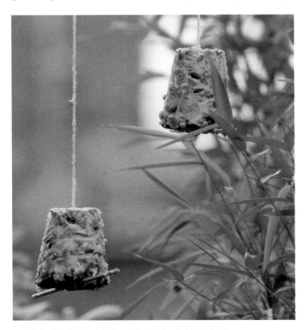

Feed the birds Suet blocks and well-stocked bird feeders will encourage birds to keep visiting your yard during the winter months when insects are hard to find.

Weather watch

Although there can be a few relatively mild December days, it's a cold month in all but the southernmost parts of the country. When a mild—or at least sunny and not too windy—day comes along, take the opportunity to have a look around your garden to make sure your plants are secure and prepared for even colder days ahead.

Cold temperatures

When the reading on the thermometer is lower than you'd like for outdoor activities, remember that cold temperatures benefit the garden by killing off pests and diseases, as well as by fulfilling the dormancy requirements that enable many plants to produce flowers and fruits when warmer days return.

Limited sun

The sun may seem like a distant memory on some December days—the combination of low-lying clouds and scant hours of daylight make for many dim days this month. The sunlight that does manage to reach us this month comes at such a low angle and stays so briefly that it rarely has time to really warm things up. The days continue growing shorter as the winter solstice approaches. Although daylight begins to increase after the solstice (around December 21), the recovery is not noticeable for at least another month.

Heavy snow

Snow blankets much of the Northern Plains, mountain regions, the upper Midwest, and New England by mid-month, although a white Christmas is by no means guaranteed in any but the northernmost parts of the country. By December's end, winter weather has settled in pretty much everywhere, meaning cold temperatures and ice and snow in the north and cool, rainy, sometimes icy conditions in the south.

plants that will attract them to your yard. Almost all of the berry-producing trees and shrubs will attract birds, and if you have room, a mixed, informal fencerow of flowering and fruiting trees and shrubs will give them both sustenance and shelter. Bare-rooted hedging plants may be available throughout the winter and can be planted whenever weather conditions are favorable. It's also a good time for taking hardwood cuttings of trees and shrubs, for an even more economical option. A small water feature will also attract birds, as they love to drink and bathe in shallow water, and unfrozen water sources may be few and far between.

Conserving warmth

Inside there will be a lot to do if you haven't yet cleaned out the greenhouse or conservatory. After doing this, insulate with bubble wrap to reduce the cost of heating. Quite a dramatic reduction in costs can be achieved by insulation and it will enable you to get your plants off to a good start early in the new year. If you don't have

Frost-hardy Brussels sprouts These come into their own this month and their taste may even be improved after a cold snap. You need to harvest them when they are still quite small, starting to pick from the bottom and working upward.

Plants for winter display

Garden centers are now packed with winter-flowering pot plants and there will be a wide variety to choose from. In very cold weather, make sure the plants are properly wrapped when you buy them, as even a short period exposed to the cold can affect the growth and flowering of these plants. A good selection includes azaleas, poinsettias, winter cyclamen, and *Solanum capsicastrum* (the winter cherry). These will fill your home with color over the holiday period. They are living decorations, so they will last longer given a little care and attention.

Another way to have color in the home at this time is by cutting shoots from winter-flowering shrubs and putting them in water; the flowers will open up in the warmth of the greenhouse, conservatory, or home. If you can do this early in December the flowers will open in time for Christmas.

Armchair gardening

If the weather is just too bad to do any work outside then it is a good idea to plan ahead and consider the plants you want to grow and the features to be created in your garden for next year. It's a pleasant occupation, leafing through seed and plant catalogs by the fireside. Getting orders off early will ensure that you get the plants you want before the nursery runs out of them. There are many specialist plant nurseries around the country and most of them produce catalogs. These can be a mine of information and you will often come across some little treasures. Vegetable seed catalogs are also a fine source of inspiration. With memories still fresh of the crops that did and didn't do well this year for you, all of the information that the best brochures give on the strengths and weaknesses of the various cultivars will probably have you planning next year's menus, never mind plantings, well in advance.

a greenhouse and don't have room for one, you should at least have a cold frame. You'll be surprised at how much more scope it will give you for propagating and sheltering plants.

Use this quiet time to sort out your tools and tidy up the shed for spring. While you're at it, you could make a list of anything you need and put it on your Christmas list. If your tools always end up in a pile on a shelf, consider adding a rack to hang them from or a set of dividers to create individual cubbyholes to tuck your tools into.

Mahonia x _media_ 'Charity'
Evergreen shrub with honey-scented flowers (see p.297)

Hippeastrum 'Apple Blossom'
One of the most spectacular bulbs to grow as a houseplant (see p.290)

Viburnum x _bodnantense_ 'Dawn'
Beautifully scented flowers on bare winter branches (see p.322)

Elaeagnus x _ebbingei_ 'Gilt Edge'
Variegated evergreen shrub for a splash of color (see p.282)

Ilex aquifolium 'Handsworth New Silver'
Variegated female holly, bearing bright berries (see p.291)

Cyclamen coum
Perennial that can be grown in pots for an indoor display (see p.279)

***Cotoneaster frigidus* 'Fructu Luteo'**
Yellow-berried shrub popular with birds (see p.278)

***Aucuba japonica* 'Variegata'**
Hedging stalwart puts on a winter show (see p.267)

***Rhododendron* 'Inga'**
Compact azalea, ideal as a winter houseplant (see p.310)

***Salix* x *rubens* 'Basfordiana'**
Prune this willow hard each year for bright stems (see p.316)

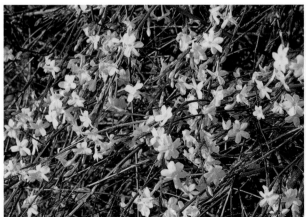

Jasminum nudiflorum
A straggly but welcome winter-flowering climber (see p.293)

***Clematis armandii* 'Apple Blossom'**
Evergreen clematis with scented winter flowers (see p.273)

What to do in December

AROUND THE YARD

There are few pests around in the garden now, but it always pays to be vigilant, as milder winters let many survive the winter when they would normally be killed.

Any plants, whether they are deciduous trees, shrubs and climbers, or herbaceous perennials, can be moved if they are growing in the wrong place or have become too big for their current position, provided that soil conditions permit. Always take as big a rootball as you can cope with when lifting larger plants. Remember to revitalize the soil both where the plant is taken from and in the new position. Stake tall plants to prevent wind rock and provide a windbreak shelter to protect from cold winds.

Protect plants vulnerable to frost. Take in any plants that have been overlooked. Perennial beds will benefit from a layer of protection. Herbaceous perennials are very easy to protect now that plants have died back—though it won't harm them even if they are in leaf. Just put a thick layer of straw or dry leaves over the crown of the plant and hold it in position with some wire netting. Taller shrubs can be insulated with straw held in place with burlap. Don't use plastic, since even when plants are dormant they still need to breathe.

Winter is pruning time for ornamental and fruiting woody plants. Consider shredding the prunings instead of burning them. Shreddings make a terrific mulch, or they can be added to the compost pile. If your yard is mostly shrubs and lawn, keep a pile of shreddings to mix in with grass clippings in the summer. These need plenty of air in them if they are to rot down properly and not form a slimy, stinking mess. Don't shred any diseased material because the disease will be spread.

Wrap insulation around outside faucets. As ice forms, water expands and this can easily burst pipes. You can insulate faucets by wrapping them in several layers of burlap, or there are products on the market especially for insulating outside faucets. If possible, turn off the supply to outside faucets and drain the pipe during the winter. This way you will avoid any possibility of burst pipes.

Continue winter digging of new planting areas and empty vegetable beds for as long as the weather permits. If the soil is so wet that it sticks to your boots, keep off it until it dries out a bit. If you have to walk on the soil when it's wet, use planks to get across. Walking on soil compacts it and, particularly if the soil is a heavy clay, the air will be driven out of it. When it does eventually dry out, it will set as hard as concrete. To prevent the soil from being completely saturated when you want to get started with the work, cover at least part of the ground with plastic sheeting to keep off the worst of the rain. When you want to work the soil, pull it back, and when you're finished cover it up again.

Keep composting Woody prunings and leaf litter decomposes faster when shredded. Try running the lawn mower over piles of fallen leaves, then collect them and add them to the compost bin.

TREES AND SHRUBS

■ **Early in December** cut a few shoots from winter-flowering shrubs such as *Viburnum* x *bodnantense* and *Prunus* x *subhirtella* 'Autumnalis'. Put the shoots in water and keep them in a cool place indoors. Soon the buds will begin to open and the beautifully scented flowers can be added to your holiday decorations.

■ **Holly trees with their red berries** are very attractive at this time of year and they provide excellent Christmas decorations for the home. But birds love to eat the berries just as much as we like to look at them. While we mustn't begrudge birds their food in harsh winter weather, it is wise to cover at least part of a holly tree with some netting to save some of the berries for the Christmas festivities. Make sure the netting is secured firmly so that birds don't get caught up in it.

■ **Check newly planted trees and shrubs,** including roses, to see if they have been loosened by winds or lifted by frost. When this happens, gaps form around the roots, causing them to dry out because they are not in close contact with the soil. If you see cracks around the plant, gently firm in with your feet. Be careful on heavy clay soils not to step down too heavily, or all the air will be driven out of the soil.

■ **Put a windbreak around newly planted evergreens.** Strong cold winds can have a devastating effect on recently planted leafy shrubs. Plants are continuously losing water from their leaves (known as "transpiration") and the rate of water loss increases with high winds passing over the surface of the leaves—just as a windy day dries laundry more quickly. The edges of the leaves dry out faster than the plant can replace the water and so cells die off. It's known as "wind scorch." To reduce damage, erect a shelter around the plants.

Ilex aquifolium **'Madame Briot'**

It can be made from any material stretched between posts, from burlap to clear plastic, or fine net mesh made specially for the purpose. If you don't have enough to go all the way around the plant, make sure it is at least on the windward side.

■ **Shake snow off trees and shrubs.** Although plants look pretty with a layer of snow on them, it can be a considerable weight and will easily bring down a branch or two. As long as the layer of snow hasn't frozen hard, brush it off as soon as possible and the damage will be slight.

Small to medium conifers that have been planted as specimen trees, where the shape of the plant is all-important, can be protected by tying thin wire or strong string around them, preventing the branches from sagging outward when the snow falls on them. Don't worry about snow lying over low plants: it actually gives them protection against cold, blanketing them from frost.

Pruning and training

■ **Prune deciduous trees and shrubs for health and to shape.** Take a look at all of the deciduous trees and shrubs in your garden to see if any need attention to

improve the health or shape of the plant. At this time of year, with no leaves in the way, it is easier to see what you are doing. You will need a good pair of pruners, a pair of loppers, and a pruning saw for cutting off larger branches. Chainsaws can be rented from hardware stores or rental centers, but unless you are familiar with these machines, they are best left to the experts; they can be extremely dangerous in inexperienced hands. Likewise, never saw through large branches, or branches high up in a tree, yourself. These are jobs for a trained arborist. If you live in an urban area or belong to a homeowners' association, check before pruning for any rules and restrictions related to trimming street trees.

■ First remove any dead or diseased wood and any crossing branches that are rubbing together, cutting out whole shoots to a joint whenever possible rather than just tipping them back.

■ If the plant is taking up too much room in a smaller garden, it can be trimmed. The main point to remember is that the harder you prune, the stronger the resulting growth will be, so when restricting size, light pruning will have a much more satisfactory effect than hacking away. Don't just give freestanding plants an all-over "haircut," as when trimming a hedge. Try to open up the center of the plant to allow air to circulate and reduce the amount of shadow cast on lower-growing plants in the border.

■ Take your time when pruning. Stand back and look at the plant often and consider what effect removing a branch will have on the appearance of the plant before making the cut. You can't stick a branch back on once it's been pruned off.

■ Most woody material can be put through a shredder to make a mulch for borders. Any diseased material should be put in the trash, taken to a municipal dump, or

Cutting off a low branch

1 First reduce the weight of the branch so that the final cut is easier to make cleanly. To prevent downward tearing, make an undercut.

2 Supporting the weight of the branch, cut downward straight through it about 2 in (5 cm) beyond the undercut.

3 Now cut back the stub cleanly, cutting just beyond the swollen ring or the "branch collar," at the point where it meets the trunk.

burned. Composting it will more than likely spread the disease.

■ Fertilize after pruning and mulch with organic matter.

■ Most plants tend to produce a mass of young shoots from the points where they were pruned. Keep an eye on this regrowth through spring and summer and remove unwanted shoots while they are still young.

■ Prune tall bush roses by half to prevent wind rock. If plants are rocked by wind, a hole will form at the base of the plant, where water will collect and cause the roots to rot. In frosty weather the water may freeze, resulting in further damage to the root system.

Planting

■ **Continue planting trees, shrubs and climbers.** As long as the soil is not frozen or waterlogged, press on with planting, as weather conditions can change quickly and short days mean there is less time to work in the garden. Heel in plants if soil conditions are not suitable for planting (see January). Plants will keep for quite a long time if planted temporarily in a corner of the yard.

Propagation

■ **Continue taking hardwood cuttings**.

Hedges

■ **Brush any heavy snow off** evergreen hedges before the weight of it splays out branches and causes damage.

■ **Prune overgrown deciduous hedges** like beech and hornbeam. No matter how often we trim hedges through the summer, they imperceptibly creep outward, taking up more space and becoming more difficult to cut. Now, while the plants are dormant, is a good time to reduce the hedge to a manageable size. On an old, established

hedge you may need loppers or a pruning saw to cut some of the larger branches.

Cut back the sides until the hedge is no more than 18–24 in (45–60 cm) wide at the top, tapering it so that the bottom of the hedge is wider. This shaping will protect the hedge from damage by heavy snowfalls. The top can be trimmed to whatever height you want. To get the top level, you may need to put up a line at the height required.

■ **Taking hardwood cuttings** is an ideal way of producing quantities of hedging plants for free. The cuttings will have rooted by next winter, when you will be able to dig them up and plant them in their permanent positions.

Alternatively, grow a deciduous hedge from hardwood cuttings *in situ*. Prepare a trench along the line of the proposed hedge as the planting area and line out cuttings along it, about 1 ft (30 cm) apart. Put a few more in at the end of the row as spares in case some of the cuttings don't root. It will take a few years but you will end up with a bargain hedge.

Clearing snow Use a sturdy broom to knock snow off hedges to avoid spoiling their shape.

CLIMBERS

■ **Brush snow off** dense evergreen climbers and wall shrubs. When heavy snow accumulates on these it can not only break stems but also puts strain on any ties and supports.

■ **Early in December** cut a few shoots from winter jasmine. Put the shoots in water and keep them in a cool place indoors. Soon the buds will begin to open and you will be able to use the beautifully scented flowers to add to your winter holiday decorations.

■ **Ornamental vines** can be pruned now to keep them from completely taking over the garden. Vines can produce growths up to 10 ft (3 m) or more in one season, and over several years, if they are not pruned, you will end up with a mess. Thin out overcrowded shoots and then prune sideshoots to two buds from the main stems kept as a framework.

■ **Take hardwood cuttings of deciduous climbers.** Remove strong woody shoots about 1 ft (30 cm) long from the plant, cutting just above a bud. Trim the base to just below a bud and cut off the tip just above a bud to leave a section of stem about 9 in (23 cm) long. Dip the cut end into hormone rooting solution. Make a slit trench in a corner of the yard with a spade, to the depth of the spade.

In heavy clay soil, put some grit in the base of the trench to help improve the drainage. Put the cuttings in to two-thirds their depth and carefully firm in with your foot. The cuttings will have rooted by next winter, when you can dig them up and plant them in their permanent positions.

PERENNIALS

■ **Continue to cut down dead growth** on herbaceous perennials and generally weed and tidy up borders. The sooner this is done, the less work there will be left in the busy spring period. But robust stems with seed heads, as on sedums, can be left uncut until the spring, as you will find they are beautiful when wrapped in a layer of frost: a lovely sight, especially on a sunny, clear morning.

■ **During periods of mild weather** when the ground is not frozen or excessively wet, you can continue to lift and divide herbaceous perennials.

■ **Root cuttings** of perennials can be taken through the winter.

Alpines

■ **Continue to clear fallen leaves from the rock garden.** Most alpine plants suffer if left covered with a damp layer of leaves for any length of time. So it is important to remove them regularly, as soon as possible. In their native mountainous regions, alpines are usually protected by a blanket of snow, which actually keeps them relatively dry. The snow generally melts quickly and the plants are then exposed to the fresh alpine air.

■ **Sow alpine seeds.** This may seem an odd time of year to do this, but in the wild, alpine seeds have to go through a period of cold weather to break the seed's dormancy. This can be imitated at home by sowing the seeds in a pot and standing the pot outside to let the seeds freeze from time to time, with a sheet of glass over the pot to protect them from excessive moisture. The seeds will germinate in the spring. If you choose to sow them later, in warmer months, then you will have to put the seeds in the refrigerator for six to eight weeks before sowing to break dormancy.

Sow the seeds in pots containing alpine potting mix, consisting of equal parts loam, sharp grit and peat-free potting mix. Water the mix before sowing and sow the seeds thinly on the surface. Cover them with horticultural grit. This will reduce the problem of algae growing on the soil surface, as the seeds can take some time to germinate. They may also germinate at different times, so don't throw away the pots until you have all the plants you need. Grow the plants on in the same type of potting mix. Alpines don't need a lot of fertilizer, so little feeding is necessary.

Covering alpine seeds

1 Cover the seeds when sown with a layer of clean, fine grit.

2 The grit will allow water to drain away from the crown of the young plant, which is prone to rot in the wet.

BULBS

■ **Check bulbs, corms, and tubers in storage** for signs of disease. Botrytis and rot can quickly spread. If diseases start to appear, remove the affected bulb or tuber—or if only part of it is affected, cut out the diseased portion and dust the cut surface with garden sulfur.

■ **Bring bulbs being forced for Christmas into light and warmth.** Bulbs such as prepared hyacinths and daffodils that were plunged outside in the fall and then brought into cool conditions a few weeks ago, can be brought into the warmth to encourage them into flower for Christmas. Hyacinths are a particular favorite as they fill the room with their scent.

■ **Bulbs that have been plunged** for forcing into flower in spring should also be inspected regularly. Check to see if they need watering. Don't overwater, especially if the bulbs are growing in bulb bowls that have no drainage holes, or rot will set in.

When the bulbs have grown about 1–2 in (2.5–5 cm) tall they should be taken indoors to a cool greenhouse or conservatory, or placed on the windowsill of a cool room. A few weeks later the bulbs can be moved to a warmer room to flower and fill the room with winter cheer. Too much warmth too early causes them to grow thin and straggly, and they don't then produce the best flowers. Turn them regularly to make sure they grow up straight. Tall narcissi often benefit from some support; a few twiggy sticks, especially bare stems of twisted hazel or willow, look attractive.

■ **Continue to pot up lilies** for a succession of blooms. Put four or five bulbs into a 7-in (18-cm) pot containing bulb mix, covering the bulbs with about 4 in (10 cm) of mix. Water them in and wait for the stunning flowers in spring.

ANNUALS AND BEDDING

■ **Get seed catalogs** and plan border designs and color schemes for next year. Even on a cold winter day, you can dream of the summer to come. The earlier you can order seeds, the less likely it is that they will be late in arriving. Seed companies get very busy in the spring, when they receive a rush of orders, because people tend to wait until the last minute to think about seeds. You'll also have a better chance of getting the varieties you want if you order early. It's always exciting to try a few new varieties each year.

■ **Sow geranium seeds this month.** It may seem early to be starting seeds into growth, but these bedding plants do need a relatively long growing period to flower the first year after sowing.

Whether you have a greenhouse or not, the ideal way to start off the seeds is in a propagator. This cuts down on the cost of having to heat a whole greenhouse. Place the propagator on the windowsill to get the maximum amount of light during the short days of winter.

A temperature of 65°F (18°C) is needed for the seeds to germinate successfully. The seeds can be sown in small pots of peat-free potting mix, watering the mix before sowing. Lightly cover them with sifted mix or vermiculite and put them in the propagator. Pot up the seedlings into larger pots when they are large enough to handle.

If you don't have room to germinate your own seeds, then you can order seedlings or young plants ("plug plants") from nurseries for delivery in spring, reducing the expense and the time needed to grow the plants at home. But order them early, as they are very popular and usually sell out fast.

CONTAINERS

■ **Permanent plants in containers** should be checked over regularly and any debris cleared out. Fallen leaves can collect around the base of plants in containers, encouraging disease and also giving pests somewhere to hibernate. They also make the plants look untidy.

■ **Move pots of borderline hardy plants** inside if you did not do this earlier. Move plants into an unheated or cool greenhouse or conservatory. Very little heat is needed, otherwise the plants will tend to grow too tall and become very straggly due to the lack of light.

Water the plants carefully, giving them enough to keep them alive. Don't overdo it or the plants may be killed. Whenever possible, ensure that there is plenty of air circulating around the plants, and open the ventilators on reasonably mild days. Be aware that damp, still air encourages diseases, such as botrytis, to set in.

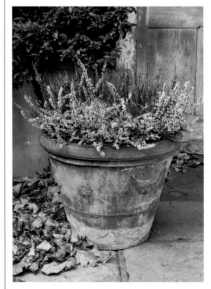

Clear out debris Don't leave fallen leaves trapped around the stems of container plants.

LAWNS

■ **Keep off the lawn** if it is frozen or wet, or put down planks to walk on. If you walk on a frozen lawn, yellow patches appear when it thaws.

■ **Repair lawns with sod.** Any worn areas of the lawn can be sodded now, working from boards to disperse your weight if the ground is very wet. Leave the sod a little higher than the surrounding lawn to allow it to settle. If you can't get hold of a small quantity of sod, or at least one that in any way resembles your own, the trick is to swap the damaged part with a good patch taken from someplace where the damaged one will be less noticeable—just as one can covertly move stained carpet tiles around.

Damaged patches on the edges of neat lawns should always be repaired by resodding, not sowing, to give the required clean, firm edge, and here as well you can swap sod sections around.

■ **Rake up any fallen leaves** that have been left lying on the lawn. If they are left, the grass will die off due to lack of light, and disease may set in due to a lack of air circulation. If a lawn has been neglected under a layer of leaves for any length of time, spiking the lawn after clearing the leaves will help to improve aeration again, especially to the roots.

New lawns

■ **If weather conditions allow**—that is, the soil is not sodden or frozen—you may continue preparing ground and laying sod.

VEGETABLES AND HERBS

■ **Cover bare beds** with clear plastic to protect the soil from winter rain. This will allow you to dig in the new year without being held up by bad weather.

■ **Make a hotbed from fresh horse manure.** This is a 19th-century practice, but it is still perfectly valid today. It makes good use of horse manure piled up to rot down. There is a lot of heat given off by manure as it breaks down and this can be harnessed to produce some early crops. Fresh horse manure is not as difficult to obtain as most people think. There are many riding stables in towns or on the edges of cities and towns and all too often they are glad to pass it on to gardeners. Some establishments may charge a modest price, but it is well worth the expense. You will almost certainly have to transport it home yourself, unless you live close to the stables.

A hotbed can be made as a free-standing pile, but the heat will be retained better in a container—a wooden compost bin is ideal. Pile it in until it is mounded above the topmost timbers. Then cap the manure with a soil mix of seven parts loam, three parts spent mushroom compost, and two parts coarse grit. Mix it well and spread a good layer on top of the heap.

Put a cold frame on top and leave it for about a week to allow the temperature to build up. It is surprising just how hot it gets—try sticking a cane into the pile and then pulling it out after a few days and you'll see just how much heat is being generated. In two or three weeks, when it has cooled a little, you can sow lettuces, carrots, radishes and turnips, and spinach for early crops.

Once these crops have finished, you can grow trailing tomatoes, cucumbers, or even melons on the heap. At the end of the season you will left with a fine pile of well-rotted manure to dig into the soil.

Mending a broken edge

1 Cut out a generous rectangle of sod around the damaged area.

2 Undercut the rectangle with a spade. Try to cut as even a thickness as possible.

3 Re-lay the piece of sod, turning it so that the broken edge faces inward.

4 Fill the hole with top-dressing and work it into the seams.

Swelling crowns You can lift celeriac throughout the winter. In frosty conditions, protect the stems with a straw mulch.

Harvesting

■ **Keep harvesting winter crops.** Brussels sprouts and parsnips fresh from the garden are treats at winter meals.

Caring for crops

■ **Earth up spring cabbages** and other winter brassicas to give them better anchorage in strong winds. Tall-growing Brussels sprouts are particularly vulnerable to being blown over. It may also be necessary to put in canes and tie the plants to them. Remove yellowing leaves regularly, as these will encourage fungal diseases. Spring cabbages are normally planted in the fall at a distance of about 6 in (15 cm) apart. During the winter, cut every other one as winter greens, leaving the others to grow on in the spring.

Sowing indoors

■ **Sow some early crops.** If you have space, you could sow a few pots or cell trays of lettuce, summer cabbages and cauliflowers, radishes, round varieties of carrots, spinach, salad onions, and turnips. These seeds don't need high temperatures to germinate; about 55°F (13°C) is adequate, so a windowsill is fine if you don't have a propagator. If you sow in pots or seed trays you will need to prick the seedlings out, spacing them about 1 in (2.5 cm) apart into another tray. Grow the young plants on in good light, watering regularly. They will be ready to put out under cloches or floating row cover in late winter for the very earliest crop.

Herbs

■ **Bay trees grown in pots** should be taken indoors, or, where hardy, they can be moved to the most sheltered part of the yard.

Potted bay tree This attractive display can be recreated next year, so move the vulnerable bay to a more sheltered spot, or even indoors.

FRUIT
Picking and storing

■ **Keep inspecting stored fruit** for signs of rot. Any that are showing symptoms of decay should be thrown out onto the lawn or vegetable garden for the birds to feed on. It will be a welcome treat for them in harsh weather.

Caring for crops

■ **Check apple and pear trees** for any signs of canker.

■ **Check that tree stakes and ties are sound.** Tree ties can easily break after a few years, so check them regularly. Also bear in mind that as a tree grows, the stem expands, making the tree tie tighter around the trunk. So on your regular inspection tours, check that ties are not too tight or they will strangle your trees.

Pruning and training

■ **Winter-prune apple and pear trees**.

■ **Finish pruning currants and gooseberries** through the winter.

■ **Prune grape vines**. Vines must only be pruned when dormant as they will "bleed" sap copiously if cut when in growth, which weakens the plant. All the laterals (sideshoots made in one season) should be pruned back to two or three buds, leaving you with long, stumpy main stems, which you can also cut back in length if overgrown.

You may feel that you are being a bit ruthless by pruning so hard, but vines produce a lot of extremely vigorous growth and you'll need to keep them in check. The new shoots that grow from the stumpy stems will grow long and bear fruit all in one season next year. You can make some of the prunings into cuttings.

Pruning vines First cut all of the fruited shoots back to two or three buds from the main stem.

Planting

■ **Plant fruit trees and bushes** whenever the soil is not frozen or too wet.

Propagation

■ **Take hardwood cuttings** of redcurrants, whitecurrants, blackcurrants, and gooseberries; all are taken in exactly the same way. Take shoots around 12 in (30 cm) long, cutting just above a bud on the parent plant. Remove the top 2 in (5 cm) of softer growth at the tip of the cutting and trim the base just below a bud. Now dip the base in hormone rooting solution. Make a slit trench. If your soil is a heavy clay, trickle sharp sand into the bottom of the trench and then line out the cuttings.

If blackcurrants have shown any signs of reversion virus or big bud mite don't propagate from them.

The new plants will have rooted by next autumn, but you can leave them for another year before moving to their permanent positions, as they will not fruit when young.

UNDER COVER

■ **Tidy up plants in the greenhouse and conservatory** regularly, removing yellowing and fallen leaves and fading flowers. The warm, moist atmosphere and short days are perfect breeding conditions for molds and other fungal diseases. Any dead plant material left lying around will encourage them.

■ **Check that greenhouse heaters** are working efficiently. If not, call an electrician.

■ **Water all plants carefully** as their growth is reduced to a minimum, unless they are flowering plants like cyclamen and indoor azaleas. Do all the watering in the early part of the day, if this is at all possible. This will give the greenhouse or conservatory time to dry out before nightfall. Cooler, damp conditions overnight are the perfect breeding ground for diseases such as botrytis (gray mold). Try to ventilate for an hour or two on mild days to keep air circulating, for exactly the same reason.

Raising plants for outdoors

■ **Sow geranium seeds.** See Annuals and Bedding.

Glasshouse and house plants

■ **Keep houseplants in good light.** During the short days of winter, plants need all the light they can get, especially houseplants that get light from only one side. Keep them at as bright a window as you can and turn them every few days so they don't grow to one side as they stretch for the light. If you can move them to a heated conservatory or greenhouse for the midwinter period, so much the better. Regularly clean the leaves of large foliage plants like rubber plants, as dust gathers on these, reducing the amount of light getting to the leaf surfaces.

Houseplants make very popular presents, but often they don't last for very long. Some of them are quite expensive, but with a little bit of care, they can last for a long time. They all need slightly different conditions in order to get the best out of them.

The ever-popular winter-flowering *Cyclamen persicum* needs a cool room and good light. When watering, try not to splash the corm or the foliage with water. It is best watered from below, standing the pot in a shallow saucer for a while.

Poinsettias, with their spectacular red, pink, or white bracts, are actually a type of euphorbia native to warm countries, where they make tall trees. They therefore need quite warm rooms and should be kept moist, but they dislike being waterlogged, so be careful when watering them.

Azaleas are pretty flowers that last a long time. They do need cool conditions and should never be allowed to dry out— not even slightly. Keep them well watered all the time. Give them good light and a cool place and they will flower for weeks.

Crops under glass

Prune grape vines under glass.

Cyclamen persicum

A–Z plant directory

This directory gives siting and growing information for all of the "Star Plants" that are featured month by month throughout the book, arranged here in A–Z order for ease of reference. We also recommend other good species and cultivars, and suggest "Perfect Partners" to look for, to help you plan your planting schemes and groupings.

Z = hardiness zone (see inside front cover for the United States Department of Agriculture Plant Hardiness Zone Map).

H = heat zone (see inside back cover for the American Horticultural Society Plant Heat Zone Map).

↕ = height; remember that trees and shrubs may take many years to reach the height given.

↔ = spread: to obtain planting distances between two different plants, add the spreads together and divide by 2.

A gorgeous display Orange heleniums, flat, yellow-headed achilleas, daisy-like echinaceas, and pink *Liatris* form a beautiful natural summer planting with drifts of tall perennials and grasses.

A

Abelia 'Edward Goucher'

Abelia

A moderately vigorous, semievergreen shrub with arching branches. Z7–9 H9–1 ‡5 ft (1.5 m), ↔8 ft (2.5 m).
■ **Seasonal highlights** Bears a mass of trumpet-shaped, lilac-pink flowers from summer to fall.
■ **Value at other times** The glossy, dark-green leaves are bronzed when young.
■ **Ideal site** Excellent in a shrub border.
■ **Cultivation** Best in fertile, well-drained soil in full sun, but tolerates light, dappled shade. Protect from cold winds. Prune after flowering. Deadhead and shorten to a strong bud any shoots that spoil the outline.
■ **Also recommended** *Abelia x grandiflora*
■ **Perfect partners** *Abelia triflora*, taller with fragrant white flowers; *Jasminum humile*, evergreen shrub with yellow flowers spring to fall.

Abutilon 'Souvenir de Bonn'

Indian mallow

Evergreen shrub or small tree. Z9–11 H12–1 ‡10 ft (3 m), ↔6–10 ft (2–3 m)
■ **Seasonal highlights** From spring to fall, it has hanging, bowl-shaped orange flowers with darker veins.
■ **Value at other times** Pale-green leaves with creamy-white margins all year.
■ **Ideal site** A sunny border, warm wall, or conservatory.
■ **Cultivation** Indoors, grow in loam-based potting soil. Grow in fertile, well-drained soil outdoors. It is best in a sheltered spot in full sun, but will tolerate dappled shade. Bring indoors for the winter in cold areas, as it will not tolerate frost.
■ **Also recommended** *Abutilon megapotamicum* with plain-green leaves and yellow and red flowers.
■ **Perfect partners** All kinds of summer bedding.

Acer palmatum

Japanese maples

Acer palmatum cultivars are deciduous, mostly mound-forming, shrubs or small trees with lobed or finely cut leaves. Most are hardy in USDA zones 6 to 8 and AHS heat zones 8 to 2.
■ **Seasonal highlights** All are valued for their habit and vibrant fall colors.
■ **Value at other times** Most have small, beautifully tinted spring flowers and winged fruits in fall.
■ **Ideal site** A sheltered shrub border or in decorative containers.
■ **Cultivation** Grow in full sun or dappled shade, in leafy, moist but well-drained soil. Mulch annually in fall. Shelter from cold winds and spring frosts.
■ **Perfect partners** Conifers and heathers.

Acer 'Bloodgood' has red-purple leaves that turn scarlet in fall. ‡↔15 ft (5 m)

Acer 'Chitose-yama' has crimson-green leaves with red-purple fall color. ‡6 ft (2 m), ↔10 ft (3 m)

Acer 'Corallinum' has red-pink young leaves that are green in summer, then red, orange, and yellow in fall. ‡6 ft (2 m), ↔10 ft (3 m)

Acer 'Garnet' has finely cut, red-purple leaves. ‡6 ft (2 m), ↔10 ft (3 m)

Acer 'Sango-kaku' has coral-red shoots and orange-yellow young leaves that turn yellow in fall. ‡6 ft (2 m), ↔10 ft (3 m)

Acer 'Linearilobum' has deeply cut leaves that turn yellow in fall. ‡6 ft (2 m), ↔10 ft (3 m)

Acer pensylvanicum 'Erythrocladum'
Moosewood

A deciduous tree with an upright habit of growth. Also known as striped maple. Z3–7 H7–1 ‡40 ft (12 m), ↔30 ft (10 m)

■ **Seasonal highlights** The bark on young shoots is a striking, brilliant coral-pink in winter, fading to orange-red with grayish-white stripes at maturity.

■ **Value at other times** In spring, clusters of yellow-green flowers hang beneath fresh green leaves, which turn yellow in fall.

■ **Ideal site** Use as a specimen or grow in a woodland garden.

■ **Cultivation** Thrives in any fertile, well-drained soil in sun or dappled shade. Provide shelter from cold winds and late frosts.

■ **Also recommended** *Acer platanoides* 'Crimson King' has leaves of the deepest red-purple.

■ **Perfect partners** Conifers and heathers.

Achillea 'Fanal'
Yarrow

A moderately vigorous, clump-forming, herbaceous perennial with fragrant leaves. Z4–8 H8–1 ‡30 in (75 cm), ↔24 in (60 cm)

■ **Seasonal highlights** Throughout summer, it bears flat heads of bright-red flowers with yellow centers.

■ **Value at other times** The flowers fade with age, but can be dried for winter flower arrangements.

■ **Ideal site** A sunny mixed or herbaceous border.

■ **Cultivation** It prefers an open site in sun, but tolerates light, dappled shade. Grow in moist but well-drained soil. Lift and divide every three or four years to maintain vigor.

■ **Also recommended** *Achillea millefolium* 'Cerise Queen' has heads of magenta-pink flowers with white centers.

■ **Perfect partners** Phlox, daylilies.

Aconitum 'Bressingham Spire'
Monkshood, Aconite

A clump-forming, herbaceous perennial of upright growth. All parts are toxic if ingested. Z3–8 H8–3 ‡to 3 ft (1 m), ↔12 in (30 cm)

■ **Seasonal highlights** Bears tall, tapered spires of deep violet-blue flowers from midsummer to fall.

■ **Value at other times** It has pretty, glossy, dark-green foliage from spring to fall.

■ **Ideal site** A mixed or herbaceous border.

■ **Cultivation** Best grown in partial shade, but tolerates full sun. Grow in moist, fertile soil enriched with organic matter. Divide the plants every three or four years in spring or fall.

■ **Also recommended** *Aconitum carmichaelii* 'Arendsii' has branched spires of clear-blue flowers in fall.

■ **Perfect partners** *Aconitum* 'Ivorine', with ivory-white flowers in late spring and early summer.

Agapanthus 'Blue Giant'
African blue lily

A clump-forming herbaceous perennial of upright habit. Z8–11 H12–1 ‡4 ft (1.2 m), ↔24 in (60 cm)

■ **Seasonal highlights** Has rounded clusters of bell-shaped, rich-blue flowers from mid- to late summer.

■ **Value at other times** Large, strap-shaped, deep-green leaves.

■ **Ideal site** A sunny border, or a tall, shapely container.

■ **Cultivation** Best in sun, but will tolerate light, dappled shade. Grow in moist but well-drained soil. Where marginally hardy, mulch in winter to protect fleshy roots from frost.

■ **Also recommended** *Agapanthus campanulatus* has pale- to dark-blue, occasionally white flowers, from mid- to late summer.

■ **Perfect partners** The strap-shaped foliage contrasts well with the bold, rounded leaves of hostas.

Alcea rosea Chater's Double Group
Hollyhock

A short-lived perennial of vigorous, upright growth. Z3–9 H10–3 ‡to 8 ft (2.5 m), ↔24 in (60 cm)

■ **Seasonal highlights** In summer, it bears peony-like flowers, ranging from white, yellow, apricot and red to lavender and purple. It attracts butterflies and bees.

■ **Value at other times** Attractive leaves for most of the year.

■ **Ideal site** The back of a sunny border, especially in cottage gardens.

■ **Cultivation** Flowers best in sun, but tolerates dappled shade. Grow in any fertile, well-drained soil. Stake in exposed sites. Treat as annuals or biennials to limit hollyhock rust.

■ **Also recommended** *Alcea rosea* 'Nigra', with single, chocolate-maroon flowers.

■ **Perfect partners** Other tall herbaceous plants like delphiniums.

A

Alchemilla mollis
Lady's mantle

Allium hollandicum
Ornamental onion

Alopecurus pratensis 'Aureovariegatus'
Foxtail grass

Alstroemeria 'Orange Glory'
Peruvian lily

Amaranthus caudatus
Love-lies-bleeding

A vigorous, clump-forming, herbaceous perennial. Z4–7 H7–1 ‡24 in (60 cm), ↔30 in (75 cm)

■ **Seasonal highlights** Bears loose clusters of tiny greenish-yellow flowers from early summer to fall.

■ **Value at other times** The hairy, soft-green leaves look especially good spangled with droplets of rain or dew.

■ **Ideal site** The front of an herbaceous border, or in paving crevices.

■ **Cultivation** Thrives in sun or partial shade. Grow in any moist, humus-rich soil. Deadhead after flowering, or it will seed itself all over the garden.

■ **Also recommended** *Alchemilla alpina* is similar but lower-growing and mat-forming.

■ **Perfect partners** It associates well with most other herbaceous perennials, but looks especially good with penstemons.

A moderately vigorous, bulbous perennial. Z4–9 H9–1 ‡3 ft (1 m), ↔4 in (10 cm)

■ **Seasonal highlights** In summer, it produces dense, rounded heads of many star-shaped, purplish-pink flowers.

■ **Value at other times** The attractive seedheads of fall can be dried for flower arrangements.

■ **Ideal site** The perfect highlight in a sunny mixed border.

■ **Cultivation** Ideally, grow in full sun, but will tolerate light shade. Grow in any fertile, well-drained soil. Plant bulbs 2–4 in (5–10 cm) deep in fall.

■ **Also recommended** *Allium caeruleum* has intense, bright-blue flowers.

■ **Perfect partners** Excellent with daylilies and achilleas, providing good contrasts of form and color.

A spreading perennial grass. Z5–8 H8–5 ‡4 ft (1.2 m), ↔16 in (40 cm), often more, but not invasive

■ **Seasonal highlights** It produces dense, cylindrical heads of pale-green to purple flowers from mid-spring to midsummer.

■ **Value at other times** Has narrow, green leaves that are striped rich yellow and arranged in basal tufts.

■ **Ideal site** A sunny mixed border or wild garden.

■ **Cultivation** Best in full sun, but it will tolerate light shade. Grow in fertile, well-drained soil. Cut back to ground level in spring for the freshest-colored foliage in summer.

■ **Also recommended** *Alopecurus lanatus* has silver-gray leaves.

■ **Perfect partners** *Hakonechloa macra* 'Aureola' and *Carex elata* 'Aurea' for contrasting golden foliage.

An upright, moderately vigorous, herbaceous perennial. Z7–11 H12–7 ‡3 ft (1 m), ↔24 in (60 cm)

■ **Seasonal highlights** For many weeks in summer, it bears showy, orange-yellow flowers with darker speckles. They are excellent for cutting.

■ **Value at other times** It has gray-green foliage.

■ **Ideal site** A mixed border or one devoted to flowers for cutting.

■ **Cultivation** Ideally, grow in full sun; it tolerates light shade. Plant carefully in late summer or early fall in any moist but well-drained soil; the fleshy roots are fragile and resent disturbance. Where marginally hardy, apply a dry winter mulch.

■ **Also recommended** *Alstroemeria hookeri*, pale-pink flowers; *A.* 'Parigo Charm' in salmon.

■ **Perfect partners** Roses, sunflowers, and border phlox.

Also known as tassel flower. A vigorous, bushy, upright perennial, usually grown as a frost-tender annual. Z10–11 H12–1 ‡3–5 ft (1–1.5 m), ↔18–30 in (45–75 cm).

■ **Seasonal highlights** From summer to fall, it produces long, hanging tassels of crimson-purple flowers.

■ **Value at other times** Lush leaves with red or purple stems. Flowers are good for dried arrangements.

■ **Ideal site** An annual or cutting border.

■ **Cultivation** Grow in full sun in humus-rich soil in a sheltered spot. It tolerates poor soil. Sow seeds indoors in early spring and plant out when the threat of frost has passed.

■ **Also recommended** *Amaranthus caudatus* 'Viridis' has green flowers that fade to cream.

■ **Perfect partners** Grow amid annual bedding as an accent plant.

Amelanchier lamarckii
Juneberry

A moderately vigorous, deciduous shrub or small tree. Z5–9 H9–5 ‡30 ft (10 m), ↔40 ft (12 m)
■ **Seasonal highlights** In mid-spring, a profusion of star-shaped, white flowers.
■ **Value at other times** The young leaves are bronzed, turning to green, then to shades of orange and red. Edible berries in early summer attract birds.
■ **Ideal site** A sunny shrub border, in an open glade in woodland garden, or as a specimen plant.
■ **Cultivation** Will tolerate light, dappled shade. Grow in nonalkaline soil that is moist but well-drained and enriched with organic matter. Tolerates hard pruning.
■ **Also recommended** *Amelanchier x grandiflora* 'Ballerina' is smaller, but similar.
■ **Perfect partners** Combine with a late, large-flowered clematis, such as 'Ville de Lyon', with bright carmine-red flowers, or 'Rouge Cardinal' with velvety crimson flowers.

Anemone blanda 'Violet Star'
Mountain windflower

A moderately vigorous, spreading, tuberous perennial. Z4–8 H8–1 ‡↔to 6 in (15 cm).
■ **Seasonal highlights** In spring, it produces clear amethyst flowers with a white reverse to the petals.
■ **Value at other times** The dark green leaves are pretty but fade away during summer dormancy.
■ **Ideal site** Excellent when naturalized in lawn or woodland and good at the front of a border.
■ **Cultivation** Plant tubers 2–3 in (5–8 cm) deep in fall, in humus-rich, well-drained soil, in sun or dappled shade.
■ **Also recommended** *Anemone blanda* 'White Splendour' has large, white flowers that are pink on the reverse.
■ **Perfect partners** Create a spring tapestry of bloom with dwarf narcissus and crocus.

Anemone x hybrida 'Max Vogel'
Japanese anemone

A vigorous, spreading, herbaceous perennial of upright growth. Z4–8 H8–1 ‡4–5 ft (1.2–1.5 m), ↔indefinite
■ **Seasonal highlights** From late summer until late fall, it bears single, light-pink flowers that become paler as the flower ages.
■ **Value at other times** The lobed, dark-green leaves make good ground cover.
■ **Ideal site** A mixed or herbaceous border, or woodland garden.
■ **Cultivation** Prefers a moist, humus-rich soil and thrives in sun or dappled shade. It is invasive, but easily controlled by digging out unwanted pieces.
■ **Also recommended** *Anemone x hybrida* 'Honorine Jobert' has white flowers.
■ **Perfect partners** Use with roses and other perennials. It looks good in an open woodland glade.

Antirrhinum majus 'Trumpet Serenade'
Snapdragon

A bushy, upright, moderately vigorous perennial that is grown as an annual. Z9–11 H12–1 ‡↔12 in (30 cm)
■ **Seasonal highlights** From summer to fall it bears spikes of open trumpet-shaped, bicolored flowers in a mixture of pastel shades.
■ **Value at other times** Has attractive, lance-shaped, somewhat glossy leaves.
■ **Ideal site** Good for bedding, containers, and for children's gardens.
■ **Cultivation** Best in full sun, but it tolerates light shade and thrives in any fertile soil. Sow seeds in late winter indoors. Set out when risk of frost has passed.
■ **Also recommended** *Antirrhinum majus* 'Jamaican Mist' is early and long-flowering, in a range of pastel colors.
■ **Perfect partners** Snapdragons associate well with a wide range of annual bedding plants.

Aquilegia vulgaris 'Nora Barlow'
Columbine

A robust, upright, moderately vigorous perennial. Z3–8 H8–1 ‡35 in (90 cm), ↔18 in (45 cm)
■ **Seasonal highlights** From late spring to early summer, it bears pom-pom flowers with narrow, spurless petals in pale green and red.
■ **Value at other times** Has pretty, dark grayish-green foliage in spring and summer.
■ **Ideal site** A sunny border, especially in a cottage garden.
■ **Cultivation** Grow in full sun or light shade, in any fertile, moisture-retentive soil. Increase is easy by division in spring, or seed sown in spring or fall and self-sown seedlings come fairly true to type.
■ **Also recommended** *Aquilegia alpina* is shorter with clear-blue flowers.
■ **Perfect partners** Roses, lupines, delphiniums, and other perennials.

A

Arctotis x hybrida 'Red Devil'
African daisy

Moderately vigorous, semierect perennial that is grown as a half-hardy annual. Z11 H9–1 ‡18–20 in (45–50 cm), ↔12 in (30 cm)

■ **Seasonal highlights** Throughout summer, it bears dark-centered, red flowerheads.

■ **Value at other times** Felted, silvery-green leaves are good for foliage contrasts.

■ **Ideal site** Sunny banks and borders, gravel gardens, and containers.

■ **Cultivation** Grow in sun, in well-drained soil. Will tolerate light, part-day shade. Sow seed indoors in early spring and set young plants out when risk of frost has passed.

■ **Also recommended** *Arctotis x hybrida* 'African Sunshine' has orange-yellow flowerheads.

■ **Perfect partners** Gazanias and other sun-loving, annual bedding plants.

Argyranthemum foeniculaceum
Marguerite

A compact, fairly vigorous subshrub, evergreen but frost-tender. Z10–11 H12–1 ‡↔to 22 in (80 cm)

■ **Seasonal highlights** It bears single, white, daisylike flowerheads with yellow centers, continuously from summer to fall.

■ **Value at other times** Fine, blue-gray leaves all year.

■ **Ideal site** Sunny borders and containers.

■ **Cultivation** Prefers full sun, but tolerates light shade. Grow in well-drained soil. Pinch out stem tips to keep plants bushy and deadhead regularly. In cold areas, overwinter indoors.

■ **Also recommended** *Argyranthemum frutescens* is similar, with less finely cut leaves.

■ **Perfect partners** *Argyranthemum* 'Jamaica Primrose' with primrose-yellow flowerheads; *A.* 'Vancouver' with pink, anemone-centered blooms.

Artemisia alba 'Canescens'
White sage

A vigorous, bushy, semi-evergreen perennial. Z6–9 H9–6 ‡18 in (45 cm), ↔12 in (30 cm)

■ **Seasonal highlights** It is grown mainly for its beautiful, aromatic, silver-gray leaves that are very finely cut.

■ **Value at other times** In late summer, it bears yellow-brown flowerheads, but most gardeners prefer to remove them.

■ **Ideal site** A hot, sunny border or gravel garden.

■ **Cultivation** Grow in any well-drained soil in sun or light, part-day shade. Dig coarse grit into heavy clay soil to improve drainage.

■ **Also recommended** *Artemisia arborescens* has finely dissected, silver-white leaves.

■ **Perfect partners** Argyranthemums and bold foliage plants, like irises and yuccas, contrast well with the fine foliage of artemisias.

Arundo donax var. *versicolor*
Giant reed

A vigorous, half-hardy, perennial grass. Z7–10 H10–1 ‡6 ft (1.8 m), ↔24 in (60 cm)

■ **Seasonal highlights** The arching, white-striped leaves are attractive all summer.

■ **Value at other times** In late summer, it bears dense heads of creamy spikelets.

■ **Ideal site** At the back of a border or in containers in a conservatory.

■ **Cultivation** Any well-drained soil is suitable. It tolerates light shade, but grows best in sun in reliably moist soil. Protect from cold winds and hard frost. Cut to the base in spring for the best-colored foliage.

■ **Also recommended** *Arundo donax* is taller, hardier, and has plain, bluish-green leaves.

■ **Perfect partners** *Pennisetum villosum* , with feathery, pale buff-purple flowerheads; *Stipa gigantea*, very tall with airy, glistening, golden spikelets.

Aster novi-belgii 'Peace'
Michaelmas daisy

An upright, moderately vigorous, herbaceous perennial. Z4–8 H8–1 ‡4 ft (1.2 m), ↔35 in (90 cm)

■ **Seasonal highlights** From late summer to mid-fall, it bears masses of single, yellow-centered, mauve flowerheads, 3 in (7 cm) across.

■ **Value at other times** Attractive lance-shaped leaves.

■ **Ideal site** Indispensable in a late summer and fall border.

■ **Cultivation** Grow in sun or light shade. Well-cultivated, moisture-retentive soil, full of organic matter, is best. Divide every three or four years. Cut down the old stems after flowering.

■ **Also recommended** *Aster amellus* 'Sonia' is shorter with pale-pink flowerheads.

■ **Perfect partners** Rudbeckias and sedums, which also provide color in late summer and fall.

Astilbe 'Bronce Elegans'
Astilbe

A moderately vigorous, clump-forming herbaceous perennial of upright growth. Z3–8 H8–2 ‡12 in (30 cm), ↔10 in (25 cm)
■ **Seasonal highlights** In late summer it produces plumes of red-pink flowers.
■ **Value at other times** The red-stemmed, dark-green leaves are good ground cover.
■ **Ideal site** A bog garden, waterside plantings, or a shady border.
■ **Cultivation** Best grown in boggy soil in sun, but will tolerate drier conditions in partial shade. Cut down old foliage in late fall. Divide every three to four years.
■ **Also recommended** *Astilbe* 'Aphrodite' has sprays of red flowers and bronze leaves.
■ **Perfect partners** Daylilies, ferns and grasses, such as squirreltail grass (*Hordeum jubatum*) with silky, beige flowerheads.

Astrantia major
Masterwort

A moderately vigorous, upright herbaceous perennial. Z4–7 H7–1 ‡12–36 in (30–90 cm), ↔18 in (45 cm)
■ **Seasonal highlights** In early and midsummer, it bears heads of tiny green, pink, or purplish-red flowers surrounded by white bracts.
■ **Value at other times** The flowerheads can be used for dried arrangements.
■ **Ideal site** A mixed or herbaceous border, especially in cottage gardens.
■ **Cultivation** Ideally, grow in full sun, but it will tolerate light shade. Plant in a humus-rich soil that doesn't dry out. Cut down dead stems when flowering is over. This plant self-seeds quite prolifically.
■ **Also recommended** *Astrantia major* subsp. *involucrata* has green-tipped white bracts.
■ **Perfect partners** Astilbes, rudbeckias, asters.

Aubrieta 'J. S. Baker'
Aubretia

A spreading, mat-forming perennial of dense and moderately vigorous growth. Z5–7 H7–5 ‡2 in (5 cm), ↔24 in (60 cm)
■ **Seasonal highlights** In spring, it produces single, white-eyed, purple flowers in profusion.
■ **Value at other times** The grayish-green leaves form dense ground cover.
■ **Ideal site** A rock garden, drystone wall, sunny bank, or border front.
■ **Cultivation** Grow in well-drained, preferably neutral to alkaline soil, enriched with organic matter. Cut back hard after flowering to maintain neat, compact plants.
■ **Also recommended** *Aubrieta* 'Joy' has double mauve flowers.
■ **Perfect partners** *Aurinia saxatilis*, with yellow flowers and most arabis, which have flowers in white or pink.

Aucuba japonica 'Variegata'
Spotted laurel

A vigorous, evergreen shrub of dense, bushy growth. Z6–10 H12–6 ‡↔to 10 ft (3 m)
■ **Seasonal highlights** Attractively variegated foliage year-round.
■ **Value at other times** Upright clusters of small, red flowers appear in mid-spring; on female plants, like this cultivar, they are followed by bright red berries.
■ **Ideal site** Grows almost anywhere, but good in dark, shady corners, in containers or as hedging.
■ **Cultivation** Exceptionally tolerant of a range of difficult sites, from deep, dry shade to coastal cliffs. It grows in any but waterlogged soil. Prune or trim hedges in spring. Very tolerant of hard pruning.
■ **Also recommended** *Aucuba japonica* 'Crotonifolia' has yellow-speckled leaves.
■ **Perfect partners** Potentillas, rhododendrons.

B

Begonia x *tuberhybrida*
Tuberous begonia

Tuberous, moderately vigorous, frost-tender perennials usually grown as annuals. ‡↔9 in (23 cm)
■ **Seasonal highlights** Throughout summer, they bear showy, mostly double, flowers, in vibrant shades of red, pink, white, and yellow. Upright and trailing cultivars are available.
■ **Value at other times** Large, glossy leaves.
■ **Ideal site** Bedding and containers.
■ **Cultivation** Best in full sun, but tolerant of partial shade. Grow in fertile, moist but well-drained soil. Bring into growth in warmth in early spring. Plant when the threat of frost has passed. Lift in fall and store dry.
■ **Also recommended** *Begonia semperflorens* cultivars are compact, with masses of small flowers throughout summer.
■ **Perfect partners** Petunias and asters.

B

Bellis perennis Tasso Series
English daisy

Moderately vigorous, rosette-forming perennial, usually grown as a biennial. Z4–8 H8–1 ↕↔2–8 in (5–20 cm).

■ **Seasonal highlights** From late winter until late summer, bears double daisy flowers in red, pink, or white.

■ **Value at other times** Attractive spoon-shaped, somewhat glossy, dark-green leaves.

■ **Ideal site** Bedding, border edging, and containers.

■ **Cultivation** Grow in any fertile, well-drained soil, in sun or light shade. Sow seeds outside in early summer or indoors in early spring. Deadhead to encourage more flowers and prevent self seeding.

■ **Also recommended** *Bellis perennis* 'Pomponette' has double flowers with quilled petals.

■ **Perfect partners** Tulips, wallflowers, forget-me-nots.

Bergenia 'Sunningdale'
Elephant's ears

Clump-forming herbaceous perennial. Z3–9 H9–1 ↕12–18 in (30–45 cm), ↔18–24 in (45–60 cm)

■ **Seasonal highlights** Rich lilac-magenta flowers on red stems appear in early and mid-spring.

■ **Value at other times** Bold, glossy dark-green leaves, which turn copper-red in winter.

■ **Ideal site** Front of a border, containers, in a woodland garden.

■ **Cultivation** Best in sun in well-drained soil enriched with plenty of organic matter, but tolerant of partial shade and poor soil. Lift and divide every three to five years to maintain vigor.

■ **Also recommended** *Bergenia* 'Ballawley' has crimson flowers and bronze-purple winter leaves.

■ **Perfect partners** Roses, hostas, fuchsias, and other herbaceous perennials.

Betula papyrifera
Paper birch, Canoe birch

A deciduous, fairly vigorous tree of conical outline. Z4–8 H8–1 ↕70 ft (20 m) or more, ↔30 ft (10 m)

■ **Seasonal highlights** The peeling white bark reveals pale orange-brown bark beneath and is beautiful when leafless in winter.

■ **Value at other times** Dark-green leaves turn yellow and orange in fall. Long, yellow catkins appear in spring.

■ **Ideal site** A fine specimen, especially in damp soil by streams or ponds.

■ **Cultivation** Grow in fertile, humus-rich soil in sun or dappled shade. In winter, prune out lowest branches when very small to create a clear trunk.

■ **Also recommended** *Betula pendula* 'Youngii' is dome-shaped and weeping.

■ **Perfect partners** Mountain ash (*Sorbus*), willows (*Salix*) and conifers.

Borago officinalis
Borage

A vigorous, branching annual, used as a culinary herb. ↕24 in (60 cm), ↔18 in (45 cm)

■ **Seasonal highlights** Throughout summer, it bears bright-blue, star-shaped flowers.

■ **Value at other times** Mounds of white-bristly, matte green leaves and hairy stems.

■ **Ideal site** Herb gardens, dry, sunny sites.

■ **Cultivation** Best in sun, in well-drained soil, but tolerates light shade. In heavy clay soil, dig in plenty of coarse grit to improve the drainage. Self-seeds freely.

■ **Also recommended** *Borago pygmaea* is mat-forming and bears hanging, clear-blue, bell-shaped flowers.

■ **Perfect partners** Mints, sage (*Salvia officinalis*), and feverfew (*Tanacetum parthenium*).

Buddleja davidii 'Fascinating'
Butterfly bush

A vigorous, deciduous shrub with arching branches. Z6–9 H9–1 ↕10 ft (3 m), ↔15 ft (5 m)

■ **Seasonal highlights** From summer to fall, it bears dense, arching spires of lilac-pink flowers.

■ **Value at other times** Attractive mid-green to gray-green foliage. It is excellent for attracting butterflies.

■ **Ideal site** Shrub or mixed borders and wildlife gardens.

■ **Cultivation** It tolerates dappled shade, but flowers best and attracts more butterflies, in full sun. Grow in any fertile, well-drained soil, rich in organic matter. Prune back the previous year's growth to a woody framework in early spring.

■ **Also recommended** *Buddleja davidii* 'White Profusion' has white flowers.

■ **Perfect partners** St. John's wort, barberry, and tree peonies.

Buddleja globosa
Orange ball tree

Vigorous, deciduous or semievergreen shrub. Z7–9 H9–7 ↕↔15 ft (5 m)
■ **Seasonal highlights** In early summer, it bears rounded clusters of fragrant, orange-yellow flowers.
■ **Value at other times** The dark-green, deeply veined leaves are handsome.
■ **Ideal site** A shrub or mixed border.
■ **Cultivation** Best grown in sun, in any fertile garden soil enriched with organic matter. It will tolerate light shade. Keep pruning to a minimum, but when mature, remove some of the oldest flowered shoots at the base, after flowering.
■ **Also recommended** *Buddleja* x *weyeriana* 'Sungold' has dark orange-yellow flowers.
■ **Perfect partners** St. John's wort, barberry, and tree peonies.

C

Caltha palustris
Kingcup, Marsh marigold

A vigorous, creeping, rhizomatous perennial. Z3–7 H7–1 ↕16 in (40 cm), ↔18 in (45 cm)
■ **Seasonal highlights** In spring it bears glossy, yellow, cup-shaped flowers, often with a second flush of bloom later in the year.
■ **Value at other times** The heart-shaped leaves are attractive for most of the year.
■ **Ideal site** A bog garden, at the waterside, or in a damp border.
■ **Cultivation** Best in full sun, but tolerates light shade. Grow in boggy, permanently moist soil at the water's edge, or in planting baskets, in water to 9 in (23 cm) deep.
■ **Also recommended** *Caltha palustris* 'Flore Pleno' has double flowers.
■ **Perfect partners** Water lilies, *Mimulus luteus*, *M. ringens*.

Camassia cusickii 'Zwanenburg'
Camassia

An upright, moderately vigorous, bulbous perennial. Z4–8 H8–1 ↕24–32 in (60–80 cm), ↔4 in (10 cm)
■ **Seasonal highlights** In late spring it bears spires of starry, deep-blue flowers.
■ **Value at other times** The grasslike leaves are ornamentally insignificant.
■ **Ideal site** An herbaceous border or wildflower meadow.
■ **Cultivation** Plant bulbs 4 in (10 cm) deep in fall. Flowers best in full sun, but tolerates light shade. Grow in deep, fertile, moisture-retentive soil. Mulch in winter where marginally hardy.
■ **Also recommended** *Camassia cusickii* has pale to deep steely-blue flowers.
■ **Perfect partners** Alliums (ornamental onions), cowslips (*Primula veris*).

Camellia x *williamsii* 'Anticipation'
Camellia

A moderately vigorous, evergreen shrub of narrowly upright growth. Z8–10 H8–7 ↕12 ft (4 m), ↔6 ft (2 m)
■ **Seasonal highlights** The beautiful, peony-like crimson flowers appear from mid-winter to mid-spring.
■ **Value at other times** The lustrous, dark-green foliage is delightful all year.
■ **Ideal site** Shrub borders, woodland gardens, and containers.
■ **Cultivation** Thrives in sun or dappled shade, but needs shade from early morning sun, which may damage flowers in frosty weather. Grow in humus-rich, acidic soil, or in acidic potting mix in containers. Trim lightly to shape after flowering, if necessary.
■ **Also recommended** *Camellia* x *williamsii* 'Donation' has semidouble, pink flowers.
■ **Perfect partners** Rhododendrons and azaleas.

Campanula lactiflora
Milky bellflower

Moderately vigorous, upright herbaceous perennial. Z4–8 H8–1 ↕4–5 ft (1.2–1.5 m), ↔24 in (60 cm)
■ **Seasonal highlights** Clusters of bell-shaped flowers from early summer to early fall are white to pale blue, lilac-blue, or violet.
■ **Value at other times** Attractive leaves from early spring to late summer.
■ **Ideal site** A mixed or herbaceous border, or woodland garden.
■ **Cultivation** Thrives in sun, but flower color is better preserved in light shade. Grow in fertile, well-drained, neutral to alkaline soil. It may need staking in exposed gardens.
■ **Also recommended** *Campanula lactiflora* 'Prichard's Variety' has violet-blue flowers.
■ **Perfect partners** Roses, *Campanula. lactiflora* 'Loddon Anna' with lilac-pink flowers, *C.* 'Elizabeth', cream flowers.

C

Carex flagellifera
New Zealand sedge

A moderately vigorous, tuft-forming, arching sedge. Z7–9 H9–7 ‡3½ ft (1.1 m), ↔35 in (90 cm)
- **Seasonal highlights** Grasslike, reddish-brown leaves all year.
- **Value at other times** Tall stems bear light-brown flower spikes in summer.
- **Ideal site** A mixed border, gravel plantings, or containers.
- **Cultivation** Grow in sun or partial shade in any soil that is not too wet or too dry. In cold areas, protect with a winter mulch.
- **Also recommended** *Carex siderosticha* 'Variegata' has pink-flushed, pale green-and-white-striped leaves.
- **Perfect partners** Use *Carex oshimensis* 'Evergold', or *Hakonechloa macra* 'Aureola' for contrasting shades of green and gold.

Carex oshimensis 'Evergold'
Golden sedge

A vigorous, evergreen, mound-forming sedge. Z4–8 H8–4 ‡12 in (30 cm), ↔14 in (35 cm)
- **Seasonal highlights** The arching, dark-green leaves have a central creamy-white stripe and remain attractive year-round.
- **Value at other times** In mid- to late spring, tall spikes of brown flowers appear.
- **Ideal site** A mixed border, gravel plantings, or containers.
- **Cultivation** Thrives in sun or partial shade. Fertile, moist but well-drained soil is required.
- **Also recommended** *Carex elata* 'Aurea' has rich-yellow leaves.
- **Perfect partners** *Polystichum setiferum* (soft shield fern) and hostas make good foliage contrasts.

Carex pendula
Weeping sedge

A vigorous, clump-forming, evergreen sedge. Z5–9 H9–5 ‡4½ ft (1.4 m), ↔5 ft (1.5 m)
- **Seasonal highlights** In late spring and early summer, arching stems bear catkinlike, dark-brown flower spikes that are erect at first, then droop with age.
- **Value at other times** Shiny mid-green leaves that are blue-green beneath.
- **Ideal site** Pondsides, damp borders, and woodland gardens.
- **Cultivation** Grow in sun or partial shade. Plant in moist, fertile soil.
- **Also recommended** *Carex grayi* (mace sedge) is shorter; its green flower spikes give rise to spiky seedheads.
- **Perfect partners** Use hostas to form a broad-leaved contrast to the narrow leaves of the sedge.

Caryopteris x clandonensis 'Kew Blue'

A moderately vigorous, arching, deciduous shrub. Z6–9 H9–1 ‡3 ft (1 m), ↔5 ft (1.5 m)
- **Seasonal highlights** From late summer to early fall, it bears spires of deep-blue flowers.
- **Value at other times** The dark gray-green leaves are silvery beneath.
- **Ideal site** A mixed or shrub border, gravel plantings, hot, dry sites.
- **Cultivation** It flowers best in full sun, but tolerates light dappled shade. Prefers light, fertile, well-drained soil. In areas with cold winters and cool summers, plant against a warm, sheltered wall. In early spring, prune it back to a permanent woody framework.
- **Also recommended** *Caryopteris* x *clandonensis* 'Worcester Gold' has golden foliage and lavender-blue flowers.
- **Perfect partners** Lavatera, fuchsias, potentillas.

Centaurea hypoleuca 'John Coutts'
Knapweed, Cornflower

A vigorous, spreading, clump-forming herbaceous perennial. Z3–9 H9–1 ‡24 in (60 cm), ↔18 in (45 cm)
- **Seasonal highlights** In summer, it bears fragrant, deep rose-pink flowers that attract bees and butterflies.
- **Value at other times** The divided, gray-green leaves are gray-white beneath.
- **Ideal site** An herbaceous border, especially in a cottage garden.
- **Cultivation** Grow this drought-tolerant plant in full sun in any well-drained soil. Regular deadheading results in more flowers later in the season. Divide every three to four years to maintain vigor.
- **Also recommended** *Centaurea dealbata* 'Steenbergii' has carmine-pink flowerheads.
- **Perfect partners** *Centaurea macrocephala*, *Lythrum*, border phlox, and other herbaceous perennials.

Chaenomeles speciosa 'Phylis Moore'
Flowering quince

Also known as japonica. A vigorous, deciduous shrub with wide-spreading branches. Z5–8 H8–5 ↕8 ft (2.5 m), ↔to 15 ft (5 m)

■ **Seasonal highlights** In spring, before, and with the new leaves, it bears large clusters of semidouble, almond-pink flowers.

■ **Value at other times** Aromatic yellow fruits appear in fall; they can be cooked in jellies or preserves.

■ **Ideal site** Shrub borders, sunny or shaded walls, and hedging.

■ **Cultivation** Grow in any fertile, well-drained soil in sun or partial shade. After flowering, shorten flowered shoots to strong buds. When mature, take out 1 in 5 of the oldest shoots.

■ **Also recommended** *Chaenomeles speciosa* 'Moerloosei' has apple-blossom-pink flowers.

■ **Perfect partners** Forsythia, pyracantha and *Ribes sanguineum* (flowering currant).

Chaenomeles x superba 'Knap Hill Scarlet'

Also known as flowering quince and japonica. A vigorous, rounded, spiny-stemmed, deciduous shrub. Z5–9 H9–5 ↕5 ft (1.5 m), ↔6 ft (2 m)

■ **Seasonal highlights** From spring to summer it bears clusters of large, scarlet flowers with golden anthers.

■ **Value at other times** Later in fall it produces golden-yellow fruits.

■ **Ideal site** Shrub borders, sunny or shaded walls, and hedging.

■ **Cultivation** Grow in any fertile, well-drained soil in sun or partial shade. After flowering, shorten flowered shoots to strong buds. When mature, take out 1 in 5 of the oldest shoots.

■ **Also recommended** *Chaenomeles x superba* 'Nicoline' has large, often semidouble, scarlet flowers.

■ **Perfect partners** Forsythia, pyracantha, and *Ribes sanguineum* (flowering currant).

Chelone obliqua
Turtlehead

A vigorous, upright, herbaceous perennial. Z3–9 H9–3 ↕16–24 in (40–60 cm), ↔12 in (30 cm)

■ **Seasonal highlights** From late summer to mid-fall, it bears dark-pink or purple flowers with yellow beards on the lower lip.

■ **Value at other times** It has attractive, lance-shaped, boldly veined leaves.

■ **Ideal site** Mixed or herbaceous borders, bog gardens.

■ **Cultivation** Grow in full sun or partial shade. Deep, fertile soil that retains moisture is ideal. Mulch well in spring before growth begins. Will tolerate heavy clay soil.

■ **Also recommended** *Chelone lyonii* is similar but taller.

■ **Perfect partners** *Coreopsis verticillata*, *Crocosmia* 'Lady Hamilton'.

Chimonanthus praecox
Wintersweet

A spreading, moderately vigorous, deciduous shrub. Z7–9 H9–7 ↕12 ft (4 m), ↔10 ft (3 m)

■ **Seasonal highlights** On bare winter shoots, it bears nodding, very fragrant, soft-yellow flowers.

■ **Value at other times** The leaves are rather coarse, but this shrub is an ideal host for late-flowering clematis.

■ **Ideal site** As a specimen, in a shrub border, against a warm wall.

■ **Cultivation** Grow in full sun or partial shade. Grow in any fertile soil. Prune after flowering, removing misplaced shoots to maintain a good shape.

■ **Also recommended** *Chimonanthus praecox* 'Grandiflorus' has larger, deeper-yellow flowers.

■ **Perfect partners** *Jasminum nudiflorum* (winter jasmine), *Mahonia x media* 'Charity'; both have yellow flowers in winter.

Chionodoxa forbesii 'Pink Giant'
Glory of the snow

A moderately vigorous, bulbous perennial. Z3–9 H9–1 ↕4–8 in (10–20 cm), ↔1¼ in (3 cm)

■ **Seasonal highlights** In early spring it bears spikes of starry, white-centered, pink flowers.

■ **Value at other times** Dies back after flowering.

■ **Ideal site** A rock garden, raised bed, beneath shrubs, in containers.

■ **Cultivation** Plant in fall 3 in (8 cm) deep. Grow in any well-drained soil in sun or dappled shade. Lift and separate the bulbs after four to five years if they become congested.

■ **Also recommended** *Chionodoxa forbesii* has white-eyed, blue flowers.

■ **Perfect partners** Grow as a carpet beneath a forsythia, with dwarf daffodils.

C

Choisya 'Aztec Pearl'
Mexican orange blossom

A bushy, fairly vigorous, evergreen shrub. Z8–10 H10–8 ‡↔ to 8 ft (2.5 m)
■ **Seasonal highlights** In both late spring and late summer, it bears clusters of pink-tinted white flowers, often with a few in fall.
■ **Value at other times** Beautiful aromatic leaves, divided into narrow, glossy dark-green leaflets.
■ **Ideal site** A shrub border, or against a warm or lightly shaded wall.
■ **Cultivation** It flowers best in sun, but will tolerate partial shade. Grow in any good garden soil. Trim after flowering in spring to improve the second flowering.
■ **Also recommended** *Choisya ternata* has broader leaves and white flowers.
■ **Perfect partners** *Choisya ternata* SUNDANCE ('Lich') has golden foliage if grown in sun, but seldom flowers.

Chrysanthemum 'Glowing Lynn'
Chrysanthemum

A bushy, upright, moderately vigorous herbaceous perennial. Z4–9 H9–1 ‡↔18 in (45 cm) or more
■ **Seasonal highlights** It bears masses of double, red-bronze flowers in late summer and fall. They make excellent cut flowers.
■ **Value at other times** Aromatic dark-green leaves.
■ **Ideal site** Borders and containers.
■ **Cultivation** Grow in full sun in fertile, well-drained soil. Plant out in late spring and pinch out the growing tips to encourage plentiful flowers. Except in very cold areas, it can be left outdoors in winter; protect the crown with a deep, dry mulch. Bring potted plants indoors for winter.
■ **Also recommended** *Chrysanthemum* 'Peach Margaret' has sprays of pale-salmon-pink flowers.
■ **Perfect partners** *Aster novi-belgii* (Michaelmas daisies), dahlias, rudbeckias.

Cimicifuga simplex 'White Pearl'
Bugbane

A robust, upright, herbaceous perennial. Z4–8 H8–1 ‡24–36 in (60–90 cm), ↔24 in (60 cm)
■ **Seasonal highlights** From early to mid-fall, it bears spires of white flowers that open from green buds.
■ **Value at other times** The divided, pale-green leaves form dense, weed-smothering ground cover.
■ **Ideal site** Damp borders and woodland gardens.
■ **Cultivation** Grow in moist, fertile, humus-rich soil in partial shade. May need staking in exposed gardens.
■ **Also recommended** *Cimicifuga simplex* var. *simplex* 'Brunette' has purplish-brown foliage and purple-tinted, white flowers.
■ **Perfect partners** *Aster* 'Violet Queen', *Salvia* x *superba*.

Cistus x cyprius
Rock rose, Sun rose

A moderately vigorous, bushy evergreen shrub. Z8–10 H10–1 ‡↔ to 5 ft (1.5 m)
■ **Seasonal highlights** During summer, it bears clusters of white flowers with crimson blotches at the bases of the petals.
■ **Value at other times** Forms a neat mound of rather sticky, dark-green leaves with wavy margins.
■ **Ideal site** Sunny banks, borders, hot, dry sites, and containers.
■ **Cultivation** Tolerant of poor and alkaline soil. Grow in well-drained soil in full sun. Set out new plants in spring, when the risk of frost has passed. Pinch out stem tips to keep the plant bushy, but don't prune hard.
■ **Also recommended** *Cistus* x *dansereaui* 'Decumbens' is low and spreading with red-blotched, white flowers.
■ **Perfect partners** Roses and lavenders.

Clarkia amoena
Satin flower

A moderately vigorous, upright, hardy annual. Z4–9 H9–1 ‡30 in (75 cm), ↔12 in (30 cm)
■ **Seasonal highlights** Throughout summer, it bears clusters of satin-textured, lilac to red-pink flowers.
■ **Value at other times** Of no real value at other times. They last for the summer only.
■ **Ideal site** Annual borders and containers.
■ **Cultivation** Best in sun in slightly acidic, moist but well-drained soil, but tolerates light shade. Rich soil encourages leafy growth at the expense of flowers. Sow seeds in the flowering site in spring or fall. Protect late-sown seedlings with cloches overwinter.
■ **Also recommended** *Clarkia amoena* 'Sybil Sherwood' has salmon-pink flowers.
■ **Perfect partners** A wide range of hardy annuals.

Clematis alpina 'Frances Rivis'
Alpine clematis

A vigorous, deciduous, twining climber. Z4–9 H9–1 ‡6–10 ft (2–3 m), ↔5 ft (1.5 m)

■ **Seasonal highlights** In spring or early summer, it bears hanging, blue flowers with slightly twisted petals.

■ **Value at other times** Has attractive foliage all summer and fluffy seedheads in late summer and fall.

■ **Ideal site** Walls, trellis, or scrambling through late-flowering shrubs.

■ **Cultivation** Tolerates sun or dappled shade, but the roots should be shaded. Grow in fertile, well-drained soil enriched with plenty of organic matter. After flowering, remove dead or damaged shoots and shorten others to confine to bounds.

■ **Also recommended** *Clematis alpina* 'Pink Flamingo' has pale-pink flowers.

■ **Perfect partners** Sturdy shrubs, like *Buddleja globosa* or *Phlomis fruticosa*.

Clematis armandii 'Apple Blossom'
Clematis

A vigorous, slightly frost-tender, evergreen climber. Z7–9 H9–1 ‡10–15 ft (3–5 m), ↔6–10 ft (2–3 m)

■ **Seasonal highlights** In early spring, it bears fragrant, pink-tinted white flowers with pink undersides.

■ **Value at other times** Has attractive foliage all year.

■ **Ideal site** A sheltered wall, through shrubs and trees, or, in cold areas, as a conservatory plant.

■ **Cultivation** Grow in sun or dappled shade in fertile, humus-rich, well-drained soil, with the roots in shade. After flowering, remove dead or damaged shoots and shorten others to contain within the available space. Use a fertile, loam-based mix for container plants and enjoy the scent at close quarters.

■ **Also recommended** *Clematis armandii* has white flowers.

■ **Perfect partners** Camellias make good hosts.

Clematis
Early-flowering clematis

These vigorous, deciduous clematis bloom in late spring and early summer, often with a second flush later in summer.

■ **Ideal site** Walls, trellises, arbors, pergolas; over shrubs, trees, or hedges.

■ **Cultivation** Grow in fertile, well-drained soil enriched with well-rotted organic matter. They flower best with top-growth in sun and roots in shade, but darker colors are better in partial shade. Plant with 4–6 in (10–15 cm) of stem below soil level to reduce danger of clematis wilt. In spring, before growth begins, cut out twiggy, dead, or damaged growth and trim remaining shoots back to strong buds. Most cultivars are hardy in USDA zones 4 to 9 and in AHS heat zones 9 to 1.

Clematis **'Fireworks'** blue-violet with a central red-purple bar, in early and late summer. ‡8 ft (2.5 m), ↔3 ft (1 m)

Clematis **'Niobe'** free-flowering with velvety deep-red flowers through most of the summer. ‡6–10 ft (2–3 m), ↔3 ft (1 m)

Clematis **'Nelly Moser'** pinkish-mauve flowers with darker central bands, in early and late summer. ‡6–10 ft (2–3 m), ↔3 ft (1 m)

Clematis VINO (**'Poulvo'**) pinkish-mauve flowers with darker central bands, in early and late summer. ‡6–10 ft (2–3 m), ↔3 ft (1 m)

Clematis **'Lasurstern'** blue flowers with cream anthers, in early summer. ‡8 ft (2.5 m), ↔3 ft (1 m)

Clematis **'Vyvyan Pennell'** double flowers with central lavender-blue petals; later flowers are single. ‡6–10 ft (2–3 m), ↔3 ft (1 m)

C

Clematis
Late-flowering clematis

The late-flowering clematis include large- and small-flowered cultivars, as well as species, which extend the flowering season from mid-summer well into fall.

■ **Cultivation** Late-flowering clematis are grown like the early-flowering ones, but are pruned differently. Cut back the previous year's stems to strong buds 9–18 in (23–45 cm) above the ground, just as the buds begin to break in spring. If new shoots are trimmed lightly when they reach 12–20 in (30–50 cm), they flower later, extending the season.

■ **Perfect partners** Since many of this group bloom well in fall, the last of their flowers will complement fall colors. The creamy and white-flowered ones, like 'Huldine', look especially good with purple-leaved shrubs such as *Cotinus coggygria*.

Clematis **'Ville de Lyon'** bears bright carmine-red flowers with darker margins and yellow anthers. ↕6–10 ft (2–3 m) ↔3 ft (1 m)

Clematis viticella is a slender but tough species and bears blue to purple and red flowers. ↕6–12 ft (2–4 m), ↔5 ft (1.5 m)

Clematis **'Jackmanii'** has large, velvety, dark-purple flowers with light greenish-brown anthers. ↕10 ft (3 m) ↔3 ft (1 m)

Clematis **'Comtesse de Bouchaud'** bears its large, single, bright mauve-pink flowers from late summer. ↕6–10 ft (2–3 m), ↔3 ft (1 m)

Clematis **'Etoile Violette'** has violet-purple flowers with contrasting yellow anthers. ↕10–15 ft (3–5 m), ↔5 ft (1.5 m)

Clematis **'Hagley Hybrid'** has large, single flowers with pinkish-mauve sepals and red anthers. ↕6 ft (2 m), ↔3 ft (1 m)

Clematis cirrhosa 'Freckles'
Winter clematis

A vigorous, slightly frost-tender, evergreen climber. Z4–9 H9–1 ↕8–10 ft (2.5–3 m), ↔5 ft (1.5 m)

■ **Seasonal highlights** In late winter and early spring, it bears creamy-white, red-speckled flowers.

■ **Value at other times** Has bronzed leaves all year and silky seedheads in summer.

■ **Ideal site** A sheltered wall, or through shrubs and trees.

■ **Cultivation** Grow in sun or dappled shade in fertile, humus-rich, well-drained soil, with the roots in shade. Protect from cold wind. After flowering, remove dead or damaged shoots; shorten others to control size.

■ **Also recommended** *Clematis cirrhosa* var. *balearica* has fragrant, red-brown speckled, cream flowers.

■ **Perfect partners** Large mahonias make good host shrubs.

Clematis macropetala 'Markham's Pink'
Clematis

A vigorous, deciduous climber. Z4–9 H9–1 ↕6–10 ft (2–3 m), ↔5 ft (1.5 m)

■ **Seasonal highlights** From spring to early summer, it bears soft sugar-pink flowers.

■ **Value at other times** Pale-green foliage and silver seedheads in summer.

■ **Ideal site** Prefers sun, but will tolerate dappled shade.

■ **Cultivation** Grow in sun or dappled shade in fertile, well-drained soil, enriched with organic matter. Site with the roots in shade. After flowering, remove dead or damaged shoots and shorten others to confine to allotted space.

■ **Also recommended** *Clematis macropetala* 'White Swan' has white flowers with creamy-white centers.

■ **Perfect partners** Forsythias, larger philadelphus, and lilacs are excellent host shrubs.

Clematis montana f. grandiflora
Clematis

A very vigorous, deciduous climber. Z4–9 H9–1 ‡30 ft (10 m), ↔12 ft (4 m)
■ **Seasonal highlights** Single, white flowers with cream anthers are produced for about four weeks in late spring and early summer.
■ **Value at other times** Attractive foliage all summer.
■ **Ideal site** A wall, fence, or large tree.
■ **Cultivation** Grow in sun or dappled shade in fertile, well-drained soil, enriched with organic matter. Site with the roots in shade. After flowering, remove dead or damaged shoots and shorten others to confine to allotted space.
■ **Also recommended** *Clematis montana* 'Elizabeth' has scented, pale-pink flowers.
■ **Perfect partners** Conifers, old fruit trees, and beech (*Fagus sylvatica*) are good hosts; they must be vigorous to carry the weight.

Clematis
GOLDEN TIARA
Late-flowering clematis

Vigorous deciduous climber. Z5–9 H9–1 ‡↔6–10 ft (2–3 m)
■ **Seasonal highlights** From late summer until fall, it produces open lantern-flowers in bright golden yellow, followed by fluffy seedheads that persist into early winter.
■ **Value at other times** Attractive foliage all through the summer.
■ **Ideal site** Walls and fences of any exposure; climbing through deciduous trees.
■ **Cultivation** Grow in moderately fertile soil enriched with organic matter. Plant deeply and shade the roots. Prune to 12 in (30 cm) from the ground in spring.
■ **Also recommended** *Clematis* 'Bill Mackenzie', similar if a little more vigorous.
■ **Perfect partners** *Clematis flammula*, flowering in white at the same time; amelanchiers and crab apples.

Cleome hassleriana 'Color Fountain'
Spider flower

A vigorous, half-hardy annual. ‡4 ft (1.2 m), ↔18 in (45 cm)
■ **Seasonal highlights** Throughout summer, it bears dense heads of scented flowers with delicate petals, in shades of pink, violet pink, or white.
■ **Value at other times** Pretty, divided leaves of fresh green.
■ **Ideal site** An annual or cutting border, or to fill seasonal gaps in an herbaceous border.
■ **Cultivation** Best in sun, but tolerates light dappled shade. Grow in light, free-draining soil. Sow seeds indoors in warmth in spring and plant out when the threat of frost has passed. Cut or deadhead regularly to prolong the flowering period.
■ **Also recommended** *Cleome hassleriana* has white, pink, or purple flowers.
■ **Perfect partners** Clarkias and rudbeckias.

Colchicum cilicicum
Autumn crocus, Naked ladies

Upright, low-growing, cormous perennials. Z4–9 H9–1 ‡4 in (10 cm), ↔3 in (8 cm)
■ **Seasonal highlights** In fall, it bears funnel-shaped, purplish-pink flowers. They appear before the leaves.
■ **Value at other times** The leaves are not ornamentally significant.
■ **Ideal site** Beneath deciduous shrubs or naturalized in grass.
■ **Cultivation** Best in an open site in full sun, but will tolerate light shade. Plant corms 4 in (10 cm) deep in late summer or early fall, in fertile, well-drained soil. If grown in grass, allow the foliage to die down naturally before mowing.
■ **Also recommended** *Colchicum autumnale* has lavender-pink flowers.
■ **Perfect partners** Hydrangeas, *Viburnum* x *bodnantense* 'Deben'.

Convallaria majalis
Lily-of-the-valley

A vigorous, spreading, upright perennial with fleshy roots. Z2–7 H7–1 ‡9 in (23 cm), ↔12 in (30 cm)
■ **Seasonal highlights** In late spring, arching stems of small, nodding, waxy, white flowers appear. They are strongly scented.
■ **Value at other times** The attractive leaves make dense ground cover.
■ **Ideal site** A shady border, woodland garden, or in containers, especially for forcing.
■ **Cultivation** Tolerates deep or partial shade. Grow in damp, leafy, fertile soil. A top-dressing of leafmold in fall is beneficial. Pot some up in fall and grow under cover for a scented display indoors.
■ **Also recommended** *Convallaria majalis* 'Flore Pleno' has double flowers.
■ **Perfect partners** Azaleas, dwarf rhododendrons, and narcissus.

C

Cornus
Dogwoods

The dogwood includes several vigorous, deciduous shrubs that are valued for their brightly colored leafless stems, which bring interest to the winter garden.

■ **Value at other times** They bear clusters of white flowers in spring and white or blue-black fruit in fall.

■ **Ideal site** A shrub border, winter garden, or beside ponds and streams.

■ **Cultivation** Grow in any moderately fertile soil. Dogwoods tolerate shade, but stems show their color best in the sun. For the best effect, prune the stems back to the base each year in early spring.

***Cornus alba* 'Aurea'** has yellow leaves, and red winter stems. Z2–8 H8–1 ‡↔10 ft (3 m)

***Cornus alba* 'Sibirica'** has glossy, bright-red winter stems. Z2–8 H8–1 ‡↔10 ft (3 m)

***Cornus alba* 'Elegantissima'** has gray-green, cream-margined leaves and red winter stems. Z2–8 H8–1 ‡↔10 ft (3 m)

***Cornus sanguinea* 'Winter Beauty'** has bright orange-yellow and red winter shoots. Z5–7 H7–1 ‡10 ft (3 m), ↔8 ft (2.5 m)

***Cornus stolonifera* 'Flaviramea'** has bright yellow-green shoots. Z2–8 H8–1 ‡6 ft (2 m), ↔12 ft (4 m)

***Cornus stolonifera* 'Kelseyi'** is compact with red-tipped, yellow-green shoots. Z2–8 H8–1 ‡30 in (75 cm), ↔5 ft (1.5 m)

Cornus mas
Cornelian cherry

Spreading, moderately vigorous, deciduous shrub or small tree. Z5–8 H8–5 ‡↔15 ft (5 m)

■ **Seasonal highlights** In late winter, it bears small but profuse clusters of yellow flowers on bare branches.

■ **Value at other times** The dark-green leaves turn red-purple in fall. It sometimes produces small bright-red fruits in fall.

■ **Ideal site** Winter garden, shrub borders, or as a specimen.

■ **Cultivation** Any fertile, well-drained soil. Best in an open, sunny site, but will tolerate light shade. Keep pruning to a minimum.

■ **Also recommended** *Cornus mas* 'Variegata' has white-margined leaves.

■ **Perfect partners** *Chimonanthus praecox*, *Viburnum* x *bodnantense* 'Dawn'.

Cortaderia selloana 'Sunningdale Silver'
Pampas grass

A vigorous perennial grass. Z7–11 H12–7 ‡10 ft (3 m) or more, ↔8 ft (2.5 m)

■ **Seasonal highlights** In late summer and fall, it sends up feathery, silvery-white flower plumes that are very weather-resistant.

■ **Value at other times** Clumps of arching bluish-green leaves year-round.

■ **Ideal site** As a specimen, at the back of a border, in woodland gardens.

■ **Cultivation** It prefers an open, sunny site, but tolerates dappled shade. Grow in fertile, well-drained soil. In late winter or early spring, carefully cut or comb out old foliage; the leaves have viciously sharp edges.

■ **Also recommended** *Cortaderia selloana* 'Albolineata' has yellow-margined leaves.

■ **Perfect partners** *Stipa gigantea*, *Arundo donax* var. *versicolor*.

Corydalis flexuosa
Fumewort

A slowly spreading, summer-dormant, herbaceous perennial. Z6–8 H7–1 ‡12 in (30 cm), ↔8 in (20 cm) or more
■ **Seasonal highlights** From late spring to summer, it produces dense clusters of slender-tubed, brilliant-blue flowers with white throats.
■ **Value at other times** Fernlike, bluish-green leaves. Dies back after flowering.
■ **Ideal site** Shady borders, rock gardens, and woodland gardens.
■ **Cultivation** Grow in a cool site in partial or dappled shade, in a humus-rich, fertile, moist but well-drained soil.
■ **Also recommended** *Corydalis fumariifolia* has azure-blue, sometimes purple, flowers.
■ **Perfect partners** *Corydalis lutea*, with yellow flowers.

Corylopsis glabrescens
Corylopsis

A moderately vigorous, deciduous shrub of open, spreading habit. Z6–9 H9–6 ‡↔ to 15 ft (5 m)
■ **Seasonal highlights** In mid-spring, it produces hanging tassels of fragrant, pale-yellow flowers.
■ **Value at other times** It has oval leaves that are pale to dark green on top and blue-green beneath.
■ **Ideal site** Shady shrub borders, woodland gardens.
■ **Cultivation** Grow in partial or dappled shade. It prefers well-drained, humus-rich, acidic soil. Prune out or shorten badly placed shoots after flowering.
■ **Also recommended** *Corylopsis pauciflora* has primrose-scented, pale-yellow flowers.
■ **Perfect partners** *Corylus avellana* 'Contorta', magnolias, *Salix lanata*.

Corylus avellana 'Contorta'
Corkscrew hazel

A fairly vigorous, deciduous shrub with twisted shoots. Z3–9 H9–1 ‡↔ to 15 ft (5 m)
■ **Seasonal highlights** The twisted shoots look good in winter, especially when snow-covered. Yellow catkins hang from bare branches in late winter or early spring.
■ **Value at other times** The heart-shaped, wrinkled leaves are also twisted.
■ **Ideal site** As a specimen or at the back of a shrub border.
■ **Cultivation** Thrives in any good garden soil in sun or partial shade. Remove any suckers that grow from the base and carefully prune out any misplaced shoots in winter.
■ **Also recommended** *Corylus maxima* 'Purpurea' has purple leaves and purple-tinted catkins.
■ **Perfect partners** Magnolias, *Salix lanata*.

Cosmos atrosanguineus
Chocolate cosmos

A spreading, herbaceous perennial with tuberous roots. Z7–11 H12–1 ‡30 in (75 cm), ↔18 in (45 cm)
■ **Seasonal highlights** From midsummer to fall, velvety, dark-maroon flowers open to release an elusive, dark-chocolate fragrance.
■ **Value at other times** Clumps of divided, fresh-green foliage.
■ **Ideal site** Warm, sheltered borders.
■ **Cultivation** Grow in fertile, well-drained soil in full sun. Deadhead regularly to prolong flowering. In cold areas, lift tubers before the first frosts and store in a dry, frost-free place.
■ **Also recommended** *Cosmos bipinnatus* is a tall annual, with white, pink or crimson flowers of similar form.
■ **Perfect partners** Achilleas, border phlox. Gray foliage and bright flowers form a good contrast to the flowers of *Cosmos atrosanguineus*.

Cosmos bipinnatus Sensation Series
Annual cosmos

A vigorous, erect, freely branching, half-hardy annual. ‡to 35 in (90 cm), ↔to 18 in (45 cm)
■ **Seasonal highlights** Large pink or white flowers are produced freely through summer and fall. They are good for cutting.
■ **Value at other times** Has feathery foliage all summer.
■ **Ideal site** Annual and cutting borders, or as gap-fillers in mixed or herbaceous borders.
■ **Cultivation** Best in full sun, but tolerates dappled shade. Grow in any well-drained, moderately fertile soil. Sow seeds indoors in early spring, or in the flowering site in late spring. Deadhead regularly.
■ **Also recommended** *Cosmos bipinnatus* Sonata Series are dwarf and good in containers.
■ **Perfect partners** *Clarkia, Chrysanthemum carinatum.*

C

Cotinus coggygria
Smoke bush

Cotinus 'Grace'
Smoke bush

Cotoneaster frigidus 'Fructu Luteo'
Cotoneaster

Crambe cordifolia
Crambe

Crataegus laevigata 'Rosea Flore Pleno'
Midland hawthorn, May

Cotinus coggygria — Smoke bush

Vigorous, mound-forming deciduous shrub. Z5–8 H8–1 ‡↔15 ft (5 m)

■ **Seasonal highlights** Plumes of tiny buff-purple flowers become smoky gray by late summer, giving rise to the common name.

■ **Value at other times** The oval green leaves turn yellow to orange and finally flaming red in fall.

■ **Ideal site** As a specimen, or in a mixed or shrub border.

■ **Cultivation** Grow in any moderately fertile, moist, but well-drained soil. For larger, brighter-colored foliage, prune back hard in spring, but allow the plant to become established before doing so.

■ **Also recommended** *Cotinus coggygria* 'Royal Purple' has dark red-purple foliage and vivid-red fall color.

■ **Perfect partners** Barberry, escallonias, weigelas.

Cotinus 'Grace' — Smoke bush

A vigorous, deciduous shrub or small tree. Z5–8 H8–3 ‡20 ft (6 m), ↔15 ft (5 m)

■ **Seasonal highlights** A haze of tiny purple-pink flowers appear in summer, giving the plant the common name of smoke bush.

■ **Value at other times** Oval purple leaves that turn a brilliant translucent red in late fall.

■ **Ideal site** As a specimen, or in a mixed or shrub border.

■ **Cultivation** Grow in any moderately fertile, moist but well-drained, soil. To get larger, brighter-colored foliage, prune all shoots back hard in spring, but let plants become well-established before doing so.

■ **Also recommended** *Cotinus coggygria* 'Notcutt's Variety' has wine-red foliage. *Cotinus* 'Flame' has good autumn color.

■ **Perfect partners** Barberry, escallonias, weigelas.

Cotoneaster frigidus 'Fructu Luteo' — Cotoneaster

A moderately vigorous, erect then spreading, deciduous tree or large shrub. Z7–8 H8–7 ‡↔to 30 ft (10 m)

■ **Seasonal highlights** Large clusters of tiny white flowers appear in summer, followed by creamy-yellow fruits in fall. The flowers attract bees; fruits are eaten by birds in hard winters.

■ **Value at other times** Has peeling bark.

■ **Ideal site** At the back of a shrub border, or as a specimen.

■ **Cultivation** Tolerates almost any soil, including dry soil, but best in moderately fertile, well-drained soil in full sun. Prune lightly to shape in winter, if necessary.

■ **Also recommended** *Cotoneaster franchettii* is semievergreen with bright orange-red fruits.

■ **Perfect partners** *Cotoneaster horizontalis*, shrubby potentillas, ceanothus.

Crambe cordifolia — Crambe

A vigorous, clump-forming herbaceous perennial. Z6–9 H9–6 ‡8 ft (2.5 m), ↔to 5 ft (1.5 m)

■ **Seasonal highlights** In early to midsummer, tall, strong stems arise bearing clouds of honey-scented white flowers.

■ **Value at other times** Forms a mound of glossy, puckered, dark-green leaves that die down in late summer.

■ **Ideal site** At the back of a mixed or herbaceous border.

■ **Cultivation** Grow in deep, fertile soil in full sun. Will tolerate partial shade. Shelter from strong winds. Is best increased by root cuttings in winter.

■ **Also recommended** *Crambe maritima* is shorter with blue-gray, puckered, twisted, wrinkled leaves and white flowers.

■ **Perfect partners** Old garden roses, philadelphus.

Crataegus laevigata 'Rosea Flore Pleno' — Midland hawthorn, May

A very hardy, deciduous tree with a rounded crown. Z5–8 H8–3 ‡↔to 25 ft (8 m)

■ **Seasonal highlights** Clusters of double pink flowers appear in late spring.

■ **Value at other times** Red fruits (haws) are produced in fall.

■ **Ideal site** As a specimen, especially in small gardens, or as hedging.

■ **Cultivation** Tolerates sun and partial shade and a wide variety of soils. Needs minimal pruning to maintain the shape and to cut out dead or damaged wood in winter.

■ **Also recommended** *Crataegus laevigata* 'Paul's Scarlet' has double, deep-pink flowers.

■ **Perfect partners** Acers, fastigiate beech (*Fagus sylvatica* 'Dawyck'), tulip tree (*Liriodendron tulipifera*).

Crocosmia x *crocosmiiflora* 'Jackanapes'

Also known as montbretia. A moderately vigorous, upright cormous perennial. Z6–9 H9–6 ‡16–24 in (40–60 cm), ↔3 in (8 cm)
■ **Seasonal highlights** In late summer it produces arching sprays of orange-red and yellow flowers.
■ **Value at other times** Handsome, sword-shaped leaves for most of the year.
■ **Ideal site** Mixed or herbaceous borders.
■ **Cultivation** Ideally, grow in full sun, but it will tolerate partial shade. Plant the corms 3–4 in (8–10 cm) deep in fertile soil. In heavy clay, plant on a layer of coarse grit. Lift and divide every three or four years, in spring.
■ **Also recommended** *Crocosmia* 'Emberglow' has dark-red flowers in summer.
■ **Perfect partners** *Crocosmia* 'Golden Fleece', with lemon-yellow flowers, asters, rudbeckias.

Crocus tommasinianus
Early crocus

A robust, cormous perennial. Z3–8 H8–1 ‡4 in (10 cm), ↔1 in (2.5 cm)
■ **Seasonal highlights** In late winter or early spring, slender, goblet-shaped flowers appear. They come in white, lilac, and red-purple, often with silvery overtones.
■ **Value at other times** No real value at other times.
■ **Ideal site** Naturalized in lawn, in borders, rock and woodland gardens.
■ **Cultivation** Best in full sun, but will tolerate dappled shade. Grow in fertile, well-drained soil. Plant corms in fall, 3–4 in (8–10 cm) deep.
■ **Also recommended** *Crocus tommasinianus* 'Albus' has starry, white flowers with golden anthers.
■ **Perfect partners** Snowdrops (*Galanthus*) and winter aconites (*Eranthis hyemalis*).

Crocus vernus 'Pickwick'
Dutch crocus

Robust, cormous perennial. Z3–8 H8–1 ‡5 in (12 cm), ↔2 in (5 cm)
■ **Seasonal highlights** From early to late spring it produces white flowers, striped pale and dark lilac, with dark-purple bases.
■ **Value at other times** No real value at other times.
■ **Ideal site** Naturalized in lawn, in borders, rock and woodland gardens, and in containers.
■ **Cultivation** Grow in sun or light dappled shade, in fertile, well-drained soil. Plant corms in fall, 3–4 in (8–10 cm) deep.
■ **Also recommended** *Crocus vernus* 'Remembrance' has glossy, violet flowers.
■ **Perfect partners** Snowdrops (*Galanthus*), winter aconites (*Eranthis hyemalis*), narcissi.

Cyclamen coum
Hardy cyclamen

Hardy cyclamen are spreading and low-growing perennials that grow from underground tubers. There are several species that flower in late summer or in fall and winter, providing carpets of color when most other plants have faded. Some flower before the leaves and others with them, but all have a delicacy that belies their tough constitution. Most self-seed freely, forming extensive colonies with time.
■ **Ideal site** Naturalized in lawn, in shady borders, beneath shrubs and trees, including conifers.
■ **Cultivation** Grow in moderately fertile well-drained soil, ideally beneath a canopy of trees or shrubs to protect them from excessive summer rain when dormant. *Cyclamen purpurascens* needs soil that does not dry out and prefers alkaline soil. Plant tubers 1¼–2 in (3–5 cm) deep in fall, or

C. coum Pewter Group
Hardy cyclamen

in early spring for *C. purpurascens*. Plants can be bought in flower and planted directly if the soil is not frozen or too wet. Give a deep, dry mulch of leafmold as the leaves wither.
■ **Recommended cyclamen** *Cyclamen coum* blooms in white and shades of pink or carmine-red, in winter or early spring, above shiny, deep-green leaves that are often marked with silver. *C. coum* Pewter Group has completely silvered leaves. ‡3 in (8 cm), ↔ 4 in (10 cm) *Cyclamen hederifolium* has small flowers in shades of white or pink in mid- to late fall. Rounded, dark, gray-green leaves, often patterned with silver, appear after the flowers. Z7–9 H9–7 ‡5 in (13 cm), ↔6 in (15 cm) *Cyclamen purpurascens* bears sweetly scented, pale to deep carmine-red flowers in mid- to late summer. Z5–9 H9–7 ‡↔ 4 in (10 cm)

C

Cytisus x praecox 'Warminster'
Warminster broom

A moderately vigorous, arching evergreen shrub. Z6–9 H9–6 ‡4 ft (1.2 m), ↔5 ft (1.5 m)
■ **Seasonal highlights** In mid- and late spring, each stem is wreathed in pealike, creamy-yellow flowers.
■ **Value at other times** Arching wandlike shoots bear small dark-green leaves.
■ **Ideal site** Shrub borders, sunny banks, hot, dry sites.
■ **Cultivation** Grow in moderately fertile, well-drained soil in full sun. Tolerates poor acidic soil. After flowering has taken place, cut back the flowered shoots to buds lower down green young wood. Don't cut into old wood.
■ **Also recommended** *Cytisus nigricans* bears yellow flowers in late summer.
■ **Perfect partners** Choisyas, camellias, and other broad-leaved evergreens.

D

Dahlia 'Bishop of Llandaff'
Dahlia

A vigorous, tuberous, frost-tender perennial. Z9–11 H12–5 ‡3½ ft (1.1 m), ↔18 in (45 cm)
■ **Seasonal highlights** From late summer until late fall, it produces peony-like, semidouble, velvety, glowing-red flowers.
■ **Value at other times** It also has very attractive dark-red, almost black, leaves.
■ **Ideal site** Bedding and mixed borders.
■ **Cultivation** Best in full sun. Dahlias are heavy feeders and need fertile, well-drained soil enriched with well-rotted organic matter. Set out in early summer when all risk of frost has passed. Lift tubers when the foliage has been blackened by fall frost. Store in a cool dry place.
■ **Also recommended** *Dahlia* 'Alloway Cottage' has soft-yellow flowers.
■ **Perfect partners** Chrysanthemums.

Daphne mezereum
Daphne

An upright, deciduous shrub. All parts are highly toxic. Z5–8 H8–5 ‡4 ft (1.2 m), ↔3 ft (1 m)
■ **Seasonal highlights** From late winter until early spring, it produces clusters of pink to purplish-pink flowers on bare branches.
■ **Value at other times** Fleshy red fruits in summer.
■ **Ideal site** Shrub borders and woodland gardens.
■ **Cultivation** Grow in sun or partial shade. Prefers slightly alkaline, humus-rich, moist but well-drained soil. Mulch to keep the roots cool. Prune only to take out dead or damaged wood, after flowering.
■ **Also recommended** *Daphne mezereum* 'Bowles's Variety' has white flowers with yellow fruit to follow.
■ **Perfect partners** Mahonias, *Viburnum* x *bodnantense* 'Dawn'.

Delphinium Black Knight Group
Delphinium

A moderately vigorous, upright, herbaceous perennial. Z3–7 H7–1 ‡5½ ft (1.7 m), ↔30 in (75 cm)
■ **Seasonal highlights** From early to midsummer, it bears long spikes of black-eyed, deep-purple flowers.
■ **Value at other times** Has attractive, deeply lobed, mid- to light-green foliage.
■ **Ideal site** A sunny border, especially in cottage gardens.
■ **Cultivation** Grow in full sun in fertile, well-drained soil enriched with plenty of organic matter. Needs staking in exposed gardens. Cut back in fall when foliage has withered.
■ **Also recommended** *Delphinium* 'Emily Hawkins' has semidouble, lilac flowers.
■ **Perfect partners** Achilleas, lupines, oriental poppies (*Papaver orientalis*).

Dianthus 'Little Jock'
Alpine pink

A low-growing, cushion-forming, evergreen perennial. Z5–9 H9–1 ‡↔4 in (10 cm)
■ **Seasonal highlights** In summer, it bears clove-scented, double, pale-pink flowers with a maroon eye and fringed petals, just above the foliage.
■ **Value at other times** Neat mounds of gray-green foliage all year.
■ **Ideal site** Rock gardens, troughs, and other containers.
■ **Cultivation** Prefers an open, sunny spot, in sharply drained, gritty, slightly alkaline soil. In clay soil, dig in plenty of grit. Good drainage is essential.
■ **Also recommended** *Dianthus alpinus* 'Joan's Blood' has deep magenta-pink flowers with crimson centers.
■ **Perfect partners** *Aurinia saxatilis* , *Saponaria caespitosa*, alpine phlox, thymes.

Diascia barberae 'Blackthorn Apricot'
Diascia

A moderately spreading, mat-forming, evergreen or semievergreen perennial. Z8–9 H9–1 ‡10 in (25 cm), ↔20 in (50 cm)

■ **Seasonal highlights** From summer until fall, it bears a profusion of apricot flowers in loose spikes.

■ **Value at other times** The mats of heart-shaped, mid-green foliage are present for most of the year.

■ **Ideal site** A sunny bank or border, in a rock garden, or raised bed.

■ **Cultivation** Grow in full sun in fertile, moist but well-drained soil. Deadhead regularly to induce more flowers. May not survive very cold, wet winters. Take stem cuttings in summer and overwinter young plants indoors.

■ **Also recommended** *Diascia rigescens* is trailing with deep-pink flowers.

■ **Perfect partners** *Veronica prostrata, V. spicata.*

Dicentra spectabilis
Bleeding heart

A vigorous, clump-forming, herbaceous perennial. Z3–9 H9–1 ‡4 ft (1.2 m), ↔18 in (45 cm)

■ **Seasonal highlights** In late spring and early summer, arching stems bear hanging, heart-shaped flowers with rose-pink outer petals and white inner ones.

■ **Value at other times** Ferny, pale-green leaves.

■ **Ideal site** Shady borders and woodland gardens.

■ **Cultivation** Best in partial shade, but will tolerate part-day sun, if soil is reliably moist. Grow in damp, fertile, preferably neutral to slightly alkaline soil. Divide every three or four years to maintain vigor.

■ **Also recommended** *Dicentra spectabilis* f. *alba* bears white flowers over longer periods.

■ **Perfect partners** Bold foliage plants such as hostas.

Dierama pulcherrimum
Angel's fishing rod

A vigorous, upright, evergreen, cormous perennial. Z8–10 H10–8 ‡3–5 ft (1–1.5 m) ↔24 in (60 cm)

■ **Seasonal highlights** In summer, it produces tall stems bearing bell-shaped, pale to deep magenta-pink flowers on very slender stalks.

■ **Value at other times** Grasslike, gray-green leaves for most of the year.

■ **Ideal site** At the front of a sunny border, or by a pond.

■ **Cultivation** Best in full sun in leafy, fertile, well-drained soil. Keep well watered in dry weather. Plant corms 2–3 in (5–7 cm) deep in spring. Divide every three or four years. Divisions may take a season to flower.

■ **Also recommended** *Dierama* 'Miranda' is shorter with bright-pink flowers.

■ **Perfect partners** Acanthus, penstemons, salvias.

Digitalis x mertonensis
Perennial foxglove

An upright, fairly vigorous herbaceous perennial. Z3–8 H8–1 ‡35 in (90 cm), ↔12 in (30 cm)

■ **Seasonal highlights** Tall spires of tubular, pinkish-buff flowers rise above the foliage in spring and early summer. They attract bees.

■ **Value at other times** Mounds of crinkled, deeply veined, dark-green leaves.

■ **Ideal site** Woodland gardens or mixed and herbaceous borders.

■ **Cultivation** Prefers partial shade and humus-rich soil, but tolerates most sites and soils if not too wet or dry. Deadhead after flowering; it self-seeds but seedlings are variable.

■ **Also recommended** *Digitalis grandiflora* has brown-veined, pale-yellow flowers.

■ **Perfect partners** *Digitalis obscura*, with yellow flowers; dicentras.

Doronicum x excelsum 'Harpur Crewe'
Leopard's bane

A vigorous, upright, and bushy herbaceous perennial. Z4–8 H8–1 ‡↔to 24 in (60 cm).

■ **Seasonal highlights** In spring, branched stems each bear 3–4 golden-yellow, daisylike flowers.

■ **Value at other times** Has attractive, soft-green, hairy, heart-shaped leaves.

■ **Ideal site** Shady borders or naturalized in woodland.

■ **Cultivation** Best in partial or dappled shade, but tolerates a more open site if soil is not too dry. Grow in fertile, moisture-retentive soil. Lift and divide every four to five years to maintain vigor.

■ **Also recommended** *Doronicum columnae* 'Miss Mason' has large, bright-yellow flowers.

■ **Perfect partners** Narcissus, pulmonarias, polyanthus primulas.

E

Echinacea purpurea 'White Swan'
Coneflower

A vigorous, upright, clump-forming herbaceous perennial. Z3–9 H12–1 ↕24 in (60 cm), ↔18 in (45 cm)
- **Seasonal highlights** From midsummer until early fall, it bears large, single, white flowers with orange-brown centers.
- **Value at other times** Has clumps of narrow, roughly hairy basal leaves.
- **Ideal site** Late-summer borders.
- **Cultivation** Best in full sun, but tolerates light, part-day shade. Grow in fertile, humus-rich, well-drained soil. Cut back the flowering stems as the blooms fade, to encourage a second flush of flowers.
- **Also recommended** *Echinacea purpurea* 'Robert Bloom' has mauve-crimson flowers with orange-brown centers.
- **Perfect partners** Achilleas, chrysanthemums, border phlox.

Elaeagnus x *ebbingei* 'Gilt Edge'
Elaeagnus

A dense, bushy, moderately vigorous evergreen shrub. Z7–11 H12–1 ↕↔ to 12 ft (4 m)
- **Seasonal highlights** All year it has lustrous dark leaves with gleaming, creamy-yellow margins.
- **Value at other times** The fall flowers are fragrant but insignificant.
- **Ideal site** Shrub borders and hedges.
- **Cultivation** The leaves color best in sun, but it tolerates dappled shade. Grow in any fertile soil that is not too dry or wet. Prune lightly to shape in mid- to late spring; cut out shoots with all-green leaves.
- **Also recommended** *Elaeagnus pungens* 'Frederici' has yellow-centered, shining, green leaves, and is slow-growing.
- **Perfect partners** Dark-leaved shrubs like hollies (*Ilex*), escallonias, and *Viburnum tinus*.

Epimedium x *warleyense*
Bishop's mitre

Also known as barrenwort. A vigorous, clump-forming, evergreen perennial. Z5–9 H9–4 ↕20 in (50 cm), ↔30 in (75 cm)
- **Seasonal highlights** From mid- to late spring, it bears sprays of nodding, yellow and orange-red flowers.
- **Value at other times** The leaves are tinted red in spring and fall and make good ground cover.
- **Ideal site** Shady mixed borders and woodland gardens.
- **Cultivation** Best in partial shade, but tolerates some sun if soil is moist. Grow in fertile, moist but well-drained soil. Shelter from cold winds. Cut back old foliage in late winter to get the best flowering display.
- **Also recommended** *Epimedium* ' Versicolor' has dark-red and yellow flowers.
- **Perfect partners** *Epimedium* x *perralchicum* (bright-yellow flowers); dwarf narcissi.

Eranthis hyemalis
Winter aconite

A vigorous perennial with small, knobbly tubers. Z4–9 H9–1 ↕2–3 in (5–8 cm), ↔2 in (5 cm)
- **Seasonal highlights** In late winter and early spring, bright-yellow flowers appear above a ruff of dissected, bright-green leaves.
- **Value at other times** No great value at other times. The foliage dies back after flowering.
- **Ideal site** Beneath deciduous trees and shrubs or naturalized in grass.
- **Cultivation** Grow in full sun, in any fertile soil that isn't very dry in summer. Plant tubers 2 in (5 cm) deep in fall, or, buy plants "in-the-green" and plant when the soil is not too wet or frozen.
- **Also recommended** *Eranthis pinnatifida* has white flowers.
- **Perfect partners** Snowdrops, crocus, hardy cyclamen.

Erica carnea 'Springwood White'
Winter heath

A vigorous, spreading, slightly trailing evergreen shrub. Z7–10 H10–5 ↕6 in (15 cm), ↔18 in (45 cm)
- **Seasonal highlights** From winter to mid-spring, it is covered with small, dense spires of white flowers.
- **Value at other times** Bright-green foliage makes good ground cover all year.
- **Ideal site** Rock gardens, especially with dwarf conifers.
- **Cultivation** Best in an open, sunny site in well-drained acidic soil; it will tolerate slightly alkaline soil. After flowering, trim off the old flowers with shears and top-dress with leafmold, garden compost, or similar.
- **Also recommended** *Erica carnea* 'Springwood Pink' has rose-pink flowers.
- **Perfect partners** Dwarf conifers and dwarf rhododendrons, shrubby potentillas, and gaultherias.

Erica x *darleyensis* 'Arthur Johnson'
Darley Dale heath

A dense, bushy, vigorous evergreen shrub.
Z7–10 H10–5 ‡3 ft (1 m), ↔30 in (75 cm)
■ **Seasonal highlights** From midwinter until spring it bears long, dense spikes of mauve-pink flowers.
■ **Value at other times** Young foliage has cream and pink tips in spring; it makes good ground cover all year.
■ **Ideal site** Rock gardens, especially with dwarf conifers.
■ **Cultivation** Best in an open, sunny site in well-drained acidic soil; it will tolerate slightly alkaline soil. After flowering, trim with shears and top-dress with leafmold or garden compost.
■ **Also recommended** *Erica* x *darleyensis* 'Darley Dale' has cream-tipped leaves in spring and shell-pink flowers.
■ **Perfect partners** Dwarf conifers and dwarf rhododendrons, shrubby potentillas, and gaultherias.

Eryngium x *tripartitum*
Sea holly

An upright, clump-forming herbaceous perennial.
Z5–8 H8–5 ‡24–36 in (60–90 cm), ↔20 in (50 cm)
■ **Seasonal highlights** From midsummer until early fall, it bears branching stems of violet-blue flowers with narrow, gray-blue bracts; they are good for drying.
■ **Value at other times** Basal clumps of shiny, slightly spiny, dark-green leaves.
■ **Ideal site** Sunny borders, seaside, and gravel gardens.
■ **Cultivation** Grow in full sun in poor, dry, gritty soil. It may need protection from excessive winter moisture, especially in cold or exposed gardens.
■ **Also recommended** *Eryngium giganteum* is a taller, self-seeding biennial with steel-blue flowers and silver bracts.
■ **Perfect partners** *Yucca gloriosa* , *Y. filamentosa.*

Erysimum cheiri Bedder Series
Wallflower

Upright, bushy, compact perennials grown as biennials.
‡12 in (30 cm), ↔9 in (23 cm)
■ **Seasonal highlights** Over long periods in spring, bear short spikes of sweetly scented, golden-yellow, orange or scarlet-red flowers.
■ **Value at other times** They are usually discarded after flowering.
■ **Ideal site** Spring bedding or containers.
■ **Cultivation** Grow in sun in well-drained, poor to moderately fertile,well-drained soil. Rich soil encourages leafy growth with fewer flowers. Sow seed in a seedbed in late spring or early summer. Prick out into a nursery bed. Plant in the flowering sites in the fall.
■ **Also recommended** *Erysimum cheiri* 'Blood Red' has luminous, deep-red flowers.
■ **Perfect partners** Forget-me-nots (*Myosotis*), tulips, polyanthus primulas.

Erythronium 'Pagoda'
Trout lily, Pagoda flower

Upright, vigorous, clump-forming, bulbous perennial.
Z4–9 H9–1 ‡6–14 in (15–35 cm), ↔4 in (10 cm)
■ **Seasonal highlights** In spring, it bears heads of nodding, brown-marked, sulfur-yellow flowers.
■ **Value at other times** Has bronze-mottled leaves that die down in summer.
■ **Ideal site** Beneath deciduous shrubs, rock and woodland gardens, or naturalized in lawn.
■ **Cultivation** Grow in partial shade in fertile, reliably moist, humus-rich soil. Plant bulbs 4 in (10 cm) deep in fall. Do not let bulbs dry out before planting, or when dormant.
■ **Also recommended** *Erythronium revolutum* has lilac-pink flowers and brown-mottled, dark-green leaves.
■ **Perfect partners** Crocus and narcissus.

Eschscholzia californica
California poppy

A moderately vigorous, mat-forming hardy annual.
‡12 in (30 cm), ↔6 in (15 cm)
■ **Seasonal highlights** From summer to fall, it bears satiny-orange, yellow, white, or red flowers.
■ **Value at other times** The flowers are followed by long, curving seed pods.
■ **Ideal site** Annual borders, dry, sunny banks, gravel gardens.
■ **Cultivation** Grow in poor, well-drained soil in full sun. Sow the seeds outdoors in early spring and thin out to about 6 in (15 cm), when the seedlings are large enough to handle. Deadhead regularly to prolong the flowering period.
■ **Also recommended** *Eschscholzia caespitosa* is dwarf, with scented, bright-yellow flowers.
■ **Perfect partners** Shirley poppies (*Papaver rhoeas* Shirley Series).

E

Euonymus alatus
Burning bush

A dense, bushy, vigorous, deciduous shrub. Z4–9 H9–1 ↕6 ft (2 m), ↔10 ft (3 m)

■ **Seasonal highlights** The leaves turn brilliant crimson in fall, setting off the red-purple fruits that split to reveal orange seeds.

■ **Value at other times** The stems have corky "wings" and the dark-green leaves are attractive all summer.

■ **Ideal site** A mixed or shrub border.

■ **Cultivation** Fall color is best in full sun, but it will tolerate partial shade. Grow in any well-drained soil. Prune in winter, if necessary, to shape and to remove any wayward, or dead and damaged shoots.

■ **Also recommended** *Euonymous alatus* 'Compactus' is similar but smaller and more dense.

■ **Perfect partners** *Euonymous fortunei* 'Emerald 'n' Gold', with gold and green leaves.

Euonymus fortunei 'Silver Queen'
Euonymus

A very hardy, vigorous, bushy, mounded, evergreen shrub. Z5–9 H9–5 ↕8 ft (2.5 m), ↔5 ft (1.5 m); ↕to 20 ft (6 m) if climbing

■ **Seasonal highlights** The shiny-green leaves with white, often pink-flushed margins make good ground cover year-round.

■ **Value at other times** Tiny, greenish-white flowers in summer, followed by pink fruits with orange seeds.

■ **Ideal site** Mixed or herbaceous borders, walls, and containers.

■ **Cultivation** Foliage color is best in full sun, but it tolerates light shade. Grow in any well-drained soil. Trim in mid- to late spring; remove any all-green shoots as soon as seen.

■ **Also recommended** *Euonymus fortunei* 'Emerald Gaiety' has white-variegated leaves.

■ **Perfect partners** *Euonymus europaeus* 'Red Cascade' has red fall leaves and fruit.

Euphorbia x martinii
Spurge

Upright, moderately vigorous, herbaceous perennial. Z7–10 H10–7 ↕↔3 ft (1 m)

■ **Seasonal highlights** From spring to midsummer, it bears heads of clustered, yellow-green flowers with dark-red nectar glands.

■ **Value at other times** Red stems and narrow green leaves that are often purple-tinged when young.

■ **Ideal site** Mixed or herbaceous borders.

■ **Cultivation** Best in full sun, but tolerant of light, dappled shade. Grow in a light, well-drained soil enriched with organic matter. In clay soil, dig in some grit to improve drainage.

■ **Also recommended** *Euphorbia mellifera* is evergreen and much taller, with honey-scented, red-brown flowers.

■ **Perfect partners** The broad, glossy leaves of bear's breeches (*Acanthus*).

Euphorbia polychroma
Spurge

A vigorous, bushy, clump-forming, herbaceous perennial. Z5–9 H9–5 ↕16 in (40 cm), ↔24 in (60 cm)

■ **Seasonal highlights** From mid-spring to midsummer, it bears long-lasting, bright yellow-green flowers at the stem tips.

■ **Value at other times** Forms a dense mound of dark green, sometimes purple-tinted, leaves.

■ **Ideal site** Herbaceous borders and decorative containers.

■ **Cultivation** Best in full sun, but tolerant of light dappled shade. Grow in a light, well-drained soil enriched with organic matter.

■ **Also recommended** *Euphorbia rigida* has thick, arching stems with gray-green leaves and yellow flowers in spring and early summer.

■ **Perfect partners** *Stachys byzantina* 'Primrose Heron'.

Euryops pectinatus
South African daisy

An upright, bushy, vigorous, half-hardy evergreen perennial. Z9–10 H10–1 ↕↔3 ft (1 m)

■ **Seasonal highlights** From early summer to mid-fall, it bears bright-yellow, daisylike flowers.

■ **Value at other times** It has gray, hairy fernlike foliage year-round.

■ **Ideal site** As a filler in herbaceous borders or in decorative pots.

■ **Cultivation** Grow in full sun, in sharply drained, moderately fertile soil. Trim after flowering to keep compact. Take stem cuttings in summer; overwinter young plants and container plants indoors.

■ **Also recommended** *Euryops acraeus* is more compact and cold-tolerant, with yellow flowers and silver-gray leaves.

■ **Perfect partners** Penstemons, osteospermums.

Exochorda x macrantha 'The Bride'

Also known as exochorda and pearl bush. A vigorous, mound-forming, deciduous shrub. Z4–8 H8–1 ‡6 ft (2 m), ↔10 ft (3 m)
- **Seasonal highlights** In late spring and early summer, the arching stems are wreathed in white flowers.
- **Value at other times** Has attractive, light-green leaves from spring to fall.
- **Ideal site** A shrub or mixed border.
- **Cultivation** Grow in full sun or partial shade, in any fertile, well-drained soil. Shorten flowered shoots to strong buds after flowering.
- **Also recommended** *Exochorda racemosa* is taller, with upright clusters of white flowers in late spring.
- **Perfect partners** Camellias as a dark-leaved backdrop; *Magnolia stellata*.

F

Forsythia x intermedia
Forsythia

A vigorous, strongly upright, deciduous shrub. Z6–9 H9–6 ‡↔to 5 ft (1.5 m)
- **Seasonal highlights** In spring, it bears bright, deep-yellow flowers all along the bare branches.
- **Value at other times** Undistinguished in summer, but a good host for clematis.
- **Ideal site** Shrub and mixed borders, or as informal hedging.
- **Cultivation** Thrives in any fertile soil in sun or light dappled shade. Shorten flowered shoots to strong buds after flowering; when established, cut out one in four of the oldest stems to encourage new growth from the base.
- **Also recommended** *Forsythia x intermedia* 'Lynwood Variety' has rich-yellow flowers in great profusion.
- **Perfect partners** Create a blue carpet beneath forsythias with *Scilla siberica*.

Freesia 'Imperial Red'
Freesia

An upright, half-hardy, bulbous perennial. Z10–11 H12–1 ‡16 in (40 cm), ↔2 in (5 cm)
- **Seasonal highlights** Bears scented, pinkish-red, creamy-throated flowers from late winter to spring.
- **Value at other times** Is grown only for its flowers.
- **Ideal site** A cool greenhouse or conservatory; prepared bulbs are summer-flowering and can be grown outdoors.
- **Cultivation** Plant bulbs in pots of loamy potting mix with added grit, in fall. Keep temperature below 55°F (13°C). Give a balanced liquid fertilizer weekly when the flower buds appear. Dry off after flowering and rest for the summer.
- **Also recommended** *Freesia*. 'Oberon' with lemon-yellow and red flowers.
- **Perfect partners** Cinerarias (*Pericallis*), paper white narcissus (*Narcissus papyraceus*).

Fremontodendron 'California Glory'
Flannel bush

A vigorous, upright then spreading, evergreen shrub Z8–10 H10–8 ‡20 ft (6 m), ↔12 ft (4 m)
- **Seasonal highlights** A long succession of saucer-shaped, deep-yellow flowers appear from late spring to mid-fall.
- **Value at other times** The lobed, dark-green leaves have tawny down beneath.
- **Ideal site** A warm, sunny, sheltered wall.
- **Cultivation** Grow in fertile, well-drained soil. Protect from cold winds. To wall-train, tie in the main stems to a support of wires or trellis. Keep pruning to a minimum; just shorten outward-growing shoots on wall-trained plants after the first flush of blooms and trim out damaged or dead wood.
- **Also recommended** *Fremontodendron* 'Pacific Sunset' has yellow flowers with pointed petals.
- **Perfect partners** *Clematis* 'Ascotiensis'.

Fritillaria imperialis
Crown imperial

A robust, strongly upright, bulbous perennial. Z4–9 H9–2 ‡to 5 ft (1.5 m), ↔10–12 in (25–30 cm)
- **Seasonal highlights** In late spring or early summer, at the tips of stout stems, bears large, nodding, orange, yellow, or red flowers crowned by leafy bracts.
- **Value at other times** Of no real value at other times.
- **Ideal site** A sunny border or raised bed.
- **Cultivation** Grow in full sun in fertile, well-drained soil. Plant bulbs in fall, at four times their own depth, setting on a layer of sharp sand to improve drainage. The bulbs will rot in wet soil.
- **Also recommended** *Fritillaria imperialis* 'Lutea' has bright-yellow flowers.
- **Perfect partners** Mid-season and late-flowering tulips.

F

Fritillaria meleagris
Snake's-head fritillary

An upright, slender bulbous perennial. Z4–9 H8–2 ‡12 in (30 cm), ↔2–3 in (5–8 cm)
■ **Seasonal highlights** In spring, it bears hanging, bell-shaped flowers in delicate, checkered shades of pink, purple, or white.
■ **Value at other times** No real value at other times.
■ **Ideal site** In a rock garden, or naturalized in lawn.
■ **Cultivation** Grow in fertile, humus-rich, moisture-retentive soil. Plant the bulbs in fall at two to three times their own depth and the same distance apart. If grown in grass, delay the first mowing until the leaves have faded naturally.
■ **Also recommended** *Fritillaria acmopetala* has pale-green, maroon-marked flowers.
■ **Perfect partners** Narcissus, camassias.

Fuchsia 'Auntie Jinks'
Fuchsia

A trailing, moderately vigorous, half-hardy shrub. Z9–11 H12–9 ‡6–8 in (15–20 cm), ↔8–16 in (20–40 cm)
■ **Seasonal highlights** From early summer until late fall, it bears masses of single flowers with pink-red tubes, cerise-margined white sepals and purple corollas.
■ **Value at other times** Of no value during winter.
■ **Ideal site** Containers, including hanging baskets, or mixed borders.
■ **Cultivation** Tolerates sun or light shade. Grow in fertile, well-drained soil or potting mix. Plant out when the threat of frost has passed. Bring indoors for the winter. Deadhead regularly. Cut back hard in spring.
■ **Also recommended** *Fuchsia* 'Celia Smedley' has pink and currant-red flowers.
■ **Perfect partners** Argyranthemums, osteospermums, geraniums.

G

Galanthus plicatus subsp. *byzantinus*
Snowdrop

A vigorous perennial bulb. Z3–9 H9–1 ‡8 in (20 cm), ↔3 in (8 cm)
■ **Seasonal highlights** In late winter or early spring, it bears nodding, honey-scented, white flowers with green markings on the inner petals.
■ **Value at other times** Of no value at other times.
■ **Ideal site** Woodland gardens, beneath trees and shrubs, or naturalized in lawn.
■ **Cultivation** Grow in dappled shade in any fertile garden soil that does not dry out in summer. Lift and divide the bulbs when congested, after flowering but before the leaves have faded. May self-seed.
■ **Also recommended** *Galanthus nivalis* has white flowers with a V-shaped green mark on each petal.
■ **Perfect partners** Winter aconites (*Eranthis hyemalis*), hardy cyclamen.

Garrya elliptica
Silk tassel bush

A dense, vigorous, bushy evergreen shrub. Z8–10 H10–8 ‡↔12 ft (4 m)
■ **Seasonal highlights** From midwinter to early spring, it bears swags of silky, hanging, gray-green catkins.
■ **Value at other times** Glossy, wavy-margined, dark grayish-green leaves all year.
■ **Ideal site** Shrub or mixed borders and shady walls.
■ **Cultivation** Grow in any fertile, well-drained soil in sun or partial shade. Shelter from cold wind. After flowering, shorten any shoots that spoil the shape, or grow away from, or in to the wall, if wall-trained.
■ **Also recommended** *Garrya elliptica* 'James Roof' has dark-sea-green leaves and very long catkins.
■ **Perfect partners** *Jasminum nudiflorum*, *Mahonia* x *media* 'Charity'.

Gazania Chansonette Series
Gazania

Vigorous, half-hardy perennial often grown as an annual. Z8–11 H12–1 ‡8 in (20 cm), ↔10 in (25 cm)
■ **Seasonal highlights** Throughout summer, it bears daisylike, dark-zoned flower heads in bronze, orange, rose-pink, salmon-pink or red.
■ **Value at other times** The glossy, dark-green leaves have silky white hair beneath.
■ **Ideal site** Bedding, containers, hot, sunny borders, seaside gardens.
■ **Cultivation** Sow seeds in warmth in spring and plant out young plants when the risk of frost has passed. Grow in full sun in light, well-drained soil. Deadhead regularly to prolong flowering.
■ **Also recommended** *Gazania* Daybreak Series has white, yellow, orange, and pink flowers.
■ **Perfect partners** Geraniums, French marigolds.

Genista aetnensis
Mount Etna broom

A vigorous, deciduous shrub or small tree with upright, then weeping, shoots. Z9–10 H10–9 ↕↔to 25 ft (8 m)
- ■ **Seasonal highlights** Fragrant, yellow, pealike flowers are borne at the stem tips in mid- to late summer.
- ■ **Value at other times** The weeping shoots are bright green and give an evergreen appearance.
- ■ **Ideal site** Sunny walls, banks, or borders.
- ■ **Cultivation** Grow in full sun in light, poor, very well-drained soil. After flowering, shorten flowered shoots to strong buds on green wood; don't cut into old wood.
- ■ **Also recommended** *Genista hispanica* is dense, spiny and much smaller with golden-yellow flowers in late spring and early summer.
- ■ **Perfect partners** *Cytisus nigricans*.

Geranium himalayense
Himalayan cranesbill

A vigorous, mound-forming herbaceous perennial. Z3–9 H9–1 ↕12–18 in (30–45 cm), ↔24 in (60 cm)
- ■ **Seasonal highlights** In early summer, it bears a profusion of white-centered, violet-blue to deep-blue flowers, and then blooms sporadically into fall.
- ■ **Value at other times** The lobed, soft-green leaves color well in fall.
- ■ **Ideal site** Mixed or herbaceous borders.
- ■ **Cultivation** Grow in any fertile, well-drained soil, in sun or partial shade. Trim after the first flush of flowers to encourage more in the fall. Divide every three or four years in spring.
- ■ **Also recommended** *Geranium endressii* has silvery-pink flowers all summer.
- ■ **Perfect partners** Achilleas, daylilies, border phlox.

Geranium psilostemon
Armenian cranesbill

A vigorous, clump-forming herbaceous perennial. Z5–8 H9–1 ↕24–48 in (60–120 cm), ↔24 in (60 cm)
- ■ **Seasonal highlights** From early until late summer, it bears sprays of upturned, brilliant-magenta flowers with black centers and veins.
- ■ **Value at other times** The leaves are tinted crimson in spring and red in fall; they make good ground cover.
- ■ **Ideal site** Mixed or herbaceous borders, especially in cottage gardens.
- ■ **Cultivation** Grow in sun or light shade, in any fertile soil. Deadhead regularly to encourage continuous blooming.
- ■ **Also recommended** *Geranium* 'Ann Folkard' is similar but more spreading.
- ■ **Perfect partners** Achilleas, border phlox, daylilies.

Geum 'Borisii'
Avens

A vigorous, clump-forming, herbaceous perennial. Z5–9 H9–5 ↕12–20 in (30–50cm), ↔12 in (30 cm)
- ■ **Seasonal highlights** From late spring to late summer, it bears long-stemmed clusters of bright, brick-red flowers with a boss of golden-yellow stamens.
- ■ **Value at other times** Basal mounds of divided, fresh green leaves.
- ■ **Ideal site** The front of sunny, mixed, or herbaceous borders, especially in cottage gardens.
- ■ **Cultivation** Grow in any fertile, well-drained soil in full sun or light, part-day shade. Lift and divide the plants every three or four years to rejuvenate.
- ■ **Also recommended** *Geum* 'Red Wings' has semidouble, scarlet flowers.
- ■ **Perfect partners** *Geum* 'Lady Stratheden' with yellow flowers.

Gunnera manicata
Gunnera

A massive, very vigorous, herbaceous perennial. Z7–11 H12–7 ↕8 ft (2.5 m), ↔10–12 ft (3–4 m)
- ■ **Seasonal highlights** The enormous, prominently veined, bright-green leaves have red-prickly stems and reach 6 ft (2 m) long.
- ■ **Value at other times** In summer, it bears fat spikes of tiny greenish-red flowers, followed by orange-red fruit.
- ■ **Ideal site** Pond- and streamsides, damp borders.
- ■ **Cultivation** Grow in sun or partial shade in deep, permanently moist, soil, enriched with plenty of organic matter. In cold areas, protect the crown in winter with a deep, dry mulch of straw or leafmold.
- ■ **Also recommended** *Gunnera tinctoria* is similar but more compact.
- ■ **Perfect partners** *Iris sibirica, Rheum palmatum* 'Atrosanguineum'.

H

Hakonechloa macra 'Aureola'
Hakonechloa

A spreading, mound-forming, deciduous grass.
Z5–9 H9–5 ‡14 in (35 cm), ↔16 in (40 cm)
■ **Seasonal highlights** The narrow, arching leaves, striped bright-yellow and green, are present for much of the year. Pale-green flower spikes appear from late summer to fall.
■ **Value at other times** Leaves turn red in fall and often persist into winter.
■ **Ideal site** The front of a border, in containers, in rock gardens, or woodland gardens.
■ **Cultivation** Grow in full sun, or for the best leaf colors, in partial shade. Grow in fertile, moist, but well-drained soil.
■ **Also recommended** *Carex elata* 'Aurea', with golden, grasslike leaves.
■ **Perfect partners** *Miscanthus sinensis* 'Gracillimus' has blue-green leaves that turn bronze in fall.

Hamamelis x *intermedia* 'Arnold Promise'

Also known as witch hazel. Slow-growing, deciduous shrub of vase-shaped outline.
Z5–9 H9–1 ‡↔to 12 ft (4 m)
■ **Seasonal highlights** Bare branches are spangled with fragrant, spidery, yellow flowers in early to midwinter.
■ **Value at other times** The leaves turn yellow before falling in fall.
■ **Ideal site** A woodland garden, as a specimen, in a shady border.
■ **Cultivation** Needs fertile, humus-rich, moisture-retentive, neutral to acidic soil and a sheltered spot in sun or partial shade. Keep pruning to a minimum, but remove crossing or damaged shoots after flowering.
■ **Also recommended** *Hamamelis* x *intermedia* 'Jelena' has coppery-orange flowers.
■ **Perfect partners** Mahonias, *Viburnum* x *bodnantense* 'Dawn'.

Hebe 'Gauntlettii'
Hebe

A bushy, upright, fast-growing, half-hardy evergreen shrub.
Z9–11 H12–9 ‡↔to 3 ft (1 m)
■ **Seasonal highlights** From late summer until late fall, it bears hanging clusters of small, pink flowers.
■ **Value at other times** Has glossy rich-green leaves.
■ **Ideal site** Sunny mixed or shrub borders, decorative containers.
■ **Cultivation** Grow in fertile, well-drained, neutral to alkaline soil in sun or dappled shade. Shelter from cold winds. Where not hardy, bring container plants into a cold greenhouse for the winter. Trim lightly to shape in spring.
■ **Also recommended** *Hebe* 'Great Orme' is hardier, with bright-pink flowers.
■ **Perfect partners** Bamboos, cotoneasters, shrubby potentillas.

Helianthemum 'Raspberry Ripple'
Rock rose, Sun rose

A spreading, low-growing, evergreen shrub.
Z6–8 H8–6 ‡8 in (20 cm), ↔12 in (30 cm)
■ **Seasonal highlights** The white flowers, irregularly marked with raspberry-pink, appear over long periods from late spring to midsummer.
■ **Value at other times** Dark grayish-green leaves.
■ **Ideal site/will tolerate** Sunny banks, borders and raised beds, hot, dry sites.
■ **Cultivation** Grow in full sun, in well-drained, neutral to alkaline soil that is not too fertile. Overly rich soil produces fewer flowers and soft growth that is more susceptible to cold damage. After flowering, trim back flowered shoots to strong young growth.
■ **Also recommended** *Helianthemum* 'Rhodanthe Carneum' has flesh-pink flowers.
■ **Perfect partners** Alpine pinks, *Phlox subulata*.

Helianthus annuus 'Teddy Bear'
Sunflower

A vigorous, upright, hardy annual. ‡35 in (90 cm), ↔12 in (30 cm)
■ **Seasonal highlights** In summer, it bears large, double, shaggy, golden-yellow flowerheads, 5 in (13 cm) wide.
■ **Value at other times** Is discarded after flowering.
■ **Ideal site** Sunny annual borders; is good for children's gardens.
■ **Cultivation** Grow in full sun in fertile, well-drained soil, in a warm, sheltered site for most prolific flowering. Sow seeds indoors in small pots in early spring, or in the flowering site in late spring.
■ **Also recommended** *Helianthus annuus* 'Sun Spot' is shorter, with larger, bright yellow flowerheads.
■ **Perfect partners** Dahlias, chrysanthemums.

Helictotrichon sempervirens
Blue oat grass

A mounded, evergreen perennial grass. Z4–9 H9–1 ↕to 4½ ft (1.4 m), ↔24 in (60 cm)
■ **Seasonal highlights** In early and midsummer, stiff, upright stems bear airy, straw-colored, purple-flushed flowering spikes.
■ **Value at other times** Spiky mounds of gray-blue leaves all year.
■ **Ideal site** The front of a border, a rock garden, or gravel garden.
■ **Cultivation** The leaves color best in full sun, but it tolerates light, dappled shade. Grow in poor, well-drained, preferably alkaline soil. Remove dead leaves and old flower spikelets in spring. Divide in spring.
■ **Also recommended** *Leymus arenarius*, a grass with bright-blue-gray leaves.
■ **Perfect partners** Purple sage (*Salvia officinalis* 'Purpurascens'), and gray-leaved *Helichrysum splendidum*.

Heliotropium 'Marine'
Heliotrope, Cherry pie

A bushy, upright, frost-tender, evergreen shrub, usually grown as an annual. Z11 H12–1 ↕to 4 ft (1.2 m), ↔12–18 in (35–40 cm)
■ **Seasonal highlights** Over long periods in summer, it bears dense heads of sweetly scented, deep-violet-blue flowers; they attract butterflies and bees.
■ **Value at other times** It has wrinkled, dark-green, purple-tinted leaves.
■ **Ideal site** Bedding and containers.
■ **Cultivation** Grow in any fertile, moist but well-drained soil in sun or partial shade. Sow seeds indoors in spring and plant out when the threat of frost has passed.
■ **Also recommended** *Heliotropium* 'Chatsworth' has deep-purple, very fragrant flowers.
■ **Perfect partners** African and French marigolds.

Helleborus niger 'Potter's Wheel'
Hellebore

Also known as Christmas rose. A robust, upright perennial. Z4–9 H9–1 ↕12 in (30 cm), ↔18 in (45 cm)
■ **Seasonal highlights** From winter to early spring, it bears bowl-shaped white flowers with green "eyes."
■ **Value at other times** Leathery, dark-green leaves on purple-marked stems.
■ **Ideal site** Shady borders, or naturalized in woodland gardens.
■ **Cultivation** Grows best in dappled shade, but tolerates a more open site if soil doesn't dry out. Grow in fertile, preferably heavy, neutral to alkaline soil. Will tolerate clay soil. Trim away old leaves before flowers emerge for the best display.
■ **Also recommended** *Helleborus purpurascens* has purplish or slate-gray flowers that are pink-flushed pale green inside.
■ **Perfect partners** Ferns, snowdrops (*Galanthus*), winter aconites (*Eranthis*).

Helleborus orientalis
Lenten rose

A vigorous, upright, evergreen perennial. Z4–9 H9–1 ↕↔18 in (45 cm)
■ **Seasonal highlights** From midwinter to spring, it bears sturdy-stemmed, white or creamy-green flowers that flush pink with age.
■ **Value at other times** Leathery, divided, deep-green basal leaves persist all year.
■ **Ideal site** Mixed or herbaceous borders, woodland gardens.
■ **Cultivation** Grows best in dappled shade, but tolerates sun if the soil is reliably moist. Grow in any good garden soil. Tolerates clay soil. Trim away old leaves before flowers emerge to display them at their best.
■ **Also recommended** *Helleborus orientalis* subsp. *guttatus* has creamy-white flowers spotted maroon within.
■ **Perfect partners** Ferns, snowdrops (*Galanthus*), winter aconites (*Eranthis*).

Hemerocallis 'Gentle Shepherd'
Daylily

A moderately vigorous, semievergreen perennial. Z3–10 H12–2 ↕26 in (65 cm), ↔4 ft (1.2 m)
■ **Seasonal highlights** The ivory-white flowers with green throats appear over long periods in midsummer.
■ **Value at other times** The slender, arching green leaves often persist through winter and make good ground cover.
■ **Ideal site** Sunny borders, gravel gardens.
■ **Cultivation** Prefers full sun, but tolerates light, dappled shade. Grow in fertile, moist but well-drained soil. Mulch in fall. Divide every three or four years, in spring, to maintain vigor.
■ **Also recommended** *Hemerocallis* 'Chorus Line' has bright-pink, yellow-marked flowers with dark-green throats.
■ **Perfect partners** Achilleas, border phlox, monardas.

H

Hippeastrum 'Apple Blossom'
Amaryllis

A robust, bulbous perennial. ‡12–20 in (30–50 cm), ↔12 in (30 cm)

■ **Seasonal highlights** In winter, it bears large, white, funnel-shaped flowers with pink-flushed petal tips.

■ **Value at other times** Has little value at other times.

■ **Ideal site** In a well-lit spot in the house or in a warm conservatory.

■ **Cultivation** Plant the bulbs in fall, with "neck and shoulders" above soil level. Water little until growth is well under way, then water freely and feed every two weeks with a balanced liquid fertilizer. After flowering, gradually reduce watering as the leaves begin to die down.

■ **Also recommended** *Hippeastrum* 'Picotee' has white flowers with red-rimmed petals.

■ **Perfect partners** Early, forced narcissus, such as *Narcissus papyraceus* and hyacinths.

Hordeum jubatum
Squirrel tail grass

A moderately vigorous, annual or perennial grass. Z4–8 H8–1 ‡20 in (50 cm), ↔12 in (30 cm)

■ **Seasonal highlights** In early and midsummer, erect stems bear nodding heads of silky, long-bristled, pale-green spikelets. They are flushed red or purple and turn buff as they age.

■ **Value at other times** Has tufts of narrow, light-green leaves. The flowerheads are good for drying.

■ **Ideal site** A wild garden or an annual, mixed or herbaceous border.

■ **Cultivation** Prefers full sun, but will tolerate light, dappled shade. Grow in any well-drained soil.

■ **Also recommended** *Stipa tenuissima* has narrow, feathery, buff-colored flowerheads in summer.

■ **Perfect partners** *Stipa gigantea, Lagurus ovatus* (hare's-tail grass).

Hyacinthoides non-scripta
Bluebell

A vigorous, clump-forming perennial bulb. Z4–9 H9–1 ‡8–16 in (20–40 cm), ↔3 in (8 cm)

■ **Seasonal highlights** In spring, sturdy stems bear nodding, sweetly scented, violet-blue flowers amid glossy, dark-green strap-shaped leaves.

■ **Value at other times** Dies back in summer.

■ **Ideal site** Woodland gardens and shady borders.

■ **Cultivation** Grow in dappled shade, in any fertile soil that does not dry out in summer. Plant the bulbs 3 in (8 cm) deep in fall. May self-seed to form extensive colonies.

■ **Also recommended** *Hyacinthoides hispanica* (Spanish bluebell) is taller, with unscented blue flowers.

■ **Perfect partners** *Erythronium* 'Pagoda', *Fritillaria cirrhosa*.

Hyacinthus orientalis 'City of Haarlem'
Hyacinth

A vigorous, upright bulb. Z5–9 H9–5 ‡8–12 in (20–30 cm), ↔3 in (8 cm)

■ **Seasonal highlights** In late spring, sturdy stems arise bearing dense spikes of highly scented, soft-primrose-yellow flowers.

■ **Value at other times** Of no value at other times.

■ **Ideal site** Spring bedding, pots indoors.

■ **Cultivation** Best in full sun. Plant bulbs in fall, 4 in (10 cm) deep, in fertile, well-drained soil. Use prepared bulbs for winter flowers indoors. Plant in bowls of pebbles with the tip of the bulb exposed. Keep in a cool, dark place for six weeks. When shoots are about 1 in (2.5 cm) long, bring into light and warmth.

■ **Also recommended** *Hyacinthus orientalis* 'Jan Bos' has cerise-red flowers.

■ **Perfect partners** Narcissus, tulips.

Hydrangea paniculata 'Grandiflora'
Hydrangea

A vigorous, deciduous shrub. Z4–8 H8–1 ‡10–22 ft (3–7 m), ↔8 ft (2.5 m)

■ **Seasonal highlights** In late summer and early fall, it produces large, conical heads of white flowers that flush pink with age.

■ **Value at other times** Handsome dark-green leaves. Flowers are good for drying.

■ **Ideal site** A shrub or mixed border or a woodland garden.

■ **Cultivation** Grow in fertile, humus-rich, moisture-retentive soil in partial shade or sun. Shelter from cold, dry winds. Needs minimal pruning, but for larger flowers, in late winter, cut back all sideshoots to within 2–3 in (5–8 cm) of the main stems.

■ **Also recommended** *Hydrangea paniculata* 'Floribunda' has narrower flowerheads.

■ **Perfect partners** St. John's wort, hostas.

I

Ilex aquifolium '**Handsworth New Silver'**

Known as English holly. A dense, vigorous, evergreen shrub of columnar outline. Z6–9 H9–7 ‡25 ft (8 m), ↔15 ft (5 m)
■ **Seasonal highlights** Bright-red berries in winter.
■ **Value at other times** All year, its dark-purple stems bear glossy dark-green leaves with spiny, cream margins.
■ **Ideal site** In a shrub border or woodland garden, or as a specimen.
■ **Cultivation** Full sun produces the best variegation, but it tolerates dappled shade. Grow in any fertile, well-drained soil. Prune to shape, if necessary, in early spring.
■ **Also recommended** *Ilex* x *altaclerensis* 'Lawsoniana'; gold-and-green leaves and red-brown berries.
■ **Perfect partners** *Mahonia* x *media* 'Charity', *Viburnum* x *bodnantense* 'Dawn'.

Impatiens **Super Elfin Series**

Busy Lizzie

Compact, frost-tender perennials grown as annuals. ‡↔to 10 in (25 cm)
■ **Seasonal highlights** Throughout summer, bears a mass of flat, spurred flowers in violet, orange, lipstick-pink, red and pastel shades.
■ **Value at other times** Can be grown in containers to flower through the winter.
■ **Ideal site** Summer bedding, containers.
■ **Cultivation** Sow seeds in warmth in early spring. Plant out when the threat of frost has passed, into moisture-retentive, fertile soil in partial or dappled shade.
■ **Also recommended** *I. walleriana* 'Starbright' has red, orange, rose-pink, and violet-blue flowers, each with a central white star.
■ **Perfect partners** Geraniums, Semperflorens begonias.

Indigofera amblyantha

Indigofera

A vigorous, deciduous shrub with arching branches. Z6–9 H8–1 ‡6 ft (2 m), ↔8 ft (2.5 m)
■ **Seasonal highlights** From early summer until early fall, it bears slender, upright clusters of pale-pink, pealike flowers.
■ **Value at other times** From spring to fall, it has elegant bright-green leaves.
■ **Ideal site** A shrub border or a specimen on a warm wall.
■ **Cultivation** Grow in full sun in fertile, moist but well-drained soil. In late winter or early spring, trim overlong, badly placed, or damaged shoots. If severely damaged by cold, prune all stems back hard to a woody framework.
■ **Also recommended** *Indigofera heterantha* has purplish pink flowers and gray-green leaves.
■ **Perfect partners** *Kalmia latifolia* (in acidic soil), escallonias.

Ipomoea tricolor '**Heavenly Blue'**

Morning glory

A vigorous, twining, frost-tender annual climber. ‡to 12 ft (4 m), ↔6 in (15 cm)
■ **Seasonal highlights** From summer until fall, it bears white-throated, funnel-shaped, deep-sky-blue flowers.
■ **Value at other times** It has heart-shaped, bright-green leaves. It is usually discarded after flowering.
■ **Ideal site** Train through shrubs, on poles and pyramids, or in decorative containers.
■ **Cultivation** Prefers a warm, sheltered site, in moderately fertile well-drained soil. It needs sun but with shade from strong midday sun. Sow seeds in spring at 64°F (18°C); grow on in warmth and set out when risk of frost has passed.
■ **Also recommended** *Ipomoea lobata* has narrowly tubular, red and yellow flowers.
■ **Perfect partners** *Tropaeolum peregrinum.*

Iris danfordiae

Dwarf iris

A small, sturdy perennial bulb. Z5–9 H8–5 ‡4–6 in (10–15 cm), ↔2 in (5 cm)
■ **Seasonal highlights** Solitary yellow flowers with greenish-yellow markings appear in late winter and early spring amid a sheaf of narrow grayish-green leaves.
■ **Value at other times** No real value at other times.
■ **Ideal site** Rock gardens, raised beds, troughs, beneath deciduous shrubs.
■ **Cultivation** Best in full sun. Plant bulbs at twice their own depth in late summer or early fall in well-drained soil. Add coarse grit to heavy clay soil to improve drainage.
■ **Also recommended** *Iris histrioides* 'Major' has deep-blue flowers.
■ **Perfect partners** Snowdrops (*Galanthus nivalis*), winter aconites, (*Eranthis hyemalis*), winter-flowering heaths (*Erica carnea*).

I

Iris foetidissima
Stinking iris

A vigorous, rhizomatous evergreen perennial.
Z7–9 H9–7 ↕↔1–3 ft (30–90 cm)

■ **Seasonal highlights** In early summer it bears subtly colored dull-purple flowers suffused with yellow.

■ **Value at other times** In fall, the seed pods split to reveal beadlike scarlet seeds. The strap-shaped, dark-green leaves give off an unpleasant scent if crushed.

■ **Ideal site** Dry, shady borders.

■ **Cultivation** Grow in any well-drained soil in sun or shade.

■ **Also recommended** *Iris foetidissima* var. *citrina* has lemon-yellow flowers.

■ **Perfect partners** Lilyturf (*Liriope muscari*), with sheaves of strap-shaped leaves and spikes of beadlike violet-mauve flowers in fall.

Iris germanica
Bearded iris

A vigorous, rhizomatous perennial.
Z3–9 H9–1 ↕2–4 ft (60–120 cm), ↔12 in (30 cm)

■ **Seasonal highlights** In late spring or early summer, upright stems bear blue-violet flowers with yellow beards.

■ **Value at other times** Fans of sword-shaped, gray-green leaves.

■ **Ideal site** Mixed or herbaceous borders, especially in cottage gardens.

■ **Cultivation** Grow in full sun or light, part-day shade in any moderately fertile well-drained soil.

■ **Also recommended** *Iris germanica* 'Florentina' has scented white flowers.

■ **Perfect partners** The broad foliage of acanthus and hostas; *Centaurea montana*.

Iris 'Harmony'
Dwarf iris

A small, sturdy perennial bulb.
Z5–8 H8–5 ↕4–6 in (10–15 cm), ↔2 in (5 cm)

■ **Seasonal highlights** Yellow-marked, royal-blue flowers appear in late winter amid a sheaf of narrow leaves.

■ **Value at other times** No real value at other times.

■ **Ideal site** Rock gardens, troughs or other containers, or beneath deciduous shrubs.

■ **Cultivation** Best in full sun. Plant bulbs at twice their own depth in late summer or early fall in well-drained soil. Add coarse grit to heavy clay soil to improve drainage.

■ **Also recommended** *Iris* 'Joyce' has deep-sky-blue flowers.

■ **Perfect partners** Snowdrops (*Galanthus nivalis*), winter aconites, (*Eranthis hyemalis*), *Erica carnea* 'Springwood White'.

Iris 'Katharine Hodgkin'
Dwarf iris

A small but vigorous, bulbous perennial.
Z5–8 H8–5 ↕5 in (12 cm), ↔1 in (5 cm)

■ **Seasonal highlights** In late winter, it bears pale-blue flowers, delicately patterned in blue and yellow.

■ **Value at other times** No real value at other times.

■ **Ideal site** Rock gardens, troughs or other containers, or beneath deciduous shrubs.

■ **Cultivation** Best in full sun. Plant bulbs at twice their own depth in late summer or early fall in well-drained soil. Add coarse grit to heavy clay soil to improve drainage.

■ **Also recommended** *Iris* 'Natascha' has very pale-blue-gray flowers.

■ **Perfect partners** Snowdrops (*Galanthus nivalis*), winter aconites, (*Eranthis hyemalis*), winter heaths (*Erica carnea*).

Iris unguicularis
Algerian iris

A vigorous, rhizomatous, evergreen perennial.
Z7–9 H9–1 ↕12 in (30 cm), ↔2 in (5 cm)

■ **Seasonal highlights** In late winter and early spring, it bears scented, pale-lavender to deep-violet, yellow-marked flowers with contrasting veins.

■ **Value at other times** Has tough, grasslike leaves throughout the year.

■ **Ideal site** Sunny borders, or at the base of a warm wall.

■ **Cultivation** Grow in full sun in poor to moderately fertile, very freely draining, neutral to alkaline soil in a sheltered spot. Once planted, leave undisturbed; they flower with increasing freedom as they settle in.

■ **Also recommended** *Iris unguicularis* 'Alba' has yellow-marked cream flowers.

■ **Perfect partners** Interplant with fall-flowering *Nerine bowdenii*.

J

Jasminum mesnyi
Primrose jasmine

A vigorous, scrambling, evergreen shrub.
Z8–10 H10–1 ↕8 ft (2.5 m), ↔10 ft (3 m)
■ **Seasonal highlights** In early spring and early summer, it bears fragrant, bright-yellow flowers.
■ **Value at other times** The divided, glossy, deep-green leaves persist all year.
■ **Ideal site** A warm, sheltered wall in mild areas, or a conservatory.
■ **Cultivation** Grow in full sun, in fertile, well-drained soil or potting mix. Tie in shoots to a support as growth proceeds. After flowering, thin out the oldest flowered shoots and shorten the remainder to strong buds.
■ **Also recommended** *Jasminum humile* is similar but hardier.
■ **Perfect partners** *Jasminum officinale* 'Argenteovariegatum' has gray-green leaves with creamy-white margins and very fragrant white flowers.

Jasminum nudiflorum
Winter jasmine

A vigorous, deciduous, scrambling shrub.
Z6–9 H9–6 ↕↔to 10 ft (3 m)
■ **Seasonal highlights** In winter and early spring, it bears masses of bright-yellow flowers on bare branches.
■ **Value at other times** The green shoots and dark-green leaves persist for most of the year.
■ **Ideal site** Tied in to supports on a sunny or lightly shaded wall, or sprawling over a sunny bank.
■ **Cultivation** Grow in any fertile garden soil. After flowering, cut back flowered shoots to strong buds. Every three or four years, take out some of the oldest growths at the base.
■ **Also recommended** *Jasminum officinale* bears fragrant white flowers from summer to fall.
■ **Perfect partners** *Daphne mezereum, Garrya elliptica.*

K

Kerria japonica 'Picta'
Kerria

An upright, moderately vigorous, deciduous shrub.
Z4–9 H9–1 ↕5 ft (1.5 m), ↔6 ft (2 m)
■ **Seasonal highlights** In mid- and late spring, it bears golden-yellow flowers.
■ **Value at other times** It has gray-green leaves with margins of creamy white.
■ **Ideal site** A mixed or shrub border.
■ **Cultivation** Grow in sun or partial shade, in any well-drained soil enriched with organic matter. After flowering, cut back flowered shoots to strong sideshoots or buds.
■ **Also recommended** *Kerria japonica* 'Pleniflora' is more vigorous with double yellow pom-pom flowers.
■ **Perfect partners** Purple-leaved barberry; *Ribes sanguineum* 'Pulborough Scarlet' (flowering currant).

Kniphofia 'Green Jade'
Red-hot poker

A vigorous, clump-forming evergreen perennial.
Z6–9 H9–6 ↕5 ft (1.5 m), ↔24–30 in (60–75 cm)
■ **Seasonal highlights** In late summer and early fall, it bears tall spikes of green flowers that fade to cream and then white. They are attractive to bees.
■ **Value at other times** Has broad, grasslike, grayish-green leaves all year.
■ **Ideal site** Mixed or herbaceous borders, gravel gardens.
■ **Cultivation** Grow in full sun in light, fertile, humus-rich, well-drained soil. Protect the crowns, of young plants especially, with a dry mulch.
■ **Also recommended** *Kniphofia* 'Prince Igor' has deep orange-red flowers.
■ **Perfect partners** Daylilies, *Knautia macedonica.*

L

Laburnum x *watereri* 'Vossii'
Golden rain

A vigorous, deciduous tree with a spreading crown.
Z5–8 H8–3 ↕↔to 25 ft (8 m)
■ **Seasonal highlights** In late spring and early summer, it produces long, hanging chains of golden-yellow flowers.
■ **Value at other times** It has lustrous, dark-green leaves from spring to fall.
■ **Ideal site** As a specimen or trained over an arbor.
■ **Cultivation** Grow in full sun in any moderately fertile soil. Prune in late winter to remove dead and damaged wood and badly placed shoots.
■ **Also recommended** *Laburnum anagyroides* is similar with shorter flower clusters.
■ **Perfect partners** *Crataegus laevigata* 'Rosea Flore Pleno', rhododendrons and azaleas (in acidic soil).

L

Lachenalia aloides 'Nelsonii'
Cape cowslip

A vigorous, frost-tender perennial bulb.
↕12–16 in (30–40 cm), ↔2 in (5 cm)
■ **Seasonal highlights** In winter or early spring, it produces dark-stemmed spikes of hanging, tubular, golden-yellow flowers.
■ **Value at other times** It has clumps of strap-shaped, smooth, green leaves.
■ **Ideal site** As a houseplant or in a greenhouse or conservatory.
■ **Cultivation** Plant bulbs 4 in (10 cm) deep in fall, in fertile potting mix. Grow in full light and water moderately when in growth. Reduce watering as the leaves fade and rest in dry conditions in summer.
■ **Also recommended** *Lachenalia aloides* has tubular, yellow flowers with scarlet tips.
■ **Perfect partners** *Cyclamen persicum* (but not in the same container).

Lagurus ovatus
Hare's-tail grass

Upright, tufted, moderately vigorous annual grass.
↕20 in (50 cm), ↔12 in (30 cm)
■ **Seasonal highlights** Throughout summer, it has dense heads of softly hairy, purple-tinted, pale-green flower spikelets that age to creamy white.
■ **Value at other times** The flowerheads can be dried and used for arrangements indoors throughout the year.
■ **Ideal site** A mixed or annual border.
■ **Cultivation** Grow in full sun in light, well-drained soil. Sow seeds directly in spring, or in containers in a cold frame in fall.
■ **Also recommended** *Hordeum jubatum* has long-bristled, silky flowerheads.
■ **Perfect partners** *Carex elata* 'Aurea'.

Lantana camara cultivars
Lantana

Vigorous, frost-tender, evergreen shrubs, often grown as annual summer bedding.
↕↔3–6 ft (1–2 m)
■ **Seasonal highlights** From late spring to fall, they bear rounded heads of small white, yellow, salmon-pink, red or purple flowers.
■ **Value at other times** The prickly stems bear finely wrinkled, deep-green leaves.
■ **Ideal site** As bedding, or in containers for patios and conservatories.
■ **Cultivation** Grow in full sun in fertile, moist but well-drained soil. Sow seeds in warmth in spring. Plant out when the risk of frost has passed. Bring patio plants indoors in fall. Prune back shoots to strong buds in late winter.
■ **Also recommended** *Lantana camara* 'Snow White' has pure white flowers.
■ **Perfect partners** Petunias and clarkias.

Lathyrus odoratus 'Colin Unwin'
Sweet pea

A hardy, vigorous annual that climbs with twining tendrils.
↕8 ft (2.5 m), ↔18 in (45 cm)
■ **Seasonal highlights** From early to midsummer, it bears frilled, soft-red flowers; many more cultivars are available, with usually fragrant flowers in white, red, pink, or blue. Flowers are good for cutting.
■ **Ideal site** In mixed borders or cottage gardens, on poles or teepees.
■ **Cultivation** Grow in sun in fertile, well-drained soil enriched with plenty of organic matter. Sow seeds indoors in late fall or late winter, or in the flowering site in spring.
■ **Also recommended** "Old-fashioned" sweet peas have small but intensely fragrant flowers.
■ **Perfect partners** Grow with lavenders and pinks, or with string beans in the kitchen garden.

Lavandula angustifolia 'Munstead'

Common name: lavender. A compact, evergreen shrub.
Z5–8 H8–3 ↕18 in (45 cm), ↔24 in (60 cm)
■ **Seasonal highlights** From mid- to late summer, it bears long-stemmed, very fragrant, blue-purple flowers.
■ **Value at other times** It has aromatic, narrow, gray-green leaves.
■ **Ideal site** Sunny, mixed, or herbaceous borders, in containers on a patio, in gravel gardens, as low hedging.
■ **Cultivation** Grow in full sun in any moderately fertile, well-drained soil. In heavy clay, incorporate plenty of grit to improve drainage. In mid-spring, cut back the previous year's growth by about 2 in (5 cm) to strong pairs of buds. Don't cut into old wood.
■ **Also recommended** *Lavandula angustifolia* 'Loddon Pink' has soft-pink flowers.
■ **Perfect partners** Roses, cistus.

Lavatera 'Barnsley'
Lavatera, Mallow

A very vigorous, bushy, semievergreen shrub. Z7–9 H9–7 ‡↔to 6 ft (2 m)
■ **Seasonal highlights** Throughout summer it produces open funnel-shaped, red-eyed, white flowers that flush soft pink with age.
■ **Value at other times** It has attractive lobed, gray-green leaves.
■ **Ideal site** A sunny shrub or mixed border, or as a specimen.
■ **Cultivation** Prefers an open, sunny site. Grow in any reasonably fertile, well-drained soil. Shelter from cold winds in exposed gardens. In spring, cut back hard to good buds low down on the shrub and apply a balanced fertilizer.
■ **Also recommended** *Lavatera cashemiriana* has clear rose-pink flowers.
■ **Perfect partners** Escallonias, lavenders, roses.

Liatris spicata 'Kobold'
Gayfeather

A delightful perennial with tightly packed flower spikes in shades of reddish purple. Z4–9 H9–1 ‡5 ft (1.5 m) ↔18 in (45 cm)
■ **Seasonal highlights** The attractive flowers are produced from late summer until fall.
■ **Value at other times** The flowers are good for cutting and the attractive swordlike foliage lasts until the first frost.
■ **Ideal site** Grow in a sunny, herbaceous or mixed border, or in containers.
■ **Cultivation** Grow in light, reasonably fertile, moist but well-drained soil in full sun. *Liatris spicata* needs soil that is reliably moist. In heavy soil, plant on a layer of coarse gravel to improve drainage or plants may rot in winter.
■ **Also recommended** *Liatris spicata* 'Alba', *L. pycnostachya*.
■ **Perfect partners** To accentuate their form, grow along with perennials that have open flowers such as erigerons, coreopsis, and geums.

Libertia ixioides
Libertia

An upright, moderately vigorous evergreen perennial. Z8–10 H10–8 ‡↔to 24 in (60 cm)
■ **Seasonal highlights** In late spring and early summer, slender stems arise bearing dense clusters of small, white flowers.
■ **Value at other times** Clusters of orange-brown seeds follow the flowers, and the narrow, leathery, dark-green leaves turn orange-brown in fall.
■ **Ideal site** A sunny mixed border.
■ **Cultivation** Grow in moist but well-drained soil in full sun. Protect with a dry mulch in winter where marginally hardy.
■ **Also recommended** *Libertia grandiflora* is similar, but taller, with white flowers.
■ **Perfect partners** *Asphodelus albus, Scilla peruviana.*

Ligularia 'The Rocket'
Ligularia

This clump-forming perennial is a striking architectural plant grown for its handsome spikes of flowers and large mid-green leaves. Z3–8 H8–1 ‡6 ft (1.8 m)
■ **Seasonal highlights** From early to late summer it produces tall "candles" of orange-yellow flowers and attractive toothed leaves with purple veins.
■ **Value at other times** In some seasons the flowers can last into fall. The foliage is attractive in its own right and will last until the first frost.
■ **Ideal site** Grow at the back of a sunny border.
■ **Cultivation** Grow in reasonably fertile, deep, and reliably moist soil, in full sun or partial shade. Provide shelter from strong winds. May need staking with twiggy sticks. Divide in spring or after flowering.
■ **Also recommended** *Ligularia* 'Greynog Gold', *L. przewalskii*
■ **Perfect partners** Grow with other moisture-loving perennials such as astilbe and daylilies.

Lilium 'Sun Ray'
Lily

A vigorous, perennial bulb. Z2–8 H8–3 ‡3 ft (1 m), ↔6 in (15 cm)
■ **Seasonal highlights** From early to midsummer, it bears bowl-shaped glossy yellow flowers with brown dots on the petals.
■ **Value at other times** No value at other times.
■ **Ideal site** Sunny borders and in containers on a patio.
■ **Cultivation** Grow in sun but shade the roots from hot sun. Best in fertile, well-drained soil enriched with leafmold or well-rotted organic matter. Plant the bulbs in fall at twice their own depth. In clay soil, plant on a layer of grit.
■ **Also recommended** *Lilium* 'Sterling Star' has scented, brown-speckled, cream-flushed-white flowers.
■ **Perfect partners** Looks good with peonies, poppies, and roses.

L

Lobelia Fan Series
Lobelia

A vigorous, clump-forming, perennial, annual, or biennial of upright growth.
Z5–8 H8–5 ‡20–24 in (50–60 cm), ↔12 in (30 cm)
■ **Seasonal highlights** From midsummer to fall, it produces long spires of bright-crimson flowers.
■ **Value at other times** The fresh bronze-red foliage will last well into autumn.
■ **Ideal site** Grow with annuals or in a mixed border in sun or part shade.
■ **Cultivation** Sow seeds indoors in a temperature of 65–70°F (18–20°C) 10–12 weeks before the last frosts. When large enough to handle, transplant into 3-in (7.5-cm) pots and grow on indoors. Transplant outdoors after hardening 12 in (30 cm) apart when the risk of frost has passed. Harmful if eaten.
■ **Also recommended** *Lobelia x gerardii* 'Vedrariensis' has violet-purple flowers.
■ **Perfect partners** Summer bedding such as antirrhinums, pelargoniums.

Lobelia Waterfall Series
Lobelia

These are mound-forming annuals covered with masses of flowers through summer.
‡10 in (26 cm), ↔12 in (30 cm)
■ **Seasonal highlights** From midsummer to late fall, the plants are covered in small, star-shaped flowers in shades of blue, light blue, or white.
■ **Value at other times** Of little value at other times.
■ **Ideal site** Grown with other annuals in borders or in containers in a sunny position.
■ **Cultivation** Sow seeds indoors in a temperature of 65–70°F (18–20°C) 10–12 weeks before the last frosts. When large enough to handle, transplant into 3-in (7.5-cm) pots and grow on indoors. Transplant outdoors when the threat of frost has passed, in a sunny position and about 6 in (15 cm) apart.
■ **Also recommended** *Lobelia erinus* Cascade Series are trailing, with carmine-red, pink, blue, or white flowers.
■ **Perfect partners** Alyssum (*Lobularia maritima*), begonias, marigolds.

Lonicera fragrantissima
Winter honeysuckle

Bushy, spreading, moderately vigorous, semievergreen shrub.
Z4–8 H9–1 ‡6 ft (2 m), ↔10 ft (3 m)
■ **Seasonal highlights** In winter and early spring, it bears very fragrant flowers.
■ **Value at other times** It has dark-green leaves that are blue-green beneath.
■ **Ideal site** A shrub border or against a warm wall; it flowers more freely in warmth with shelter.
■ **Cultivation** Grow in any fertile, well-drained soil in sun or light shade. After flowering, prune back flowered shoots to strong buds or shoots lower down the stems.
■ **Also recommended** *Lonicera x standishii* is similar and flowers from late fall to early spring.
■ **Perfect partners** *Jasminum nudiflorum*; use a late-season clematis like *Clematis* 'Ernest Markham' for interest in late summer.

Lonicera x heckrottii
Honeysuckle

A vigorous, semievergreen, twining climber.
Z6–9 H9–5 ‡15 ft (5 m), ↔10 ft (3 m)
■ **Seasonal highlights** From mid- to late summer, it bears clusters of fragrant coral-pink flowers that are orange-yellow within.
■ **Value at other times** Has dark-green leaves with blue-green undersides and sometimes bears glossy, red berries in fall.
■ **Ideal site** A wall, fence, or trellis.
■ **Cultivation** Grow in any fertile, moist but well-drained soil. In early spring, shorten shoots to strong buds or shoots lower down the stems.
■ **Also recommended** *Lonicera periclymenum* 'Graham Thomas' has yellow flowers.
■ **Perfect partners** *Clematis* 'Huldine', *Clematis* 'Ville de Lyon'.

Lonicera x purpusii
Winter honeysuckle

A moderately vigorous, semievergreen or deciduous shrub.
Z7–9 H9–7 ‡6 ft (2 m), ↔8 ft (2.5 m)
■ **Seasonal highlights** In winter and early spring, it bears small clusters of very fragrant white flowers with conspicuous yellow anthers.
■ **Value at other times** It has purple shoots and dark-green leaves for the summer.
■ **Ideal site** A shrub border, or against a warm wall; it flowers most freely in warmth with shelter.
■ **Cultivation** Grow in any fertile, well-drained soil in sun or dappled shade. After flowering, cut back flowered shoots to strong buds, but only to control size.
■ **Also recommended** *Lonicera x purpusii* 'Winter Beauty' is very free-flowering.
■ **Perfect partners** *Daphne mezereum*, mahonias, sarcococca.

Lupinus 'The Page'
Lupine

A vigorous, clump-forming herbaceous perennial. Z3–8 H8–1 ‡35 in (90 cm), ↔30 in (75 cm)

■ **Seasonal highlights** It produces dense spires of pealike, carmine-red flowers in early and midsummer.

■ **Value at other times** Cut back after the first flush for a few more flowers later in summer. The attractive foliage fades after flowering.

■ **Ideal site** A mixed or herbaceous border, cottage gardens.

■ **Cultivation** Grow in light, fertile, well-drained, preferably slightly acidic soil in sun; it tolerates part-day shade. Take basal cuttings in mid-spring; lupines are often short-lived.

■ **Also recommended** *Lupinus* 'Chandelier' has bright-yellow flowers.

■ **Perfect partners** Delphiniums, Oriental poppies (*Papaver orientalis*), pyrethrums.

Lychnis chalcedonica
Maltese cross

A moderately vigorous, herbaceous perennial. Z3–8 H8–1 ‡3–4 ft (0.9–1.2 m), ↔12 in (30 cm)

■ **Seasonal highlights** In early and midsummer, it produces rounded clusters of cross-shaped scarlet flowers at the tips of upright stems.

■ **Value at other times** Has basal clumps of bright-green leaves.

■ **Ideal site** A mixed or herbaceous border.

■ **Cultivation** Grow in any fertile, moist but well-drained soil in sun or light shade. Provide support. Deadhead to prolong flowering. Divide in spring or fall. Self-seeds freely.

■ **Also recommended** *Lychnis coronaria* has gray leaves and magenta flowers.

■ **Perfect partners** Aquilegias, lupines, oriental poppies (*Papaver orientalis*).

Lysichiton americanus
Skunk cabbage

A very vigorous, spreading herbaceous perennial. Z7–9 H9–7 ‡3 ft (1 m), ↔4 ft (1.2 m)

■ **Seasonal highlights** In early spring, before the leaves appear, it bears clublike spikes of tiny green flowers surrounded by large, glossy, yellow spathes.

■ **Value at other times** The large, paddle-shaped leathery, green leaves elongate after flowering.

■ **Ideal site** Pond- or streamsides.

■ **Cultivation** Grow in full sun or light, dappled shade in moist, fertile, humus-rich soil. Allow plenty of room for the leaves to grow.

■ **Also recommended** *Lysichiton camtschatcensis* has creamy-white flower spathes.

■ **Perfect partners** *Caltha palustris*.

M

Magnolia stellata
Star magnolia

Compact, bushy, slow-growing, deciduous shrub. Z5–9 H9–5 ‡9 ft (3 m), ↔12 ft (4 m)

■ **Seasonal highlights** In early and mid-spring, the silky buds open to star-shaped, white flowers.

■ **Value at other times** Has a neat habit and attractive leaves for the summer.

■ **Ideal site** As a specimen, or in a shrub or mixed border.

■ **Cultivation** Grow in moist but well-drained, fertile, humus-rich soil in sun or dappled shade. It tolerates slightly acidic or slightly alkaline soil. Shelter from cold winds and late frosts, which may damage the flowers. Little or no pruning is required.

■ **Also recommended** *Magnolia stellata* 'Waterlily' has larger, double, white flowers.

■ **Perfect partners** Camellias, flowering quince (*Chaenomeles*).

Mahonia x *media* 'Charity'
Mahonia

An upright, bushy, vigorous evergreen shrub. Z8–9 H9–8 ‡to 15 ft (5 m), ↔12 ft (4 m)

■ **Seasonal highlights** From late fall to early spring, it bears long spikes of fragrant, deep-yellow flowers.

■ **Value at other times** During the rest of the year, it has attractive, glossy dark-green, sharply toothed leaves.

■ **Ideal site** In a shrub border, woodland garden, or as a specimen.

■ **Cultivation** Grow in moist but well-drained, humus-rich soil, in partial shade or in sun if soil is reliably moist. It needs little pruning; if it becomes leggy or outgrows its allotted space, prune after flowering.

■ **Also recommended** *Mahonia repens* 'Rotundifolia' is shorter and spreading with dark-yellow flowers in spring.

■ **Perfect partners** *Viburnum tinus*, *Daphne mezereum*.

M

Malus
Crab apples

Deciduous, mostly vigorous, small trees that are ideal as specimens for smaller yards. Most crab apples grow well in USDA hardiness zones 5 to 8 and AHS heat zones 8 to 1. Choose a cultivar that is suited to your local conditions.

■ **Seasonal highlights** In spring, they bear masses of blossom ranging from white to pink and purplish reds.

■ **Value at other times** In fall, they bear crab apples in colors ranging from yellow to red; the leaves turn yellow and orange too.

■ **Cultivation** Grow in any fertile, well-drained soil in sun to light shade. Purple-leaved varieties are best in sun. Remove misplaced shoots or dead or damaged wood in winter.

Malus x hartwigii **'Katherine'** has small, red-flushed, yellow fruit.
↕↔20 ft (6 m)

Malus **'Royalty'** has flowers of crimson-purple.
↕↔25 ft (8 m)

Malus **'John Downie'** has white flowers.
↕30 ft (10 m), 20 ft (6 m)

Malus pumila **'Cowichan'** has rose-pink flowers.
↕↔25 ft (8 m)

Malus x zumi **'Professor Sprenger'** has white flowers.
↕↔22 ft (7 m)

Malus x moerlandsii **'Liset'** has purple-red fruit.
↕↔20 ft (6 m)

Matthiola Brompton Group
Brompton stocks

Vigorous, bushy, woody-based perennials grown as annuals or biennials.
↕18 in (45 cm), ↔12 in (30 cm)

■ **Seasonal highlights** From late spring to summer, they bear densely packed spikes of scented, single or double flowers in pink, red, purple, yellow and white. They are excellent cut flowers.

■ **Value at other times** No real value at other times.

■ **Ideal site** Cottage gardens, cutting borders, and mixed borders.

■ **Cultivation** Grow in full sun in fertile, well-drained soil. Sow seeds in warmth in spring and set out when the risk of frost has passed. For larger, earlier flowers, sow in fall and overwinter in a cold frame.

■ **Also recommended** *Matthiola* 'Giant Excelsior Column' has tall spires of double flowers.

■ **Perfect partners** China asters, border carnations.

Miscanthus sinensis 'Silberfeder'
Miscanthus

Vigorous, upright, deciduous perennial grass.
Z4–9 H9–1 ↕8 ft (2.5 m), ↔4 ft (1.2 m)

■ **Seasonal highlights** It has silvery, pinkish brown flowerheads in early to mid-fall; these and the dry leaves persist through winter.

■ **Value at other times** Has arching blue-green leaves.

■ **Ideal site** Mixed or herbaceous borders.

■ **Cultivation** Grow in any fertile, moist but well-drained soil in full sun; it tolerates light shade. Cut old growth to the ground in spring. Divide congested clumps in spring.

■ **Also recommended** *Miscanthus sinensis* 'Zebrinus' has green leaves horizontally banded with yellow.

■ **Perfect partners** *Stipa gigantea, Glyceria maxima* 'Variegata'.

N

Monarda 'Mahogany'
Bergamot, Bee balm

A vigorous, clump-forming, herbaceous perennial. Z3–9 H9–1 ‡35 in (90 cm), ↔18 in (45 cm)

■ **Seasonal highlights** From midsummer until fall, it bears whorls of wine-red flowers at the stem tips. The flowers attract bees.

■ **Value at other times** Has aromatic, red-veined, dark-green leaves.

■ **Ideal site** A mixed or herbaceous border, or herb garden.

■ **Cultivation** Best in sun, but will tolerate light, dappled shade. Grow in any fertile, well-drained soil that doesn't dry out in summer. Divide overcrowded clumps in spring.

■ **Also recommended** *Monarda* 'Cambridge Scarlet' has scarlet-red flowers.

■ **Perfect partners** Achilleas, border phlox, sunflowers (*Helianthus*).

Muscari armeniacum
Grape hyacinth

A vigorous, bulbous perennial. Z4–8 H8–1 ‡8 in (20 cm), ↔2 in (5 cm)

■ **Seasonal highlights** In spring, it produces spikes of tubular, bright-blue flowers with white mouths.

■ **Value at other times** Of no value at other times.

■ **Ideal site** A rock garden, the front of a mixed or herbaceous border, in containers.

■ **Cultivation** Grow in full sun in any well-drained, moderately fertile soil. Plant bulbs, 4 in (10 cm) deep, in fall. Lift to divide congested clumps as the leaves fade in summer.

■ **Also recommended** *Muscari botryoides* f. *album* has fragrant, white flowers.

■ **Perfect partners** Erythroniums, crocus.

Narcissus 'Cheerfulness'
Double narcissus

Robust, bulbous perennial. Z3–9 H9–1 ‡16 in (40 cm), ↔3 in (8 cm)

■ **Seasonal highlights** In mid-spring, each stem produces several sweetly scented, double, white flowers with clustered, creamy-white segments at the center.

■ **Value at other times** Of no value at other times.

■ **Ideal site** Borders, and containers indoors and outside.

■ **Cultivation** Grow in sun or light, dappled shade. Plant the bulbs in fall at twice their own depth, in any fertile, well-drained soil. If flowering declines and bulbs are congested, allow the foliage to die down naturally and lift and divide the clumps.

■ **Also recommended** *Narcissus* 'Yellow Cheerfulness' has golden-yellow flowers.

■ **Perfect partners** Forsythia, doronicums, crocus.

Narcissus cyclamineus
Wild narcissus

A vigorous, perennial bulb. Z3–9 H9–1 ‡6–8 in (15–20 cm), ↔1 in (2.5 cm)

■ **Seasonal highlights** In early spring, it bears nodding, golden-yellow flowers with backswept petals.

■ **Value at other times** Of no value at other times.

■ **Ideal site** Naturalized in lawn or in rock or woodland gardens.

■ **Cultivation** Grow in sun or dappled shade in any moderately fertile, well-drained soil. Plant bulbs in fall at twice their own depth. If grown in lawn, allow foliage to fade naturally before mowing.

■ **Also recommended** *Narcissus* 'Jumblie' has similar but larger flowers with golden-orange cups.

■ **Perfect partners** Crocus, chionodoxas.

Narcissus 'Dutch Master'
Trumpet daffodil

A vigorous perennial bulb. Z3–9 H9–1 ‡14 in (35 cm), ↔3 in (8 cm)

■ **Seasonal highlights** In mid-spring it bears large golden-yellow flowers, with short, slightly frilled trumpets.

■ **Value at other times** Can be grown in containers to flower earlier indoors.

■ **Ideal site** Naturalized in grass, in borders, or containers.

■ **Cultivation** Grow in sun or dappled shade in fertile, well-drained soil. Plant bulbs in fall at twice their own depth. For forcing, plant in pots and plunge in a cold frame for about 8 weeks or until shoots appear. Bring into a cool greenhouse, and take indoors as flower buds begin to open.

■ **Also recommended** *Narcissus* 'Little Beauty' is shorter with creamy-white, yellow-cupped flowers.

■ **Perfect partners** Crocus, chionodoxas.

N

Nemesia caerulea
Perennial nemesia

A vigorous, bushy, woody-based perennial.
Z9–10 H10–1 ‡24 in (60 cm), ↔12 in (30 cm)
■ **Seasonal highlights** Clusters of yellow-throated, pink, pale-blue, lavender-blue or white flowers appear from early summer to fall.
■ **Value at other times** It has dark-green leaves.
■ **Ideal site** Borders, raised beds, and decorative containers.
■ **Cultivation** Grow in a sheltered site in full sun in moderately fertile, well-drained soil. It may not survive very cold winters. If container-grown it can be brought into a greenhouse in fall. Otherwise, take stem cuttings in summer and overwinter young plants indoors.
■ **Also recommended** *Nemesia caerulea* 'Innocence' has white flowers.
■ **Perfect partners** Argyranthemums, osteospermums.

Nemesia strumosa 'KLM'
Annual nemesia

Bushy, free-flowering annual. Z9–10 H10–1 ‡7–12 in (18–30 cm), ↔4–6 in (10–15 cm).
■ **Seasonal highlights** Bears bicolored, blue and white flowers with pink throats and yellow beards, from mid- to late summer.
■ **Value at other times** Can be grown as an early spring-flowering house plant.
■ **Ideal site** Bedding, hanging baskets, other containers.
■ **Cultivation** Grow in full sun or light, dappled shade in any moderately fertile, well-drained soil. Sow seeds in warmth in spring and plant out when the risk of frost has passed. Or sow in fall and overwinter indoors for early flowers indoors.
■ **Also recommended** *Nemesia strumosa* 'Prince of Orange' has orange flowers.
■ **Perfect partners** Clarkias and petunias.

Nepeta x faassenii
Catmint, catnip

A vigorous, clump-forming, herbaceous perennial.
Z3–8 H8–1 ‡↔18 in (45 cm)
■ **Seasonal highlights** From early summer to early fall, it bears fragrant, pale lavender-blue flowers with darker purple spots. Attracts bees, moths, and butterflies.
■ **Value at other times** It also has wrinkled, hairy, aromatic, gray-green leaves.
■ **Ideal site** Mixed or herbaceous borders, cottage and wildlife gardens.
■ **Cultivation** Grow in any fertile, well-drained soil. Trim hard after the first flush of flowers to keep plants neat and encourage more flowers. Rejuvenate old plants by dividing in spring or fall.
■ **Also recommended** *Nepeta sibirica* is taller with blue to lavender-blue flowers.
■ **Perfect partners** Alchemillas, lavenders, roses.

Nerine bowdenii
Nerine

A moderately vigorous, perennial bulb.
Z8–10 H10–8 ‡18 in (45 cm), ↔3 in (8 cm)
■ **Seasonal highlights** In fall it bears rounded heads of funnel-shaped, faintly scented pink flowers. The strap-shaped leaves emerge after flowering.
■ **Value at other times** Of no value at other times.
■ **Ideal site** At the base of a warm, sunny wall, or in raised beds.
■ **Cultivation** Grow in full sun in sharply drained soil in a warm, sheltered site. Provide a dry winter mulch where marginally hardy. Plant in summer with the nose (tip) of the bulb just at soil level.
■ **Also recommended** *Nerine bowdenii* 'Alba' has white, often pink-flushed flowers
■ **Perfect partners** *Schizostylis, Scilla scilloides*.

Nicotiana x sanderae Starship Series
Tobacco plant

Upright, bushy, moderately vigorous, half-hardy annuals.
‡12 in (30 cm), ↔4 in (10 cm)
■ **Seasonal highlights** From summer until fall, bears a profusion of pink, red, rose-pink, white, or lime-green flowers.
■ **Value at other times** Of no value at other times.
■ **Ideal site** Annual and mixed borders, decorative containers.
■ **Cultivation** Grow in full sun or light, dappled shade in any fertile, well-drained soil. Sow seeds indoors in early spring and plant out when the danger of frost has passed.
■ **Also recommended** *Nicotiana* Domino Series 'Salmon Pink' is compact with upturned salmon-pink flowers.
■ **Perfect partners** Geraniums, petunias, asters.

Nicotiana sylvestris
Tobacco plant

A vigorous biennial or short-lived perennial. Z10–11 H12–1 ‡5 ft (1.5 m), ↔24 in (60 cm)

■ **Seasonal highlights** It bears loose heads of white, trumpet-shaped flowers that are very fragrant when they open in the evening.

■ **Value at other times** It has a basal rosette of large, dark-green leaves.

■ **Ideal site** Mixed or herbaceous borders, or woodland gardens.

■ **Cultivation** Grow in light, dappled shade in any fertile, moist but well-drained soil. Tolerates full sun in reliably moist soil. Sow seeds in indoors in early spring. Plant out when the threat of frost has passed. Provide a deep winter mulch in cold areas.

■ **Also recommended** *Nicotiana* 'Lime Green' is annual with lime-green flowers.

■ **Perfect partners** *Eremurus*, roses.

Nigella damascena 'Miss Jekyll'
Love-in-a-mist

A vigorous annual. ‡20 in (50 cm), ↔9 in (23 cm)

■ **Seasonal highlights** During summer, it produces sky-blue flowers, surrounded by a ruff of slender leaves.

■ **Value at other times** It has finely divided, feathery foliage. The seedpods can be dried for indoor arrangements.

■ **Ideal site** Annual borders, cutting borders, cottage gardens.

■ **Cultivation** Grow in full sun in any moderately fertile, well-drained soil. Sow seeds in the flowering site in spring and thin seedlings to 9 in (23 cm) apart. May also be sown in fall for earlier flowers. Protect with cloches in areas with very cold wet winters.

■ **Also recommended** *Nigella hispanica* 'Curiosity' has scented, dark-eyed, bright-blue flowers.

■ **Perfect partners** Clarkias and calendulas.

Nymphaea
Waterlilies

These submerged aquatic perennials mostly have a spread of 3–7 ft (0.9–2.2 m); *Nymphaea tetragona* 'Helvola', only 10–16 in (25–40 cm) across, work in very small ponds. Hardy waterlilies grow in USDA hardiness zones 3 to 11 and in AHS heat zones 12 to 1.

■ **Seasonal highlights** In summer, they bear large single or double flowers in white and shades of pink, red, or yellow. There are frost-tender species, like *Nymphaea capensis* (Z10–11 H12–1) with fragrant, pale-blue flowers, grown in indoor ponds in cold areas.

■ **Value at other times** The large, flat leaves float on the water's surface, providing shelter for fish and helping shade out algal growth. Most are glossy dark green, but several, like 'Marliacea Chromatella', have attractive bronze or purple markings.

■ **Ideal site** Ponds with still water.

■ **Cultivation** Grow in full sun. Plant in aquatic planting baskets of loamy soil and cover the surface with pea gravel to prevent the soil muddying the water. Remove yellowing leaves through the summer. Lift and divide when leaves become crowded.

Nymphaea 'Fire Crest'

Nymphaea 'Marliacea Chromatella'

Nymphaea tetragona 'Helvola'

Nymphaea capensis

Nymphaea alba

Nymphaea 'Rose Arey'

O

Oenothera fruticosa 'Fyrverkeri'
Evening primrose

Also known as sundrops. An upright, vigorous, herbaceous perennial.
Z4–8 H8–1 ‡12–36 in (30–90 cm), ↔12 in (30 cm)
■ **Seasonal highlights** From late spring until late summer, cupped yellow flowers open from red buds.
■ **Value at other times** It has red-tinted stems and maroon-flushed leaves.
■ **Ideal site** Mixed or herbaceous borders.
■ **Cultivation** Easily grown in moderately fertile, moist but well-drained soil in full sun.
■ **Also recommended** *Oenothera macrocarpa* is trailing with golden-yellow flowers.
■ **Perfect partners** *Coreopsis verticillata*, border phlox, *Lychnis chalcedonica*.

Osteospermum jucundum
Osteospermum

A vigorous, clump-forming, evergreen perennial.
Z9–11 H6–1 ‡4–20 in (10–50 cm), ↔20–36 in (50–90 cm)
■ **Seasonal highlights** From late spring to fall, it bears mauve-pink to magenta, daisylike flowerheads.
■ **Value at other times** The dense mat of gray-green leaves are good ground cover.
■ **Ideal site** Beds and borders, especially in hot, dry sites.
■ **Cultivation** Grow in sun in any well-drained soil. Deadhead regularly to prolong flowering. May not survive cold wet winters, so take stem cuttings in late summer; overwinter young plants indoors.
■ **Also recommended** *Osteospermum* 'Buttermilk' bears primrose-yellow flowers with a bronze reverse.
■ **Perfect partners** Argyranthemums, pyrethrums, chrysanthemums.

P

Peonies
Herbaceous peonies

Vigorous, long-lived, herbaceous perennials.
■ **Seasonal highlights** From early to midsummer, they bear very showy, bowl-shaped, single or double flowers in white and shades of red and pink.
■ **Value at other times** The dark or grayish-green leaves often color well in fall.
■ **Ideal site** Mixed or herbaceous borders, especially in cottage gardens.
■ **Cultivation** Best in full sun, but tolerant of dappled shade for part of the day. Grow in deep, fertile, moist but well-drained soil that is enriched with plentiful organic matter. The large-flowered sorts may need unobtrusive, grow-through supports in exposed gardens.
■ **Perfect partners** Hostas, Oriental poppies (*Papaver orientalis*), roses.

Paeonia lactiflora **'Laura Dessert'** has double flowers with pale-pink outer petals. Z3–8 H8–1 ‡↔30–32 in (70–75 cm)

Paeonia lactiflora **'Ballerina'** has large, double, pink flowers. Z3–8 H8–1 ‡↔36–39 in (90–100 cm)

Paeonia lactiflora **'Kelway's Supreme'** bears fragrant, semidouble pale-pink flowers. Z3–8 H8–1 ‡↔36–39 in (90–100 cm)

Paeonia lactiflora **'Bowl of Beauty'** has carmine-red and creamy-white petals. Z3–8 H8–1 ‡↔32–39 in (80–100 cm)

Paeonia lactiflora **'Sarah Bernhardt'** has double, rose-pink flowers with a silvery sheen. Z3–8 H8–1 ‡↔36–39 in (90–100 cm)

Paeonia officinalis **'Rubra Plena'** bears large, double, satin-textured, rich crimson flowers. Z3–8 H8–1 ‡↔30–32 in (70–75 cm)

Paeonia mlokosewitschii
Caucasian peony

A vigorous, clump-forming herbaceous perennial.
Z3–8 H8–1 ‡↔26–36 in (65–90 cm)

■ **Seasonal highlights** In late spring and early summer, it bears single, bowl-shaped, lemon-yellow flowers.

■ **Value at other times** The bluish-green leaves are heavily suffused with red-purple as they emerge.

■ **Ideal site** Mixed or herbaceous borders.

■ **Cultivation** Grow in full sun or part-day shade in deep, fertile, moist but well-drained soil enriched with organic matter. Shelter from strong winds.

■ **Also recommended** *Paeonia emodi* has nodding, pure-white flowers in late spring.

■ **Perfect partners** *Aquilegia alpina, Polemonium carneum.*

Paeonia officinalis 'Rubra Plena'
Common peony

A vigorous, clump-forming herbaceous perennial.
Z3–9 H8–1 ‡↔30–32 in (70–75 cm)

■ **Seasonal highlights** In early and midsummer it bears large, double, satin-textured, rich, crimson flowers.

■ **Value at other times** Deep-green, divided, leaves.

■ **Ideal site** Mixed or herbaceous borders, especially in cottage gardens.

■ **Cultivation** Grow in full sun or part-day shade in deep, fertile, moist but well-drained soil enriched with organic matter. Provide a grow-through support in exposed gardens.

■ **Also recommended** *Paeonia officinalis* 'Rosea Superba Plena' has large, double, rose-pink flowers.

■ **Perfect partners** Lavenders, roses, campanulas.

Papaver orientale 'Cedric Morris'
Oriental poppy

A vigorous, clump-forming, herbaceous perennial.
Z3–9 H9–1 ‡18–36 in (45–90 cm), ↔24–36 in (60–90 cm)

■ **Seasonal highlights** From late spring to midsummer, it bears bowl-shaped, satiny, soft-pink flowers with frilled petals, each with a black basal mark.

■ **Value at other times** The bristly, jagged leaves die back soon after flowering.

■ **Ideal site** Mixed or herbaceous borders, especially in cottage gardens.

■ **Cultivation** Grow in full sun, in deep, fertile, well-drained soil. Cut back hard after flowering, to produce fresh foliage and a few later flowers.

■ **Also recommended** *Papaver orientalis* 'Beauty of Livermere' has large, glossy, scarlet-crimson flowers.

■ **Perfect partners** Lupines, daylilies.

Papaver rhoeas Shirley Series
Shirley poppy

Vigorous, free-flowering hardy annuals.
‡35 in (90 cm), ↔12 in (30 cm)

■ **Seasonal highlights** During summer, bears bowl-shaped, single or semidouble flowers in white and shades of yellow, pink, orange and red.

■ **Value at other times** They have hairy stems with downy, light-green leaves.

■ **Ideal site** Annual and mixed borders, especially in cottage gardens.

■ **Cultivation** Grow in sun in any poor to moderately fertile, well-drained soil. Sow seeds in spring in the flowering site. Self-seeds freely, but seedlings are variable.

■ **Also recommended** *Papaver somniferum* 'Paeony Flowered' has large, double, frilly flowers in white and shades of red, pink, and purple.

■ **Perfect partners** Clarkias, escholschzias, nigellas.

Parthenocissus tricuspidata
Boston ivy

A very vigorous, deciduous, self-clinging climber.
Z4–8 H8–1 ‡↔to 70 ft (20 m)

■ **Seasonal highlights** The leaves turn brilliant red and deep purple in fall.

■ **Value at other times** Has lobed, bright-green leaves from spring onward.

■ **Ideal site** Large walls, fences, or growing through large trees.

■ **Cultivation** Grow in any fertile, well-drained soil in sun or shade. Guide young plants into the support until they cling for themselves. Prune in late winter, if necessary, to limit size.

■ **Also recommended** *Parthenocissus henryana* has dark-green, often pink-flushed, leaves with silver veins; they turn bright red in fall.

■ **Perfect partners** *Jasminum nudiflorum*, late-flowering clematis.

P

Pelargonium 'Apple Blossom Rosebud'
Zonal geranium

Frost-tender, evergreen, fleshy-stemmed perennial.
↕16 in (40 cm), ↔10 in (25 cm)
- **Seasonal highlights** From summer to fall, it bears large clusters of white flowers with pink margins.
- **Value at other times** Rounded, pale-green leaves.
- **Ideal site** Containers on a patio, or in the home or conservatory.
- **Cultivation** Grow in fertile, well-drained soil or potting mix in full sun. Set out when risk of frost has passed. Give a high-potash fertilizer weekly. Deadhead regularly. Take stem cuttings during spring or summer and overwinter indoors.
- **Also recommended** *Pelargonium* Horizon Series are seed-raised and good for bedding; they have flowers in white and shades of pink and red.
- **Perfect partners** Annual lobelias, fuchsias.

Pennisetum alopecuroides 'Hameln'

Also known as fountain grass. A vigorous, clump-forming evergreen grass.
Z5–9 H9–1 ↕↔4 ft (1.2 m)
- **Seasonal highlights** In summer and fall it bears cylindrical, feathery, greenish-white flowerheads that mature to pale gray.
- **Value at other times** The dark-green leaves turn golden yellow in fall. The flowerheads can be dried for indoor flower arrangements.
- **Ideal site** Mixed or herbaceous borders.
- **Cultivation** Grow in light, well-drained soil in full sun. Cut back dead top growth in spring. Plant and divide overcrowded clumps in late spring.
- **Also recommended** *Pennisetum villosum* is shorter and deciduous, with feathery, pale-green then purple flowerheads.
- **Perfect partners** *Lagurus ovatus, Stipa gigantea.*

Penstemon
Penstemons

Vigorous, evergreen or semievergreen perennials of upright growth.
- **Seasonal highlights** From summer to late fall, they bear bell-shaped, foxglovelike flowers in white and shades of red, pink, lilac, and maroon.
- **Value at other times** Form dense clumps of fresh, green leaves.
- **Ideal site** Mixed or herbaceous borders.
- **Cultivation** Best in sun, but tolerant of dappled, part-day shade. Grow in fertile, well-drained soil. Incorporate grit into heavy clay soil. Deadhead regularly. May not survive cold wet winters, so take stem cuttings in late summer and overwinter indoors.
- **Perfect partners** Achilleas, border phlox, cranesbills, *Phygelius*.

Penstemon **'Alice Hindley'** has lilac-blue flowers.
Z7–10 H10–7 ↕35 in (90 cm), ↔18 in (45 cm)

Penstemon **'Apple Blossom'** has white-throated, pink flowers.
Z7–10 H10–7 ↕↔18–24 in (45–60 cm)

Penstemon **'Burgundy'** has wine-red flowers.
Z7–10 H10–7 ↕35 in (90 cm), ↔18 in (45 cm)

Penstemon **'Chester Scarlet'** has large scarlet flowers.
Z7–10 H10–7 ↕24 in (60 cm), ↔18 in (45 cm)

Penstemon **'Maurice Gibbs'** bears white-throated, cerise-pink blooms.
Z7–10 H10–7 ↕30 in (75 cm), ↔18 in (45 cm)

Penstemon **'Stapleford Gem'** has large, lilac-purple flowers suffused with pink and white within. Z7–10 H10–7 ↕24 in (60 cm)

Perovskia 'Blue Spire'
Russian sage

A moderately vigorous, deciduous subshrub. Z3–9 H9–1 ‡4 ft (1.2 m), ↔3 ft (1 m)
■ **Seasonal highlights** In late summer and early fall, it bears tall spires of violet-blue flowers.
■ **Value at other times** It has gray-white stems and silver-gray leaves.
■ **Ideal site** Sunny borders, especially in hot, dry sites, or seaside gardens.
■ **Cultivation** Grow in poor to moderately fertile, well-drained soil in full sun. In early spring, cut back all shoots to within 12 in (30 cm) of the ground.
■ **Also recommended** *Perovskia* 'Hybrida' has dark lavender-blue flowers.
■ **Perfect partners** Roses, hardy fuchsias, lavenders.

Petunia Million Bells Pink
Petunia

Vigorous, half-hardy perennials grown as annuals. ‡↔to 12 in (30 cm)
■ **Seasonal highlights** From early summer until late fall, bears masses of small, trumpet-shaped, bright magenta-pink flowers.
■ **Value at other times** Cuttings can be taken and plants grown inside to flower in winter and early spring.
■ **Ideal site** Bedding and containers, including hanging baskets.
■ **Cultivation** Grow in full sun in light, well-drained soil. Shelter from strong winds. This cultivar is usually sold as "plugs" or young plants.
■ **Also recommended** *Petunia* Surfinia Series are vigorous with large, white, pink, red, magenta, or violet-blue flowers.
■ **Perfect partners** Geraniums, fuchsias, annual lobelias, and nasturtiums (*Tropaeolum majus*).

Philadelphus microphyllus
Mock orange

A vigorous, deciduous shrub. Z4–8 H8–1 ‡↔to 3 ft (1 m).
■ **Seasonal highlights** In early and midsummer, it bears single, very fragrant, pure-white flowers.
■ **Value at other times** It has peeling, dark chestnut-brown bark and glossy leaves.
■ **Ideal site** A mixed or shrub border.
■ **Cultivation** Grow in full sun or light, dappled shade, in any moderately fertile, well-drained soil. After flowering, shorten flowered shoots to strong buds. When mature, cut back one in five of the oldest stems at the base.
■ **Also recommended** *Philadelphus* 'Buckley's Quill' is taller, with scented, very double white flowers packed with quill-like petals.
■ **Perfect partners** *Jasminum humile*, shrubby potentillas, roses.

Phlox paniculata 'Eva Cullum'
Border phlox

A vigorous, strongly upright herbaceous perennial. Z4–8 H8–1 ‡4 ft (1.2 m), ↔to 3 ft (1 m)
■ **Seasonal highlights** From summer to mid-fall, it bears bright, deep-pink flowers with darker-pink centers and a heady scent. Excellent for cutting.
■ **Value at other times** Fresh-green leaves from spring onward.
■ **Ideal site** Mixed or herbaceous borders.
■ **Cultivation** Grow in fertile, moist soil in sun or light dappled shade. Divide every 3–4 years in fall or spring to maintain vigor. Take basal cuttings in spring or root cuttings in fall or winter.
■ **Also recommended** *Phlox paniculata* 'Windsor' has purple-eyed, red-pink flowers.
■ **Perfect partners** Roses, penstemons, cranesbills.

Phygelius x rectus 'Salmon Leap'
Phygelius

A vigorous, suckering, upright, evergreen shrub. Z8–9 H9–8 ‡4 ft (1.2 m), ↔5 ft (1.5 m)
■ **Seasonal highlights** Throughout summer and into fall it produces curving, tubular, orange flowers that hang from slender stalks.
■ **Value at other times** Glossy dark-green leaves look good for most of the year.
■ **Ideal site** A shrub or mixed border or against a sunny wall.
■ **Cultivation** Grow in sun in fertile, moist but well-drained soil. Deadhead regularly. Give a deep winter mulch where marginally hardy. Needs little pruning; cut back frost-damaged growth to strong buds in spring, to the base if necessary.
■ **Also recommended** *Phygelius aequalis* 'Yellow Trumpet' has creamy-yellow flowers.
■ **Perfect partners** Cranesbills, daylilies, penstemons.

P

Physalis alkekengi
Chinese lanterns

A vigorous, rhizomatous, herbaceous perennial.
Z3–9 H8–1 ‡2–2½ ft (60–75 cm), ↔35 in (90 cm)
■ **Seasonal highlights** Nodding, bell-shaped, creamy-white flowers in midsummer.
■ **Value at other times** In late summer and fall, inflated, papery, red lanterns enclose orange-red fruits. They can be used in dried-flower arrangements.
■ **Ideal site** Mixed or herbaceous borders.
■ **Cultivation** Grow in full sun in any well-drained soil. Cut stems for drying just as the lanterns begin to color.
■ **Also recommended** *Physalis alkekengii* var. *franchetii* is similar, with smaller flowers.
■ **Perfect partners** *Lychnis chalcedonica*.

Pieris 'Flamingo'
Pieris

A dense, bushy, moderately vigorous evergreen shrub.
Z6–8 H8–6 ‡to 12 ft (4 m), ↔10 ft (3 m)
■ **Seasonal highlights** In late winter and spring, it bears hanging clusters of urn-shaped, dark flamingo-pink flowers that open from dark-red buds.
■ **Value at other times** The glossy, green leaves are attractive year-round.
■ **Ideal site** Shrub borders, as specimens, in woodland gardens.
■ **Cultivation** Grow in leafy, moist but well-drained, acidic soil in sun or dappled shade. Shelter from cold, dry winds. Keep pruning to a minimum.
■ **Also recommended** *Pieris japonica* 'White Cascade' bears long clusters of white flowers over long periods.
■ **Perfect partners** Winter heaths (*Erica carnea* cultivars), rhododendrons, and azaleas.

Plumbago auriculata
Cape leadwort

A frost-tender, scrambling, or climbing evergreen shrub.
Z9–11 H12–10 ‡10–20 ft (3–6 m), ↔3–10 ft (1–3 m)
■ **Seasonal highlights** From summer until late fall, it bears long-tubed, sky-blue flowers in clusters at the stem tips.
■ **Value at other times** The smooth, often bluish-green-tinged leaves look good for most of the year.
■ **Ideal site** Greenhouse or conservatory.
■ **Cultivation** Grow in fertile free-draining potting mix in full sun. Tie stems in to a support as growth proceeds. Prune all sideshoots to within 3–4 buds of the main stems in spring.
■ **Also recommended** *Plumbago indica* is shrubby with rose-pink flowers in winter.
■ **Perfect partners** *Jasminum mesnyi*, *J. polyanthum*.

Polemonium carneum
Jacob's ladder

A moderately vigorous, bushy herbaceous perennial.
Z4–9 H9–1 ‡4–16 in (10–40 cm), ↔8 in (20 cm)
■ **Seasonal highlights** In early summer it bears loose clusters of shallowly bell-shaped, pale-pink, yellow, occasionally dark-purple or lavender flowers.
■ **Value at other times** It has attractive divided leaves.
■ **Ideal site** Herbaceous or mixed borders and rock gardens.
■ **Cultivation** Grow in full sun or light, dappled shade in any fertile, well-drained soil. Add grit to heavy clay soil to improve drainage. Deadhead regularly to encourage more flowers.
■ **Also recommended** *Polemonium caeruleum* is taller with lavender-blue flowers.
■ **Perfect partners** *Tradescantia* 'Purple Dome', *Erigeron* 'Serenity', *Potentilla atrosanguinea*.

Potentilla fruticosa
PRINCESS ('Blink')
Shrubby potentilla

A compact but vigorous, deciduous shrub.
Z3–7 H7–1 ‡24 in (60 cm), ↔to 3 ft (1 m).
■ **Seasonal highlights** From late spring until mid-fall, it produces saucer-shaped, pale-pink flowers that fade to white.
■ **Value at other times** It has dense, dark-green leaves that make good ground cover.
■ **Ideal site** Mixed or shrub borders, containers, as low hedging.
■ **Cultivation** Prefers full sun, but tolerates light, dappled shade. Grow in poor to moderately fertile, well-drained soil. In early spring, cut back all stems to within 1 in (2.5 cm) of the old growth. The easiest way is to use a pair of shears.
■ **Also recommended** *Potentilla fruticosa* 'Elizabeth' has bright-yellow flowers.
■ **Perfect partners** *Philadelphus microphyllus*, St. John's wort.

Primula denticulata
Drumstick primula

A vigorous, rosette-forming herbaceous perennial. Z2–8 H8–1 ↕↔to 18 in (45 cm)

■ **Seasonal highlights** In mid-spring and early summer, stout stems bear dense, spherical clusters of purple, yellow-eyed flowers.

■ **Value at other times** It has handsome rosettes of mid-green leaves that are white-mealy beneath.

■ **Ideal site** Rock gardens, at the front of beds and borders.

■ **Cultivation** Grow in sun or dappled shade in moist, fertile soil. Divide every three to four years in fall or spring.

■ **Also recommended** *Primula florindae* is taller with clusters of fragrant, bell-shaped, sulfur-yellow flowers.

■ **Perfect partners** *Euphorbia polychroma*, Welsh poppy (*Meconopsis cambrica*).

Primula Gold-laced Group
Polyanthus primula

A rosette-forming evergreen or semievergreen perennial. Z5–8 H8–5 ↕10 in (25 cm), ↔30cm

■ **Seasonal highlights** In mid- to late spring, it produces clusters of velvety mahogany-red flowers, each petal having a gold margin.

■ **Value at other times** The rosettes of mid-green leaves are tinged with red.

■ **Ideal site** Borders, bedding, containers, rock garden, or cold greenhouse.

■ **Cultivation** Grow in moist, fertile, humus-rich, neutral to acidic soil. Indoors, grow in loam-based potting mix.

■ **Also recommended** *Primula* 'Blossom' has gold-centered, crimson flowers.

■ **Perfect partners** Sweet violets (*Viola odorata*) and violas.

Primula 'Miss Indigo'
Primula

Vigorous, evergreen, or semievergreen perennial. Z4–8 H8–4 ↕8 in (20 cm), ↔14 in (35 cm).

■ **Seasonal highlights** From late winter to late spring it produces clusters of double, indigo-purple flowers with creamy-white tips.

■ **Value at other times** Has rosettes of wrinkled, bright-green leaves for most of the year.

■ **Ideal site** Shady borders, bedding, containers.

■ **Cultivation** Grow in dappled shade in damp, fertile, humus-rich soil. Divide after flowering to maintain vigor.

■ **Also recommended** *Primula vulgaris* 'Marie Crousse' has double violet flowers.

■ **Perfect partners** Sweet violets (*Viola odorata*), and violas, pulmonarias.

Prunus avium 'Plena'
Gean, Wild cherry

A vigorous, deciduous tree with a wide-spreading crown. Z4–9 H9–1 ↕↔ 40 ft (12 m)

■ **Seasonal highlights** In mid-spring, it bears hanging clusters of double white flowers.

■ **Value at other times** The leaves are bronze when they emerge and turn red, yellow, and orange in fall.

■ **Ideal site** Perfect as a specimen tree.

■ **Cultivation** Grow in any moist, but well-drained soil. Needs minimal pruning; remove badly placed or crossing branches in summer, because of risk of silverleaf infection.

■ **Also recommended** *Prunus avium* has single flowers.

■ **Perfect partners** Crab apples (*Malus*), laburnums.

Prunus padus 'Watereri'
Bird cherry

A vigorous, deciduous tree with a spreading crown. Z4–8 H8–1 ↕50 ft (15 m), ↔30 ft (10 m)

■ **Seasonal highlights** In late spring, it bears long, slender spires of many small, fragrant, white flowers.

■ **Value at other times** The dark-green leaves turn red and yellow in fall. In mid- to late summer it bears small, black cherries that attract birds.

■ **Ideal site** As a specimen, or in woodland gardens.

■ **Cultivation** Grow in any moist but well-drained soil. Needs minimal pruning; remove badly placed or crossing branches in winter, or in midsummer if silverleaf disease is a problem in your area.

■ **Also recommended** *Prunus padus* 'Colorata' has red-purple leaves and pink flowers.

■ **Perfect partners** Crab apples (*Malus*).

P

Prunus
Japanese cherries

Vigorous, free-flowering deciduous trees. Z6–8 H8–1 ↕30–40 ft (10–12 m), ↔25–30 ft (8–10 m)
- **Seasonal highlights** They bear a profusion of fragrant blossom in spring.
- **Value at other times** Most have fine fall color.
- **Ideal site** All of the recommended cultivars are beautiful specimen trees.
- **Cultivation** Grow in any moist, but well-drained soil. Need minimal pruning; remove badly placed or crossing branches in winter, or in midsummer if silverleaf disease is a problem in your area.
- **Perfect partners** Crab apples (*Malus*), laburnum, amelanchier.

Prunus **'Amanogawa'** is narrowly upright with semidouble, pale-pink flowers

Prunus **'Kiku-shidare-zakura' (syn. 'Cheal's Weeping')** is weeping, with double, bright-pink flowers

Prunus **'Kwanzan'** is vase-shaped with double, deep-pink flowers

Prunus **'Shirotae' (syn. 'Mount Fuji')** is arching and spreading with single or semidouble white flowers

Prunus **'Spire'** is vase-shaped with single, pale-pink flowers

Prunus **'Ukon'** is vigorous and spreading with pink-flushed, creamy-white flowers

Prunus sargentii
Sargent's cherry

A vigorous, deciduous tree with a wide-spreading crown. Z5–9 H9–1 ↕to 60 ft (20 m), ↔50 ft (15 m)
- **Seasonal highlights** In early to mid-spring it bears hanging clusters of large, single, pale-pink flowers.
- **Value at other times** The bark is a shining, dark chestnut brown. The elliptical leaves have long, tapering tips and are bronze-red as they emerge with the flowers. Cherries follow the flowers and attract birds.
- **Ideal site** A beautiful specimen tree, it also thrives in woodland gardens.
- **Cultivation** Grow in moist, well-drained soil. It needs minimal pruning; remove crossing branches in winter, or in midsummer if silverleaf disease is a problem.
- **Also recommended** *Prunus sargentii* 'Columnaris' is a narrowly upright form that reaches 10 ft (3 m) tall.
- **Perfect partners** Crab apples (*Malus*), laburnum and juneberry, with underplantings of crocus, narcissi, and daffodils.

Prunus serrula
Tibetan cherry

A moderately vigorous, rounded, deciduous tree. Z6–8 H8–1 ↕↔30 ft (10 m)
- **Seasonal highlights** In late spring, it bears small, single, bowl-shaped, white flowers.
- **Value at other times** The polished mahogany bark is beautiful throughout the year. The leaves turn yellow in fall.
- **Ideal site** A perfect specimen tree for small gardens.
- **Cultivation** Grow in fertile, moist but well-drained soil in sun or light, dappled shade. It needs minimal pruning (in late summer); when young, remove sideshoots from the trunk when very small, to display the bark at its best.
- **Also recommended** *Prunus maackii* has coppery bark.
- **Perfect partners** *Betula papyrifera*, crocus, and colchicums.

Prunus x *subhirtella* 'Autumnalis Rosea'
Higan cherry, Rosebud

A moderately vigorous, spreading, deciduous tree. Z6–8 H8–1 ‡↔25 ft (8 m)
■ **Seasonal highlights** From late fall to spring, it bears small, semidouble, pale-pink flowers.
■ **Value at other times** Leaves are bronzed when young and yellow in fall.
■ **Ideal site** A perfect specimen tree for small gardens.
■ **Cultivation** Grow in fertile, moist but well-drained soil in sun or light, dappled shade. It needs minimal pruning, in late summer, to remove damaged or badly placed shoots.
■ **Also recommended** *Prunus autumnalis* 'Pendula Rosea' has weeping branches and rose-pink flowers.
■ **Perfect partners** Underplant with crocus (for spring) and colchicums (for fall).

Pulmonaria angustifolia 'Azurea'
Lungwort

A vigorous, spreading, herbaceous perennial. Z4–8 H8–1 ‡10 in (25 cm), ↔18 in (45 cm)
■ **Seasonal highlights** From early to late spring, it bears funnel-shaped, bright-blue flowers, tinted red in bud.
■ **Value at other times** It has smooth, unspotted, glistening dark-green leaves that make good ground cover.
■ **Ideal site** Shady borders and wild or woodland gardens.
■ **Cultivation** Grow in deep or dappled shade, in damp, humus-rich soil. Cut back after flowering for a fresh crop of new leaves. Divide every three to four years to maintain vigor.
■ **Also recommended** *Pulmonaria rubra* 'Redstart' has coral-red flowers from midwinter to spring.
■ **Perfect partners** Narcissus, crocus, doronicums, and primroses.

Pulsatilla vulgaris
Pasque flower

A clump-forming, moderately vigorous herbaceous perennial. Z5–7 H7–5 ‡4–8 in (10–20 cm), ↔8 in (20 cm)
■ **Seasonal highlights** Nodding, bell-shaped, silky-hairy flowers in shades of purple, or occasionally white, appear in spring.
■ **Value at other times** The finely divided, hairy leaves grow taller after flowering. Silky, silvery seedheads follow the flowers.
■ **Ideal site** A rock garden or raised bed.
■ **Cultivation** Grow in fertile, gritty, sharply drained soil in sun. Protect from excessive winter moisture. Pulsatillas dislike being disturbed, so choose the site with care.
■ **Also recommended** *Pulsatilla alpina* has white flowers.
■ **Perfect partners** Dwarf tulips, *Aubrieta*, scillas.

Pyracantha 'Golden Charmer'
Firethorn

A vigorous, bushy, spiny evergreen shrub. Z7–9 H9–7 ‡↔to 10 ft (3 m)
■ **Seasonal highlights** Has bright-orange berries from fall through winter.
■ **Value at other times** Clusters of small, white flowers in early summer; glossy, bright-green leaves all year.
■ **Ideal site** Sunny or shady walls; as a specimen or as hedging.
■ **Cultivation** Grow in any fertile, well-drained soil. Trim hedging in summer. On wall-trained plants, shorten outward- and inward-growing shoots in mid-spring. Trim sideshoots to 2–3 leaves after flowering to expose the berries.
■ **Also recommended** *Pyracantha* 'Orange Glow' has dark orange-red berries.
■ **Perfect partners** *Jasminum nudiflorum, Garrya elliptica*.

Pyrus salicifolia 'Pendula'
Weeping pear

A vigorous, weeping, deciduous tree. Z5–9 H9–5 ‡15 ft (5 m), ↔12 ft (4 m)
■ **Seasonal highlights** Creamy-white flowers in spring, followed by small, hard, unpalatable green pears.
■ **Value at other times** The stiffly weeping branches bear willowlike, gray-hairy leaves from spring to fall.
■ **Ideal site** A fine specimen tree for small gardens.
■ **Cultivation** Grow in sun in any fertile soil. It needs little pruning other than routine removal of any dead, damaged, or crossing growth in winter.
■ **Also recommended** *Pyrus ussuriensis* is taller with large clusters of white flowers in spring and green leaves that turn red-bronze in fall.
■ **Perfect partners** *Betula pendula* 'Youngii', crab apples (*Malus*) or mountain ash (*Sorbus*).

R

Rhodochiton atrosanguineus
Rhodochiton

A frost-tender, herbaceous perennial climber.

‡10 ft (3 m), ↔30 in (75 cm)

■ **Seasonal highlights** From summer to fall, it bears hanging, tubular, deep-red-purple flowers with a "skirt" of rose-pink calyces.

■ **Value at other times** It has attractive, heart-shaped, rich-green leaves.

■ **Ideal site** A warm wall, conservatory, containers, hanging baskets.

■ **Cultivation** Grow in sun or light shade, in humus-rich, moist but well-drained soil or potting mix. Trim in summer, if necessary, to limit size. Bring indoors for the winter.

■ **Also recommended** This is the only species in common cultivation.

■ **Perfect partners** Annual lobelias (in hanging baskets); twining through sweet peas (*Lathyrus odoratus*).

Rhododendrons and azaleas

Evergreen rhododendrons

With over 500 species and thousands of cultivars, rhododendrons are extremely variable, ranging from tiny alpine shrubs to huge, treelike species.

■ **Seasonal highlights** Most bear flowers between early spring and early summer.

■ **Value at other times** Lustrous, usually dark-green leaves persist all year.

■ **Ideal site** Shrub borders and woodland gardens. If you garden in alkaline soil, grow them in large containers filled with acidic potting mix.

■ **Cultivation** All rhododendrons and azaleas must have acidic, moist but well-drained, leafy, humus-rich soil. Grow in light, dappled shade with shelter from cold, dry winds. Plant with the top of the root ball no deeper than it was in the pot. Keep pruning to a minimum; shorten any overlong shoots that spoil the shape after flowering.

Rhododendron **'Hydon Dawn'** Large clusters of pale-pink flowers with dark-pink centers in spring. ‡↔5 ft (1.5 m)

Rhododendron cinnabarinum **subsp.** *xanthocodon* has yellow flowers mid-spring to summer. Z8–9 H9–1 ‡20 ft (6 m), ↔6 ft (2 m)

Rhododendron **'Beauty of Littleworth'** has huge trusses of fragrant, white flowers in late spring. Z7–9 H9–1 ‡↔12 ft (4 m)

Rhododendron **'Golden Torch'** has trusses of soft-yellow flowers late spring and early summer. Z7–9 H9–1 ‡↔5 ft (1.5 m)

Rhododendron **'Halfdan Lem'** has rounded trusses of dark-spotted red flowers in mid- to late spring. Z7–9 H9–1 ‡↔8 ft (2.5 m)

Rhododendron **'Polar Bear'** Beautiful clusters of white flowers in late spring. ‡15 ft (5 m) ↔12 ft (4 m)

Rhododendron 'Inga'
Indica azalea

A compact, frost-tender, evergreen shrub.

‡↔20 in (50 cm)

■ **Seasonal highlights** In winter, it bears funnel-shaped, pink flowers with white margins to the slightly frilled petals.

■ **Value at other times** Small, glossy, dark-green leaves throughout the year.

■ **Ideal site** Use as a houseplant.

■ **Cultivation** Grow in pots of acidic potting mix in bright light, but shaded from direct sun. Keep just moist and mist daily until the flower buds show color. Keep the temperature no higher than 55–61°F (13–16°C). Repot after flowering. Plunge them in a shaded cold frame for the summer and keep them cool and moist. Bring back indoors in early winter.

Rhododendron 'Vuyk's Scarlet'

Evergreen azalea

A hardy evergreen shrub. Z6–9 H9–1 ‡30 in (75 cm), ↔4 ft (1.2 m)
■ **Seasonal highlights** In mid-spring is covered in funnel-shaped, scarlet flowers with frilled petals. Container plants flower earlier if brought into a cool greenhouse at the end of fall.
■ **Value at other times** Glossy, dark leaves all year.
■ **Ideal site** Shrub borders, rock gardens and woodland gardens, containers.
■ **Cultivation** Grow in acidic, moist but well-drained, humus-rich soil, or in large pots in acidic potting mix, in dappled shade or full sun. Shelter from cold, dry winds. Trim shoots that spoil the form after flowering.
■ **Also recommended** *Rhododendron* 'Vuyk's Rosyred' has deep rose-pink flowers.
■ **Perfect partners** Japanese maples; smoke bush.

Rhododendron yakushimanum

Rhododendron

A very hardy, vigorous, evergreen shrub. Z5–9 H9–1 ‡to 6 ft (2 m)
■ **Seasonal highlights** In mid-spring, it bears trusses of funnel-shaped flowers that open from deep-pink buds and fade gradually to white.
■ **Value at other times** The glossy, dark-green leaves are clothed in dense tawny down when young.
■ **Ideal site** Shrub borders, woodland gardens.
■ **Cultivation** Grow in acidic, moist but well-drained, leafy, humus-rich soil in dappled shade or full sun. Shelter from cold, dry winds. Trim any shoots that spoil the shape and deadhead after flowering.
■ **Also recommended** *Rhododendron yakushimanum* 'Ken Janeck' has white flowers, lined with pink-purple and green spots.
■ **Perfect partners** Conifers; heathers; birch)

Rhododendron 'Freya'

Azalea

Azaleas are a sub-section of the genus *Rhododendron* that have smaller leaves and bear profuse trusses of small, often vividly colored flowers in spring or early summer. Many of the deciduous azaleas also have brilliant fall color.
■ **Ideal site** Rock and woodland gardens, shrub borders and containers.
■ **Cultivation** Grow in acidic, moist but well-drained, leafy, humus-rich soil in dappled shade or sun. Deciduous azaleas are more tolerant of open sites in sun than evergreen rhododendrons, but are best sited so that they do not receive early morning sun, as this will exacerbate damage to the flowers in frosty weather. Plant with the top of the root ball no deeper than it was in the pot; they will not tolerate deep planting. Keep pruning to a minimum; just shorten any overlong shoots that spoil the shape, after flowering. Deadhead carefully, if practical.

Rhododendron 'Strawberry Ice'

Azalea

■ **Recommended** *Rhododendron* 'Freya' is a compact shrub with small leaves bearing dense trusses of small, funnel-shaped "hose-in-hose" flowers (one flower within another) in late spring and early summer. They are fragrant, pink-flushed salmon-orange. It enjoys full sun. Z5–8 H9–1 ‡↔5 ft (1.5 m) *Rhododendron* 'Strawberry Ice' is bushy and compact with rounded trusses of widely funnel-shaped flowers in late spring. They are a soft flesh-pink with darker veins and deeper pink at the petal margins. Z5–8 H8–9 ‡↔6 ft (2 m)
■ **Perfect partners** Conifers; heathers.

Rhus typhina

Staghorn sumac

A vigorous, suckering, deciduous shrub or small tree. Z3–8 H8–1 ‡15 ft (5 m), ↔20 ft (6 m)
■ **Seasonal highlights** In summer, it bears spires of yellow-green flowers that give rise, on female plants, to dense clusters of hairy, deep-crimson-red fruits.
■ **Value at other times** In fall, the divided leaves turn brilliant orange-red.
■ **Ideal site** Mixed and shrub borders, or as a specimen.
■ **Cultivation** Gives the best fall color in sun, but tolerates light shade. Grow in any moist but well-drained soil. Can be pruned hard in spring to within two or three buds of the base for larger, lusher leaves.
■ **Also recommended** *Rhus glabra* has smooth shoots and glossy blue-green leaves.
■ **Perfect partners** *Cotoneaster frigidus* 'Cornubia', *Cotinus* 'Grace'.

R

Ribes sanguineum
Flowering currant

A vigorous, deciduous shrub. Z6–8 H8–6 ‡↔to 6 ft (2 m)
■ **Seasonal highlights** In spring, it bears hanging clusters of tiny, deep-pinkish-red flowers.
■ **Value at other times** It has dense, aromatic, dark-green foliage from spring to fall. Flowers are followed by small, blue-black fruits.
■ **Ideal site** A mixed or shrub border, or as informal hedging.
■ **Cultivation** Grow in full sun or light, dappled shade in any fertile soil. Prune flowered shoots back to strong buds, or shoots lower down the shrub, after flowering, to keep compact and bushy. Trim hedging after flowering.
■ **Also recommended** *Ribes odoratum* has fragrant yellow flowers.
■ **Perfect partners** Forsythias, *Chaenomeles x superba* 'Rowallane'.

Rosa
Hybrid tea and floribunda roses

The hybrid tea or large-flowered roses are upright, freely branching bushes.
■ **Value at other times** All have attractive dark green leaves from spring to fall.
■ **Ideal site** Rose beds, mixed and shrub borders, or as informal hedges.
■ **Cultivation** Grow in full sun in deep, fertile, moist but well-drained soil. They thrive in heavy clay soil. Apply a balanced fertilizer and mulch in late winter or early spring. Prune large-flowered roses in late winter or early spring, cutting the main stems back to strong, outward-facing buds, 8–10 in (20–25 cm) above the ground. Reduce sideshoots to 2–3 buds. For cluster-flowered roses, prune back main stems to 10–18 in (25–45 cm) above ground and shorten sideshoots to 2–3 buds. Deadhead to encourage more flowers.

Rosa AMBER QUEEN ('Harroony') has fragrant, cupped, double, amber-yellow flowers. Z5–9 H9–5 ‡20 in (50 cm), ↔24 in (60 cm)

Rosa 'Crimson Glory' A classic hybrid tea rose with brilliant-scarlet flowers. Z5–9 H9–5 ‡↔24 in (60 cm)

Rosa 'Elizabeth Harkness' A hybrid tea rose with white flushed-pink flowers from early to late summer. ‡32 in (80 cm) ↔24 in (60 cm)

Rosa HANNAH GORDON ('Korweiso') bears cupped, double pale blooms with dark pink margins. Z4–11 H12–1 ‡32 in (80 cm), ↔26 in (65 cm)

Rosa FRAGRANT CLOUD ('Tanellis') A favorite, classic hybrid tea rose with scented red flowers. ‡30 in (75 cm) ↔24 in (60 cm)

Rosa BLUE MOON ('Tannacht') has large, high-centered, double flowers of soft lilac-mauve. ‡3 ft (1 m), ↔28 in (70 cm)

Rosa ANNA FORD
('Harpiccolo')
Patio rose

These dwarf, cluster-flowered roses make compact, deciduous shrubs. From summer to fall, they bear clusters of rounded, single to fully double flowers. They have abundant, glossy, dark-green leaves. ANNA FORD has urn-shaped, semidouble, orange-red flowers. Z5–9 H9–5 ‡18 in (45 cm), ↔16 in (40 cm)
■ **Ideal site** In containers, in mixed borders, as border edging.
■ **Cultivation** Grow in fertile, well-drained soil in full sun. Prune in the dormant season, as for floribunda roses. Cut back the main stems and sideshoots by no more than a third to a half of their length.
■ **Also recommended** QUEEN MOTHER ('Korquemu') has semidouble, clear-pink flowers.
■ **Perfect partners** Lavenders and pinks.

Rosa 'Chinatown'
Modern shrub rose

Diverse in size, habit, and flower form, modern shrubs are vigorous, deciduous and flower freely from summer to fall. They bear single to fully double flowers in few- to many-flowered clusters and are often beautifully scented. 'Chinatown' has double, pink-flushed yellow flowers. Z5–9 H9–5 ‡4 ft (1.2 m), ↔3 ft (1 m)
■ **Ideal site** Shrub and mixed borders, as hedges, or as specimen plants.
■ **Cultivation** Grow as for bush roses. Prune only for health and to reduce overcrowding. Every 3–4 years, cut an older stem or two to the base of the plant.
■ **Also recommended** 'Buff Beauty' has fragrant, double, apricot-buff flowers.
■ **Perfect partners** Lavanders, cistus, *Anemone* x *hybrida*.

Rosa
English roses

A group of modern shrub roses that have been bred to combine the shapes, colors, and scents of the Old garden roses with the vigor, disease-resistance, and repeat-flowering virtues of the modern shrubs. They are graceful, deciduous, or semievergreen shrubs and flower almost continuously from early summer to fall. Many are exquisitely scented.
■ **Ideal site** Mixed and shrub borders, and as specimens.
■ **Cultivation** Grow as for bush roses. Prune as for floribunda bush roses, but much more lightly, to maintain the shrub's stature.
■ **Perfect partners** Lavenders, pinks, and border phlox go well with most roses.

Rosa BROTHER CADFAEL ('Ausglobe') Clear-pink peony-like flowers with a strong fragrance. ‡4 ft (1.2 m) ↔3 ft (1 m)

Rosa DARCEY BUSSELL ('Ausdecorum') The rich, crimson flowers produced in summer have a fruity fragrance. ‡3 ft (1 m) ↔24 in (60 cm)

Rosa EGLANTYNE ('Ausmark') has strongly scented, cupped, fully double flowers of pale pink. Z4–9 H9–4 ‡4 ft (1.2 m), ↔5 ft (1.5 m)

Rosa GRAHAM THOMAS ('Ausmas') has cupped, fully double, yellow flowers with a fruity scent. Z4–9 H9–4 ‡4 ft (1.2 m), ↔5 ft (1.5 m)

Rosa GERTRUDE JEKYLL ('Ausbord') Large rosette-shaped flowers of rich pink with strong fragrance. ‡4 ft (1.2 m) ↔3 ft (1 m)

Rosa WILL SHAKESPEARE 2000 ('Ausromeo') has fully double, fragrant flowers of crimson. Z4–9 H9–4 ‡4 ft (1.2 m), ↔5 ft (1.5 m)

Rosa gallica var. *officinalis* 'Versicolor'

Also known as old garden rose (gallica), rosa mundi. Dense, vigorous, thorny, free-branching shrub. Z3–9 H9–1 ‡32 in (80 cm), ↔to 3 ft (1 m)
■ **Seasonal highlights** In midsummer, bears scented, semidouble, pale-pink flowers striped with darker pink in small clusters.
■ **Ideal site** Beds, borders, and as hedging.
■ **Cultivation** Grow as for bush roses. To encourage bushy growth, after flowering, cut back any overlong shoots by up to one third and sideshoots by two-thirds.
■ **Also recommended** *Rosa* 'Charles de Mills' has very fragrant, fully double, deep-mulberry-pink flowers.
■ **Perfect partners** Lavanders, cistus, *Anemone* x *hybrida*.

R

Rosa
Climbing and rambling roses

■ **Seasonal highlights** Deciduous, thorny, stiff-stemmed climbing shrubs bear single to fully double, often fragrant flowers, singly or in clusters, from summer to fall. Rambling roses have very vigorous, deciduous, or semievergreen climbers with long, flexible, thorny stems. Unlike climbers, they bloom only once in summer, bearing single to fully double, often scented flowers, usually in many-flowered clusters. They have more or less glossy, pale to dark-green leaves with small leaflets.

■ **Value at other times** Deciduous, thorny, stiff-stemmed climbing shrubs grow best on pillars, walls, or fences, while rambling roses favor arbors and arches, and growing through large, old trees.

Rosa 'Golden Showers' has large, fragrant, double, yellow blooms.
Z5–9 H9–5 ↕10 ft (3 m), ↔ 8 ft (2.5 m)

Rosa HANDEL **('Macha')** has double white with pink petal margins.
Z5–9 H9–5 ↕10 ft (3 m), ↔7 ft (2.2 m)

Rosa 'New Dawn' A vigorous, hardy climbing rose with fragrant, cupped, double, pale pearl-pink flowers. ↕10 ft (3 m) ↔8 ft (2.5 m).

Rosa 'Albertine' has double, soft, salmon-pink flowers.
Z5–9 H9–5 ↕15 ft (5 m), ↔12 ft (4 m)

Rosa 'American Pillar' bears single, white-eyed, carmine-red flowers.
Z5–9 H9–5 ↕15 ft (5 m), ↔12 ft (4 m)

Rosa 'Bobbie James' has sprays of semidouble, scented, creamy-white flowers.
Z5–9 H9–5 ↕30 ft (10 m), ↔20 ft (6 m)

Rosa 'Königin von Dänemark'
Old garden rose (Alba)

Vigorous shrub of arching growth with gray-green leaves.
Z3–9 H9–1 ↕5 ft (1.5 m), ↔ 4 ft (1.2 m)

■ **Seasonal highlights** Flowers profusely over long periods in midsummer, bearing fully double, intensely fragrant, pink flowers with a green eye.

■ **Ideal site** In mixed or shrub borders or as specimens.

■ **Cultivation** Grow as for bush roses. Albas tolerate shade better than most roses. To encourage bushy growth, after flowering, reduce main stems by a third of their height and sideshoots by two-thirds.

■ **Also recommended** *Rosa* 'Alba Semiplena' has flat, semidouble white flowers.

■ **Perfect partners** Lavanders, cistus, *Anemone* x *hybrida*.

Rosa moyesii
Wild or Species rose

A vigorous, upright, open deciduous shrub with long, arching branches.
Z4–9 H9–1 ↕ to 12 ft (4 m), ↔10 ft (3 m)

■ **Seasonal highlights** Single, cupped, sealing-wax red flowers in summer, very attractive to honey bees.

■ **Value at other times** In fall, it produces large, crimson, flask-shaped hips.

■ **Ideal site** Grow as a specimen.

■ **Cultivation** Grow in any fertile, moist but well-drained soil in sun or light, dappled shade. Every 3–4 years, in winter, cut one or two old shoots to the ground. Overlong, wayward shoots can be shortened at any time.

■ **Also recommended** *Rosa moyesii* 'Geranium' is more compact with brighter, cherry-red flowers.

■ **Perfect partners** *Clematis florida* 'Sieboldii', *Tropaeolum speciosum*.

Rosa 'Noisette Carnée'
Noisette rose

Also known as old climbing garden rose (noisette). A moderately vigorous climber, with smooth stems. Z6–9 H9–1 ↕6–12 ft (2–4 m), ↔6–8 ft (2–2.5 m)
■ **Seasonal highlights** From summer until fall, it bears sprays of cupped, double, pale-pink flowers with a spicy fragrance.
■ **Ideal site** A warm, sheltered wall.
■ **Cultivation** The noisettes need more warmth and shelter than most climbers to flower and repeat well, otherwise grow as for bush roses and prune as for climbers.
■ **Also recommended** *Rosa* 'Madame Alfred Carrière', with tea-scented, fully double creamy-white flowers. *Rosa* 'Gloire de Dijon' with fully double, quartered, fragrant, creamy-buff flowers.
■ **Perfect partners** *Clematis* 'Etoile Voilette', *C.* 'Lasurstern'.

Rosa rugosa
Rugosa rose

A vigorous, deciduous shrub of dense, prickly growth. Z2–9 H9–1 ↕↔3–8 ft (1–2.5 m)
■ **Seasonal highlights** In summer, it bears single, spicily fragrant, magenta to carmine-red or white flowers with a boss of yellow stamens.
■ **Value at other times** Each flower produces a large, round, bright tomato-red hip and flowers and hips are present at the same time.
■ **Ideal site** In a border, or as an informal hedge; thrives in coastal sites.
■ **Cultivation** Grow in any fertile, moist but well-drained soil in sun or light-dappled shade. Every three or four years, in winter, cut out one or two old shoots to the ground. Shorten wayward shoots at any time.
■ **Also recommended** *Rosa rugosa* var. *alba* has clove-scented, white flowers.
■ **Perfect partners** *Tropaeolum speciosum.*

Rosa 'William Lobb'
Old garden rose (moss)

Vigorous, upright, or arching shrub with dark-green leaves. Z4–9 H9–4 ↕↔6 ft (2 m)
■ **Seasonal highlights** In midsummer, bears fully double, intensely fragrant red-purple flowers that fade with lavender-gray tints, on thorny shoots with dense, mossy growth on the stem tips.
■ **Ideal site** Beds and borders.
■ **Cultivation** Grow as for bush roses. To encourage bushy growth, after flowering, reduce main stems by one-third of their height and sideshoots by two-thirds.
■ **Also recommended** *Rosa* 'Nuits de Young', shorter, with dense brown-green moss and deep-maroon flowers.
■ **Perfect partners** Lavanders, cistus, *Anemone* x *hybrida.*

Rudbeckia 'Herbstsonne'
Coneflower

Vigorous, clump-forming, herbaceous perennial. Z3–7 H7–1 ↕to 6 ft (2 m), ↔35 in (90 cm)
■ **Seasonal highlights** From midsummer until early fall, it bears daisylike, bright-yellow flowerheads with cone-shaped centers.
■ **Value at other times** It has attractive, prominently veined, glossy, green leaves.
■ **Ideal site** Mixed or herbaceous borders, or naturalized in woodland.
■ **Cultivation** Best in full sun, but tolerates light, dappled shade. Grow in fertile, preferably heavy, soil. After three or four years, lift and divide in spring or fall to rejuvenate.
■ **Also recommended** *Rudbeckia laciniata* 'Goldquelle' is shorter, with double, lemon-yellow flowers.
■ **Perfect partners** *Sedum spectabile, Aster novi-belgii* (Michaelmas daisies).

S

Salix caprea 'Kilmarnock'
Kilmarnock willow

A top-grafted, stiffly weeping, deciduous tree. Z6–8 H8–6 ↕5–6 ft (1.5–2 m), ↔6 ft (2 m)
■ **Seasonal highlights** In mid- and late spring, it produces gray male catkins, studded with yellow anthers, on bare shoots.
■ **Value at other times** Forms a dense umbrella of stout, yellow-brown stems and narrow dark-green leaves that are gray-green beneath.
■ **Ideal site** As a specimen, or in large containers.
■ **Cultivation** Grow in full sun or light shade, in any moist but well-drained soil. Prune annually between late fall and early spring to thin out congested shoots.
■ **Also recommended** *Salix exigua* is taller and upright with narrow, silvery leaves.
■ **Perfect partners** *Betula pendula* 'Youngii', *Corylopsis glabrescens.*

S

Salix x rubens 'Basfordiana'
Hybrid crack willow

Vigorous, upright, deciduous tree; pruned regularly, it makes a twiggy shrub.
Z4–7 H7–1 ‡50 ft (15 m), ↔30 ft (10 m)
■ **Seasonal highlights** It has bright orange-yellow young shoots in winter.
■ **Value at other times** In spring it bears slender, yellow catkins with the emerging, narrow, gray-green leaves that become glossy, bright green in summer.
■ **Ideal site** In a shrub border or by the water's edge.
■ **Cultivation** Grow in any moist but well-drained soil. Cut all stems back hard each or, for catkins, every other year in early spring, to the ground or to a short trunk. Young shoots have the best color.
■ **Also recommended** *Salix daphnoides* 'Aglaia' has glossy mahogany-red shoots.
■ **Perfect partners** Corylopsis, dogwoods.

Salvia coccinea 'Lady in Red'
Salvia

An upright, bushy, half-hardy perennial, often grown as an annual.
Z11 H12–1 ‡16 in (40 cm), ↔12 in (30 cm)
■ **Seasonal highlights** From summer to fall, it bears slender open spikes of luminous-red flowers.
■ **Value at other times** It has heart-shaped, toothed and veined, dark-green leaves.
■ **Ideal site** Bedding, borders, and containers.
■ **Cultivation** Grow in full sun in any moderately fertile, well-drained soil. May not survive cold, wet winters, so take softwood cuttings in spring or summer and overwinter young plants indoors.
■ **Also recommended** *Salvia patens* 'Cambridge Blue' has pale-blue flowers.
■ **Perfect partners** Osteospermums and argyranthemums.

Santolina chamaecyparissus 'Lemon Queen'

Also known as cotton lavender. A vigorous, evergreen shrub.
Z6–9 H9–1 ↔24 in (60 cm)
■ **Seasonal highlights** From mid- to late summer, it bears lemon-yellow pom-pom flowerheads.
■ **Value at other times** It has white, woolly young shoots that carry slender, finely divided leaves with a wonderful sharp fragrance.
■ **Ideal site** Mixed or herbaceous borders.
■ **Cultivation** Best in full sun, but will tolerate light, part-day shade. Grow in any moderately fertile, well-drained soil. In heavy clay soil, dig in coarse grit to improve drainage. In early spring, trim over plants with shears to keep them bushy and compact.
■ **Also recommended** *Santolina pinnata* subsp. *neapolitana* 'Sulphurea' is slightly taller.
■ **Perfect partners** *Salvia officinalis* 'Tricolor'.

Sarcococca hookeriana var. humilis

Also known as Christmas box and sweet box. A moderately vigorous, suckering evergreen shrub.
Z6–9 H9–1 ‡24 in (60 cm), ↔to 3 ft (1 m)
■ **Seasonal highlights** In winter, it bears clusters of tiny, honey-scented, pink-tinted white flowers, followed by round, dark-blue fruits.
■ **Value at other times** The glossy, dark-green leaves make good ground cover.
■ **Ideal site** In a woodland garden or shrub border, or as low, informal hedging.
■ **Cultivation** Grow in fertile, moist but well-drained soil in deep or partial shade, or in sun if soil remains moist. Needs little pruning. Dig out suckers at the margins of the clump if it encroaches on other plants.
■ **Also recommended** *Sarcococca confusa* is taller but similar.
■ **Perfect partners** *Helleborus niger, Viburnum* x *bodnantense* 'Dawn', *V. tinus*.

Scabiosa 'Butterfly Blue'
Scabious

Also known as pincushion flower. A clump-forming, spreading herbaceous perennial.
Z3–8 H8–1 ↔16 in (40 cm)
■ **Seasonal highlights** From mid- to late summer, it bears wiry-stemmed, lavender-blue flowers that attract bees and butterflies.
■ **Value at other times** It has divided, gray-green basal leaves.
■ **Ideal site** A mixed or herbaceous border, especially in cottage gardens; wildlife gardens.
■ **Cultivation** Grow in any moderately fertile, well-drained soil in full sun, or light part-day shade.
■ **Also recommended** *Scabiosa caucasica* 'Miss Willmott' has white flowerheads.
■ **Perfect partners** Lavenders, pinks (*Dianthus*) and herbaceous potentillas, such as 'Yellow Queen'.

Scaevola aemula
Fairy fan-flower

A tufted, frost-tender, evergreen perennial, grown as an annual in cold areas. Z11 H12–1 ↕↔to 20 in (50 cm)

■ **Seasonal highlights** Throughout summer, it bears leafy, trailing spikes of small, fan-shaped, purple-blue or blue flowers.

■ **Value at other times** Is discarded after flowering.

■ **Ideal site** Containers, hanging baskets.

■ **Cultivation** Grow in full sun or light, dappled shade, in any moist but well-drained, fairly fertile soil or potting mix. Take stem cuttings in spring or summer and overwinter indoors, or sow seed in warmth in spring. Set out when risk of frost has passed.

■ **Also recommended** *Scaevola* 'Mauve Clusters' has lilac-mauve flowers.

■ **Perfect partners** Fuchsias, geraniums, French marigolds (*Tagetes*).

Schizostylis coccinea **'Sunrise'**
Kaffir lily

A vigorous, evergreen, rhizomatous perennial. Z7–9 H9–1 ↕24 in (60 cm), ↔12 in (30 cm)

■ **Seasonal highlights** From late summer to early winter, it bears spikes of glossy, salmon-pink flowers. They are good for cutting.

■ **Value at other times** The narrowly sword-shaped, bright-green leaves persist for most of the year.

■ **Ideal site** Mixed or herbaceous borders, or in containers.

■ **Cultivation** Grow in a fertile, moist but well-drained soil. Shelter from cold winds. It benefits from an organic mulch in winter where marginally hardy.

■ **Also recommended** *Schizostylis coccinea* 'Major' has glossy, scarlet flowers.

■ **Perfect partners** Asters (Michaelmas daisies), *Sedum spectabile*, rudbeckias.

Scilla siberica **'Spring Beauty'**
Squill

A slender, perennial bulb. Z2–7 H8–1 ↕8 in (20 cm), ↔2 in (5 cm)

■ **Seasonal highlights** In spring it bears loose spikes of small, nodding, deep-blue flowers amid narrow, strap-shaped, shining, green leaves.

■ **Value at other times** Of no value at other times.

■ **Ideal site** A rock garden, at the front of a mixed border; in containers.

■ **Cultivation** Grow in full sun or light, dappled shade, in any fertile, humus-rich soil. Plant the bulbs in fall at twice their own depth.

■ **Also recommended** *Scilla peruviana* 'Alba' is taller with white flowers.

■ **Perfect partners** Grow with chionodoxas and *Anemone blanda* cultivars beneath forsythias.

Sedum spectabile **'Brilliant'**
Ice plant

A vigorous, clump-forming, herbaceous perennial. Z4–9 H9–1 ↔18 in (45 cm)

■ **Seasonal highlights** From late summer until late fall, it bears large, flat heads of many tiny, star-shaped, bright-pink flowers. An excellent plant for attracting butterflies.

■ **Value at other times** The fleshy, slightly scalloped, gray-green leaves are handsome throughout spring and summer.

■ **Ideal site** Mixed or herbaceous borders; is good in hot, dry sites.

■ **Cultivation** Grow in fertile, well-drained, preferably neutral to slightly alkaline, soil in sun. Divide in spring, every three or four years to maintain vigor.

■ **Also recommended** *Sedum spectabile* 'Iceberg' has pale-green leaves and white flowers.

■ **Perfect partners** Asters, rudbeckias, *Schizostylis*.

Skimmia japonica
Skimmia

A vigorous, dome-shaped, evergreen shrub. Z7–9 H9–7 ↕to 15 ft (5 m), ↔5 ft (1.5 m)

■ **Seasonal highlights** In winter, it produces dense clusters of pink buds that open in mid- to late winter to reveal scented white flowers.

■ **Value at other times** It has slightly aromatic, glossy dark-green leaves all year. Female plants bear red berries, if male and female plants are grown together.

■ **Ideal site** A shrub or mixed border.

■ **Cultivation** Grow in dappled or deep shade, in any fertile, humus-rich soil. It needs little, if any, pruning other than to shape, if necessary, after flowering.

■ **Also recommended** *Skimmia japonica* 'Bronze Knight' is shorter, male, and has dark, bronze-red buds in winter.

■ **Perfect partners** Gaultherias, winter heaths (*Erica carnea*).

S

Solanum crispum 'Glasnevin'
Chilean potato tree

Solenostemon 'Brightness'
Coleus

Solidago 'Goldenmosa'
Goldenrod

Sorbus commixta
Mountain ash

Spiraea 'Arguta'
Bridal wreath

A very vigorous, evergreen or semievergreen, scrambling shrub or climber.
Z9–11 H12–1 ↕↔to 20 ft (6 m)

■ **Seasonal highlights** Throughout summer, it bears fragrant, deep purple-blue flowers at the stem tips, followed by pale-yellow fruit.

■ **Value at other times** It has handsome dark-green leaves for most of the year.

■ **Ideal site** On a warm, sunny wall.

■ **Cultivation** Grow in full sun, or light, part-day shade, in neutral to slightly alkaline, fertile, well-drained soil. After flowering, shorten sideshoots to three or four buds.

■ **Also recommended** *Solanum jasminoides* 'Album' has white flowers.

■ **Perfect partners** *Clematis* 'Pagoda'; climbing or rambling roses.

A bushy, fast-growing, frost-tender perennial, often grown as a foliage annual.
↕18 in (45 cm), ↔12 in (30 cm)

■ **Seasonal highlights** All year it has rust-red leaves, edged with pale green.

■ **Ideal site** As a houseplant, or outdoors as bedding or in containers.

■ **Cultivation** Grow in a sheltered, sunny site, in fertile, moist but well-drained soil or potting mix. Sow seed in warmth in early spring and plant out when the risk of frost has passed. Pinch out shoot tips to promote bushiness and also any flowers to preserve good leaf color and condition. Take stem cuttings in summer.

■ **Also recommended** *Solenostemon scutellarioides* Wizard Series has leaves patterned in green, red, cream, yellow, and purple.

■ **Perfect partners** French marigolds (*Tagetes*), geraniums.

A vigorous, bushy, herbaceous perennial.
Z5–9 H9–1 ↕30 in (75 cm), ↔18 in (45 cm)

■ **Seasonal highlights** In late summer and early fall, it bears feathery, conical plumes of yellow-stalked, bright-yellow flowers.

■ **Value at other times** It has wrinkled, mid-green leaves. The flowers are good for cutting.

■ **Ideal site** An herbaceous border or wild garden.

■ **Cultivation** Grow in full sun in any poor to moderately fertile soil. Every three or four years, lift and divide in spring or fall to maintain vigor. Cut off the flowers as they fade to prevent them from seeding.

■ **Also recommended** *Solidago* 'Golden Wings' is taller, with horizontally spreading plumes of golden yellow.

■ **Perfect partners** Rudbeckias, *Sedum spectabile*.

A vigorous, broadly conical, deciduous tree.
Z6–8 H8–1 ↕30 ft (10 m), ↔22 ft (7 m)

■ **Seasonal highlights** In late spring, it bears broad heads of tiny white flowers.

■ **Value at other times** In fall, clusters of orange-red berries festoon the branches and the divided leaves turn yellow to red and purple. The berries attract birds.

■ **Ideal site** A beautiful specimen tree.

■ **Cultivation** Grow in any fertile, moist, but well-drained, neutral to acidic soil. Little pruning is necessary except to remove any crossing or damaged branches in winter.

■ **Also recommended** *Sorbus sargentiana* is similar, with many small, bright-red berries.

■ **Perfect partners** Maples (*Acers*) and birches (*Betula*).

A vigorous, deciduous shrub with arching branches.
Z5–8 H8–1 ↕↔8 ft (2.5 m)

■ **Seasonal highlights** In spring, clusters of tiny, bright white flowers wreathe the branches.

■ **Value at other times** It has attractive leaves of fresh, bright green.

■ **Ideal site** A mixed or shrub border.

■ **Cultivation** Best in full sun, but tolerates light, part-day shade. Grow in any fertile, moist but well-drained soil. After flowering, cut back the flowered shoots to strong buds. Every three or four years, cut out one in three of the oldest flowered stems to the base to encourage strong, new growth.

■ **Also recommended** *Spiraea japonica* 'Little Princess' is compact with pink flowers.

■ **Perfect partners** *Chaenomeles* x *superba* 'Nicoline', *Cytisus* x *praecox*.

Stipa gigantea
Golden oats, giant feather grass

A vigorous, evergreen or semievergreen perennial grass.
Z8–10 H12–1 ↕8 ft (2.5 m), ↔4 ft (1.2 m)
■ **Seasonal highlights** In summer, tall arching stems bear open flowerheads of silvery, purple-green spikelets that turn gold as they ripen.
■ **Value at other times** It forms arching clumps of narrow green leaves.
■ **Ideal site** A fabulous specimen, border, or container plant.
■ **Cultivation** Grow in full sun in any moderately fertile soil. It tolerates light shade and heavy clay soil. Cut down the old growth in spring.
■ **Also recommended** *Stipa tenuissima* is shorter with filament-like leaves and feather-fine flowerheads.
■ **Perfect partners** *Hakonechloa macra* 'Aureola', *Carex pendula*.

Syringa vulgaris
Lilacs

Vigorous, deciduous shrubs or small trees. Most lilacs grow well in USDA hardiness zones 3 to 8 and in AHS heat zones 8 to 3. ↕↔22 ft (7 m)
■ **Seasonal highlights** In late spring and early summer they bear dense, conical clusters of intensely fragrant flowers.
■ **Value at other times** They have heart-shaped, dark-green leaves from spring to late fall.
■ **Ideal site** In a shrub border or as specimens.
■ **Cultivation** Grow in any fertile, neutral to alkaline soil. Deadhead young plants, cutting back to strong buds lower down on the shrub. If necessary, prune to shape after flowering.
■ **Perfect partners** Hawthorn (*Crataegus*) and laburnums.

Syringa vulgaris **'Charles Joly'** has double dark-purple flowers.

Syringa vulgaris **'Charles X'** has single purple-red flowers.

Syringa vulgaris **'Katherine Havemeyer'** has double lavender-blue flowers, which are purple in bud.

Syringa vulgaris **'Madame Lemoine'** has double white blooms.

Syringa vulgaris **'Président Grévy'** has large spires of double lilac-blue flowers with red-violet buds.

Syringa vulgaris **'Primrose'** has soft primrose-yellow flowers.

T

Tagetes 'Naughty Marietta'
French marigold

A compact, bushy, vigorous, half-hardy annual.
↕↔12–16 in (30–40 cm)
■ **Seasonal highlights** From early to late summer, deep-yellow flowerheads with maroon-red marks emerge atop the dark-green leaves.
■ **Value at other times** They are consigned to the compost pile after flowering.
■ **Ideal site** Bedding, border edging, and containers.
■ **Cultivation** Grow in sun in moderately fertile, well-drained soil. Sow seeds in warmth indoors in spring and set out when risk of frost has passed; or sow in the flowering site in late spring. Deadhead regularly to prolong the flowering period.
■ **Also recommended** *Tagetes* 'Tangerine Gem' has deep-orange flowers.
■ **Perfect partners** Geraniums, annual lobelias, fuchsias.

T

Tamarix tetrandra
Tamarisk

A vigorous, open, deciduous shrub or small tree.
Z5–9 H9–5 ↕↔10 ft (3 m)
■ **Seasonal highlights** In mid- to late spring, it bears short spikes of many tiny, pale dusky-pink flowers all along the arching branches.
■ **Value at other times** It has purple-brown shoots and small, needle- or scalelike green leaves.
■ **Ideal site** In a shrub border, or as a specimen; it does especially well in coastal gardens.
■ **Cultivation** Grow in full sun, in moist but well-drained soil. Shelter from cold, dry winds. It is resistant to strong winds in coastal areas. After flowering, shorten flowered shoots to strong buds lower down the shoots.
■ **Also recommended** *Tamarix ramosissima* 'Pink Cascade' has pink flowers in late summer.
■ **Perfect partners** *Syringa*, *Spiraea* 'Arguta'.

Thunbergia alata
Black-eyed Susan

A frost-tender, evergreen perennial climber, grown as an annual in cold areas.
↕8 ft (2.5 m), ↔18 in (45 cm)
■ **Seasonal highlights** From summer to fall, the twining stems bear single, orange or yellow, occasionally creamy-white flowers; some have chocolate-purple centers.
■ **Value at other times** It has pretty, heart-shaped, toothed, mid-green leaves.
■ **Ideal site** In containers, on supporting teepees, or poles.
■ **Cultivation** Grow in sun in any moist but well-drained soil. Sow the seeds in spring in heat; plant in containers and grow on in warmth. Set out when the weather is warm and settled. Take stem cuttings in summer and overwinter indoors.
■ **Also recommended** *Thunbergia gregorii* has orange flowers.
■ **Perfect partners** *Ipomoea tricolor*.

Trollius x *cultorum* 'Earliest of All'
Globeflower

A moderately vigorous, clump-forming herbaceous perennial.
Z5–8 H8–5 ↕20 in (50 cm), ↔16 in (40 cm)
■ **Seasonal highlights** The bowl-shaped, shining, clear-yellow flowers arise on strong stems from mid-spring to midsummer.
■ **Value at other times** It has basal mounds of lobed, toothed, glossy, green leaves.
■ **Ideal site** Bog gardens and stream- or pondsides, damp borders, or meadow gardens.
■ **Cultivation** Best in full sun, but tolerant of partial shade. Grow in reliably moist, deep, fertile soil. Lift and divide the plants every three or four years to rejuvenate them.
■ **Also recommended** *Trollius* x *cultorum* 'Alabaster' has pale creamy-yellow flowers.
■ **Perfect partners** *Caltha palustris*, *Lysichiton americanus*, *Darmera peltata*.

Tropaeolum speciosum
Flame creeper

A moderately vigorous, herbaceous perennial climber.
Z8–10 H10–1 ↕↔to 10 ft (3 m) or more.
■ **Seasonal highlights** From summer to fall, the slender stems form swags of long-spurred, vermilion flowers.
■ **Value at other times** It has very attractive, lobed, bright-green leaves.
■ **Ideal site** Grow through dark-leaved shrubs or hedges, like yew, or with creamy-flowered roses.
■ **Cultivation** Grow in moist, reasonably fertile, preferably slightly acidic soil, with its roots in cool shade and head in sun. It can be difficult to establish, as the long, fleshy white roots are fragile; plant carefully.
■ **Also recommended** *Tropaeolum tuberosum* is a frost-tender, tuberous perennial with orange and yellow flowers.
■ **Perfect partners** *Tropaeolum peregrinum*, a yellow-flowered annual.

Tulipa 'Spring Green'
Viridiflora tulip

A moderately vigorous, bulbous perennial.
Z3–8 H8–1 ↕16 in (40 cm), ↔3 in (8 cm)
■ **Seasonal highlights** In late spring it produces very elegant, green-feathered, ivory-white flowers.
■ **Value at other times** Of little value at other times.
■ **Ideal site** Bedding, borders, and decorative containers.
■ **Cultivation** Grow in full sun, in any moderately fertile, well-drained soil. Add coarse grit to heavy clay soil. Plant bulbs 4–6 in (10–15 cm) deep in late fall. Lift bulbs once the leaves fade and ripen in a cool greenhouse.
■ **Also recommended** *Tulipa* 'Queen of Night' has glossy, dark, maroon-purple flowers in late spring.
■ **Perfect partners** Wallflowers (*Erysimum*), polyanthus primulas, winter-flowering pansies.

V

Tulipa tarda
Species tulip

A vigorous, perennial bulb. Z3–8 H8–1 ‡ to 6 in (15 cm), ↔ 2 in (5 cm)
■ **Seasonal highlights** In early and mid-spring it produces open, starry, greenish-white flowers that are yellow inside.
■ **Value at other times** Of no value at other times.
■ **Ideal site** Rock gardens, borders, and containers.
■ **Cultivation** Best in full sun, but it will tolerate light, part-day shade. Grow in any poor to moderately fertile, well-drained soil. Add coarse grit to heavy clay soil. Plant the bulbs at twice their own depth in late fall.
■ **Also recommended** *Tulipa turkestanica* has starry white flowers.
■ **Perfect partners** Scillas and chionodoxas.

Verbascum 'Cotswold Queen'
Mullein

An upright, moderately vigorous perennial. Z5–9 H9–5 ‡ 4 ft (1.2 m), ↔ 12 in (30 cm)
■ **Seasonal highlights** From early until late summer, erect spires bear saucer-shaped yellow flowers with red-purple centers.
■ **Value at other times** It has striking basal rosettes of wrinkled, gray-green leaves.
■ **Ideal site** Sunny banks and borders.
■ **Cultivation** Best in full sun in poor, well-drained, preferably slightly alkaline, soil. Too-rich soil produces soft, floppy stems that then need staking. May be short-lived, so divide in spring or fall, or take root cuttings in winter.
■ **Also recommended** *Verbascum chaixii* f. *album* has white flowers with mauve centers.
■ **Perfect partners** Delphiniums, monkshood, border phlox.

Verbena 'Showtime'
Bedding verbena

Bushy, half-hardy perennial grown as an annual. ‡ ↔ 10 in (25 cm)
■ **Seasonal highlights** From summer until fall, it produces masses of flowers in shades of rose-pink to magenta, scarlet, or white, some with white centers. The toothed, dark-green leaves form dense, neat mounds.
■ **Value at other times** Discard after flowering.
■ **Ideal site** Annual borders, edging, containers, or hanging baskets.
■ **Cultivation** Grow in sun, in well-drained, not-too-fertile soil or potting mix. Sow seeds in early spring in warmth. Plant out when the risk of frost is past.
■ **Also recommended** *Verbena* 'Peaches n' Cream', with pale orange-pink to apricot-yellow flowers.
■ **Perfect partners** Clarkias, busy Lizzies (*Impatiens*), geraniums.

Verbena bonariensis
Verbena

A vigorous, frost-hardy, clump-forming perennial. Z7–11 H11–1 ‡ to 6 ft (2 m), ↔ 18 in (45 cm)
■ **Seasonal highlights** From midsummer to fall, wiry, branching stems bear heads of lilac-purple flowers.
■ **Value at other times** It has attractive, toothed, dark-green basal leaves.
■ **Ideal site** Mixed or herbaceous borders, gravel gardens, especially in hot, dry sites.
■ **Cultivation** Grow in any moderately fertile soil in full sun. It may not survive cold, wet winters, so provide a dry winter mulch. Take stem-tip cuttings in late summer. Overwinter young plants indoors.
■ **Also recommended** *Verbena corymbosa* is more densely clump-forming, with red-purple flowers.
■ **Perfect partners** Verbascums, *Cynara cardunculus*, *Ferula communis*.

Veronica gentianoides
Speedwell

A moderately vigorous, mat-forming herbaceous perennial. Z4–7 H7–1 ‡ ↔ to 18 in (45 cm)
■ **Seasonal highlights** In early summer it produces upright stems of shallowly cupped, pale-blue flowers.
■ **Value at other times** It has attractive basal rosettes of slightly scalloped, glossy, dark-green leaves.
■ **Ideal site** At the front of a border or in a rock garden.
■ **Cultivation** Best in full sun, but tolerates light, part-day shade. Grow in moderately fertile, well-drained soil. Plants begin to lose vigor after two or three years, so divide in fall or spring to rejuvenate.
■ **Also recommended** *Veronica longifolia* is much taller, with lilac-blue flowers.
■ **Perfect partners** Lavenders, cranesbills.

V

Viburnum x *bodnantense* 'Dawn'
Viburnum

A sturdy, upright, vigorous deciduous shrub.
Z7–8 H8–1 ‡10 ft (3 m), ↔to 6 ft (2 m)

■ **Seasonal highlights** From late fall to early spring, it bears small, rounded clusters of fragrant pink flowers, on bare branches.

■ **Value at other times** It has deeply pleated, bright-green leaves that are bronze when young.

■ **Ideal site** Shrub borders, woodland gardens, or informal hedging.

■ **Cultivation** It thrives in any reasonably fertile, well-drained soil in sun or dappled shade. It needs little pruning other than to shorten any shoots that spoil the shape and to thin out congested shoots on mature plants. Prune after flowering.

■ **Also recommended** *Viburnum farreri* has white, often pink-flushed winter flowers.

■ **Perfect partners** Mahonias, sarcococcas.

Viburnum x *juddii*
Viburnum

A rounded, deciduous shrub.
Z5–9 H9–1 ‡4 ft (1.2 m), ↔4 ft (1.2 m).

■ **Seasonal highlights** In mid- to late spring, it bears rounded clusters of fragrant, pink-tinted, white flowers that open from pink buds.

■ **Value at other times** In fall, the dark-green leaves turn dark red.

■ **Ideal site** A mixed or shrub border.

■ **Cultivation** Grow in full sun. Tolerates partial shade. Grow in any reasonably fertile, well-drained soil. After flowering, shorten any shoots that spoil the outline.

■ **Also recommended** *Viburnum carlesii* is similar but taller and has red fruits in fall.

■ **Perfect partners** *Daphne retusa, Prunus tenella*.

Viburnum opulus 'Compactum'
European cranberry bush

A sturdy but slow-growing deciduous shrub.
Z4–8 H8–1 ‡↔to 5 ft (1.5 m)

■ **Seasonal highlights** In late spring and early summer, it produces showy, flat, "lacecap" clusters of white flowers at the stem tips.

■ **Value at other times** In fall, the glossy, bright-red fruits nestle among the bright-red fall leaves.

■ **Ideal site** Shrub borders, woodland gardens, or informal hedging.

■ **Cultivation** It thrives in any reasonably fertile, well-drained soil in sun or dappled shade. It needs little pruning other than to shorten any shoots that spoil the shape after flowering.

■ **Also recommended** *Viburnum opulus* 'Xanthocarpum' has yellow fruits.

■ **Perfect partners** *Ceratostigma willmottianum, Lonicera* x *purpusii*.

Viburnum plicatum 'Mariesii'
Japanese snowball tree

A vigorous, spreading, deciduous shrub with distinctively tiered branches.
Z4–8 H8–1 ‡↔to 12 ft (4 m)

■ **Seasonal highlights** In late spring it produces flat "lacecap" white flowerheads.

■ **Value at other times** It has heart-shaped leaves that turn red-purple in fall.

■ **Ideal site** Shrub and mixed borders, woodland gardens.

■ **Cultivation** Grow in any reasonably fertile, well-drained soil in sun or partial shade. After flowering, lightly prune any shoots that spoil the outline of the shrub.

■ **Also recommended** *Viburnum plicatum*; both the shrub and the flowerheads are more rounded in shape.

■ **Perfect partners** *Osmanthus delavayi*.

Viburnum sargentii 'Onondaga'
Sargent viburnum

A bushy, moderately vigorous, deciduous shrub.
Z4–7 H7–1 ‡10 ft (3 m), ↔6 ft (2 m)

■ **Seasonal highlights** In late spring, it bears flat "lacecap" heads of pink-flushed, white flowers.

■ **Value at other times** The maplelike leaves are purple-bronze in spring, green in summer and dark red-purple in fall.

■ **Ideal site** Shrub and mixed borders, woodland gardens.

■ **Cultivation** Grow in any reasonably fertile, well-drained soil in sun or partial shade. After flowering, lightly prune any shoots that spoil the outline of the shrub.

■ **Also recommended** *Viburnum sieboldii* is taller, with open clusters of small white flowers in late spring and pink fruit.

■ **Perfect partners** Mahonias, *Daphne mezereum*, sarcococcas.

Viburnum tinus
Laurustinus

A dense, moderately vigorous, evergreen shrub. Z8–10 H10–1 ↕↔to 10 ft (3 m)

■ **Seasonal highlights** Over long periods in winter and spring, it bears flattened clusters of white flowers.

■ **Value at other times** The glossy, dark-green leaves are attractive all year.

■ **Ideal site** In shrub borders or as informal hedging.

■ **Cultivation** Grow in sun or partial shade in any fertile, moist but well-drained soil. Trim hedging after flowering and, on free-standing specimens, shorten any overlong shoots that spoil the outline.

■ **Also recommended** *Viburnum rhytidophyllum* is very tall, with deeply veined, leathery, dark-green leaves.

■ **Perfect partners** Forsythias, mahonias, *Rubus thibetanus*.

Vinca minor
Lesser periwinkle

A dense, vigorous, trailing evergreen shrub. Z4–9 H9–1 ↕to 8 in (20 cm), ↔indefinite

■ **Seasonal highlights** From spring until fall it bears blue-violet, occasionally pale blue, red-purple, or white flowers.

■ **Value at other times** The attractive lance-shaped, glossy, dark-green leaves make excellent ground cover.

■ **Ideal site** Shady or sunny banks and borders or woodland gardens.

■ **Cultivation** Grow in any but the driest soil in partial or deep shade. In sun, the soil needs to be reliably moist. Prune as hard as necessary to limit spread.

■ **Also recommended** *Vinca major* 'Variegata' spreads rampantly and has larger, cream-variegated leaves.

■ **Perfect partners** *Euonymus fortunei* 'Emerald 'n' Gold'.

Vitis coignetiae
Ornamental vine

A vigorous, deciduous climber. Z5–9 H9–1 ↕50 ft (15 m), ↔indefinite

■ **Seasonal highlights** Undoubtedly at its best in the fall when the large, heart-shaped leaves turn gold, then brilliant red and purple.

■ **Value at other times** The deep-green, spring and summer leaves are wrinkled and deeply veined with thick brown felt beneath.

■ **Ideal site** On large walls, through tall trees, to disguise unsightly garden structures.

■ **Cultivation** Grow in sun or partial shade in well-drained, preferably neutral to slightly alkaline soil. Prune in winter and again in summer, as needed, to limit size.

■ **Also recommended** *Vitis vinifera* 'Purpurea' has purple leaves (red in fall).

■ **Perfect partners** *Parthenocissus thompsonii*, *Tropaeolum tuberosum*.

W

Wisteria floribunda 'Multijuga'
Japanese wisteria

A very vigorous, deciduous twining climber. Z5–9 H9–1 ↕↔28 ft (9 m) or more

■ **Seasonal highlights** In early summer it bears hanging chains of fragrant, pealike, lilac-blue flowers.

■ **Value at other times** It has attractive, fresh green leaves from spring to fall.

■ **Ideal site** Walls, arbors, arches, trees.

■ **Cultivation** Grow in sun in any fertile, well-drained soil. Avoid east-facing walls; early sun will exacerbate damage to frosted flower buds. Train main stems on to supporting wires. In summer, cut back the leafy sideshoots to 5–6 buds from the main stems, and again in winter, shortening them to 2–3 buds.

■ **Also recommended** *W. sinensis* 'Alba' has chains of white flowers.

■ **Perfect partners** Late-flowering clematis.

Z

Zinnia elegans 'Dasher Scarlet'
Zinnia

Bushy, half-hardy annual. ↕↔12 in (30 cm)

■ **Seasonal highlights** From early summer to fall, it bears semidouble heads of scarlet, weatherproof flowers above dense mounds of pale- to mid-green leaves.

■ **Value at other times** Is discarded after flowering.

■ **Ideal site** Bedding and edging, containers, window boxes.

■ **Cultivation** Grow in sun, in any moderately fertile, well-drained soil. Sow seeds in warmth in early spring. For a longer succession of blooms, sow some in the flowering site in late spring. Deadhead regularly to keep more flowers coming.

■ **Also recommended** *Zinnia haageana* 'Orange Star' has orange flowerheads.

■ **Perfect partners** French marigolds, tuberous begonias, nemesias.

Index

Page numbers in *italics* indicate an illustration or boxed text. Page numbers in **bold** indicate a main topic. Species are listed before cultivation entries

Acknowledgments

Author's acknowledgments

I wish to express my heartfelt thanks to all of the people involved with this book project, for without their help and encouragement I would never have finished it. Firstly I must thank the publisher, Dorling Kindersley, and the Royal Horticultural Society for having faith in me and allowing the project to go ahead. Individually I must thank David Lamb, Louise Abbott, Alison Donovan, Anna Kruger, Lee Griffiths and Viv Watton. They have all been very professional, excellent company and I have learned a lot from all of them. Thanks to all the team at the RHS too for their editorial input. And to anyone not mentioned my apologies and special thanks.

I would also like to thank Lin Hawthorne for editing the Plant Directory. Other people to thank include Mr Chris Ayton for information on Yoder chrysanthemums from Littlehampton in West Sussex.

I also wish to express special thanks to Lynda Hamilton for the use of her garden as a setting for photography.

Lastly, but by no means least, my thanks to Steve Hamilton for taking the photographs for each of the monthly projects. He showed extreme patience, especially considering my carpentry skills!

Publisher's acknowledgments

Dorling Kindersley would like to thank Susanne Mitchell, Karen Wilson, Barbara Haynes, Andrew Halstead and Chris Prior of the Royal Horticultural Society; Annelise Evans and Lin Hawthorne for editorial assistance, Stephen Josland for design assistance, and Murdo Culver for technical assistance.

US Adult Editor Rebecca Warren
Index Michèle Clarke
Illustrator Karen Gavin
Media resources DK Image Library

AHS Plant Heat Zone Map reproduced with permission of the American Horticultural Society (www.ahs.org).

Picture Credits

The publisher would like to thank the following for their kind permission to reproduce their photographs:
(Key: a-above; b-below/bottom; c-centre; f-far; l-left; r-right; t-top)

John Amand and Winchester Growers Ltd: John Amand 55tl, 299ftr; **David Austin Roses www.davidaustinroses.com:** 313br, 313clb, 313tr, 314tr, 315tc; **Gillian Beckett:** 215cr, 308fcla; **Corbis:** AgStock Images 72; Michelle Garrett 112tl; Patrick Johns 69tl, 265ftl; Dency Kane/Beateworks 2, 120; moodboard 173t; Robert Pickett 40br; **DK Images:** Airedale Publishing 92, 148t, 222, 223 (all), 243; Airedale Publishing/Sarah Cuttle 102, 162; **Eric Crichton Photos:** 127cr, 128br, 155cr, 214cl, 273ftl, 278tr, 308tr (sargentii), 320ftl, 321tr; **GAP Photos:** Richard Bloom 1, 6bl, 10bl, 23bl, 28, 50, 226; Christina Bollen 230, 231; Elke Borkowski 10br, 91; Jonathan Buckley - Design: John Massey Location: Ashwood Nurseries 13b; Jonathan Buckley - Design: Sarah Raven, Perch Hill 52t; Carole Drake - Location: The Sir Harold Hillier Gardens/Hampshire County Council 244; Carole Drake - Location: The Sir Harold Hillier Gardens/Hampshire County Council 7br; Victoria Firmston 221; John Glover 232tr, 258b, 272tc, 296ftl; Jerry Harpur 170; Neil Holmes 143t, 305ftl; Geoff Kidd 238bl; Jenny Lilly - Location: David Austin Roses 313cra; Brian North 63bl; Rice / Buckland 161bl; S & O 14br, 76-77, 174tl, 277tr (Chocolate cosmos), 296ftr; Jason Smalley 30bl; Friedrich Strauss 89br, 100, 112br, 155bl, 296tl; Graham Strong - Design: Sue Jollans 53; Visions Premium 6br, 144; Jo Whitworth 250cl; **Garden Picture Library:** Mark Bolton 192; Mark Boulton 276br; Ron Evans 174bl, 267ftr; John Glover 263ftl; Neil Holmes 35cl, 271ftl; Lamontagne 310bl; Zara McCalmont 276fclb; Howard Rice 33, 54cr, 315ftr; Friedrich Strauss 305tl; Paul Windsor 125; **The Garden Collection:** Liz Eddison 147; **Getty Images:** Chris Everard 168; GAP Photos/Victoria Firmston 87br, 237b; GAP Photos 140; GAP Photos/Neil Holmes 48; Image Source 146, 158; GAP Photos/Zara Napier 246; Martin Page 251tr; GAP Photos/Juliette Wade 189, 259br; **Marianne Majerus Garden Images:** Andrew Lawson 248-249; **Clive Nichols:** 8; Bassibones Farm, Bucks 98; Design:Rupert Golby - Chelsea 95 148b; Leeds City Council, Chelsea 98 149; Clive Nichols/ Lady Farm, Somerset 260-261; **Photolibrary:** 291tc; Michele Lamontagne 225; Mark Turner 153br; Francesca Yorke 3, 173b; **Photos Horticultural:** 34br, 54tl, 57br, 57tl, 74, 103, 107tr, 129br, 176br, 177cl, 179br, 195, 196bl, 214br, 233cr, 250tl, 262br, 264tr ('Orange Glory'), 265ftr, 269tc, 271tl, 271tr, 273crb ('Nelly Moser'), 274cla (viticella), 276fcla, 278ftl, 281ftr, 283ftl, 285tc, 294ftr, 294tr, 297ftr, 311ftr, 314ftr, 321ftl, 322ftr, 322tl, 323ftr; **Science Photo Library:** Leslie J. Borg 233br, 292ftl; Ron Chapman 307ftl; Anthony Cooper 12, 251cr, 316ftl; Ian Gowland 35tl, 274tr; R. Greenwood 267tr ('Variegata'); Ray Lacey 128cl, 264ftl; Jiri Loun 304tl; Adrian Thomas 280tr; H. Thomson 57cl, 285tl; **Wildlife Matters:** 104tl, 129cl, 152cl, 215br, 232cl, 233cl, 251bl, 272ftl, 273tl, 275tl ('Golden Tiara'), 293ftr, 295tc, 312tl, 315tl, 318ftl, 322tr; Debi Wagner Stock Pics 236; Nancy Rothwell 292ftr; Steffie Shields 56bl, 320ftr

All other images © Dorling Kindersley.   For further information see: www.dkimages.com